The Natural Divisions of Missouri

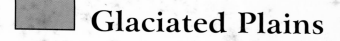 **Big Rivers**

Glaciated Plains

Mississippi Lowlands

Osage Plains

Ozark

Ozark Border

Vicki,

Merry Christmas. I love you!

Love
Bob

Cover: Wild azalea, *Rhododendron roseum.* Photo by Don Kurz

Shrubs and Woody Vines
of Missouri

*This book is dedicated to those who
appreciate and want to learn more
about our native shrubs and woody vines.*

Disclaimer

Medicinal uses for plants described in this book are for informational
purposes only, and should not be read as promotions for medical or
herbal prescriptions for self healing.

Missouri Department of Conservation
P.O. Box 180
Jefferson City, MO 65102-0180

Shrubs and Woody Vines
of Missouri

by

Don Kurz

illustrations by Paul Nelson

Bernadette Dryden, editor and designer
Libby Block, production assistant

Acknowledgments

I want to thank fellow workers, family, and friends for their interest and support over the years while this book was being written. The publication of this book would not have been possible without the approval of Assistant Director Allen Brohn and Natural History Division Chief John E. Wylie. Their vision for the usefulness of such a book is appreciated. I also want to thank former and present Natural History Division Chiefs Dr. James H. Wilson and Richard H. Thom for their interest and encouragement.

While most of this book was written on my own time, which, I feel, qualifies as a true labor of love, I do appreciate the Conservation Department's support of this project. This work was made much easier with clerical help from Barbara Singleton who typed the species list and proofread the county distribution maps; to Debra Hardin for merging 170 text files into one; to Niki Aberle and Jason Jett for creating the natural division and North American maps; and to Shelley Daniels and Amy Linsenbardt for photocopying illustrations and state distribution maps for each species.

Editing, design and layout of the book was in the very capable hands of Bernadette Dryden. Her comments and questions also added to the clarity of what I was trying to accomplish. Thanks also to Libby Block for assisting in making editorial changes in the text. The introduction, taxonomic keys and species descriptions were reviewed by botanist Tim Smith. His close attention to details added accuracy to the final product. My sincere gratitude is extended to Carol Davit for her meticulous attention to proofing the final draft.

Appreciation also goes to Dr. George Yatskievych, author of the upcoming revision of the "Flora of Missouri," for his comments, and for providing location information on some of the rarer shrubs and woody vines.

Probably the most important decision I made early on in the development of this book was not to use color photographs. It would have been very time consuming to try to capture on film the images of the leaves, flowers and fruit of each species.

I was fortunate to have been able to enlist the help of Paul Nelson, an outstanding botanical illustrator. His keen eye for detail, and the desire to capture a plant's growth habit by drawing from fresh material, adds special three-dimensional qualities to his work. I am honored to have his drawings in this book.

Contents

Introduction

Trees in a natural community dominate the setting, and understandably so, since they dwarf the vegetation growing underneath them. But beneath that canopy layer grows a variety of shrubs and woody vines that boast their own individual character, form and color.

The purpose of this book is to provide information on the identification, uses, care and propagation techniques of shrubs and woody vines; its goal is to foster an increased understanding and appreciation of these important plants.

There are various definitions that differentiate trees from shrubs. The American Forestry Association describes a tree as a woody plant with a single stem or trunk at least 3 inches in diameter at breast height (4 1/2 feet above ground). A tree is also at least 13 feet tall, with a definite crown of foliage. A shrub has multiple stems arising from the ground and is generally smaller than a tree.

Since some small trees such as Eastern redbud and flowering dogwood can appear shrubby in open situations, they also are included in this book. Woody vines have stems that require support, either by creeping along the ground or climbing by way of tendrils or by other means such as the coiling of its stems.

Some plants that are considered woody farther south die back to the ground in Missouri and states farther north due to colder winter temperatures. Only plants that retain some woody tissue above or at ground level are included here. Shrubs and woody vines classified as rare, endangered, or thought to be eliminated from the flora of the state also are described and illustrated, with the hope that new locations will be found.

Exotic species also are included in this book. These are plants that are considered to be non-native, originating in Europe or Asia, and introduced into the United States. Many of these exotic plants escape from their original plantings and invade nearby natural communities. They often become a nuisance, with eradication proving costly and time-consuming.

Native shrubs and woody vines have adapted throughout thousands of years to local growing conditions, and wildlife have come to depend on them for food and cover. Exotic plants disrupt this balance, and the planting of those species known to be invasive should be discouraged. The exotic shrubs and woody vines covered in this book possess those undesirable qualities.

The native shrubs and woody vines of Missouri are found in a variety of habitats or natural communities. Some of these woody species, however, are restricted to certain regions of the state. These regions or natural divisions (see inside front cover) are based on geologic history, soils, topography, plant and animal distribution and other natural features. There are six major regions and 18 subregions which are termed natural divisions and sections.

Ozark Natural Division: This is a region of extensive forested hills and valleys. The division has an ancient geological history which included several periods of slow uplift, accompanied by deep erosion by its streams. This land mass has been exposed for more than 250 million years, while surrounding regions were repeatedly covered by glaciers, seas or floods. This long exposure, together with a diversity of bedrock and soil types, has created habitats for more species of plants and animals than exists in any other part of the state.

Glaciated Plains Natural Division: The landscape of this natural division has been dramatically affected by major glacial events that ended approximately 500,000 years ago. The glaciers leveled north Missouri and deposited silts, sands, gravels and boulders. Erosion throughout time has produced rolling plains that once were home to extensive prairies, interrupted only by scattered savannas and forested river valleys.

Ozark Border Natural Division: This is a transition zone between the Ozarks and other regions of the state. The landscape is Ozarklike, but the soils are deeper and more productive. Plant and animal ranges in the Ozarks and Glaciated Plains overlap in this natural division.

Big Rivers Natural Division: The Missouri and Mississippi rivers and their flood plains and terraces occupy this natural division. Although greatly altered today with locks and dams, levees and agriculture, the remaining forested land and aquatic features provide important habitat for a variety of plants and animals.

Mississippi Lowlands Natural Division: More than 24 million years ago, this region was the northern boundary of the Gulf of Mexico. Much later, during the time of the glaciers, melt-water from the retreating ice formed the Ohio and Mississippi river systems, which scoured and deposited sediments, and reshaped the land to what it is today. Up until 100 years ago, extensive bottomland forests and swamps dominated the region. Today, massive ditches and extensive agriculture have eliminated most of the habitat for unique plants and animals that have a southern coastal plain origin.

Osage Plains Natural Division: Like the Ozarks, this region is also unglaciated. The gently rolling hills and plains once were dominated by prairie. Although the deeper soils have been plowed for row crops and the thinner soils pastured, there are still areas of prairie — although measured in acres instead of square miles.

(Note: For a technical discussion of this subject see "The Natural Divisions of Missouri" by R.H. Thom and J.H. Wilson in "Transactions of the Missouri Academy of Science," Vol. 14, 1980, pp. 9-23; or, for a more general description, obtain a copy of the "Directory of Missouri Natural Areas," Missouri Conservation Department, 1996, which is available at Conservation Department offices.)

How to Use This Book

PLANT NAMES

Common names for plants are easy to learn, but they sometimes lead to confusion and misunderstanding because one species may have several names, and one name sometimes can be applied to more than one plant. Eastern witch hazel, for example also is called common witch hazel, witch hazel, hamamelis, long boughs, pistachio, snapping hazel, snapping hazelnut, southern witch hazel, spotted alder, striped, tobacco, white hazel, winterbloom, and wood tobacco. These names are frequently local and vary from place to place, but there is only one scientific

name, *Hamamelis virginiana*, and that is used worldwide. An example of a common name that is used for more than one plant is bowman's root. It is a synonym for hemp dogbane, spotted spurge and Culver's root — three completely different plants.

Scientific names are in classical Latin or Greek, which are adopted throughout the world, regardless of spoken language. They are also binomial, composed of the genus name followed by the specific name. The genus name is a noun, often commemorating noted botanists, or is simply the classical name for the group. The first letter of the genus is always capitalized. The species name is an adjective, modifying the noun, and is always written in lowercase letters. The scientific name for every shrub or woody vine covered in this book has an explanation for the derivation of the genus and species names.

Following the scientific name is the name, usually abbreviated, of the botanist who named the species; if two botanists are responsible for the binomial combination, the first is placed in parenthesis. The common and scientific names used in this book follow either Julian A. Steyermark's "Flora of Missouri" or George Yatskievych and Joanna Turner's "Catalogue of the Flora of Missouri."

USE OF KEYS

If you know the common name of a plant covered in this book, a quick check in the index can direct you to the page number for the species. Another method would be to thumb through the book and look for an illustration of a plant similar to the one you are trying to identify. But if the plant differs slightly and you cannot find it, it is time to use the keys.

Taxonomic keys provide a convenient shortcut method of identifying plants by outlining and grouping related types. They consist of a series of couplets, with a choice of contrasting statements. The first choice may sound like the right description, but read both categories to make sure. The second category, by contrast, may actually help to explain the first one. After a choice is made, a number at the end of the category directs you to either the page for the plant description or to the next couplet.

The keys and species descriptions were written

in a way to avoid botanical terms as much as possible. When terms are used, they are immediately defined in parenthesis. This method saves time and eliminates the need for a glossary or having to memorize such terms as obovate, cuneate, etc. Often, more than one character is used to identify plants in the key. Leaves, flowers and fruit commonly are described, but winter characters such as leaf scars and buds are not.

NOTES ON SPECIES DESCRIPTIONS

The shrubs and woody vines are grouped separately, and listed by scientific name in alphabetical order. Both common and scientific names can be found in the index. When a scientific name has changed, the older name or less commonly used name is mentioned in the "Remarks" section under species descriptions. All names mentioned, both common and scientific, are listed in the index.

The state maps, showing counties in which the particular species has been found, are taken from Julian A. Steyermark's "Flora of Missouri." This 1963 publication is being revised and updated by George Yatskievych, Missouri Conservation Department. Subsequent revisions of the "Shrubs and Woody Vines of Missouri" will add the new distribution maps from the revised flora.

Landscaping With Native Shrubs and Woody Vines

Maybe it is a part of human nature, or maybe we have been conditioned, to always want to look for something new and different; this desire is nowhere more apparent than with the pursuit of new plants. Seed and plant catalogs and garden nurseries strive to offer the "improved" variety that displays a different flower shape or color or some other characteristic that sets it apart from past examples.

Unfortunately, along with the desire for something bigger and better or new and improved, comes the feeling that the plant has to be exotic; that is, from another country. We have been so conditioned this way that we often are surprised

when we see something "native" that catches our eye, and wonder where it has been all the while.

Native plants have been ignored too long because of the attention that has been focused on the use of exotics. But the natives slowly are gaining the attention of people that are concerned about the threat exotics pose to our diminishing natural communities. Even exotics planted in backyards can spread into nearby habitats. They often out-compete native trees, shrubs and wildflowers, and as a result, reduce the diversity of plants that wildlife depend upon for food and cover.

A drive through the residential areas of St. Louis County in April underscores the severity of this problem. The understory along the highways' wooded corridors is solid with the green foliage of bush honeysuckle. This aggressive shrub is early to leaf out in the spring and one of the last to drop its leaves in autumn, thereby robbing seedling trees, shrubs and showy wildflowers of the necessary sunlight to grow. This is one example among many where exotic plants have been highly promoted; once established, many have proved to be hard or almost impossible to eradicate.

Native shrubs and woody vines contain many fine attributes worthy of ornamental use. They are very economical, since they are long-lived and seldom need replacing. They have adapted throughout thousands of years to the local climate and soils, so they are more likely to survive the extremes of heat, cold and drought. They are easy to grow, and do not require constant attention once they are established. There is a variety of heights and shapes, foliage patterns, and colors and shapes of flowers and fruits from which to choose.

On the following pages is a list of selected shrubs and woody vines. The plants are grouped by habitat desirability or by features of interest for landscaping purposes.

Shrubs and Woody Vines for Use in Moist Sites or Along Stream Banks

Shrubs

Amorpha fruticosa, false indigo
Aronia melanocarpa, black chokeberry
Arundinaria gigantea, giant cane
Cephalanthus occidentalis, button bush
Cornus foemna, stiff dogwood
Cornus obliqua, swamp dogwood
Dirca palustris, leatherwood
Hamamelis vernalis, Ozark witch hazel
Hamamelis virginiana, Eastern witch hazel
Ilex verticillata, winterberry
Itea virginica, Virginia willow
Lindera benzoin, spice bush
Rosa palustris, swamp rose
Salix species, willows
Sambucus canadensis, common elderberry
Sambucus racemosa, red-berried elder
Spiraea alba, meadow-sweet
Spiraea tomentosa, hardhack
Staphylea trifoliata, American bladdernut
Styrax americanum, snow-bell

Woody Vines

Ampelopsis arborea, pepper vine
Aristolochia tomentosa, woolly pipe-vine
Bignonia capreolata, cross vine
Vitis palmata, red grape
Vitis riparia, riverbank grape
Vitis rupestris, sand grape
Vitis vulpina, frost grape
Wisteria frutescens, wisteria

Shrubs and Woody Vines With Interesting Fruit

Shrubs

Aesculus glabra, Ohio buckeye ■ leathery capsule, shiny brown seed
Aesculus pavia, red buckeye ■ leathery capsule, shiny brown seed
Amelanchier arborea, service berry ■ red
Aralia spinosa, Hercules club ■ large black clusters
Callicarpa americana, beauty berry ■ bright violet
Cornus alternifolia, alternate-leaved dogwood ■ blue-black
Cornus florida, flowering dogwood ■ bright red
Cornus foemina, stiff dogwood ■ bright blue
Cornus obliqua, swamp dogwood ■ pale blue
Corylus americana, hazelnut ■ brownish acornlike, edible
Cotinus obovatus, smoke tree ■ smokey appearance when in fruit
Crataegus species, hawthorns ■ red
Euonymous americanus, strawberry bush ■ warty red capsule, scarlet seed
Euonymous atropurpureus, wahoo ■ red capsule, scarlet seed
Ilex decidua, possum haw ■ red
Ilex verticillata, winterberry ■ red
Lindera benzoin, spice bush ■ bright red
Prunus americana, wild plum ■ red
Prunus angustifolia, chickasaw plum ■ reddish-yellow
Prunus virginiana, choke cherry ■ dark red
Ptelea trifoliata, hop tree ■ large waferlike wings
Quercus prinoides, dwarf chinquapin oak ■ small acorns
Rhamnus caroliniana, Carolina buckthorn ■ shiny black
Rhus copallina, winged sumac ■ red clusters
Rhus glabra, smooth sumac ■ red clusters
Ribes species, gooseberries and currants ■ edible
Rosa blanda, smooth wild rose ■ large red rose hips, edible
Rosa palustris, swamp rose ■ red rose hips, edible
Rosa setigera, prairie rose ■ red rose hips, edible
Rubus species, blackberries and raspberries ■ red to black, edible
Sambucus canadensis, common elderberry ■ purplish-black clusters
Sambucus racemosa, red-berried elder ■ red clusters
Staphylea trifoliata, American bladdernut ■ large inflated capsules
Symphoricarpos occidentalis, wolfberry ■ white clusters
Vaccinium species, blueberries ■ bluish-black, edible
Viburnum species, arrow woods ■ bluish-black

Woody Vines

Aristolochia tomentosa, woolly pipe-vine ■ a large dry capsule
Celastrus scandens, American bittersweet ■ scarlet capsule, red seeds
Clematis virginiana, virgin's bower ■ clusters of long white hairs
Lonicera species, honeysuckles ■ red
Parthenocissus quinquefolia, Virginia creeper ■ dark purple
Parthenocissus vitacea, woodbine ■ bluish-black
Vitis species, grapes ■ red to dark purple, edible

Shrubs and Woody Vines For Fall Color

Shrubs

Aesculus glabra, Ohio buckeye ■ yellow
Aesculus pavia, red buckeye ■ yellow
Amelanchier arborea, service berry ■ orange
Callicarpa americana, beauty berry ■ yellow
Cercis canadensis, Eastern redbud ■ yellow
Cornus florida, flowering dogwood ■ red to purple
Cotinus americanus, smoke tree ■ reddish-orange
Dirca palustris, leatherwood ■ yellow
Hamamelis vernalis, Ozark witch hazel ■ yellow
Hamamelis virginiana, Eastern witch hazel ■ yellow
Lindera benzoin, spice bush ■ yellow
Ptelea trifolia, hop tree ■ yellow
Rhamnus caroliniana, Carolina buckthorn ■ yellow
Rhus aromatica, fragrant sumac ■ reddish-yellow to red
Rhus copallina, winged sumac ■ red
Rhus glabra, smooth sumac ■ red

Woody Vines

Celastrus scandens, American bittersweet ■ yellow
Cocculus carolinus, Carolina moonseed ■ bright red
Parthenocissus quinquefolia, Virginia creeper ■ red
Parthenocissus vitacea, woodbine ■ red
Vitis species, grapes ■ yellow

Spring-Flowering Shrubs

Aesculus glabra, Ohio buckeye
Aesculus pavia, red buckeye
Amelanchier arborea, service berry
Amorpha canescens, lead plant
Amorpha fruticosa, false indigo
Ceanothus americanus, New Jersey tea
Ceanothus herbaceus, redroot
Cercis canadensis, Eastern redbud
Chionanthus virginicus, fringe tree
Cornus species, dogwoods
Cotinus obovatus, smoke tree
Crataegus species, hawthorns
Dirca palustris, leatherwood
Euonymus atropurpureus, wahoo
Hydrangea arborescens, wild hydrangea
Lindera benzoin, spice bush
Neviusia alabamensis, snow wreath
Philadelphus pubescens, mock orange
Physocarpus opulifolius, ninebark
Prunus species, wild plums
Rhododendron roseum, wild azalea

Ribes species, gooseberries and currants
Styrax americanum, snow-bell
Vaccinium species, blueberries
Viburnum species, arrow woods

Summer-Flowering Shrubs

Aralia spinosa, Hercules club
Callicarpa americana, beauty berry
Cephalanthus occidentalis, buttonbush
Hypericum prolificum, shrubby St. John's-wort
Spiraea alba, meadow-sweet
Spiraea tomentosa, hardhack

Tall Shrubs or Small Trees

Aesculus glabra, Ohio buckeye
Amelanchier arborea, service berry
Aralia spinosa, Hercules club
Bumelia lanuginosa, woolly buckthorn
Cercis canadensis, Eastern redbud
Chionanthus virginicus, fringe tree
Cornus species, dogwoods
Cotinus obovatus, smoketree
Crataegus species, hawthorns
Hamamelis vernalis, Ozark witch hazel
Hamamelis virginiana, Eastern witch hazel
Ilex decidua, possum haw
Prunus species, wild plums
Rhamnus caroliniana, Carolina buckthorn
Rhamnus lanceolata, lance-leaved buckthorn
Viburnum species, arrow woods

Low-Growing Shrubs

Amorpha canescens, lead plant
Ascyrum hypericoides, St. Andrew's cross
Polygonella americana, jointweed
Rosa arkansana, Arkansas rose
Rosa carolina, pasture rose
Rubus flagellaris, dewberry
Vaccinium vacillans, lowbush blueberry

This list is by no means inclusive. These are plants, however, that may be more readily available from plant nurseries. You do have the option of broadening your selection by collecting and propagating seeds and cuttings, or by layering. All of these techniques are discussed in the section on propagation. Digging plants from the wild is not recommended. Most plants do not survive from the shock of transplanting, and the practice is not desirable from a conservation standpoint.

Charles Schwartz

Landscaping to Help Bring Wildlife to Your Backyard

Some of our fondest childhood memories involve wildlife discoveries made in our own backyard. Remember the thrill of watching a colorful butterfly flutter and alight on a flower, or a squirrel scamper up a tree? How about the delight of discovering your first robin's eggs in a mud-lined nest? All these experiences can help nurture a lifelong interest in nature.

Wildlife will not be drawn to urban backyards, however, unless you can provide a habitat composed of three basic ingredients: food, water and shelter. Food comes from plants that produce fruits, berries, grains, seeds, acorns, nuts or nectar. The plants can be herbaceous annuals, biennials and perennials, or trees, shrubs and woody vines.

Mixtures of all these types provide a variety of foods that are available throughout the year for butterflies and other insects, birds and mammals. In addition, insects — many of which feed on plant parts — provide protein for other insects, reptiles, amphibians, birds and mammals.

Native shrubs and woody vines that attract butterflies, moths and their caterpillars

Shrubs

Aesculus glabra, Ohio buckeye
Aesculus pavia, red buckeye
Ceanothus americanus, New Jersey tea
Cephalanthus occidentalis, buttonbush
Cercis canadensis, Eastern redbud
Crataegus species, hawthorns
Lindera benzoin, spice bush
Malus species, wild crab apples
Prunus species, wild plums and cherries
Rhus aromatica, fragrant sumac
Rhus copallina, winged sumac
Rhus glabra, smooth sumac
Ribes species, gooseberries and currants
Rubus species, blackberries and dewberries
Spiraea alba, meadow-sweet
Spiraea tomentosa, hardhack
Vaccinium species, blueberries
Viburnum species, arrow woods

Woody Vines

Aristolochia tomentosa, woolly pipe-vine
Lonicera species, honeysuckles

Native shrubs and woody vines especially attractive to birds

Shrubs

Amelanchier arborea, service berry
Aralia spinosa, Hercules club
Callicarpa americana, beauty berry
Cornus species, dogwoods
Crataegus species, hawthorns
Euonymus atropurpureus, wahoo
Ilex decidua, possum haw
Ilex verticillata, winterberry
Lindera benzoin, spicebush
Malus species, wild crab apples
Physocarpus opulifolius, ninebark
Prunus species, wild plums and cherries
Rhus species, sumacs
Ribes species, gooseberries and currants
Rosa species, roses
Rubus species, blackberries and raspberries
Sambucus canadensis, common elderberry
Sambucus racemosa, red-berried elder
Symphoricarpos orbiculatus, buckbrush

Vaccinium species, blueberries
Viburnum species, arrow woods

Woody Vines

Campsis radicans, trumpet creeper
Celastrus scandens, bittersweet
Lonicera species, honeysuckles
Parthenocissus quinquefolia, Virginia creeper
Parthenocissus vitacea, woodbine
Vitis species, wild grapes

A source of water will more than double the numbers and variety of wildlife that will be attracted to your backyard habitat. A bird bath, water garden or frog pond will provide a local source for water, and eliminate the time wildlife would spent searching for it elsewhere.

Shelter or cover is the last ingredient for attracting wildlife to your property. Birds, especially, need places where they can hide from predators and escape from severe weather. Densely branching shrubs also provide good nesting places for birds and excellent cover for their fledglings. Shrubs that spread by suckering to create dense thickets ideal for nesting cover include wild plums and cherries, and blackberries and raspberries.

For more information on ways to attract wildlife to your property, consult Carrol Henderson's "Landscaping for Wildlife," listed on page 381. Also, ask the Missouri Department of Conservation for a copy of "Landscaping for Backyard Wildlife." Additional worthwhile references are listed under Selected References.

David Besenger

Planting and Maintenance

Whether buying nursery stock or growing plants yourself, the same common sense gardening techniques used for growing and caring for traditional garden plants can be applied to native shrubs and woody vines. There are many excellent publications on the subject, some of which are free. Be sure to contact the university extension service (located in most counties) or the Missouri Conservation Department's Forestry Division for publications on the planting and maintenance of trees and shrubs.

There are some basic rules of thumb that should be practiced to ensure successful plant establishment. The best time to plant nursery stock is in late fall to early winter. This gives the plant some time to get established, and allows the roots to continue growing in all but the coldest of temperatures. If the container-grown plant is potbound, unravel the roots and spread them out before covering with soil. Prune the shrub about one-third off the top to aid in its establishment. This also will produce a denser crown, which can attract songbirds seeking nesting sites and cover.

Mulch around the shrub with leaves, grass clippings, wood chips, or straw to reduce weeds and hold moisture. Add fertilizer in spring when growth appears. A light application of a balanced fertilizer such as 10-10-10 will work. Some shrubs that need a more acid soil, such as vacciniums and rhododendrons, require an acid fertilizer that can be purchased at most garden supply stores. Water frequently during the first growing season to aid the roots in getting established.

Shrubs are very low-maintenance plants. Their dense shapes are often used to form hedges or screens along a boundary or to separate one part of the property from the garden area. They also are well-suited for parks and open spaces, especially along highway roadsides. Woody vines, on the other hand, need a little more attention since they have a tendency to wander and climb. They can be used effectively on trellises or allowed to sprawl over rocky exposed areas. They also can be used on slopes to curtail bank erosion and allowed to climb fences to aid in screening. A few, such as the native raccoon grape, trumpet creeper and the exotic Japanese honeysuckle, are very aggressive; their planting is not recommended.

Control Recommendations: It is sometimes necessary to treat undesirable shrubs and woody vines, especially if they are not native. The simplest method to eradicate shrubs is to cut the plant off at the base and treat with a herbicide. Roundup herbicide (a formulation of glyphosate) is available at most garden and farm supply stores. Buy the liquid herbicide in concentrated form and dilute to 20 percent with water; apply within minutes to the freshly cut stump. A brush or sponge applicator is very effective and minimizes waste. Plastic bottles with mist sprayers also may be used.

The cut-stump treatment is most effective July to September when the sap is traveling down into the roots, carrying the herbicide with it. Treatment in winter has also proved effective. Avoid applications when the plant is actively growing. Sap is moving up and into the branches, keeping the herbicide from entering the roots.

Since Roundup is a nonselective herbicide, it is not recommended as a foliar spray because the drift would contact, and possibly kill, non-target species. Follow the same recommendations for treating unwanted woody vines. A foliar spray of 2 to 3 percent can be applied to the leaves if the surface area is solid vines. This is often the case with Japanese honeysuckle where rampant growth smothers other vegetation. Since this exotic vine is semi-evergreen, the leaves can be sprayed in November after a hard frost. By then, most native plants have gone dormant, except for Japanese honeysuckle.

Propagation

Growing shrubs and woody vines from seeds, cuttings or by layering is an enjoyable and inexpensive way of adding diversity to your backyard. Unfortunately, many of the plants described in this book are not available from nurseries or plant catalogues. But, with a little background knowledge on plant propagation, an afternoon's walk can yield a variety of interesting plants whose seeds can be collected and grown with little cost and effort. Time and patience, and a little attention, are the main requirements for successful plant propagation.

The collecting of seeds on public land is usually permissible, but digging plants is not. In 1993, Missouri passed a plant digging law (Revised Statute of Missouri Law No. 229.475) that makes it illegal to dig plants from roadsides of county, state, or interstate highways unless a person is granted special permission from the agency responsible for administering the roadside. The collection of above-ground plant parts is allowed, as long as the collection is not for commercial purposes. Digging and transplanting plants from the wild also is not recommended because of the low rate of recovery from loss and damage to the plant's root system.

Where available, nursery-grown stock is the easiest to work with; potted shrubs and vines already have a few years growth, which enables them to flower sooner. This is particularly advantageous if the flowers and fruits are the most worthwhile features. Most nurseries are limited in their supply of native plants, but ask if they can order what you want. Listed in Appendix B, page 380, are mail-order nurseries that sell native woody plants.

Growing plants from seeds is a cheap and easy alternative to nursery-grown plants, although it may take three to five years before the plant is old enough to flower. When collecting seeds be sure that the fruit appears ripe or mature. Fleshy fruit often changes color and softens, which indicates the seeds are ready. The seeds must be separated from the pulp and allowed to dry.

Other plants produce capsules that turn brown and split open when the seeds are ready. Seeds should be collected in a paper bag or envelope. Avoid putting any seeds in plastic bags or glass jars. These airproof containers can cause the seed to rot from excess moisture. Store seeds away from excessive heat and the sun's rays until you are ready to plant them.

Few seeds are capable of germinating right away. Many require certain conditions, such as a rest or dormant period.

Other seeds with thick coats, such as legumes, need scarification — a process whereby the seed's outer layer is worn down or cracks from cycles of heat or cold. Once the seed coat is damaged, water enters the seed to start the growing process. It may take a few years for this to occur in nature, but by nicking the seed coat with a file the swelling can occur overnight. Be sure to cut on the opposite side of where the seed was attached, and use a triangular file to make a notch deep enough so that you see a change in color.

Some seeds are not fully mature when they leave their parent plant. The embryo needs additional time to fully grow and develop. This can happen during a process called stratification, where the seeds are exposed to warm and/or cold temperatures for several weeks or months.

In both cases the seeds need moisture. Fringe tree seeds, for example, exhibit what is called a double dormancy. The seeds are produced during the growing season, overwinter, and receive warm stratification the following summer; after winter's cold treatment, the seeds germinate the following spring. Fortunately, this two-year process happens in only a few other shrubs, such as witch hazel, spice bush, hop hornbeam, elderberry and viburnums.

Most seeds simply need cold stratification. This is easily accomplished by placing the seeds in a plastic bag mixed with equal parts of coarse sand, sphagnum moss or peat moss that is moist, but not excessively wet. (If sand is used, be sure to boil it first to destroy insect eggs and any fungus that might be present.) Then place the bag in the refrigerator for a couple of months at around 40 degrees Fahrenheit.

This is best done in February and March for planting in April, either in the ground or in pots for later transplanting. Seed treatment requirements for many of the plants described in this book may be found in "Seeds of Woody Plants in the United States" (USDA Forest Service, Agriculture Handbook No. 450, 1974. Ask your local library or garden center for a copy.

The easiest way to propagate plants from seed is simply to plant the seed directly in soil, usually at a depth of twice its diameter. If the seed is collected from plants and sown within their normal range, chances are they will successfully germinate. Attention also must be given to planting them in soil conditions similar to that of the parent plant's. Seeds planted out of the natural range of the parent plants often will not germinate. Flowering dogwood is a good example. The range for this plant is in the southern half of Missouri. Apparently, the seeds are sensitive to the colder winter temperatures of northern latitudes.

On the other hand, more northern ranging plants such as red-berried elder and pussy willow may find either the winters not cold enough or the summers too hot for seed germination, or maybe a combination of both. Stratifying seeds and planting them in pots under controlled conditions, such as in your house or in a cold frame, is a sure way to start plants.

Growing plants from cuttings takes a little more effort and attention, but it allows you to start plants faster. With a cutting, flowering time often can be shortened to two years; with seeds, however, it may take from three to five years for most shrubs and vines. Also, the desirable characteristics of the parent plant will be duplicated in the cutting, because it is just an extension of the same genes.

With seeds, the new plants may or may not look exactly like the parent plant because the genetic makeup of each seed is not exactly the same. If you find a flowering dogwood with a pink flower, for example, you will produce offspring with that same characteristic by growing new plants from cuttings. Seeds typically will revert to the flowering dogwood's normal color of white.

The best time to take cuttings is at the plant's softwood stage. This is usually after the twig has finished producing new leaves, which is around late June through July. The twig is just beginning to harden or become firm, and the bark is still partly green. Early in the morning is the best time to take cuttings — before wind and sun begin drawing moisture out of the twigs and leaves. With a sharp knife, cut 6- to 8-inch sections off the tips of branches and place them in either a moist plastic bag or in water until they are ready to be planted.

Next, strip the lower leaves, leaving 2 to 3 inches of the twig bare. With a sharp knife, cut a shallow slice along one side of the bare part of the twig, removing only the thin bark. At this stage, dusting the wound with rooting hormone will stimulate the roots to grow faster. Rooting hormone is available at most nursery supply stores, with certain types specifically formulated for use on woody plants.

Place the cuttings in a medium composed of moistened sphagnum moss, or a combination of peat or perlite — also available at stores selling plants. Sterilized sand also may be used, but it must be coarse to allow air spaces for the roots. The container should be covered with a plastic bag or plastic wrap, which provides humidity and keeps the soil from drying out. A six-pack styrofoam cooler works very well; be sure to punch drainage holes in the bottom. Place the container in a shaded location with an air temperature of between 70 and 80 F.

The cuttings should root in about three weeks and begin new top growth in six weeks. Gently tug at the cutting, and if it resists, the roots have developed. Gradually remove the covering to allow the plants to "harden off"; this refers to the plants' need to adapt to the conditions of wind and lower humidity. The rooted cuttings may be either planted or left in the container to overwinter for spring planting. In the latter case, the container should overwinter on the north side of a building, and be mulched to protect the new plants from severe cold temperatures.

Layering requires the least amount of attention, but the practice is not as reliable in producing new plants. A young limb of a shrub or a portion of a vine is wounded by scraping away a small section of bark on the underside of the twig. Bury the section in a shallow trench, anchor it and cover with soil; be sure to leave the tip above ground. After about two years, the newly rooted branch or vine can be separated just below the roots and planted. Sometimes this form of propagation happens naturally and a spade or trowel is all that is needed to retrieve a rooted section of stem or vine for transplanting.

Keys to the Shrubs

1. Small trees or shrubs 2
1. Vines, climbing and twining or sprawling, p. 30

2. Plants somewhat parasitic upon the branches of trees . . . Mistletoe, *Phoradendron flavescens*, p. 164
2. Plants not parasitic upon the branches of trees and with stems or trunk emerging from the ground 3

3. Plants consisting of a cluster of long, swordlike leaves emerging from the base. 4
3. Plants without basal leaf cluster; leaves arranged along stem 6

4. Flowering or fruiting main stem with several long conspicuous side branches; leaves shorter than the base of the flowering or fruiting part of the stem; main leaves 1 1/4 to 1 3/4 inches wide . . . Spanish bayonet, *Yucca smalliana*, p. 298
4. Flowering or fruiting main stem unbranched; leaves longer than the base of the flowering or fruiting portion of the stem; main leaves 1/4 to 1 inch wide 5

5. Plants of hill prairies of northwestern Missouri; leaves stiff and rigid, 1/4 to 1/2 inch wide; petals pointed at tip . . . Soapweed, *Yucca glauca* var. *glauca,* p. 296
5. Plants of glades of southernmost counties of Missouri; leaves rather soft and flexible, 1/2 to 1 inch wide; petals mostly blunt at tip . . . Soapweed, *Yucca glauca* var. *mollis*, p. 296

6. Plants with hollow-jointed bamboolike stems with base of leaves enclosing the stem; leaves with parallel veins . . . Giant cane, *Arundinaria gigantea*, p. 56
6. Plants with various stems, but not hollow and jointed. 7

7. Leaves scalelike or needlelike, less than 1/4 inch wide 8
7. Leaves not scalelike or needlelike, more than 1/4 inch wide **10**

8. Large shrub to small tree, evergreen, with minute scalelike leaves; leaves opposite or whorled; plants of glades, woodlands and old fields 9
8. Small shrub to 4 feet, deciduous, with needlelike leaves; leaves alternate; plants of open areas with sandy soil . . . Jointweed, *Polygonella americana*, p. 170

9. Shrub or small tree to 30 feet in height; trunk of tree more or less branched at base; bark with conspicuous white blotches on the trunk and branches; leaves bright green in winter; short branchlets holding the scalelike leaves soft to the touch . . . Ashe's juniper, *Juniperus ashei*, p. 136
9. Medium-sized tree to 60 feet in height; trunk of tree solitary, unbranched at the base; bark lacking white blotches on trunk and branches; leaves rust-colored in winter; short branchlets holding the scalelike leaves rough to prickly to the touch . . . Eastern red cedar, *Juniperus virginiana*, a tree, not covered in this book.

10. Leaves simple 11
10. Leaves compound 12

11. Leaves opposite or whorled. . . . Key A, p.16
11. Leaves alternate . . . . Key B, p.19

12. Leaves opposite . . . . Key C, p.26
12. Leaves alternate . . . . Key D, p.26

KEY A. Shrubs With Leaves Simple and Opposite or Whorled

1. Leaves whorled . . . Buttonbush, *Cephalanthus occidentalis*, p. 76
1. Leaves opposite 2

2. Leaves with toothed margins. 3
2. Leaves with entire margins 18

3. Twigs often ending in a spine . . . Common buckthorn, *Rhamnus cathartica*, p. 194
3. Twigs not ending in a spine. 4

4. At least some of the leaves with petioles more than 1 1/2 inches long . . . Wild hydrangea, *Hydrangea aborescens*, p. 124
4. Petioles less than 1 1/2 inches long 5

5. Undersurface of leaves, petioles and twigs covered with dense, star-shaped hairs . . . Beauty berry, *Callicarpa americana*, p. 66
5. Leaves, petioles and twigs smooth or with hairs not star-shaped. 6

6. Twigs green and somewhat 4-sided or with 4 prominent lines 7
6. Twigs neither green or 4-sided. 9

7. Petioles (leaf stalk) of leaves at tip of stem more than 1/4 inch long 8
7. Petioles of leaves at tip of stem less than 1/4 inch long or absent 10

8. Leaves hairy beneath; stems not prominently winged; flowers 7 to 15, purple; fruit purple to rose-colored; coating covering seed scarlet . . . Wahoo, *Euonymous atropurpureus*, p. 110
8. Leaves smooth beneath; stems prominently winged; flowers 2 to 8, yellowish-green; fruit pink; coating covering seed orange to red . . . Winged euonymus, *Euonymous alatus*, p. 106

9. Stems trailing and rooting when in contact with soil; leaves thin, those at tip of stem inverted egg-shaped, mostly broadest in upper half; plants of shaded rocky, mainly dolomite, north-facing bluffs and slopes . . . Running strawberry bush, *Euonymus obovatus*, p. 112
9. Stems erect or sprawling, or the lower branches sometimes rooting; leaves thick, those at tip of stem lance- to egg-shaped, broadest at middle or lower half; plants of low sandy woods along spring branches, low moist woods, moist wooded slopes and moist stream banks . . . Strawberry bush, *Euonymus americanus*, p. 108

10. Leaf bases narrowly wedge-shaped; flowers and fruits in clusters on stem of previous year . . . Swamp privet, *Forestiera acuminata*, p. 114
10. Leaf bases usually rounded to heart-shaped; flowers and fruits in clusters on stem of current year. 11

11. Leaves with 1 or 2 pairs of side veins originating near the base of the blade and curving sharply toward the leaf tip and not toward the immediate margin . . . Mock orange, *Philadelphus pubescens*, p. 162
11. Leaves with several pairs of side veins originating along the central vein and directed toward the margin, not curving sharply toward the leaf tip 12

12. Margins of leaves normally with many fine, narrow, closely crowded teeth; side veins branching and joining before reaching the margin; petiole flat 13
12. Margins of leaves normally with coarse, broad or triangular more loosely-spaced teeth; side veins simple, each vein extending to a tooth. 15

13. Rust-colored hairs or numerous dots on lower surface of leaves, especially along the central vein, also on petioles; leaf blades leathery, glossy on upper surface . . . Southern black haw, *Viburnum rufidulum*, p. 294
13. Few or no rust-colored hairs or dots on lower surface of leaves, or along central vein or petioles; leaf blades rather thin, not leathery, dull on upper surface 14

14. Rarely encountered; all or most of leaf blades abruptly slender and long-pointed at tip; teeth of leaf blades conspicuously pointing outward; margins of petioles (leaf stalks) wavy . . . Nannyberry, *Viburnum lentago*, p. 284
14. Commonly encountered throughout Missouri; leaf blades blunt or short-pointed at the tip; teeth of leaf blades curved inward or upward toward the tip, shorter and less conspicuous; margins of petioles (leaf stalks) not at all or only slightly wavy . . . Black haw, *Viburnum prunifolium*, p. 288

15. Petioles (leaf stalks) 3/8 inch long or less, nearly absent on some leaves (particularly those below the flower clusters); usually 4 to 10 teeth along the margin on each side of the leaf blade . . . Downy arrow wood, *Viburnum rafinesquianum*, p. 290
15. Petioles (leaf stalks) over 3/8 inch long, 10 to 30 teeth along the margin on each side of the leaf blade 16

16. Leaves usually deeply heart-shaped at the base; usually 16 to 30 teeth along the margin on each side of the leaf blade; outer bark loose and peeling off . . . Arrow wood, *Viburnum molle*, p. 286

16. Leaves usually rounded or narrowed at base, not deeply heart-shaped; mostly 10 to 15 teeth along the margin on each side of the leaf blade; outer bark tight, not peeling off 17

17. Flower stalks, petioles (leaf stalks), and both surfaces of leaf blades smooth . . . Arrow wood, *Viburnum recognitum*, p. 292

17. Flower stalks, petioles (leaf stalks), and both surfaces of leaf blades more or less hairy . . . Southern arrow wood, *Viburnum dentatum*, p. 282

18. Plants somewhat parasitic upon the branches of trees . . . Mistletoe, *Phoradendron flavescens,* p. 164

18. Plants not parasitic upon the branches of trees and with stems or trunk emerging from the ground 19

19. Flowers in clusters at the end of twigs . . . 20
19. Flowers in clusters along the leaf axils . . . 26

20. Leaves with the main veins curving, tending to parallel the margin and to meet at or near the leaf tip 21

20. Leaves with the main veins extending toward the margin with little curvature toward the leaf tip . . . Buttonbush, *Cephalanthus occidentalis*, p. 76

21. Leaves alternate, but often crowded at ends of twigs and appearing whorled; most of the leaf stalks 3/4 to 2 1/4 inches long . . . Alternate-leaved dogwood, *Cornus alternifolia*, p. 82

21. Leaves opposite; most of the leaf stalks 1/4 to 3/4 inch long 22

22. Flowers greenish-yellow in a dense headlike cluster surrounded by 4 large white or pink petallike bracts; fruit bright red; small trees up to 40 feet . . . Flowering dogwood, *Cornus florida*, p. 86

22. Flowers white or creamy-white in an open broad cluster, not surrounded by bracts; fruit blue or white; shrubs 3 to 20 feet tall 23

23. Lower surface of leaves woolly with loose curled or curving hairs; upper surface of leaves rather rough-hairy (rarely smooth) . . . Rough-leaved dogwood, *Cornus drummondii*, p. 84

23. Lower surface of leaves either lacking hairs or slightly hairy with minute hairs lying close against the surface; upper surface of leaves smooth 24

24. Lower surface of leaves green and without any hairs; pith of the twigs of the present year and up to 2 years old white and less than 1/3 the diameter of the twig . . . Stiff dogwood, *Cornus foemina*, p. 88

24. Lower surface of leaves whitish, grayish or gray to silvery green with minute colorless hairs lying close against the surface; pith of the twigs of the present year and up to 2 years old pale brown or tan; or, if white, the pith at least half the diameter of the twig 25

25. Youngest twigs densely hairy; older branches reddish-brown; fruit bluish; flower cluster flat or indented at the summit, broader than high; stalks of the flowers yellow brown . . . Swamp dogwood, *Cornus obliqua*, p. 90

25. Youngest twigs lacking hairs; older branches gray; fruit white on red stalks; flower cluster dome- or globe-shaped; stalks of the flowers red . . . Gray dogwood, *Cornus racemosa*, p. 92

26. Leaves long and narrow, up to 1/2 inch wide 27

26. Leaves more than 1/2 inch wide 28

27. Plant upright, 1 to 6 feet tall; leaves usually with smaller ones in their axils . . . Shrubby St. John's-wort, *Hypericum prolificum*, p. 128

27. Plant small, up to 3 feet tall or sprawling; leaves without smaller ones in their axils . . . St. Andrew's cross, *Hypericum hypericoides*, p. 126

28. Leaves large, from 4 to 8 inches long, often clustered at the tip and may appear whorled . . . Fringe tree, *Chionanthus virginicus*, p. 80

28. Leaves smaller, up to 3 inches long, not clustered at the tip and clearly opposite 29

29. Fruit black; flowers tubular shaped; petals 4; stamens 2 . . . California privet, *Ligustrum ovalifolium*, p. 140

29. Fruit white, pink or red; flowers bell-shaped with 5 petals or tubular with 2 lips and showy 30

30. Flowers showy, fragrant, tubular and 2-lipped, 1 lip with 4 lobes, the other lip with 1 lobe; leaf tip abruptly pointed; leaf margin fringed with fine hairs . . . Bush honeysuckle, *Lonicera maackii*, p. 146

30. Flowers small, not showy or fragrant; with 5 petals; leaf tip round to blunt or if pointed, not abruptly; leaf margin lacking a fringe of fine hairs 31

31. Flower about 1/8 inch long, greenish to purplish; fruit usually coral-pink, purplish-red or red . . . Buckbrush, *Symphoricarpos orbiculatus*, p. 272

31. Flower about 1/4 inch long, pale pink; fruit white or greenish white . . . Wolfberry, *Symphoricarpos occidentalis*, p. 270

KEY B. Shrubs With Leaves Simple and Alternate

1. Leaves entire 2
1. Leaves toothed or lobed 25

2. Thorns or prickles present 3
2. Thorns or prickles absent 5

3. Fruit red; twigs with prominent thorns at the axil of each leaf bundle; flowers 2 to 4 per cluster; petals 6; stamens 6 . . . Japanese barberry, *Berberis thunbergii*, p. 60

3. Fruit black; twigs with scattered thorns, not at the axil of each leaf bundle; flowers 10 to 50 per cluster; petals 5; stamens 5 4

4. Lower surface of leaves densely hairy; twigs more or less hairy . . . Woolly buckthorn, *Bumelia lanuginosa*, p. 62

4. Lower surface of leaves smooth or nearly so; twigs smooth or nearly so . . . Southern buckthorn, *Bumelia lycioides*, p. 64

5. Leaves grasslike with parallel veins . . . Giant cane, *Arundinaria gigantea*, p. 56

5. Leaves with veins arising from the base (palmate) or along the main vein (pinnate) 6

6. Plants rare; catkins flowering before leaves emerge . . . Corkwood, *Leitneria floridana*, p. 138

6. Conditions not as above 7

7. Leaves heart-shaped, broadly rounded, or as broad as or broader than long . . . Eastern redbud, *Cercis canadensis*, p. 78

7. Leaves not heart-shaped or broader than long 8

8. Young twigs and at least lower side of leaves covered with a dense silvery or whitish hairiness 9

8. Young twigs and leaves not covered with a dense silvery or whitish hairiness 11

9. Leaves densely silvery-scaly on at least lower side and often on both sides; outside of flowers silvery-scaly; flowers not in catkins . . . Autumn olive, *Eleaegnus umbellata*, p. 104

9. Leaves silvery- or whitish-hairy but not silvery-scaly; outside of flowers not silvery-scaly; flowers in catkins 10

10. Lower side of leaf more or less hairy; twigs often hairy; low shrub mainly 3 to 9 feet tall; occurs in prairies, hill prairies, open woods, rocky draws or washes, rocky slopes, and thickets . . . Prairie willow, *Salix humilis*, p. 248

10. Lower side of leaf smooth; mature twigs smooth or nearly so; large shrub to small tree to 16 feet tall; occurs in very wet areas along creeks and rivers in open or wooded areas . . . Pussy willow, *Salix discolor*, p. 246

11. Leaves with 3 main veins arising from the same place at the very base of the leaf blade at junction with petiole 12

11. Leaves with one main vein with side veins arising at various locations along it and not from the base of the leaf 13

12. Shrub or small tree growing in glades or other dry rocky exposed situations; leaves of

fruiting branches more than 1/2 as broad as long, egg-shaped, tip blunt or ending at a sharp angle; grayish green on both surfaces or darker above . . . Dwarf hackberry, *Celtis tenuifolia*, p. 74

12. Usually medium to large tree of low wet bottomland along streams and in valleys, but also small trees on glades and bluffs; leaves of fruiting branches less than 1/2 as broad as long, mostly narrowly lance-shaped, tapering to a long slender tip, which is often curved to one side; both leaf surfaces pale or dull green . . . Sugarberry, *Celtis laevigata*, a tree, not covered in this book.

13. Leaf blades near the tip of twigs about 6 inches long; crushed leaves and bark aromatic 14
13. Leaf blades near the tip of twigs less than 6 inches long; crushed leaves and bark not aromatic. 15

14. Rare shrub; leaf blades drooping, thin, green on both surfaces . . . Pond berry, *Lindera melissifolia*, p. 144
14. Common shrub; leaf blades erect or ascending, rather firm and thickish; upper surface dark green, lower surface pale or grayish . . . Spice bush, *Lindera benzoin*, p. 142

15. All the leaves less than 3/4 inch long; broken leaves or stems with milky sap . . . Buck brush, *Andrachne phyllanthoides*, p. 50
15. All the leaves more than 3/4 inch long; broken leaves or stems without milky sap. . . 16

16. Next year's leaf buds hidden and covered by base of leaf stalk; leaf stalk hollow; twigs enlarged at joints, very tough, hard to tear or break and very flexible, capable of being tied into a knot; flowers appearing before the leaves . . . Leatherwood, *Dirca palustris*, p. 102
16. Buds not covered by base of leaf stalk; leaf stalk not hollow; twigs not enlarged at joints, either easily broken or torn, not easily tied into a knot; flowers appearing with leaves present. 17

17. Buds naked (not covered by scales), densely hairy, slender and elongated . . . Carolina buckthorn, *Rhamnus caroliniana*, p. 192
17. Buds covered by scales, short and cone- or egg-shaped 18

18. Larger leaf blades usually less than 1 1/2 inches wide. 19
18. Leaf blades usually more than 1 1/2 inches wide 24

19. Flowers large and showy, at least 1 1/2 inches long, 1 1/2 to 2 inches wide; leaves usually clustered at or near the tips of twigs . . . Wild azalea, *Rhododendron roseum*, p. 198
19. Flowers smaller, 1/4 to 1/2 inch long, about 1/4 inch wide; leaves scattered all along the length of the twigs, not clustered at the tip 20

20. At least the lower leaf surfaces marked with resin dots or scales; winter twigs predominantly black . . . Black huckleberry, *Gaylussacia baccata*, p. 116
20. Lower and upper leaf surface without any resin dots or scales; winter twigs green, gray or brown. 21

21. Rare plant; flowers 3/8 to 1/2 inch long; fruit a dry capsule . . . Stagger bush, *Lyonia mariana*, p. 150
21. Common plant; flowers about 1/4 inch long; fruit a dry or fleshy berry 22

22. Leaves mostly rounded or blunt at tip, or with a short abrupt point at tip, leathery, thick, firm, dark green on upper surface, sometimes evergreen; tall shrubs or small crooked tree to 15 feet tall . . . Farkleberry, *Vaccinium arboreum*, p. 276
22. Leaves mostly short- to long-pointed at tip, thin, soft, pale green or pale grass-green on upper surface, leaves dropping; small shrubs, rarely more than 6 feet tall 23

23. Small leaves (bracts) present at the base of flower and fruit stalks (pedicels); flowers broadly bell-shaped, wider than long, with the stamens extending beyond the flower . . . Deerberry, *Vaccinium stamineum*, p. 280
23. No small leaves (bracts) at the base of any flower or fruit stalks (pedicels); flowers cylinder-shaped, longer than broad, with the stamens not extending beyond the flower . . . Lowbush blueberry, *Vaccinium pallidum*, p. 278

24. Leaves rounded or blunt at the tip, upper surface bluish-green; leaf stalk and lower leaf

surface smooth; flower and fruit stalks slender, conspicuously purple or brown with gland-tipped hairs . . . Smoke tree, *Cotinus obovatus*, p. 96

24. Leaves short- to long-pointed at the tip, upper surface dark green; either the leaf stalk and lower leaf surface somewhat hairy; flower stalks without a feathery hairiness or sometimes smooth . . . Alternate-leaved dogwood, *Cornus alternifolia*, p. 82

25. Leaves lobed, the lobes toothed or toothless 26
25. Leaves not lobed, teeth present and wavy, rounded or pointed, short or long 37

26. Leaves with one main vein, the side veins arising at different levels along the main vein and not from the base of the leaf blade 27
26. Leaves with 3 or more main veins arising from the same place at the base of the leaf blade at the junction with the petiole . . . 32

27. Petals absent, flowers in catkins; fruit an acorn (a scaly cup surrounding base of nut); leaves large, oaklike; thorns or spines absent. 28
27. Petals present, showy; flowers not in catkins; fruit fleshy or dry, but not an acorn; leaves smaller, not oaklike; thorns or spines or spurs (short compact twigs resembling spines) present 29

28. Usually a shrub to 8 feet tall; teeth of leaf mostly 4 to 8 on each side, typically blunt but also pointed; leaves mainly 1 1/2 to 4 inches long; petioles 1/4 to 3/4 inch long . . . Dwarf chinquapin oak, *Quercus prinoides*, p. 190
28. Usually a medium to large tree, to 70 feet tall, but sometimes shrubby and only 7 feet tall; teeth of leaf mainly 8 to 13 on each side, typically sharp, pointed, and prominent, but varying to blunt, low, and less prominent; leaves mainly 4 to 8 inches long; petioles 3/4 to 1 1/4 inches long . . . Chinquapin oak, *Quercus muehlenbergii*, a tree, not covered in this book.

29. Prominent thorns or spines present on

stems; fruit less than 3/4 inch across . . . Frosty hawthorn, *Crataegus pruinosa*, p. 98
29. Thorns or spines absent or nearly so, stems with spurs (short compact twigs resembling spines); fruit more than 3/4 inch across. . . 30

30. Leaves narrow, broadest in the middle and tapering at both ends to lance-shaped . . . Narrow-leaved crab apple, *Malus angustifolia*, p. 152
30. Leaves not narrow, often egg-shaped to sometimes triangular-shaped 31

31. Lower surface of leaf with densely matted hairs; green cup-shaped receptacle at the base of the petals densely hairy on the outside . . . Prairie crab apple, *Malus ioensis*, p. 156
31. Lower surface of leaf slightly hairy when young, smooth later; green cup-shaped receptacle at the base of the petals smooth . . . Sweet crab apple, *Malus coronaria*, p. 154

32. Fruit, a large capsule, dry, splitting into 5 parts, upright, 3/4 to 1 inch long; stamens arranged on a long column . . . Rose of Sharon, *Hibiscus syriacus*, p. 122
32. Fruit small, fleshy and berrylike or dry and splitting along 2 sides, drooping; less than 1/2 inch long; stamens not arranged on a long column 33

33. Bark shredding; flowers white, upright; stamens 30-40; leaves mostly longer than broad or some as broad as long . . . Ninebark, *Physocarpus opulifolius*, p. 166
33. Bark not shredding; flowers yellow or greenish, often nodding; stamens 5; leaves mostly as broad or broader than long 34

34. Spines or prickles present on some of the stems or branches. 35
34. No spines or prickles on any stem or branch. . . 36

35. Fruit covered by slender prickles; flowers yellowish-green; both leaf surfaces hairy . . . Prickly gooseberry, *Ribes cynosbati*, p. 208
35. Fruit without prickles; flowers whitish-green; upper leaf surface smooth, lower surface hairy . . . Missouri gooseberry, *Ribes missouriense*, p. 210

36. Leaves and twigs with minute orange dots;

flowers greenish-white or yellowish; plants found in the extreme northern part of Missouri . . . Wild black currant, *Ribes americanum*, p. 206

36. Leaves and twigs without minute orange dots; flowers golden yellow; plants found in southwestern Missouri . . . Golden currant, *Ribes odoratum*, p. 212

37. Thorns, spines or prickles on twigs or stems. . . 38
37. No thorns, spines or prickles on twigs or stems 39

38. Small shrub to 3 feet tall; twigs bearing 3 spines and a leaf bundle at each axil . . . American barberry, *Berberis canadensis*, p. 58
38. Shrub to small tree, more than 3 feet tall; twigs bearing 1 spine or spur (short compact twigs resembling spines), leaves not in bundles . . . 39

39. Prominent thorns or spines present on stems; fruit less than 3/4 inch across . . . Frosty hawthorn, *Crataegus pruinosa*, p. 98
39. Thorns or spines absent or nearly so, stems with spurs (short compact twigs resembling spines); fruit more than 3/4 inch across . . . 40

40. Leaves narrow, broadest in the middle and tapering at both ends to lance-shaped . . . Narrow-leaved crab apple, *Malus angustifolia*, p. 152
40. Leaves not narrow, often egg-shaped to sometimes triangular-shaped 41

41. Lower surface of leaf with densely matted hairs; green cup-shaped receptacle at the base of the petals densely hairy on the outside . . . Prairie crab apple, *Malus ioensis*, p. 156
41. Lower surface of leaf slightly hairy when young, smooth later; green cup-shaped receptacle at the base of the petals smooth . . . Sweet crab apple, *Malus coronaria*, p. 154

42. At least 2 of the lowest side veins conspicuous and arising at the very base of the leaf blade, there joining the base of the central vein 41
42. Lowest side veins joining the central vein above the very base of the leaf blade. . . . 43

43. Leaf blade more or less lopsided (asymmetrical)

with one half longer or broader than the other half, most noticeable at the base. 44
43. Leaf blade not lopsided, each half the same length and width as the other half. 45

44. Shrub or small tree; leaves of fruiting branches more than 1/2 as broad as long, egg-shaped, tip blunt or ending at a sharp angle; grayish-green on both surfaces or darker above . . . Dwarf hackberry, *Celtis tenuifolia*, p. 74
44. Usually medium to large tree; leaves of fruiting branches less than 1/2 as broad as long, mostly narrowly lance-shaped, tapering to a long slender tip which is often curved to one side; both leaf surfaces pale or dull green . . . Sugarberry, *Celtis laevigata*, a tree, not covered in this book.

45. Leaf margins wavy-edged and lacking prominent teeth; flowers yellow, orange or red, blooming from January-April or September-December, usually preceding the appearance of the new leaves or after the fall of the old ones; petals 4; ribbonlike; stamens 4 46
45. Leaf margins not wavy-edged and with prominent teeth; flowers white, blooming from May-June with new leaves present; petals 5, not ribbonlike; stamens 5 47

46. Flowering from September to the end of December; flowers yellow; twigs smooth or slightly hairy . . . Eastern witch hazel, *Hamamelis virginiana*, p. 120
46. Flowering from January-April; some part of the flower usually tinged with orange, reddish or salmon; twigs densely hairy or woolly . . . Ozark witch hazel, *Hamamelis vernalis*, p. 118

47. Main flower or fruit stalk longer than the leaf arising directly below it; main flower or fruit stalk bare or with a few small leaves; leaf blades broadly egg-shaped, tip somewhat pointed . . . New Jersey tea, *Ceanothus americanus*, p. 70
47. Main flower or fruit stalk usually shorter than the leaf arising directly below it; main flower or fruit stalk not bare and with a few small leaves; leaf blades narrow and lance-shaped, tip mostly blunt . . . Redroot, *Ceanothus herbaceus*, p. 72

48. Flowers white, approximately 1/4 inch long, drooping; petals 5 . . . Snowbell, *Styrax americanum*, p. 268
48. Without the above combination of characters. 49

49. Buds covered by 1 scale; all the flowers in catkins (a slender column of small flowers); the flowers bearing staminate (male flowers) and pistillate (female flowers) in clusters on separate plants; seeds with a tuft of silky hairs 50
49. Buds with 2 or more scales; flowers either not in catkins, or arranged other than that described in alternate section above; seeds without any hairy tuft 51

50. Leaves green on both sides (those at tips of shoots sometimes covered with silvery-silky hairs) 51
50. Leaves silvery, grayish white, pale bluish-green, or with a whitish coating on lower side . . . 61

51. Teeth on margins of leaves scattered and unevenly spaced, only 3 to 12 to an inch; leaves with very short stalks (petioles) or stalkless . . . Sandbar willow, *Salix interior*, p. 250
51. Teeth on margins of leaves closely and equally spaced, mostly 13 to 25 to an inch; stalks (petioles) of leaves 1/8 to 3/4 inch long . . . Heart-leaved willow, *Salix rigida*, p. 254

52. Margins of leaves entire (without teeth), edges slightly wavy, or with only 2 to 11 broad low teeth to an inch 53
52. Margins of leaves finely and distinctly toothed, the teeth more crowded, 12 to 25 to an inch. 54

53. Lower side of leaf more or less hairy; twigs often hairy; low shrub to 5 feet tall . . . Prairie willow, *Salix humilis*, p. 248
53. Lower side of leaf smooth (lacking hairs), mature twigs smooth or nearly so . . . Pussy willow, *Salix discolor*, p. 246

54. Lower side of (surface or veins or both) of some or all of the leaves more or less hairy. 55
54. Lower side of leaves smooth (without hairs) or mainly so 59

55. Youngest twigs or topmost part of twigs or branchlets hairy 56
55. Youngest twigs or topmost part of twigs or branchlets smooth or nearly so 57

56. Leaves up to 7 inches long, narrowly lance-shaped . . . Carolina willow, *Salix caroliniana*, p. 244
56. Leaves up to 3 inches long, broadest in the middle and tapering at both ends . . . Heart-leaved willow, *Salix rigida*, p. 254

57. Stipules (leafy appendage at base of leaf stalk) conspicuous (1/4 to 3/4 inches long), egg-shaped, and mostly persistent on the young or new leafy shoots . . . Carolina willow, *Salix caroliniana*, p. 244
57. Stipules either none or minute or lance-shaped, small and inconspicuous, or not persisting. 58

58. Teeth occur along margins of leaves from base to tip and teeth not tipped with glands; stipules of shoots lance-shaped, eventually falling; twigs easy to break, brittle . . . Silky willow, *Salix sericea*, p. 256
58. Teeth do not occur at base of leaf, and teeth that are present are tipped with glands; stipules none or very tiny and quickly disappear; twigs hard to break or tear . . . Meadow willow, *Salix petiolaris*, p. 252

59. Youngest twigs or topmost part of twigs hairy or mainly so . . . Carolina willow, *Salix caroliniana*, p. 244
59. Youngest twigs or topmost part of twigs smooth. 60

60. Strong leafy sprouts with conspicuous, nearly circular stipules occurring at the base of the leaf stalks . . . Heart-leaved willow, *Salix rigida*, p. 254
60. Strong leafy sprouts with no stipules, or stipules minute and quickly disappearing . . . Meadow willow, *Salix petiolaris*, p. 252

61. Flowers without petals or sepals or both . . . 62
61. Flowers with both petals and sepals 68

62. Rare shrub; sepals 5, free and separate to

their base, persisting, green, leaflike, and spreading after flowering; stamens white, numerous, usually more than 100 in each flower . . . Snow wreath, *Neviusia alabamensis*, p. 158

62. Commonly found small trees and shrubs in all sections of Missouri; sepals either 2 to 4 parted or 3 to 9 lobed, with the base united in a short conspicuous tube; stamens 2 to 9 to a flower 63

63. Leaf blades often more or less lopsided (asymmetrical) with one half longer or broader than the other half, most noticeable at the base; some or all the flowers complete with stamens and pistils; all the flowers with the sepals united into a bell-shaped tube . . . Water elm, *Planera aquatica*, p. 168

63. Leaf blades usually not lopsided, each half the same length and width as the other half; flowers are separated into stamen-bearing (staminate) and pistil-bearing (pistillate) flowers in separate parts of the same plant; either the staminate or pistillate flowers without sepals 64

64. Lower surface of leaves whitish or grayish white; bark peeling off in reddish-brown papery strips, exposing a pale smooth layer . . . River birch, *Betula nigra*, a tree, not covered in this book.

64. Lower surface of leaves green or pale green, not white or grayish-white; bark smooth or rough, not peeling. 65

65. Leaf blades with a blunt or rounded tip and rounded teeth . . . Alder, *Alnus serrulata*, p. 42

65. Leaf blades with a pointed tip or pointed teeth, or both 63

66. Leaf blade usually with 5 to 8 veins on each side of the central vein . . . Hazelnut, *Corylus americana*, p. 94

66. Leaf blade usually with 9 to 15 veins on each side of midrib 67

67. Bark smooth, twisty, bluish-gray; lower surface of fully grown leaves smooth (without hairs), except for some hairy tufts in the axils of the veins; none of the large side nerves forked . . . Hornbeam, *Carpinus caroliniana*, p. 68

67. Bark scaly, light brown or brownish-gray; lower surface of fully grown leaves mostly hairy; some of the lower large side nerves forked . . . Hop hornbeam, *Ostrya virginiana*, p. 160

68. Petals united into a short bell-shaped to cylindrical tube so that the attempt to remove one portion disturbs the neighboring section of the flower; stamens 10 69

68. Petals free from each other, separated all the way down to their base, so that one petal can be removed without tearing or disturbing the other petals; stamens 4, 5 to 8, or 10 to 50 71

69. Leaves mostly rounded or blunt at tip, or with a short abrupt point at tip, leathery, thick, firm, dark green on upper surface, sometimes evergreen; tall shrubs or small crooked tree to 15 feet tall . . . Farkleberry, *Vaccinium arboreum*, p. 276

69. Leaves mostly short- to long-pointed at tip, thin, soft, pale green or pale grass-green on upper surface, leaves dropping; small shrubs, rarely more than 6 feet tall 70

70. Small leaves (bracts) present at the base of flower and fruit stalks (pedicels); flowers broadly bell-shaped, wider than long, with the stamens extending beyond the flower . . . Deerberry, *Vaccinium stamineum*, p. 280

70. No small leaves (bracts) at the base of any flower or fruit stalks (pedicels); flowers cylinder-shaped, longer than broad, with the stamens not extending beyond the flower . . . Lowbush blueberry, *Vaccinium pallidum*, p. 278

71. Lower surface of leaves white or rusty with densely hairy matted wool . . . Hardhack, *Spiraea tomentosa*, p. 264

71. Lower surface of leaves pale to dark green, not white or rusty, with densely hairy matted wool 72

72. Flowers of a single sex, the staminate (male) and pistillate (female) found on separate plants 73

72. Flowers with both stamens and pistils in the same flower and on the same plant 75

73. Leaves thick, leathery, evergreen, usually with a few (0 to 8) remote, stiff, spiny teeth on each side . . . American holly, *Ilex opaca*, a tree, not covered in this book.

73. Leaves not thick nor leathery, not evergreen, with several to many teeth (usually 8 to 25) along each margin. 74

74. Teeth of leaves rounded or blunt; tip of leaf rounded or blunt . . . Possum haw, *Ilex decidua*, p. 130

74. Teeth of leaves sharp-pointed; tip of leaf tapering to a point . . . Winterberry, *Ilex verticillata*, p. 132

75. Petals 4; sepals 4; stamens 4, opposite the petals, alternate with the sepals 76

75. Petals 5; sepals 5; stamens 5 or 10 to 50, alternate with the petals 78

76. Leaf blades with mostly 3 to 4 veins on each side of the central vein; some leaves appearing alternate, but most are opposite; leaf blades abruptly pointed at the tip; twigs often ending at a spiny tip . . . Common buckthorn, *Rhamnus cathartica*, p. 194

76. Leaf blades usually with 4 to 10 veins on each side of the central vein; leaves mainly alternate; leaf blades gradually pointed at the tip; none of the twigs ending in a spiny tip 77

77. Margin of leaf blade with many fine teeth; largest leaf blades 1 1/2 to 3 1/2 inches long; buds for next year covered with scales; fruit 2-seeded; sepals, petals and stamens 4 . . . Lance-leaved buckthorn, *Rhamnus lanceolata*, p. 196

77. Margin of leaf blade faintly toothed; largest leaf blades 3 to 7 inches long; buds for next year naked, with dense brown hairs; fruit 3-seeded, sepals, petals and stamens 5 . . . Carolina buckthorn, *Rhamnus caroliniana*, p. 192

78. Pith of branches chambered, or interrupted by partitions; stipules (leaf parts at the base of the leaf stalks) or their scars absent; stamens 5; fruit consisting of a dry 2-celled capsule . . . Virginia willow, *Itea virginica*, p. 134

78. Pith of branches solid and continuous; stipules (leaf parts at the base of the leaf stalks) or their scars present; stamens 10 to 60;

fruit consisting of 5 dry follicles (dry capsules splitting on one side) or of a fleshy berry or rose hip. 79

79. Small shrub growing to 4 feet tall; flowers small, about 1/8 inch across, numerous; fruit in 5 pod-shaped follicles (dry capsules splitting on one side) . . . Meadow-sweet, *Spiraea alba*, p. 262

79. Shrub to small tree more than 4 feet tall; flowers more than 1/8 inch across, not numerous (less than 10 per cluster); fruit fleshy 80

80. Central vein of the upper surface of the leaves with small glands present; fruit small, about 1/4 inch long and wide, purplish-black . . . Black chokecherry, *Aronia melanocarpa*, p. 54

80. Central vein lacking small glands; fruit more than 1/4 inch in length and width, reddish-black, red, green or yellowish-green 81

81. Bark light gray and smooth when young, becoming dark gray with shallow furrows and long ridges when older; among the first woody plants to bloom in early spring . . . Service berry, *Amelanchier arborea*, p. 44

81. Bark dark red to reddish or grayish brown, breaking into thin, scaly plates; not one of the first woody plants to bloom in early spring. 82

82. Leaves broadly egg-shaped to rather round, not much, if any longer than broad, the base heart-shaped to broadly rounded . . . Perfumed cherry, *Prunus mahaleb*, p. 178

82. Leaves lance-shaped, narrowly egg-shaped but obviously longer than broad, the base not heart-shaped or broadly rounded. . . . 83

83. A colored, usually brownish-red or brownish (sometimes pale) gland at tip or side of the teeth along the leaf margin 84

83. No gland arising from teeth of leaves . . . 86

84. Mature leaf blades mainly 3/4 to 2 inches long, 1/4 to 3/4 inch wide . . . Chickasaw plum, *Prunus angustifolia*, p. 174

84. Mature leaf blades mainly 2 to 4 1/2 inches long, 1 to 2 1/4 inches wide 85

85. Gland arising from the very tip of each tooth of the leaf; teeth of leaves pointed, conspicuous, spreading away from the margin; fully grown leaves flat with each half spread out, not folded . . . Wild goose plum, *Prunus hortulana*, p. 176

85. Gland arising from that end of each tooth facing the indented lower side of the margin; teeth of leaves low or not pointed, not conspicuous or spreading; fully grown leaves more or less folded lengthwise, troughlike . . . Wild goose plum, *Prunus munsoniana*, p. 182

86. Buds strongly hairy; fruit velvety hairy; stone deeply pitted and sculptured; leaves troughlike, the halves more or less folded lengthwise, conspicuously drooping . . . Peach, *Prunus persica*, p. 184

86. Buds smooth (without hairs) or with a few hairs; fruit smooth; stone not sculptured; leaves not folded, not conspicuously drooping 87

87. Flowers and fruits in elongated clusters longer than broad, with 15 to 30 fruits; clusters appearing on stems of the new year's growth; mature fruits approximately 3/8 inch across. 88

87. Flowers and fruits with 1 or 2 to 5 in a cluster; clusters appearing on stems of preceding year; mature fruits about 1 inch across. . . 89

88. Teeth of leaf margin sharp or conspicuously pointed, spreading upward, but not curved inward; leaf blades rather thin, dull green, abrupt and short pointed at the tip, egg-shaped or inverted egg-shaped; low shrub or small tree . . . Choke cherry, *Prunus virginiana*, p. 186

88. Teeth of leaf margin blunt, short and curved-in along the margin; leaf blades thick, firm, dark green, shiny, gradually tapering to the longer tip, broadly lance-shaped to broadly egg-shaped; tree becoming 100 feet or more tall . . . Black cherry, *Prunus serotina*, a large tree, not covered in this book.

89. Leaf stalks hairy all around; twigs more or less hairy; lower surface of mature leaf blades hairy; fruit eventually turning grayish-blue or grayish-lavender . . . Big tree plum, *Prunus mexicana*, p. 180

89. Leaf stalks smooth (without hairs); twigs smooth; lower surface of mature leaf blades smooth or sparsely hairy on the main veins; fruit eventually turning red . . . Wild Plum, *Prunus americana*, p. 172

KEY C. Shrubs With Leaves Compound and Opposite

1. Leaflets 3 . . . American bladdernut, *Staphylea trifoliata*, p. 266
1. Leaflets 5 to 11 2

2. Leaves palmately compound, all the leaflets attached to and spreading from the same point at the tip of the main leaf stalk 3
2. Leaves pinnately compound, with some leaflets attached at different levels on the leaf axis or with the leaflet at the tip on a longer stalk than the other leaflets 4

3. A small to medium-sized tree, petals more or less equal, greenish-yellow; stamens long, extending beyond the petals; fruit prickly; leaflets mainly 7, bluish-green or grass-green on upper surface . . . Ohio buckeye, *Aesculus glabra*, p. 38
3. A shrub to small tree; petals unequal in length, width and shape, red or rarely yellow; stamens shorter than or only slightly longer than the upper petals; fruit smooth; leaflets mainly 5, dark green on upper surface . . . Red buckeye, *Aesculus pavia*, p. 40

4. Common species, found throughout the state; flowering and fruiting clusters in flat-topped heads; fruits usually purplish-black, rarely red . . . Common elderberry, *Sambucus canadensis*, p. 258
4. Rarely found; flowering and fruiting clusters cone- or pyramid-shaped; fruits usually red . . . Red-berried elder, *Sambucus racemosa*, p. 260

KEY D. Shrubs With Leaves Compound and Alternate

1. Thorns or prickles on at least the stems or branches of the plant 2
1. Thorns or prickles absent on all parts of the plant 25

2. Leaves palmately compound, all the leaflets attached to and spreading from the same

point at the tip of the main leaf stalk (petiole) 3

2. Leaves pinnately compound, with some leaflets attached at different levels on the leaf axis 15

3. Lower surface of leaflets white or whitened . . . 4
3. Lower surface of leaflets green or grayish-green, but not white or whitened 6

4. Flowers or fruits 2 to 7 in a short, flat or rounded cluster; fruit separating when ripe from the central green receptacle, the receptacle remaining attached to the stalk of the fruit 5
4. Flowers or fruits in a pyramid-shaped cluster; fruit remaining attached to the central green receptacle, even when ripe . . . Twice-leafed blackberry, *Rubus bifrons*, p. 234

5. Some of the stems whitened with a coating that can be rubbed off; fruit black when ripe; stalks of flowers or fruits bearing thorns or prickles (a small, slender thorn); stems bearing thorns or prickles; common species . . . Black raspberry, *Rubus occidentalis*, p. 238
5. Stems not whitened with a coating that can be rubbed off; fruit red when ripe; stalks of flowers or fruits bearing bristles but not thorns or prickles; stems bearing bristles but no thorns or prickles; rare species . . . Red raspberry, *Rubus strigosus*, p. 238

6. Canes (stems) of first year and usually of second year and leaf stalks (petioles) bearing purplish red bristles or hairs . . . Southern dewberry, *Rubus trivialis*, p. 242
6. Canes (stems) and leaf stalks (petioles) smooth, spiny or hairy, but without purplish-red bristles 7

7. Main stems trailing, sprawling, low-arching or forming domes over the ground, the tips or branches of the first year's vegetative canes rooting at the tip 8
7. Main stems erect to ascending with arching tips, but not with rooting or trailing tips . . . 10

8. Flower stalks (pedicels) with gland-tipped hairs . . . Dewberry, *Rubus invisus*, p. 236

8. Flower stalks (pedicels) without gland-tipped hairs 9

9. Terminal (topmost) one of the 3 leaflets of the flowering cane egg-shaped, broadest near the base or below the middle, the sides curved or rounded . . . Dewberry, *Rubus flagellaris*, p. 236
9. Terminal (topmost) one of the 3 leaflets of the flowering cane broadly lance-shaped or inverse egg-shaped, broadest at or above the middle, narrowed toward the wedge-shaped base, with the sides straight or nearly so below the middle . . . Southern dewberry, *Rubus enslenii*, p. 236

10. Numerous gland-tipped hairs present on the stalks of the flowers and fruits, and often on other parts of the flower cluster and younger parts of the main stem of the vegetative cane of the first year's growth 11
10. Gland-tipped hairs mostly absent on the stalks of the flowers and fruits and the young growth (a few inconspicuous ones may be present) 12

11. The main developed flower clusters 2 to 4 times as long as thick, rather elongated and cylinder-shaped; topmost (terminal) leaflet of leaves of the first year's canes narrowly egg-shaped or 2 or 3 times longer than broad . . . Highbush blackberry, *Rubus allegheniensis*, p. 230
11. The main developed flower clusters as long as thick or at most 2 times as long as thick, broadest at the summit or with the flowers mostly crowded at the summit; topmost (terminal) leaflet of leaves of the first year's canes broadly egg-shaped to nearly round in shape . . . Highbush blackberry, *Rubus orarius*, p. 230

12. The upper 3 leaflets of fully grown leaves of the vegetative first year's canes (without flowers) 2 to 3 times as long as broad; flowers medium size, the petals narrow, about 3/8 inch broad . . . Highbush blackberry, *Rubus argutus*, p. 232
12. The upper 3 leaflets of fully grown leaves of the vegetative first year's canes (without flowers) usually less than twice as long as broad; flowers medium to large, with broad rounded petals 1/2 to 3/4 inch broad. . . . 13

13. Main fully developed flower clusters short cylinder-shaped, not broadened across the top and with an elongated cluster stalk . . . Highbush blackberry, *Rubus mollior*, p. 232

13. Main fully developed flower clusters broadened across the top with a short cluster stalk 14

14. Leaflike bracts 7 to 12 in the flower cluster, a large bract at the base of each or nearly each flower or fruit stalk; topmost (terminal) leaflet of the 5 leaflets of the first year's vegetative canes (without flowers) widest toward the base, broadly egg-shaped; main flower clusters short and rather hidden in the leaves attached just below . . . Highbush blackberry, *Rubus pensilvanicus*, p. 240

14. Leaflike bracts fewer in the flower cluster, found only at the base of the lower and middle flower or fruit stalks; topmost (terminal) leaflet of the 5 leaflets of the first year's vegetative canes (without flowers) widest near the middle; main flower clusters standing above the leaves attached just below . . . Highbush blackberry, *Rubus ostryifolius*, p. 240

15. Leaves more than once-compound, with the side leaf divisions further divided into additional leaflets . . . Hercules club, *Aralia spinosa*, p. 52

15. Leaves once-compound, with the side leaf divisions attached directly to the main stalk and not further divided into additional leaflets 16

16. Leaflets with transparent dots between the veins (hold leaf to light); leaf lacking stipules (small bracts at base of main leaf or leaf stalk) or stipels (tiny bracts or appendages at base of leaflets); flowers and fruit clustered at nodes along the stem . . . Prickly ash, *Zanthoxylum americanum*, p. 300

16. Leaflets lacking transparent dots; stipules present at base of main leaf stalk, either free or united with the stalk or minute stiples present at base of the leaf stalks of the leaflets at least on young leaves; flowers and fruit not clustered at nodes along the stem 17

17. Leaflets without teeth (entire); stipels (tiny bracts or appendages at base of leaflets) present at base of the leaf stalks of the leaflets,

but stipules (small bracts at base of main leaf or leaf stalk) absent at base of main leaf stalk; flower lacking typical petals but pea-shaped, the petals of a flower of different sizes and shapes 18

17. Leaflets with teeth; stipels absent at base of the leaflets, but stipules present at base of main leaf stalk, either united to it or free at the base; flower with typical petals, not pea-shaped, the petals similar in sizes and shapes 19

18. Flowers white with a yellow blotch on the uppermost petal; twigs smooth with paired spines at base of leaves . . . Black locust, *Robinia pseudo-acacia*, a common, medium to large tree, not covered in this book.

18. Flowers rose or rose-purple; twigs bristly . . . Bristly locust, *Robinia hispida*, p. 214

19. Stems almost entirely smooth, with few prickles or thorns 20

19. Stems with several to many prickles or thorns 21

20. Stems more or less straight and upright, usually 1 1/2 to 3 feet tall . . . Smooth wild rose, *Rosa blanda*, p. 218

20. Stems long and spreading, whiplike, downward-arching or climbing, commonly 6 feet or more long . . . Prairie rose, *Rosa setigera*, p. 228

21. Stipules (small leaflike growth along leaf stalk) deeply dissected, fringed and comb-like; flowers small, 3/4 to 1 1/2 inches across . . . Multiflora rose, *Rosa multiflora*, p. 224

21. Stipules not as above; flowers medium to large, 1 to 3 inches across 22

22. Leaves on old stems mainly with 3 leaflets, on new stems 3 or 5; stems arching, recurved, climbing or sprawling. 23

22. Leaves on old and new stems mainly with 5 to 11 leaflets, or if 3 to 5, then the stems erect, ascending or forming a bush 24

23. Flower petals 5 . . . Prairie rose, *Rosa setigera*, p. 228

23. Flower petals 6 to 9 . . . Damask rose, *Rosa X damascena*, p. 222

24. Tip of rose hips (fruit) with persistent lobes; flower stalk smooth . . . Prairie wild rose, *Rosa arkansana*, p. 216
24. Tip of rose hips (fruit) lacking lobes; flower stalk with gland-tipped hairs, often disappearing in fruit 25

25. Large shrubs of swamps or wet ground, mostly 5 to 8 1/2 feet tall; leaves finely toothed; stipules (leafy growth along the leaf stalk) rolled up along the leaf stalk . . . Swamp rose, *Rosa palustris*, p. 226
25. Plants mainly of glades, prairies and dry or rocky ground, usually less than 3 feet tall; leaves coarsely toothed; stipules flat . . . Pasture rose, *Rosa carolina*, p. 220

26. All of the leaflets 3 27
26. Some or all of the leaflets 5 or more to a leaf. 30

27. Leaflet margins smooth or finely toothed . . . Hop tree, *Ptelea trifoliata*, p. 188
27. Leaflet margins lobed or coarsely toothed . . . 28

28. Leaves fragrant when crushed; middle (terminal) one of the three leaflets without any stalk before joining the main leaf stalk; flowers yellow, in crowded clusters appearing before or with the leaves; mature fruit red, covered with hairs or glands . . . Fragrant sumac, *Rhus aromatica*, p. 200
28. Leaves not fragrant; middle (terminal) one of the three leaflets on a long stalk more than 3/4 inch long before joining main leaf stalk; flowers greenish, greenish-white, or yellowish-green, in loose open clusters appearing with grown leaves; mature fruit grayish-white or yellowish-white, smooth or with short, hairy and warty projections 29

29. Middle (terminal) one of the three leaflets with a short- to long-pointed tip; leaflets coarsely or wavily toothed or without any teeth; stems sometimes appearing shrublike, but mostly climbing with aerial roots; leaves scattered along the stem; fruit usually smooth . . . Poison ivy, *Toxicodendron radicans*, p. 358
29. Middle (terminal) one of the three leaflets with a rounded or blunt tip; leaflets with usu-

ally 2 to 4 lobes or large teeth on each side; stems short, never climbing; leaves mostly clustered near the summit; fruit minutely short hairy and with warty projections . . . Poison oak, *Toxicodendron toxicarium*, p. 274

30. Leaves more than once-compound, with the side leaf stalks or leaf divisions further divided into additional leaflets 31
30. Leaves once-divided, with the side leaflets attached directly to the main stalk and not further divided into additional leaflets. . . 33

31. Compound leaves with an even number of leaflets, or with a pair of leaflets at the tip . . . Prairie acacia, *Acacia angustissima*, p. 36
31. Compound leaves with an odd number of leaflets, or with 1 leaflet at the tip 32

32. Low plants mostly less than 3 feet tall; the compound leaf without a stalk or barely visible; leaflets rarely more than 3/4 inch long . . . Lead plant, *Amorpha canescens*, p. 46
32. Taller plants mainly 3 to 12 feet tall; compound leaves distinctly stalked; leaflets usually 3/4 to 1 1/2 inches long . . . False indigo, *Amorpha fruticosa*, p. 48

33. Branches and leaf stalks smooth; leaflets coarsely toothed; main stalk where leaflets are attached not winged in the spaces between the leaflets . . . Smooth sumac, *Rhus glabra*, p. 204
33. Branches and leaf stalks covered with a minute hairiness; leaflets smooth, teeth minute or absent; main stalk where leaflets are attached winged in the spaces between the leaflets . . . Winged sumac, *Rhus copallina*, p. 202

Keys to the Woody Vines

1. Vines, climbing and twining or sprawling. . . 2
1. Small trees or shrubs. . . . . p. 16

2. Leaves compound. 3
2. Leaves simple 11

3. Leaves opposite 4
3. Leaves alternate 6

4. Leaflets lacking teeth, 2 per leaf . . . Cross vine, *Bignonia capreolata*, p. 276
4. Leaflets toothed or lobed, 3 or more per leaf. . . 5

5. Leaflets 3 per leaf . . . Virgin's bower, *Clematis virginiana*, p. 326
5. Leaflets 5 or more per leaf . . . Trumpet creeper, *Campsis radicans*, p. 318

6. Plants climbing by aerial roots; leaflets 3 . . . Poison ivy, *Toxicodendron radicans*, p. 358
6. Plants climbing by twining or tendrils; leaflets 3 to many. 7

7. Stems twining; plants without tendrils; fruit a bean . . . Wisteria, *Wisteria frutescens*, p. 376
7. Stems not twining; plants with tendrils; fruit a berry 8

8. All the leaves either divided into 3 leaflets or deeply 3-parted; leaves very fleshy or succulent (thick); petals and stamens 4 . . . Marine vine, *Cissus incisa*, p. 324
8. Most of the leaves divided into 5 to 34 leaflets, rarely only 3; leaves not fleshy or succulent; petals and stamens 5 9

9. All the leaves divided into 3 to 7 leaflets, palmately arranged (all the leaflets attached to and spreading from the same point at the tip of the main leaf stalk) 10
9. All the leaves divided into 9 to 34 leaflets, not palmately arranged . . . Pepper vine, *Ampelopsis arborea*, p. 304

10. Leaves dull on the upper surface, not glossy; tendrils many-branched, ending in large suckers or adhesive disks; 25 to 200 or more flowers per cluster; fruit about 1/4 inch across . . . Virginia creeper, *Parthenocissus quinquefolia*, p. 346
10. Leaves glossy on upper surface; tendrils few-branched, slender-tipped, not ending in suckers or adhesive disks; 10 to 60 flowers per cluster; fruit about 3/8 inch across . . . Woodbine, *Parthenocissus vitacea*, p. 348

11. Leaves opposite 12
11. Leaves alternate 20

12. Plants low-growing, ground-hugging, not climbing; upper surface of leaves shiny . . 13
12. Plants climbing by twining; upper surface of leaves not shiny 14

13. Leaves opposite throughout stem; flowers white or pinkish, sometimes tinged with purple, up to 1/2 inch across; fruit red, shiny . . . Partridge berry, *Mitchella repens*, p. 344
13. Leaves at end of stem often in clusters of 3 to 4; flowers lilac to blue, about 1 inch across; fruit a dry capsule, rarely produced . . . Common periwinkle, *Vinca minor*, p. 362

14. In winter, stems dying back to a woody base; sap milky; tip of leaves ending in an abrupt point or long and tapering . . . Climbing dogbane, *Trachelospermum difforme*, p. 360
14. Stems not dying back to the base; sap not milky; tip of leaves blunt to slightly pointed 15

15. Leaves evergreen, with thick waxy coating, margin of leaves irregularly toothed; flowers small, about 1/8 inch long; petals 4 . . . Wintercreeper, *Euonymus fortunei*, p. 330
15. Leaves not evergreen, margin of leaves lacking teeth; flowers 3/4 to 1 1/2 inches long; petals 2 16

16. None of the leaves joined at their bases . . . Japanese honeysuckle, *Lonicera japonica*, p. 336
16. Uppermost leaves joined at their bases . . 17

17. Flowers deep red on outside, 1 1/2 to 2 inches long; stamens barely extending

beyond the flower . . . Trumpet honeysuckle, *Lonicera sempervirens*, p. 340

17. Flowers orange, yellow, cream-color, 3/4 to 1 1/4 inches long; stamens much extending beyond the flower 18

18. A white coating occurs on the upper surface of the uppermost leaves, which are joined at their bases; the uppermost joined leaves forming a more or less circular or nearly circular form, broader than long; flowering and fruiting clusters arranged in 2 to 6 whorls (in circles around the stalk), which are usually separated . . . Grape honeysuckle, *Lonicera reticulata*, p. 338

18. Upper surface of the uppermost joined leaves green or barely whitened; the uppermost joined leaves forming a longer than broad disc; flower and fruit clusters in 1 to 3 crowded whorls (in circles around the stalk) 19

19. Lower surface of leaves conspicuously whitened or silvery-blue; flower tube slightly enlarged on one side at the base; flower yellow or greenish-yellow tinged with purple, rose or brick red, 1/2 to 3/4 inch long . . . Limber honeysuckle, *Lonicera dioica*, p. 332

19. Lower surface of leaves slightly gray-green or pale, but not noticeably whitened; flower tube slender without any enlargement on one side at the base; flower orange, orange-yellow, or creamy-yellow, but lacking purple, rose or brick red, 3/4 to 1 1/4 inches long . . . Yellow honeysuckle, *Lonicera flava*, p. 334

20. Tendrils arising in pairs at the base of leaf stalks; prickles or spines sometimes present on stem 21

20. Tendrils absent, or, if present, not arising in pairs from the base of leaf stalks; prickles or spines absent 24

21. Lower surface of leaves whitened, bluish-gray or silvery . . . Greenbrier, *Smilax glauca*, p. 352

21. Lower surface of leaves about the same green color as the upper surface 22

22. Leaf margin much more thickened than the rest of the leaf blade; at least the older stems more or less with tufts of small star-shaped hairs; toothlike projections on the margins

of leaves colored; leaf blades sometimes with white blotches; leaves sometimes fiddle-shaped; veins thickened and conspicuous in a network over the leaf surface . . . Catbrier, *Smilax bona-nox*, p. 350

22. Leaf margin not thicker than rest of leaf blade; stem smooth throughout; toothlike projections on the margins of leaves colorless; leaf blades lacking white blotches; leaves never fiddle-shaped; slender veins forming delicate network, which is not thickened conspicuously 23

23. Prickles or spines of stem pale or with a dark tip, flattened and with a broad base; stalk bearing the flowering or fruiting clusters shorter than or equaling the leaf stalk; fruit bluish-black, covered with a grayish-blue coating; seeds 2 to 3 in each berry . . . Greenbrier, *Smilax rotundifolia*, p. 356

23. Mature prickles or spines black throughout, round, and bristlelike; stalk bearing the flowering or fruiting clusters much longer than the leaf stalk; fruit black without coating; seeds 1 in each berry . . . Bristly greenbrier, *Smilax hispida*, p. 354

24. Plants climbing by twining or sprawling, tendrils absent. 25

24. Plants climbing by tendrils 31

25. Leaves pinnately veined, with one main vein with side veins arising at various locations along it and not from the base of the leaf. . . 26

25. Leaves palmately veined, with veins arising from the same place at the very base of the leaf blade, at the junction with the leaf stalk . . . 28

26. Side veins of leaves nearly straight, evenly spaced and parallel . . . Supple-jack, *Berchemia scandens*, p. 310

26. Side veins of leaves variously arranged, not as above 27

27. Leaves egg-shaped to oval, margin with finely pointed teeth . . . American bittersweet, *Celastrus scandens*, p. 322

27. Leaves circular to broadly inverted egg-shaped, margin with small rounded teeth . . . Round-leaved bittersweet, *Celastrus orbiculatus*, p. 320

28. Leaves heart-shaped; margin entire; both leaf surfaces with woolly hairs; flowers solitary, strongly curved; fruit a dry capsule . . . Woolly pipe-vine, *Aristolochia tomentosa*, p. 308

28. Leaves variable with margins lobed; upper leaf surface smooth, lower leaf surface smooth to hairy but not woolly hairy; flowers in clusters, not curved, radially symmetrical; fruit berry-shaped 29

29. Usually some leaf blades longer than broad, egg-shaped or triangular, densely hairy on lower surface; fruit red . . . Carolina moonseed, *Cocculus carolinus*, p. 328

29. Leaf blades usually as broad as long or broader than long, only sparsely hairy on lower surface or smooth; fruit bluish-black or black 30

30. Top of leaf stalk joining the leaf on the lower side of the leaf blade near the lower margin of the blade; leaves shallowly 3 to 7 angled or lobed; lower surface of leaf blade pale gray or silvery-gray; leaf blade firm and thickish . . . Moonseed, *Menispermum canadense*, p. 342

30. Top of leaf stalk joining the leaf directly at the edge or base of the leaf blade; leaves deeply 3 to 7 lobed with long-pointed lobes; lower surface of leaf blade green, scarcely paler than the upper surface . . . Cupseed, *Calycocarpum lyoni*, p. 316

31. Leaves entire . . . Ladies' eardrops, *Brunnichia ovata*, p. 314

31. Leaves toothed 32

32. Pith white, continuous, not interrupted at the nodes (where buds or leaf stalks arise) by a cross partition; flowering or fruiting clusters much broader than long; petals all separate from one another, spreading at flowering time, falling away singly; fruit not edible; bark tight, not loosening into flaky or ropy strands or shreds . . . Raccoon grape, *Ampelopsis cordata*, p. 306

32. Pith brown, interrupted at each node (where buds or leaf stalks arise) by a cross partition (except in *Vitis rotundifolia*); flowering or fruiting clusters much longer than broad; petals joined at their tips, and falling as one caplike piece before the flower opens; fruit

edible; bark of old stems loosening into flaky or ropy strands or shreds (except in *Vitis rotundifolia*) 33

33. Lower surface of fully grown leaf blades either whitened with light rusty cobwebby hairs or dull green with a grayish or ashy covering of hairs lying against the surface 34

33. Lower surface of fully grown leaf blades green and lacking hairs or with short straight hairs standing erect from the surface, not cobwebby 35

34. Some of the leaves shallowly or deeply 3- to 5-lobed; lower surface of fully grown leaf blades whitish with light rusty cobwebby hairs; small branches round, not angled . . . Summer grape, *Vitis aestivalis*, p. 364

34. Leaves not deeply lobed but may have 2 shallow lobes; lower surface of fully grown leaf blades dull green with a grayish or ashy more or less uniform, continuous covering of hairs; small branches angled . . . Winter grape, *Vitis cinerea*, p. 366

35. Pith continuous through the nodes; bark of branches and main stem tight, not shredding off; tendrils simple, not forked . . . Muscadine, *Vitis rotundifolia*, p. 372

35. Pith interrupted at the nodes by a cross partition; bark of older branches and main stem loosening and shredding; tendrils when present, forked 36

36. Leaf blades usually broader than long, sometimes shaped like a lima or kidney bean; leaf blade folded upward or trough-shaped to expose the pale green lower surface; tendrils absent or opposite only uppermost leaves or at tips of flowering or fruiting branches; plants rarely climbing . . . Sand grape, *Vitis rupestris*, p. 372

36. Leaf blades longer than broad with a conspicuous triangular tip, generally heart-shaped, broadly egg-shaped, or triangular egg-shaped; leaf blade relatively flat, not folded or trough-shaped; tendrils present; plants climbing 37

37. Leaf blades merely toothed, or if lobed, the 2 side lobes short, shoulderlike; leaves of

flowering or fruiting branches not 3-lobed
. . . Frost grape, *Vitis vulpina*, p. 374

37. Leaf blades with usually 2 prominent side lobes which are generally long-pointed and tapering; leaves of flowering or fruiting branches 3-lobed. 38

38. New branches of the current season bright red or purplish red; fruit black, without a whitish coating; margins of leaf blades scarcely or not at all lined with fine hairs; leaf blades of flowering or fruiting branches 1 1/2 to 3 1/2 inches broad . . . Red grape, *Vitis palmata*, p. 368

38. New branches of the current season green, gray or brown, not red; fruit grayish-blue with a whitish coating that can be rubbed off; margins of leaf blades lined with fine hairs; leaf blades of flowering or fruiting branches 3 to 6 inches broad . . . Riverbank grape, *Vitis riparia*, p. 370

Shrubs

Prairie acacia

Acacia angustissima (Miller) Kuntze

Mimosa family (Mimosaceae)

Field Identification: Rarely more than 2 feet tall, this **semi-woody shrub, with its fernlike leaves,** winterkills to the ground in the northern part of the United States, but maintains a woody base in its southern range.

Flowers: Late June-October, **in short globe-shaped clusters emerging from the axils of leaves,** clusters white, about 1/2 inch across with 6 to 15 flowers; petals 5, greenish-white, 1/8 inch long; stamens numerous, from 50 to 100 or more, extending beyond the flower.

Fruit: August-September, **pods solitary or in clusters,** 2 to 3 inches long, about 1/4 inch wide, dark brown, thin, flat, dry, constricted between the seeds, tip blunt, pod splitting to release 3 to 6 seeds; seeds about 1/8 inch long and wide, broadly egg-shaped, brown, often mottled, flattened.

Leaves: Alternate, **twice-pinnately compound,** 2 to 5 inches long; leaflets averaging 20 to 33 pairs on a pinnae (first division of a compound leaf), **end leaflets a pair instead of one end or terminal leaflet;** leaflets 1/8 to 1/4 inch long, mostly linear, tip blunt; both surfaces pale green, smooth or with a few hairs; petioles 1/2 to 1 1/2 inches long with a grooved upper surface, hairs flattened.

Twigs: Long, slender, brown, deeply grooved, somewhat hairy, often dies back to near the ground in winter.

Trunk: Bark greenish-brown, ribbed, tight; wood soft, white, with a large brown pith, barely woody.

Habitat: Occurs on dolomite glades, open hillsides and exposed ledges along bluffs in the extreme southwestern part of the state.

In Missouri it is not known from prairies.

Range: Louisiana to Texas, north to Missouri, and west to southeastern Kansas and Oklahoma.

Wildlife Uses: The seeds have a high protein content, which rates it as a good wildlife food. The seeds are known to be eaten by mourning dove, bobwhite quail and small mammals.

Remarks: There are several varieties of *Acacia angustissima,* and the one in Missouri is referred to as var. *hirta* (Nutt.) Robinson. It strongly resembles the herbaceous Illinois bundleflower *(Desmanthus illinoensis)* but lacks glands on the petioles, the stamens are numerous instead of 5, and the fruit is about twice as wide as the latter.

Its fernlike leaves and drought tolerance makes prairie acacia a good candidate for rock gardens.

Acacia is an ancient word meaning "a hard, sharp point," with reference to the presence of spines in many species; *angustissima* refers to the very narrow leaflets.

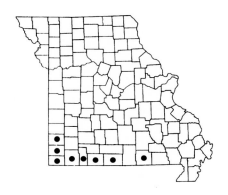

Acacia angustissima ✻ a. Growth form, b. Flower cluster, c. Fruit

Ohio buckeye

Aesculus glabra Willd.

Horse chestnut family (Hippocastanaceae)

Field Identification: Variable from a shrub to medium-sized tree, depending upon site conditions; branches drooping with upcurved ends.

Flowers: April-May, clustered along an axis 4 to 8 inches long, 2 to 3 inches wide on the tips of twigs; **flowers greenish-yellow**, 1/2 to 3/4 inch long, in the shape of a tube; petals 4, two upright and two lateral, **equal in length**; stamens 8, **longer than the petals**.

Fruit: September-October, capsule leathery, 1 to 2 1/4 inches across, globe to inverted egg-shaped, light brown, **roughened by blunt spines**, splitting into three parts; seeds 3, sometimes flattened by pressure against each other, shiny, brown, 1 to 1 1/2 inches wide.

Leaves: Opposite, palm-shaped with **mainly 7 leaflets**, broadest in the middle and tapering at both ends to egg-shaped, tip pointed, base wedge-shaped, margin finely toothed, leaflet 4 to 6 inches long, 1 1/2 to 2 1/2 inches wide; upper surface bluish- or grass-green, smooth; lower surface paler, smooth, sometimes hairy on the veins; leaves turning yellow in early autumn, foul smelling when crushed; petioles 4 to 6 inches long.

Twigs: Reddish-brown to gray, hairy at first, smooth later; lenticels (pores) orange; leaf scars large.

Trunk: Bark dark brown when young, smooth; older bark gray and broken into plates roughened by small numerous scales, foul smelling; wood whitish, fine-grained, soft, sapwood hardly distinguishable.

Habitat: Occurs in rich or rocky woods of valleys, ravines, gentle or steep slopes, base of bluffs, edge of low woods, thickets, and occasionally on edges of limestone glades. Throughout Missouri, except for the extreme southeastern region.

Range: Northern Alabama, northern Mississippi, northeastern Texas, Arkansas, and Oklahoma, north to Pennsylvania and west to Ohio, Michigan, Iowa, northeastern Nebraska and Kansas.

Wildlife Uses: The tubular greenish-yellow flowers are frequented by ruby-throated hummingbirds for their nectar. The seeds and young foliage are considered poisonous although the seeds are reported to be eaten by squirrels.

Medicinal Uses: People have carried buckeyes in their pockets to prevent rheumatism. The bark or nuts have been used to cure skin sores and ulcers, the flowers to treat rheumatism, and the bark and fruit as a tonic and to treat fever.

Remarks: Ohio buckeye is sometimes planted for ornament in the Eastern United States and in Europe. It has been in cultivation since 1809. The leaves are the first to emerge in early spring before any other tree. It is a short-lived tree. The wood is easy to carve and resists splitting. It is used for fuel, paper pulp, artificial limbs, splints, woodenware, boxes, crates, toys, furniture, veneer for trunks, drawing boards and occasionally for lumber. The seeds are considered poisonous, but are rendered harmless after boiling or roasting; they were roasted and eaten by Native Americans as a starchy meal.

Aesculus is the ancient name for a European mast-bearing (seed-bearing) tree; *glabra* refers to the smooth leaves.

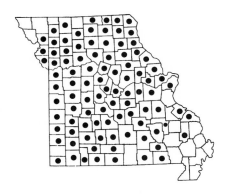

Aesculus glabra ❧ a. Growth form, b. Flower cluster, c. Fruit, d. Seed

Red Buckeye

Aesculus pavia L.

Horse chestnut family (Hippocastanaceae)

Field Identification: Shrub, or, more rarely, a small tree. The crown is usually dense and the branches short, drooping with upcurved ends.

Flowers: April-June, clustered along an axis 4 to 8 inches long, flowers red, 3/4 to 1 1/2 inches long, in the shape of a tube 3/8 to 5/8 inch long ending in 2 upright and 2 lateral **petals unequal in length; stamens 8, shorter than or only slightly longer than the upper petals.**

Fruit: September-November, capsule 1 to 2 inches in diameter, leathery, somewhat globe- or egg-shaped, light brown, **smooth but finely pitted**, splitting into three parts; seeds 1 to 3, rounded or flattened by pressure against each other, shiny, light to dark brown, about 1 inch in diameter.

Leaves: Opposite, **palm-shaped with 5 leaflets**, lance-shaped with the broadest toward the tip or inverted egg-shaped, tip terminating in a sharp angle to abruptly pointed, base gradually narrowed, margin coarsely toothed, leaflet length 3 to 6 inches, width 1 to 1 1/2 inches; **upper surface shiny, dark green**, smooth with a few hairs on the veins, lower surface paler, smooth to matted hairs; petioles nearly smooth or with varying degrees of hairiness, red, 3 to 7 inches long.

Twigs: Green to gray or brown, drooping with upcurved ends, stout, smooth; lenticels (pores) pale brown to orange; leaf scars large.

Trunk: Bark gray to brown, smooth on young branches, on old trunks roughened into short plates that flake off in small, thin scales.

Habitat: Occurs in low rich woods in valleys, at the base of bluffs, low slopes and along streams. Also it persists in old pastures, clearings, and along utility rights-of-way. **Found wild only in southeastern Missouri.**

Range: Florida to central Texas, north to Virginia, Tennessee, southern Illinois, southeastern Missouri and Oklahoma.

Wildlife Uses: The tubular red flowers are frequented by ruby-throated hummingbirds for their nectar. The seeds and young foliage are considered poisonous, although the seeds are reported to be eaten by squirrels.

Medicinal Uses: It is reported that the powdered bark is used in domestic medicine for toothache and ulcers.

Remarks: This shrub, with its red flowers and palmately shaped foliage, is a popular ornamental that flowers in just a few years when grown from seed. The seeds and young foliage are poisonous to livestock. The powdered seeds have been used in ponds and slow-moving water to catch fish, which become groggy and float to the surface. The roots contain soap-foaming properties and have been used for washing clothes.

Aesculus is the ancient name for an old mast-bearing (seed-bearing) tree; *pavia*, honors Peter Paaw (died 1617), of Leyden, a northeastern suburb of London.

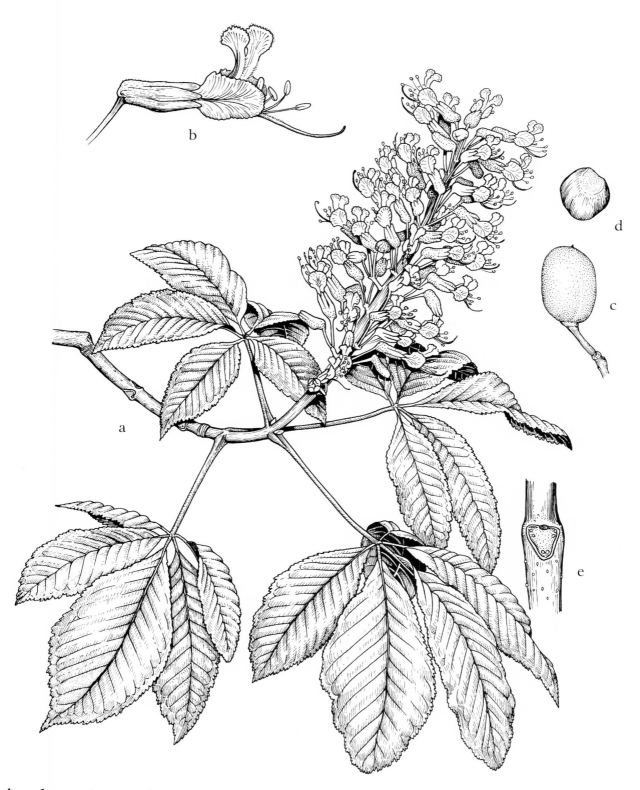

Aesculus pavia ❦ a. Growth form, b. Flower, c. Fruit, d. Seed, e. Leaf scar

Alder

Alnus serrulata (Ait.) Willd.

Birch family (Betulaceae)

Also called common alder, smooth alder, tag alder

Field Identification: Irregularly shaped shrub or slender tree to 20 feet.

Flowers: March-April, borne in separate staminate (male) and pistillate (female) catkins; staminate catkins in clusters of 2 to 5, 2 to 4 inches long, cylindric, drooping; stamens 3 to 6; pistillate catkins in clusters of 2 to 3, about 1/4 inch long, green to purple.

Fruit: September-October, about 3/4 inch long, oval-shaped, a conelike cluster of woody bracts each below a nutlet; nutlet small, oval, flattened, sharp-angled, less than 1/8 inch long.

Leaves: Alternate, simple, deciduous, thick blades 1 to 5 inches long, inverted egg-shaped to oval, **blunt or rounded at the tip**, terminating at a sharp angle or wedge-shaped at the base, **margin with teeth blunt or rounded**, rather dark green on both sides, and somewhat hairy or smooth beneath, veins prominent; petioles smooth or hairy, 1/3 to 1/2 inch long.

Twigs: Reddish-brown to brown, hairy at first, smooth later, slender, flexible.

Trunk: Bark reddish-brown to brown, with horizontal lenticels (pores); bark with narrow grooves starting as a vertical row of dots and eventually opening to a narrow crack; wood lightweight, not strong, light brown.

Habitat: Occurs along stream banks, springs, spring branches and fens.

Range: From Florida, Louisiana and eastern Texas, north to Nova Scotia, Maine, New Hampshire, Vermont, New York, West Virginia, Ohio, Minnesota, Iowa, Missouri and Oklahoma.

Wildlife Uses: The fruit is eaten by several species of birds. Woodcock and ruffed grouse eat the buds, catkins and seeds. Alder provides cover for woodcocks from early spring through fall for nesting, feeding and resting. Beavers commonly use alders in dam construction.

Medicinal Uses: The dried, powdered bark steeped in water has been used for eye infections. Tea made from the bark has been used to treat diarrhea and as a blood purifier. Native Americans applied an extract of the inner bark to poison ivy rash.

Remarks: Alder, with its dense mass of roots, is sometimes planted to prevent erosion on stream banks. Alder roots also enrich the soil, for in association with certain bacteria, they absorb atmospheric nitrogen and make it available to neighboring plants. Alder easily spreads by vegetative growth, either by sprouting new shoots from the base of older plants; by sending up shoots from underground stems; or by layering, a process in which a branch that has come in contact with the ground sends down roots and sends up shoots.

The woody, conelike female catkins are sometimes plated with gold or silver and used for jewelry.

Alnus is the classical name of the alder; *serrulata* refers to the finely toothed leaves.

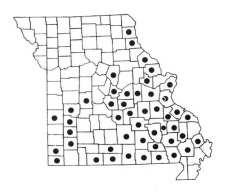

Alnus serrulata ❧ a. Growth form, b. Winter twig, c. Male catkin, d. Female catkin, e. Fruit

Service berry

Amelanchier arborea (Michx. f.) Fern.

Rose family (Rosaceae)

Also called shadbush, sarvice berry, sarviss tree, June berry, shadblow, sugar plum, Indian cherry

Field Identification: Tall shrub or small tree, rarely up to 30 feet tall.

Flowers: March-May, often appearing before the leaves; flower clusters 3 to 7 inches long, **rather dense, erect or nodding, silky-hairy**, fragrant, 6 to 12 flowered; petals 5, white, widest at the middle, rounded to flat-tipped, 1/2 to 1 inch long; stamens about 20.

Fruits: June-July, borne on long pedicels, globe-shaped, 1/4 to 1/2 inch diameter, dry, **reddish-purple**, tasteless or sweetish; seeds small and numerous (4 to 10).

Leaves: Alternate, simple; blades 2 to 5 inches long, 1 to 2 inches wide; oval to longer than broad, tip pointed, base rounded or heart-shaped, sharply and finely toothed on the margin; smooth or nearly so above, young leaves paler and hairy beneath, usually smooth when mature; petioles 1 1/2 to 2 inches long, slender, hairy at first but smooth later.

Twigs: Reddish-brown, slender, rather crooked, somewhat hairy when young but smooth later; lenticels (pores) numerous and pale.

Trunk: Bark light gray and smooth when young, becoming dark gray with shallow furrows and long ridges; wood dark brown, with a wide, white sapwood, sometimes used for making tool handles. It ranks with persimmon as the heaviest wood among North American trees, and as fifth in hardness.

Habitat: Open rocky woods, bluffs; usually on well-drained slopes.

Range: Florida to Missouri, Oklahoma and northeastern Texas, north to Minnesota, Michigan, Ontario, Quebec, New Brunswick and Maine.

Wildlife Uses: Service berry is a valuable wildlife plant, with at least 35 species of birds eating the fruit and 11 species of mammals either eating the fruit or browsing the twigs and foliage.

Remarks: The showy white flowers are among the first woody plants to bloom in spring, appearing before the leaves open. It is occasionally used in landscaping for its showy white flowers and red fruit. The fall foliage is very colorful, turning a pale orange or gold blended with red and green. The fruit is edible and varies in sweetness. It can be eaten raw or cooked in pies, puddings or muffins. Native Americans used the fruit in breadmaking, first making a paste from it, then drying it and mixing it with cornmeal.

The word "service" is a derivation of *sarviss*, which is said to be a modified form of *sorbus*, the name applied to a fruit known to the Romans and resembling that of *Amelanchier*. Shadbush was so named by the European settlers along the Atlantic Coast for the timing of the blooms with the spawning runs of shad.

Amelanchier is from the name of a French province; *arborea* refers to the treelike character of this species.

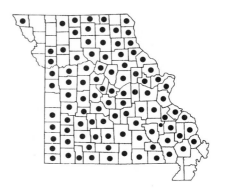

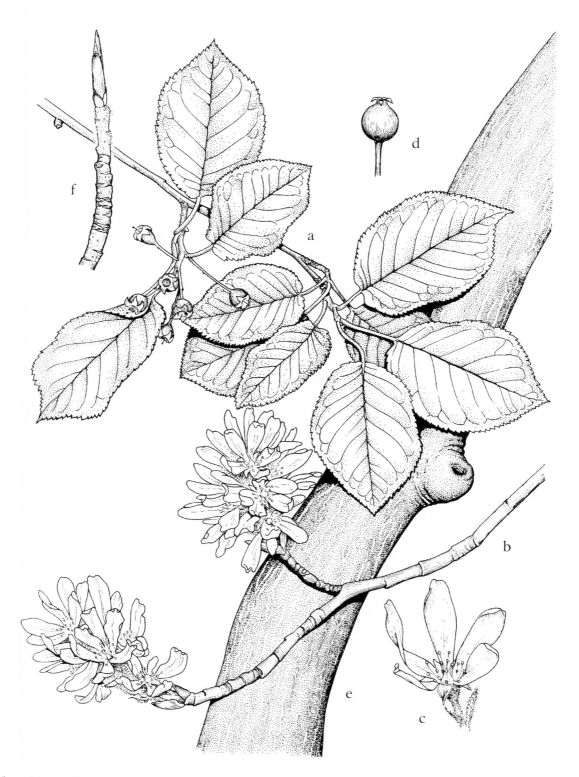

Amelanchier arborea ❀ a. Growth form with fruit cluster, b. Twig with flower clusters, c. Flower, d. Fruit, e. Stem with bark, f. Winter twig

Lead plant

Amorpha canescens Pursh

Bean family (Fabaceae)

Field Identification: An erect or ascending shrub 1 to 3 feet, leafy to the base.

Flowers: May-August, in slender, dense, flower clusters, often with lateral clusters below the terminal ones, clusters up to 10 inches long on a densely hairy stalk, flower tube-shaped with the tip lobed, 1/4 inch long, bluish-purple; stamens 10.

Fruit: August-September, individual pods 1/6 to 1/5 inch long, often no pods at the tip, pods 1/6 to 1/5 inch long, densely hairy; seed solitary, longer than broad, brown, shiny, about 1/8 inch long.

Leaves: Pinnately compound, 1 1/2 to 5 inches long, each leaf with from 13 to 49 leaflets; **leaflets small, less than 3/4 inch long**, widest in the middle to egg-shaped, tip and base rounded, margin entire; upper surface with flattened hairs, **lower surface with gray hairs; petiole absent or barely visible.**

Twigs: Flexible, **densely hairy**, gray-brown, pith white.

Trunk: Bark gray, smooth; wood white, hard, no differentiation of heartwood and sapwood.

Habitat: Occurs in prairies, glades and woodlands.

Range: From Michigan to Saskatchewan and North Dakota, south to Louisiana, and west to New Mexico.

Wildlife Uses: The flowers are a nectar source for butterflies and bees. Cottontail rabbits browse on the stems in winter.

Medicinal Uses: The leaves can be used to make a pleasant-tasting yellow-brown tea. The Omaha Indians powdered the dried leaves and blew them into cuts and open wounds to help promote scab formation. The Potawatomis made a leaf tea to kill pinworms and other intestinal worms. They also steeped the leaves to make a liquid to cure eczema.

Remarks: The occurrence of lead plant is indicative of a high-quality prairie or glade. Since it is palatable to livestock, lead plant is found less frequently on grazed prairies. It is sometimes grown as an ornamental plant because of its showy purple flower spikes and grayish-white foliage. This species may die back to the ground and appear as an herbaceous plant. In other cases, several inches of above-ground stem overwinters and new growth originates from previous year's stems.

Amorpha means "without form," referring to the solitary tube-shaped petal; *canescens* refers to the dense, gray hairs. The name lead plant refers to the leaden hue of the leaves.

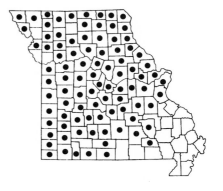

Amorpha canescens ❧ a. Growth form with flower clusters, b. Flower, c. Twig with fruit clusters

False indigo

Amorpha fruticosa L.

Bean family (Fabaceae)

Also known as indigo bush

Field Identification: Shrub often clumped, **branching to 12 feet high.**

Flowers: May-June, flower clusters dense, sometimes with lateral branches below the terminal ones, 2 1/2 to 6 inches long on a hairy stalk, flower tube-shaped with the tip lobed, about 1/4 inch long, purplish-blue; stamens 10.

Fruit: August-September, individual pods 1/4 to 3/8 inch long, smooth with resinous dots; seed about 1/6 inch long, lance- to egg-shaped, curved at one end, brown and glossy.

Leaves: Pinnately compound, 2 1/2 to 10 inches long; leaflets 9 to 27, **3/4 to 1 1/2 inches long**, 3/8 to 3/4 inch wide, oval to longer than broad, tip rounded to abruptly pointed, base rounded or wedge-shaped, margin entire; upper surface dull green and smooth; lower surface paler and smooth or finely hairy; **petioles 3/4 to 2 inches long**, smooth or with long, soft hairs.

Twigs: brown or gray, with scattered long, soft hairs becoming smooth with age.

Trunk: Bark of young trunks smooth, brown-gray, with prominent lenticels (pores), old trunks with slight cracks; wood hard, porous, yellowish, with prominent rays.

Habitat: Found in moist ground in thickets along streams, rocky banks, borders of ponds, and low open wet woods.

Range: From Florida to Louisiana, Texas, Mexico and California, north to New Hampshire, Massachusetts, Manitoba, Saskatchewan and Minnesota.

Wildlife Uses: Butterflies and bees frequent the flowers for nectar. Bobwhite quail eat the seeds. It is not a dense bush, but red-winged blackbirds often use it as a nesting site.

Medicinal Uses: The roots and stems of both false indigo and lead plant contain rotenone, which is used as an insecticide and fish poison. This substance has shown anti-cancer activity in lymphocytic leukemia and nasopharyngeal tumor systems.

Remarks: False indigo is a variable species throughout its wide range. It has been cultivated since 1724, and is useful for landscape planting, erosion control and game food.

A closely related species, smooth false indigo, *Amorpha nitens*, has not been found in Missouri, but does occur in southern Illinois, western Kentucky, northern Arkansas and northeastern Oklahoma. It differs from *Amorpha fruticosa* by having smooth leaflets and branches and with the seed pod lacking resinous dots. It may well be found in southern Missouri in the future.

Amorpha means "without form," referring to the solitary tube-shaped petal; *fruticosa* is for the shrubby character of the plant. The common name, false indigo, comes from the commercial use of some species that yield a poor indigo (blue) dye.

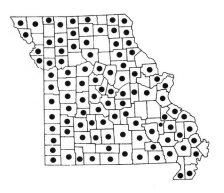

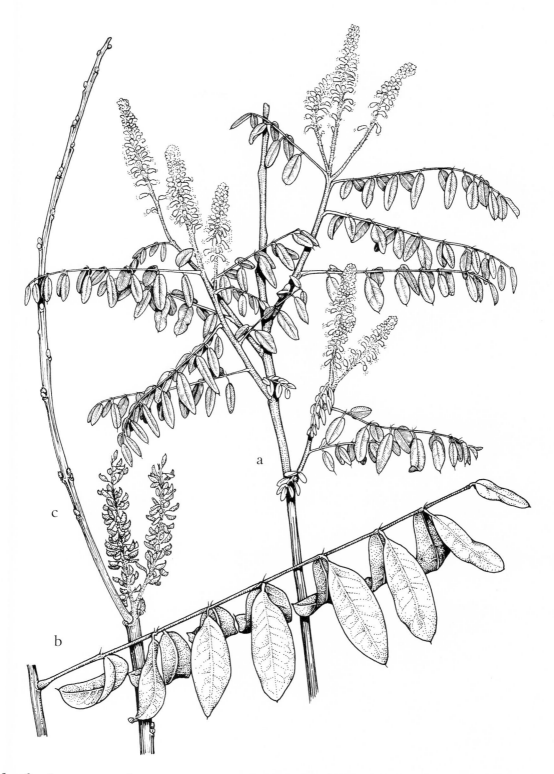

Amorpha fruticosa a. Growth form with flower clusters, b. Pinnately compound leaf, c. Winter twig with fruit clusters

Buck brush

Andrachne phyllanthoides (Nutt.) J. Coulter

Spurge family (Euphorbiaceae)

Also known as Missouri maiden-bush

Field Identification: An upright or straggling branched shrub, 1 to 3 feet tall.

Flowers: May-October, small, greenish-yellow, emerging from the angle of where leaf joins stem, solitary, on smooth stalks 1/4 to 5/6 inch long, with both male and female flowers found on the same plant and about 1/4 inch wide; male flowers with 5 to 6 stamens (shown in illustration).

Fruit: August-October, capsule globe-shaped, 1/4 to 1/3 inch in diameter, 3-lobed, dry, 6-seeded; seeds rough, minute (not shown in illustration).

Leaves: Numerous, simple, alternate, oval to inverted egg-shaped, tip blunt to rounded, base rounded or sharply tapering, margin entire, length 1/3 to 7/8 inch, 2/5 to 3/5 inch wide, thin, rather soft and more or less translucent, under surface yellowish-green and smooth, lower surface paler with veins finely networked; **leaves with milky sap when broken**; petioles short or absent.

Twigs: Leafy, ascending, simple, slender and wiry, smooth, reddish-brown to light brown or grayish when older, shiny; **twigs with milky sap when broken.**

Trunk: Bark light brown to gray with shaggy plates.

Habitat: Occurs on rocky ledges of dolomite bluffs, dolomite glades, and along dry gravelly washes of rocky stream beds.

Range: From Missouri to Arkansas, Oklahoma and northern, central and western Texas.

Remarks: The color and shape of its leaves adds to the ornamental value of this small shrub. Branch dieback can occur north of its natural range in Missouri after very cold winters. It has been cultivated since 1899. This low shrub is the only woody member of the predominately tropical spurge family to extend its range as far north as Missouri; the other woody members of the family in the New World extend southward into Mexico, and Central and South America.

Andrachne is the classical Greek name for the purslane or spurge; *phyllanthoides* indicates that it resembles the phyllanthus plant.

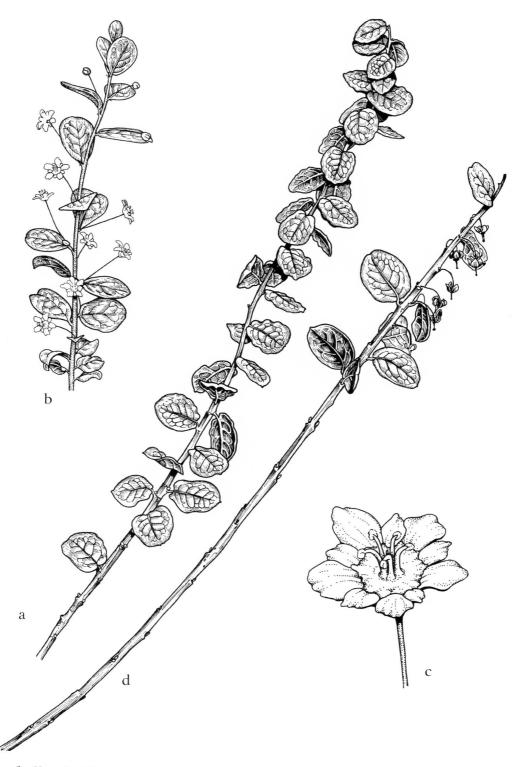

Andrachne phyllanthoides ❧ a. Growth form, b. Stem with leaves and flowers, c. Flower, d. Stem with fruit capsules

Hercules club

Aralia spinosa L.

Ginseng family (Araliaceae)

Also known as devil's walking stick, tear-blanket, angelica tree

Field Identification: Spiny, few-branched shrub or slender, flat-topped small tree to 35 feet.

Flowers: July-September, the large, branched cluster of flowers is very conspicuous, stalks below the flowers are light yellow, flowers are white, 1/8 inch across, petals 5, white; stamens 5.

Fruit: September-October, in large clusters; fruit black, juice purple, diameter about 1/4 inch; seed solitary, longer than broad, rounded at ends, flattened, dry, brittle, brownish.

Leaves: Alternate, compound, **leaves more than simply once-compound, with the side leaf divisions further divided into additional leaflets; compound leaves generally borne at the top of the trunk; blades 3 to 4 feet long, 2 to 4 feet wide**, each stalk with 5 to 6 pairs of leaflets with a terminal leaflet; leaflets dark green above, paler beneath, 1 to 4 inches long, tiny prickles often on center vein of leaflet, yellow in autumn; petioles 18 to 20 inches long, clasping the base of the stem, prickly.

Trunk: Bark dark brown, cracks shallow, ridges irregular, **armed with stout, light brown to orange prickles**, inner bark yellow, **leaf scars abundant and conspicuous**; wood brown to yellow, weak, soft, light, close-grained.

Habitat: Low upland sandy woods, thickets, wooded slopes, bluffs and ravines.

Range: From Florida to east Texas and Oklahoma, north to New Jersey, Pennsylvania, New York, Ohio, Indiana, Illinois and Iowa.

Wildlife Uses: The seeds are eaten by many birds and the leaves browsed by white-tailed deer.

Medicinal Uses: Native Americans drank a watered extraction of the bark and root to purify the blood and to treat fever. The water that fresh roots were stored in has been used to treat irritated eyes. At one time the inner bark was used for curing toothaches.

Remarks: The author's first encounter comes from a painful appreciation for the stem's armor when reaching for a trunk to stabilize footing on an unstable slope. The shrub has high ornamental value and is often planted in Europe. It has been cultivated since 1688. The wood was once used for small articles such as pen racks, button boxes, photograph frames, stools and rocking chair arms. The black fleshy fruits at one time were used for dyeing hair black.

Aralia is from the French-Canadian *Aralie*, the name appended to the original specimens sent to Tournefort, a French botanist, by the Quebec physician, Sarrasin; *spinosa* refers to the spiny trunk and branches.

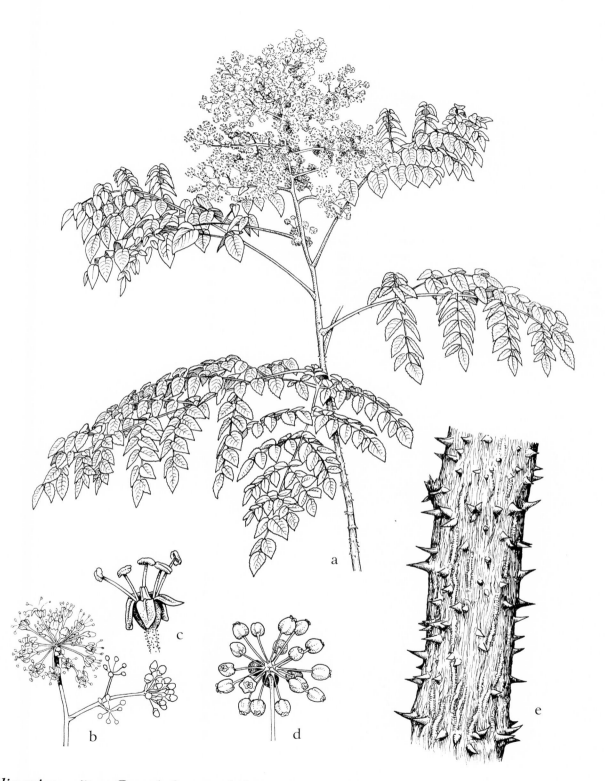

Aralia spinosa ❀ a. Growth form with flower clusters, b. Flower cluster, c. Flower, d. Fruit cluster, e. Stem with prickles

Black chokeberry

Aronia melanocarpa (Michaux) Elliott

Rose family (Rosaceae)

Field Identification: Small shrub to 9 feet, mostly single-stemmed, thickets are not dense and sucker sprouts from roots are not apparent.

Flowers: April-May, in clusters of about 6 to 8 flowers at the ends of twigs, 1 to 2 inches broad; flowers white to pinkish, about 1/2 inch across; petals about 1/4 inch long, oval, tip round, base tapering; stamens 15 to 25.

Fruit: September-October, **purplish-black, about 1/4 inch long and wide**, oval to globe-shaped, tip rounded, base flattened.

Leaves: Simple, alternate, 1 1/2 to 4 inches long, longer than broad and tapering at both ends, sometimes egg-shaped, tip pointed, base wedge-shaped, margin finely toothed with a small gland at the end of each tooth, dark green, **upper surface with reddish dots (glands) along the main vein**, veins sunken below the surface; lower surface paler, smooth with a few scattered hairs; petioles about 1/4 inch long.

Habitat: Known only from sandy wet or boggy ground along seeps at the base of Crowley's Ridge.

Range: Georgia, Tennessee, Arkansas, southeastern Missouri, north to Newfoundland, and west to Ontario and Minnesota.

Wildlife Uses: The fruit is eaten by several species of birds.

Remarks: Black chokeberry is listed as endangered in Missouri. A few small populations grow along seep branches at the base of Crowley's Ridge. Although the ridge runs from Scott City in Scott County south to about 20 miles southwest of Dexter in Stoddard County, there are only a few areas that provide suitable habitat for the shrub. Mining for sand and gravel, and clearing hills for pastures and homesites on Crowley's Ridge north of Dexter is destroying habitat for the black chokeberry and several other rare or endangered plant species.

One area that has been protected, Holly Ridge Conservation Area, provides habitat for black chokeberry and several other unique plants. Here American holly *(Ilex opaca)*, screw-stem *(Bartonia paniculata)*, swamp oats *(Trisetum pensylvanicum)*, blue curls *(Trichostema setaceum)*, and netted chain fern *(Woodwardia areolata)* grow along seep branches at the base of wooded slopes.

Black chokeberry is often grown as an ornamental for its showy clusters of white flowers. The purple-black fruit is about the size of blueberries, but they are less sweet and far more chewy. With their high pectin content, they are good for making jelly and jams.

Aronia is from the Greek name *aria*, for whitebeam (a species of *Sorbus*, mountain ash), the fruits of which resemble chokeberry; *melanocarpa* refers to the black *(melano)* fruit *(carpa)*. It is difficult to determine why chokeberry got a reputation so bad as to account for its common name. The fruits are not bitter, especially when compared to chokecherry, for which it may once have been mistaken.

Aronia melanocarpa ❀ a. Growth form with flower clusters, b. Flower, c. Fruit

Giant cane

Arundinaria gigantea (Walter) Muhlenb.

Grass family (Poaceae)

Field Identification: Bamboolike canes, woody, branched above, rarely more than 16 feet tall. Grows in dense colonies due to vegetative spread by rhizomes.

Flowers: April-May, flowers between long intervals, borne in clusters composed of larger, flattened flower stalks from branches on the old wood; flower stalks 1 1/2 to 2 1/2 inches long, mostly 5 to 15 flowered, petals absent.

Fruits: Grain is furrowed, enclosed in flattened spikelets.

Leaves: Somewhat crowded at ends of branches, blades 4 to 12 inches long, 5/6 to 1 1/3 inches wide. longer than broad and lance-shaped to long and narrow, tip pointed, rounded or tapering at the base and enclosing the stem, margin with small, sharp teeth; **leaf blade grasslike with parallel veins.**

Stems: Smooth with hollow segments separated by solid joints, green turning light brown with age.

Habitat: Found in the lowlands and along larger streams and at the base of dolomite cliffs.

Range: From Florida to Texas, north to southern New Jersey, and the southern parts of Ohio, Indiana, Illinois and Missouri.

Wildlife Uses: The young shoots were once eaten by the woods bison, woods elk and black bear. Cane is used for nesting by the Swainson's warbler, which is now endangered due to drastically reduced cane stands.

Remarks: Giant cane is Missouri's only native grass that is woody by nature. Giant cane has suffered greatly from loss of habitat due to impoundments, grazing and the clearing of valleys for cultivation. Native Americans and early European settlers used the seeds for food. The young shoots were used as a pot herb in the same manner as the bamboo shoots of tropical countries. Livestock eat the shoots and fruit. Canes also are used for fishing poles and for mats.

Giant cane is occasionally planted north of its natural range, but it will be killed back to the ground during cold winters. Spreading by rhizomes, this grass can be difficult to contain in a home landscape. The dense stand can make an effective screen or border.

Arundinaria is derived from the word *arundo*, the Latin name for "reed"; *gigantea* refers to the "gigantic" stature of the plant.

Arundinaria gigantea ❀ a. Detailed view of stem with leaves, b. Flower stalks

American barberry

Berberis canadensis Miller

Barberry family (Berberidaceae)

Field Identification: Small, spiny shrub, sparsely branched, less than 3 feet tall.

Flowers: May, clustered, arising from the leaf/stem axis on a stalk, usually 5 to 10 flowers per cluster, petals 6, yellow; stamens 6.

Fruit: June-July, red, a 1-seeded berry, about 3/8 inch long.

Leaves: Spines at the axils are actually three-branched leaf remnants that bear clusters of small leaves at their base; leaves broadest above the middle and narrowly tapering to the base, 3/4 to 2 1/2 inches long, tip rounded or ending at a sharp angle, margin bears several small teeth 2 to 11 on each side leaf, small veins indistinct beneath.

Twigs: Bearing three spines and a leaf cluster at each axil, two-year-old branches orange or reddish-brown.

Habitat: Occurs on rocky, wooded — usually north-facing — upper ledges of bluffs along the Jacks Fork and Eleven Point rivers on dolomite or sandstone.

Range: From West Virginia and Virginia to Georgia and Alabama, and in Indiana and Missouri.

Wildlife Uses: Birds are known to eat the fruits. White-tailed deer browse on the leaves, which have a pleasant acidic flavor, very similar to that of sheep-sorrel leaves.

Remarks: There are few sites for this shrub in Missouri and it is classified as rare on the list of endangered species for the state. It may never have been very common — being on the western edge of its distribution — but open-range grazing, which ended in the 1960s, may have contributed to its current status. In areas where it is more common, the berries are known to make a good jam, some say one of the best to be had from wild fruits. The fruits are best just after they ripen, for later in the summer they are said to be relatively tasteless. The same holds true for the leaves, which become bitter later in the summer.

This shrub serves as an alternate host for black stem rust, an economically serious disease affecting wheat. In some parts of its range, American barberry plants have been killed to eliminate it as a disease host.

Berberis is from *Berberys*, the Arabic name of the fruit; *canadensis* mistakingly attributes this plant as to have come from Canada.

Berberis canadensis ❀ a. Growth form with fruit, b. Winter twig with fruit, c. Stem with flower clusters, d. Flower

Japanese barberry

Berberis thunbergii DC.

Barberry family (Berberidaceae)

Field Identification: Densely branched, spiny shrub to 7 feet tall.

Flowers: April-May, clustered, arising from the leaf/stem axis on a stalk, usually 2 to 4 flowers per cluster, petals 6, yellow; stamens 6.

Fruits: June, **red**, a 1-seeded berry, about 3/8 inch long.

Leaves: Spine at each axil is actually a leaf remnant with small leaf clusters at its base; leaves in small clusters, broadest above the middle and narrowly tapering to the base, up to 2 inches long, tip rounded or ending at a sharp angle, margin smooth edged, small veins indistinct beneath.

Twigs: Bearing a prominent single spine and leaf cluster at each axil; wood yellow.

Habitat: Commonly cultivated as a hedge plant, sometimes escaping into old fields and open woods.

Range: Native of Japan; introduced and naturalized from Nova Scotia to Michigan, south to North Carolina and Missouri.

Remarks: Another exotic shrub — common barberry, *Berberis vulgaris* — can be distinguished from American and Japanese barberry by its clusters of 10 to 20 flowers at an axil, teeth of mature leaves ending in a bristle, usually 13 to 20 teeth on a side, 2-year-old branches gray, and small veins distinct beneath. It is a native from Europe. Like Japanese barberry, it is known to escape from cultivation into pastures, open woods and occasionally along rocky spring branches.

Berberis is from *Berberys*, the Arabic name of the fruit; *thunbergii* is for Carl Peter Thunberg (1742-1828), a Swedish botanist whose personal herbarium collection, which he gave to the University of Uppsala, is considered one of the most important historical collections today.

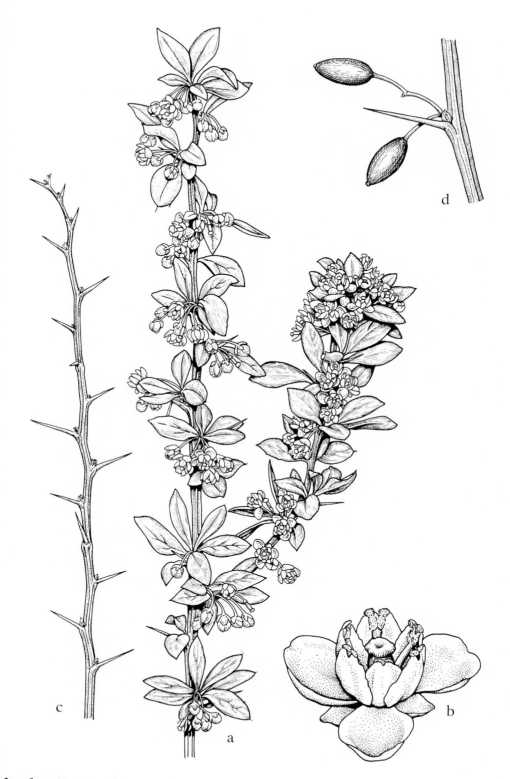

Berberis thunbergii ✽ a. Growth form with flower clusters, b. Flower, c. Winter twig with spines, d. Winter twig with fruit and spine

Woolly buckthorn

Bumelia lanuginosa (Michaux) Pers.

Sapodilla family (Sapotaceae)

Also called chittim wood, false buckthorn, gum-elastic

Field Identification: Shrub or an irregularly shaped tree to 40 feet with thorns, short spur branches and milky sap.

Flowers: June-July, in dense clusters of 5 to 30 flowers at the leaf/stem axis, flowers white, petals 5, each 3-lobed, middle lobe longest, fragrant; stamens 5.

Fruit: September-October, borne on slender, drooping stalks, oval to inverted egg-shaped, 1/3 to 1 inch long, shiny, black, fleshy; seed solitary, large, brown, rounded, 1/4 to 1/2 inch long.

Leaves: Alternate or clustered, often on short lateral spurs, longer than broad, widest near the tip, tip rounded or blunt, base wedge-shaped, margin entire, blade length 1 to 3 inches, width to 1 inch, leathery, shiny green and smooth above, **lower surface varying from rusty to white or gray-woolly**; petioles short, averaging about 1/2 inch long, densely hairy with matted wool.

Twigs: Gray to reddish-brown, zigzag, slender, stiff, with **thorns, twigs hairy at first with gray, white or rusty matted hairs.**

Trunk: Dark brown or grayish, with shallow furrows and forming a network of ridges with thickened scales; wood hard, heavy, yellow or brown, close-grained.

Habitat: Found in dry or open rocky woodlands, glades and bluff escarpments, crevices of bluffs, usually on upland ridges and slopes, rarely in valleys and ravine bottoms.

Range: From Florida to east Texas, north to Virginia and Illinois, Missouri, Kansas and Oklahoma; also in Mexico.

Wildlife Uses: Birds are very fond of the fruit, eating it as soon as it is barely ripe. White-tailed deer eat the fruit and the leaves, and cave-dwelling wood rats take leaves into their dens.

Remarks: This is the last of the native shrubs or small trees to come into flowering in Missouri. The foliage is long-persisting, and in late autumn turns a yellowish-green. The black fruit is edible, but not tasty, and has been reported to produce stomach disturbances and dizziness if eaten in quantity. The wood is used in small quantities for tool handles and cabinet-making. A milky-colored gum is freely exuded from wounds on the trunk and branches. The tree has been in cultivation since 1806.

Bumelia is the ancient Greek name for the European Ash; *lanuginosa* refers to the woolly hairs of the leaf.

Bumelia lanuginosa ❧ a. Growth form, b. Twig with flower cluster, c. Fruit on short spur branch, d. Winter twig with short spur branches and thorns

Southern buckthorn

Bumelia lycioides (L.) Pers.

Sapodilla family (Sapotaceae)

Also called Carolina buckthorn, ironwood, smooth bumelia

Field Identification: Large shrub or small tree to 25 feet with spreading branches, milky sap, spur branches, and stout thorns.

Flowers: June-July, in dense clusters of 10 to 50 flowers at the leaf/stem axis, flowers white, about 1/5 inch wide, 5-lobed, lobes each 3-parted (or toothed); stamens 5.

Fruit: September-October, oval to egg-shaped, black 1/4 to 2/3 inch long, thin-skinned, pulpy, bittersweet; seed solitary, large, smooth, egg-shaped, abruptly pointed at the tip.

Leaves: Solitary or clustered on short lateral spurs, except on vigorous growth, simple, alternate, blades 2 to 6 inches long, 1/2 to 2 inches wide, margin entire, tip pointed, rarely blunt, base gradually tapering; upper surface bright green and smooth, **lower surface smooth**, paler, veins netlike; petioles slender, 1/3 to 1 inch long, hairy at first but smooth later.

Twigs: Rather stout, thick, with lateral spurlike branchlets, with or without stout thorns at the leaf base, **twigs smooth**, shiny, reddish-brown to gray.

Trunk: Smooth, thin, reddish-brown to gray, scales small and thin; wood brown to yellow, close-grained, heavy, hard, not strong.

Habitat: Found in low alluvial woods of floodplains and river bottom land, and thickets along streams. Known only from the Bootheel in southeastern Missouri.

Range: From Florida to eastern Texas, north to Virginia, Kentucky, Indiana, Illinois and Missouri.

Wildlife Uses: The fruit is eaten by a number of species of birds. The leaves are browsed by white-tailed deer.

Remarks: Missouri specimens of southern buckthorn frequently have thickened, spindle-shaped swellings of woody stems with small holes, apparently resulting from an insect laying its eggs in the plant tissue. This shrub is considered uncommon in southeastern Missouri due to loss of habitat. The Missouri Bootheel has experienced widespread clearing of once extensive bottomland forests and swamps for agricultural purposes. Recent surveys on Missouri Department of Conservation lands have located small populations of southern buckthorn.

Bumelia is the ancient Greek name for the European Ash; *lycioides* applies to the Lyciumlike fruit, which in turn is named for Lycia, an ancient country in Asia Minor.

Bumelia lycioides ✻ a. Growth form with flower cluster and thorns, b. Stem with fruit and thorn

Beauty berry

Callicarpa americana L.

Vervain family (Verbenaceae)

Also called American beauty berry, French mulberry

Field Identification: A many-branched shrub to 9 feet.

Flowers: June-August, numerous, borne in the leaf/stem axils, rose to pink or pale blue (rarely white), small, tubular, 4-lobed; stamens 4.

Fruit: August-November, berrylike, borne in conspicuous expanded clusters in leaf axils, **rose to purple or violet to blue**, globe-shaped, fleshy, 1/8 to 1/4 inch long, sweet; seeds 4, about 1/16 inch long, light brown.

Leaves: Simple, aromatic, opposite, margin coarsely toothed near the ends, oval, broadest in the middle, or inverted egg-shaped, tip pointed, base wedge-shaped, 3 to 9 inches long, 1 1/2 to 5 inches wide, dark green and smooth or powdery above, paler with dense, star-shaped hairs beneath; petioles slender, 3/4 to 2 inches long, with **dense, star-shaped hairs.**

Twigs: Circular to 4-sided, slender, gray to reddish-brown, with dense, star-shaped hairs, smooth later.

Trunk: Bark on old stems smooth, tight or somewhat roughened with small, thin scales below.

Habitat: Occurs on wooded dolomite slopes bordering the White River. Historical sites have been destroyed by the impounded waters of Table Rock Dam, but two small populations have been found growing just above the high-water mark along Bull Shoals Lake. Another site was recently discovered in Ripley County.

Range: From Florida to Texas, north to Maryland, Tennessee, Missouri, Arkansas and Oklahoma. Also in northern Mexico and the West Indies.

Wildlife Uses: At least 10 species of birds feed on the fruit, especially bobwhite quail. Also known to be eaten by raccoon, opossum, and gray fox.

Remarks: Beauty berry is endangered in Missouri. The damming of the White River destroyed most of the habitat for this shrub. Since Missouri is the northern edge of its range, it was probably never abundant in the state. The plant is common in Arkansas. The unique color of the berries adds to its ornamental value. The related, but non-native species, *Callicarpa dichotoma* and *Callicarpa japonica*, are similar in appearance to *Callicarpa americana* and are planted as ornamentals. They are more cold-tolerant than the native beauty berry.

Callicarpa is from the Greek word *kallos* ("beauty") and *karpos* ("fruit"); *americana* refers to the country in which it was discovered.

Callicarpa americana ❀ a. Growth form with fruit clusters, b. Stem with flower clusters

Hornbeam

Carpinus caroliniana Walter

Birch family (Betulaceae)

Also called blue beech, musclewood

Field Identification: Tall shrub or small tree to 35 feet, with a gray trunk and pendulous branches.

Flowers: April-May, staminate (male) and pistillate (female) flowers separate but on the same tree; staminate flowers green, borne in long cylinder-shaped catkins (a hanging spike of flowers), 1 to 1 1/2 inches, scales of catkin triangular-shaped, tip pointed, green below, reddish above; stamens numerous; pistillate catkins about 1/2 inch.

Fruit: August-October, nutlet or seed about 1/3 inch long, oval, borne at base of a 3-lobed bract (modified leaf), many together forming long hanging clusters 3 to 6 inches long. The middle lobe of the bract is lance-shaped and entire or toothed, and much longer than the lateral lobes.

Leaves: Simple, alternate, longer than broad, egg-shaped, tip pointed, base rounded, wedge-shaped, or heart-shaped, margin sharply double-toothed, dull bluish-green and smooth above, paler and hairy in axils of the veins below; leaf blade usually with 9 to 15 veins on each side of central vein; petioles about 1/3 inch long, slender, hairy.

Twigs: Slender, zigzag, gray or red.

Trunk: Bark **smooth, tight, thin, bluish-gray**, sometimes blotched with darker or lighter (some gray blotches may be due to crustose lichens), **trunk fluted into musclelike ridges**; wood light brown, sapwood lighter, strong, hard, tough, heavy, close-grained.

Habitat: Found on north-facing bluffs, in rich woods at the base of bluffs, rocky slopes along streams, ravine bottoms, low wooded valleys, and moist woodland.

Range: From Florida to east Texas, and north to Nova Scotia and west to Minnesota.

Wildlife Uses: The seed is eaten by at least nine species of birds. Catkins and buds rank as one of the most important ruffed grouse foods by volume consumed during late autumn, winter and early spring. Quail occasionally eat the seeds, which are also considered a preferred winter food of turkeys. Small amounts of seeds, bark and wood are eaten by cottontail rabbits, beavers, and fox and gray squirrels. White-tailed deer will browse the twigs and foliage.

Remarks: The wood is used for golf clubs, handles, fuel, mallets, cogs, levers and wedges. It ranks as one of the hardest and strongest woods known in eastern North America — surpassing oak, hickory, locust and persimmon. Only flowering dogwood is harder. The tree has been cultivated as an ornamental since 1812.

Carpinus is the classical name for hornbeam; *caroliniana* refers to the states of Carolina, probably where it was first described.

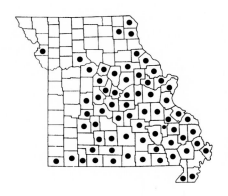

Carpinus caroliniana ❀ a. Growth form with hanging fruit clusters in bracts, b. Pair of three-lobed bracts, c. Male (l) and female (r) flower clusters, d. Male flower, e. Female flower, f. Stem

New Jersey tea

Ceanothus americanus L.

Buckthorn family (Rhamnaceae)

Also called wild snowball

Field Identification: Shrub to 3 feet. Branches spreading, herbaceous above, woody toward the base.

Flowers: May-June, borne in sometimes branched clusters at the base of leaves, showy, fragrant, usually 2 to 5 inches long, 3/4 to 1 1/4 inches diameter; stalk bearing the flower clusters 2 to 10 inches long, **stalk bare and arising above the leaf directly below it**, petals 5, hooded, usually notched, each resembling a miniature ladle, white; stamens 5.

Fruit: July-August, a drupe (seed covered by fleshy pulp), round, three-parted, 1/5 to 1/4 inch long, black; nutlets 3, seed coat smooth, reddish-brown.

Leaves: Simple, alternate, **broadly egg-shaped** to somewhat longer than broad, margin toothed, **tip somewhat pointed**, base heart-shaped to rounded; upper leaf surface green, hairy; lower leaf surface gray, densely and velvety hairy, 2 to 4 inches long, 1 to 2 1/2 inches wide; petioles about 1/2 inch long.

Twigs: Flexible, densely hairy, dark gray-green.

Trunk: Bark greenish-brown with wide splits showing a brown inner bark; old stems brown, sometimes flaky; wood soft, white.

Habitat: Found in upland or rocky prairies, glades, open woods, and thickets, sometimes along railroads. Found possibly in every county.

Range: The type commonly encountered in Missouri is known as var. Pitcheri, which occurs from Georgia to Texas, north to Indiana, Illinois, Iowa and Kansas.

Wildlife Uses: The leaves are eaten by white-tailed deer, and the fruits by wild turkey. Some birds are known to eat the seeds.

Medicinal Uses: The root, which imparts a red color to water, causes blood vessels to contract and increases the coagulability of the blood. *Ceanothus* was once used in treating syphilis, but the results were of no value. A drink from the boiled leaves and seeds has been used to cure ulcerated sore throat.

Remarks: The leaves were used by Native Americans to make a drink like tea. On the buffalo hunt, when timber was scarce, the great gnarled woody roots of this shrub, often larger than the part above ground, were used for fuel. Tribes along the Atlantic Coast probably taught the colonists the use of New Jersey tea, which was used as a patriotic substitute for black tea during the American Revolution after British tea was dumped in Boston Harbor. This shrub makes an attractive ornamental.

    Ceanothus is from an obscure name given by the Greek, Theophrastus; it is probably misspelled and not for this genus; *americanus* refers to its being found growing in North America.

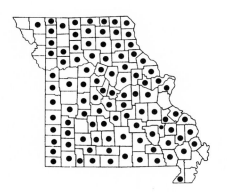

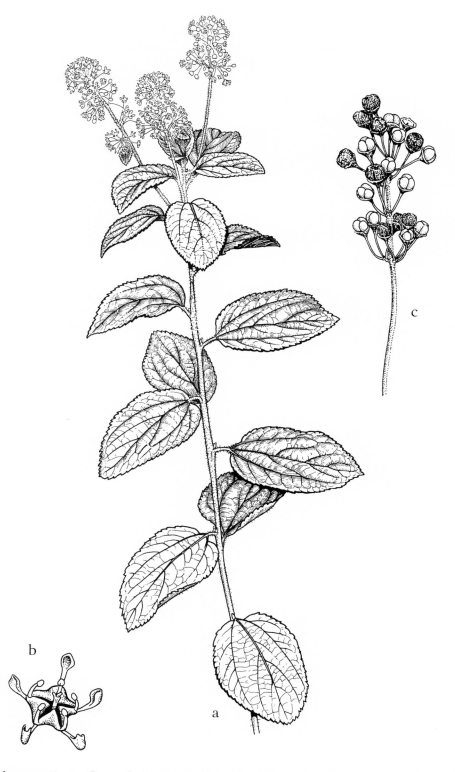

Ceanothus americanus ❀ a. Growth form with flower clusters, b. Flower, c. Stem with fruit clusters

Redroot

Ceanothus herbaceus Raf.

Buckthorn family (Rhamnaceae)

Also called inland New Jersey tea

Field Identification: An upright shrub attaining a height of 3 feet, with slender, upright, hairy branches.

Flowers: Late April-June, short flower clusters ending on new, leafy stems; stalk bearing the flower cluster about 3/8 inch long, **stalk with a few small leaves and usually shorter than the leaf arising directly below it**; petals 5, hooded, each resembling a miniature ladle, white; stamens 5.

Fruit: August-September, a drupe (seed covered by fleshy pulp), round, 3-parted, about 1/5 inch long, dark brown; nutlets 3, seed coat smooth, shiny, reddish-brown.

Leaves: Simple, alternate, 1 1/2 to 2 1/2 inches long, 1/2 to 1 inch wide, **leaf blades overall very narrow but broad in the middle**, margin somewhat toothed, **tip mostly blunt**, base wedge-shaped to rounded, upper surface dark green, smooth to hairy, lower surface paler, hairy; petioles 1/8 to 1/2 inch long, hairy to smooth later.

Twigs: Slender, brittle, young ones green to brown or straw-colored, hairy; older ones brown to dark gray, smooth.

Trunk: Bark gray-brown, thin, the outer bark cracked into short slits; wood medium-hard, pale red-brown.

Habitat: Occurs in upland and rocky prairies, loess hill prairies, glades, open and rocky woodlands. Mostly in western Missouri and scattered eastward.

Range: From Ontario to Wisconsin, Minnesota, Manitoba, South Dakota and Colorado, south to Florida, Louisiana, Oklahoma and central Texas.

Wildlife Uses: The leaves are eaten by white-tailed deer and the fruits by wild turkey. Some birds are known to eat the seeds, including bob-white quail.

Medicinal Uses: The root, which imparts a red color to water, causes blood vessels to contract and increases the coagulability of the blood. *Ceanothus* was at one time used in treating syphilis, but the results were of no value. A drink from the boiled leaves and seeds has been used to cure ulcerated sore throat.

Remarks: Like New Jersey tea, the leaves were used by Native Americans to make a tealike drink. On the buffalo hunt, when timber was scarce, the great gnarled woody roots of this shrub, often larger than the part above ground, were used for fuel. The roots are a deep red and can be used to make a good dye, hence the name redroot. The roots also form nitrogen-fixing nodules with bacteria and perform some service in enriching the soil, an ability few other non-legumes possess.

Ceanothus is from an obscure name given by the Greek, Theophrastus; it is probably misspelled and not for this genus; *herbaceus* refers to the leafy small branches.

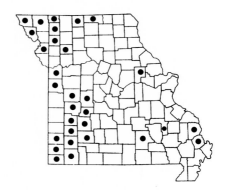

Ceanothus herbaceus ❀ a. Growth form with flower clusters, b. Flower, c. Stem with fruit clusters

Dwarf hackberry

Celtis tenuifolia Nutt.

Elm family (Ulmaceae)

Field Identification: A shrub to small tree up to 24 feet tall, **often somewhat scraggly.**

Flowers: April-May, small clusters of staminate (male) flowers in leaf axils, near the base of a short new branch; pistillate (female) flowers in leaf axils, toward the tip of the same new shoot. Pistillate flowers contain disproportionately large stigmas (central column), an adaption useful in capturing the plant's wind-dispersed pollen.

Fruit: September-October, drupe (a seed covered by fleshy pulp), globe-shaped, about 1/4 inch long, orange to brown or red; seed brown; stalk hairy, about 3/8 inch long.

Leaves: Simple, alternate, broadly egg-shaped to triangular, **leaf blade lopsided (asymmetrical) with one half longer or broader than the other half**; tip pointed, **base slanting with unequal sides**, margin mostly entire, blade length 3/4 to 4 inches, width 1/2 to 1 3/4 inches, thin, sometimes leathery in texture, upper surface dark green, rough, lower surface hairy to smooth; petioles 1/4 to 3/8 inch long, hairy.

Twigs: Slender, reddish-brown, hairy at first, later smooth and darker brown to gray; **bark often with corky ridges**.

Trunk: Bark light gray, furrowed, the ridges short, warty, and with vertical sides; wood light, soft, nearly white, with a wide, white sapwood.

Habitat: Occurs in rocky open woods, dolomite glades and along bluffs.

Range: From northern Florida to Louisiana and eastern Oklahoma, north to Virginia, Kentucky, Indiana, Missouri and Kansas.

Wildlife Uses: Fruits are eaten by raccoons, squirrels, wild turkeys and ruffed grouse.

Remarks: On dry, thin-soiled glades, dwarf hackberry exhibits an interesting stunted, gnarly appearance. The fruits are edible, and probably were used by Native Americans to flavor meat, as other species of hackberries were. The berries were pounded fine and mixed with a little fat and parched corn.

Celtis is the name given by the Greek, Pliny, to a sweet-fruited African lotus; *tenuifolia* refers to the thin leaves.

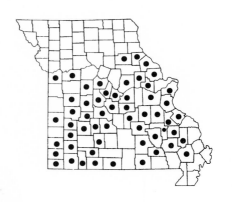

Celtis tenuifolia ❀ a. Section of trunk showing growth form, b. Branch with leaves, c. Male flowers, d. Female flower, e. Fruit

Buttonbush

Cephalanthus occidentalis L.

Madder family (Rubiaceae)

Also called globe flower, honeyball, swamp sycamore, pond dogwood

Field Identification: Shrub or small tree to 18 feet, growing in low areas, often swollen at the base.

Flowers: June-August, borne on stalks 1 to 3 inches long, white, fragrant, **clustered in globe-shaped heads** 1 to 1 1/2 inches in diameter; flower 1/4 to 1/2 inch long, tubular with 4 short, spreading lobes; stamens 4.

Fruit: September-October, a round cluster of reddish-brown nutlets; nutlets dry, pyramidlike, 1/4 to 1/3 inch long.

Leaves: Opposite but more commonly **in whorls of 3**, blades 2 to 8 inches long, 1 to 3 inches wide; leaves oval or lance-shaped, tip pointed, base rounded or narrow, margin entire; dark green and smooth above, somewhat paler with a few hairs along the veins and in the axils of the veins; petioles smooth, stout, 1/2 to 3/4 inch long.

Twigs: Dark reddish-brown to gray-brown, shiny, smooth, with a few light lenticels (pores), pith yellow.

Trunk: Bark thin, gray to brown, thick, later with flattened ridges and deep fissures; wood soft, lightweight, white.

Habitat: Found in low wet woods, swamps and thickets, borders of streams and sloughs, and in upland sinkhole ponds, river bottom oxbow lakes and ponds.

Range: Florida to Mexico, north to Nova Scotia, and west to Quebec, Ontario and California; also West Indies and Central America.

Wildlife Uses: The nutlets are eaten by at least 25 species of birds (mostly water birds, including wood ducks). The fragrant flowers are a favorite nectar source for honeybees. Song sparrows and red-winged blackbirds, as well as other birds, nest in its branches. Animals may be poisoned by feeding on the leaves.

Medicinal Uses: Native Americans induced vomiting with a tea made from the inner bark. The bark was used as a laxative and tonic, also in the form of a tea, and has been chewed to relieve toothache. A tincture (extraction by alcohol) of the bark has been used to treat fever, coughs and venereal disease. The root, boiled and mixed with honey to make a syrup, has been used to treat pleurisy.

Remarks: Buttonbush is frequently planted as an ornamental. Along margins of sinkhole ponds, sloughs and swamps it can form almost impenetrable thickets. Although the shrub is of no commercial value, it could be planted to protect lakeshores from wave action.

Cephalanthus is a Greek name for "head-flower"; *occidentalis* means "western." The common name, buttonbush, refers to the similarity of the flowering and fruiting heads to spherical buttons, a style more popular in earlier times.

Cephanlanthus occidentalis ✄ a. Growth form, b. Stem with flower clusters, c. Flower, d. Fruit cluster

Eastern redbud

Cercis canadensis L.

Senna family (Caesalpiniaceae)

Field Identification: Shrub or small tree to 40 feet. Distinctly ornamental in spring with small, clustered, rose-purple flowers covering the bare branches before the leaves.

Flowers: Late March-early May, **flowering before the leaves**, in clusters of 2 to 8, on stalks 1/4 to 3/4 inch long; flowers 1/4 to 2/5 inch long, **rose-purple**, petals 5, of the three upper petals, the two outer ones longer than the central one, the two lower petals joined together to form a keel; stamens 10, shorter than the petals.

Fruit: September-October, persistent on the branches, often abundant; pod 3 to 4 inches long, about 1/2 inch wide, tapering at both ends, leathery, reddish-brown; seeds several, egg-shaped, flattened, 1/6 to 1/5 inch long.

Leaves: Simple, alternate, 2 to 6 inches long, 1 1/4 to 6 inches, **oval to heart-shaped or as broad as or broader than long**, tip pointed, base heart-shaped, margin entire; upper surface dark green, smooth; lower surface paler and smooth with some hairs along the veins and in the vein axils; petioles 1 1/4 to 5 inches long, smooth.

Twigs: Slender, smooth, brown to gray, often zigzag, pith white.

Trunk: Bark reddish-brown to gray, thin and smooth when young, older ones with long cracks and short, thin, blocky plates; wood heavy, hard, brown, with a thin, white sapwood.

Habitat: Found in open woodland, borders of woods, thickets, dolomite glades, and along rocky streams and bluffs. Occurs in every county in Missouri.

Range: From Florida to Texas and northeastern Mexico, north to Connecticut and Ontario, and west to Michigan, Missouri, Nebraska and Kansas.

Wildlife Uses: The seeds are eaten by several species of birds, and the foliage browsed by white-tailed deer. Eastern redbud also is a nectar source for bees.

Remarks: Eastern redbud has been used as an attractive ornamental since 1641. It usually blooms a couple of weeks before flowering dogwoods, and, on rare occasions, the two overlap in flowering. Eastern redbuds begin to bear pods at five years of age; the maximum age is about 75 years. Good crops of pods generally occur on alternate years. The leaves turn a yellow or pale greenish-yellow in autumn. The sour- or pea-flavored flowers are sometimes used raw or pickled in salads; in Mexico they are fried.

Cercis is the ancient name of the closely related Judas-tree of Europe and Asia. According to legend, Judas hanged himself from a branch of the tree. The species name, *canadensis*, literally means "of Canada," where it is rather uncommon. Or perhaps it refers to northeastern North America, before political boundaries were drawn.

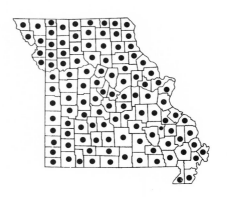

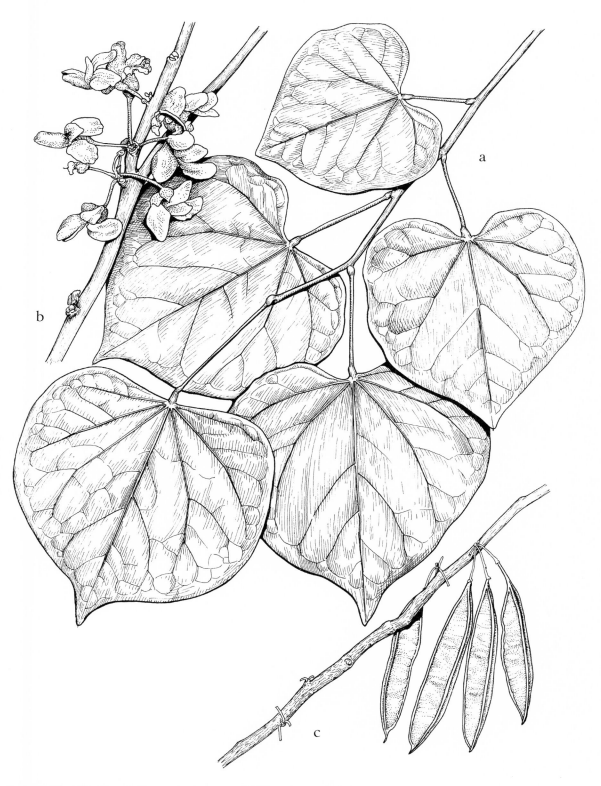

Cercis canadensis ❧ a. Growth form, b. Flowers, c. Fruit

Fringe tree

Chionanthus virginicus L.

Olive family (Oleaceae)

Also called old man's beard, graney gray-beard

Field Identification: Usually a shrub with crooked branches, but sometimes a tree to 35 feet.

Flowers: April-May, **in delicate drooping bundles** 4 to 6 inches long; stalks hairy; petals 4 to 6, narrow, tip pointed, about 1 inch long, white with purple spots near the base, fragrant; stamens 2.

Fruit: August-October, drupe (a seed covered by fleshy pulp) borne in clusters, bluish-black, smooth, globe- to egg-shaped, to 3/4 inch long, 1 to 3 seeds each about 1/3 inch long, oval, brown. Plants 5 to 8 years old begin to produce seed.

Leaves: Simple, opposite, **may appear whorled near the tip, large**, 4 to 8 inches long, 1 to 4 inches wide, oval to egg-shaped or lance-shaped, tip blunt to pointed, base wedge-shaped, margin entire or wavy, dark green and smooth above, paler below with hairs on the veins; petioles to 1 inch long, hairy.

Twigs: Stout, hairy, light brown to orange, later gray.

Trunk: Bark brown to gray, thin, close, flattened, broken into small thin scales; wood light brown, sapwood lighter, hard, heavy, close-grained.

Habitat: Occurs along rocky dolomite wooded ledges and bluffs, and along the edges of dolomite glades in southwestern Missouri, and along wooded slopes of small creeks and wet woods in southeastern Missouri.

Range: Florida to Texas, north to New Jersey, Pennsylvania, West Virginia, Ohio, Missouri and Oklahoma.

Medicinal Uses: Native Americans boiled the bark in water and used the liquid to bathe wounds and treat fever associated with malaria. Pioneers applied an application of crushed bark to cuts and bruises. In Appalachia, a solution from boiled bark is used to treat skin inflammations. The leaves and flowers have been used to treat inflammations and sores, ulcers in the mouth and throat, and diarrhea.

Remarks: Fringe tree provides a showy display of late spring flowers clustered in drooping fringes. Fruits resemble small olives, at first green but turning black at maturity. It does well in landscaped settings. The leaves turn a rich yellow in autumn. Fringe tree has been grown as an ornamental since 1736, but is often difficult to find at nurseries.

Chionanthus is a combination of two Greek words meaning "snow flower"; *virginicus* refers to the state of Virginia, probably where it was first found and described.

Chionanthus virginicus ❁ a. Growth form with flower clusters, b. Flower, c. Fruit

Alternate-leaved dogwood

Cornus alternifolia L.

Dogwood family (Cornaceae)

Also known as pagoda dogwood, green osier, pigeon berry and blue dogwood

Field Identification: Shrub or small tree to 18 feet. Branches often in tierlike layers. Easily mistaken for flowering dogwood when not in flower.

Flowers: May-June, white to cream-colored, inflorescence broad or flat-topped, 1 1/4 to 2 1/2 inches broad, sepals minute or absent; petals 4, small, about 1/8 inch long; stamens 4.

Fruit: July-September, borne on red pedicels, drupe (a seed covered by fleshy pulp) bluish-black, stone deeply pitted at the summit.

Leaves: Mostly alternate, a few opposite, but often crowded near the end of twig, margin entire, leaves 2 to 5 inches long, 3/4 to 2 1/2 inches wide, either egg-shaped, longer than broad, or widest in the middle, tip pointed, base wedge-shaped; upper surface smooth, dark green; lower surface paler, hairy, **lateral veins 4 to 6 on each side, conspicuous; petioles 3/4 to 2 1/4 inches long**, somewhat hairy.

Twigs: Often horizontal or ascending, slender, smooth, glabrous, green, pith white and small.

Trunk: Bark thin, dark reddish-brown, smooth or fissured and cross-checked; wood hard, with reddish-brown heartwood and thick, paler sapwood.

Habitat: Found along wooded north-facing slopes and along wooded banks of streams.

Range: From Newfoundland and Nova Scotia to Ontario and Minnesota, south to Florida, Georgia, Alabama and Arkansas.

Wildlife Uses: Its leaves are browsed by white-tailed deer and cottontail rabbit. The fruit are eaten by at least 11 species of birds, including warbling vireos and ruffed grouse. Black bears may be especially fond of this fruit.

Remarks: Alternate-leaved dogwood is a popular ornamental, first introduced into cultivation in 1760. It prefers naturalized plantings in partial shade. It is a good replacement for the cold-sensitive flowering dogwood in the northern part of the state. In the fall, the leaves turn yellow to red.

Cornus is from the Latin word *cornu*, "a horn," in reference to the hard wood; *alternifolia* means "alternate leaves."

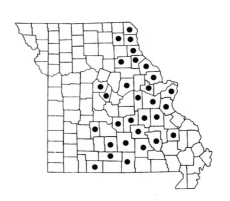

Cornus alternifolia ❀ a. Growth form with flower clusters, b. Flower, c. Fruit

Rough-leaved dogwood

Cornus drummondii C. Meyer

Dogwood family (Cornaceae)

Field Identification: Irregularly branched shrub or small spreading tree.

Flowers: May-June, yellowish-white, borne in terminal spreading, long-stalked clusters 1 to 3 inches across; flower stalks 1 to 2 inches long, hairy, petals 4, spreading, pointed at the tip.

Fruit: August-October, globe-shaped drupe (a seed covered by fleshy pulp), **white**, style (small stalk) on tip of drupe persistent, 1 to 2 seeds, slightly furrowed.

Leaves: Simple, opposite, margins entire, leaves 1 to 5 inches long, 1/2 to 2 1/2 inches wide, conspicuously veined, egg- to lance-shaped, or longer than broad to widest in the middle, tip pointed, base rounded to wedge-shaped, upper surface olive-green and rather **rough-hairy above**, lower surface paler with **woolly, loose curled or curving hairs**; petioles 1/4 to 3/4 inch long, slender, rough-hairy, green to reddish.

Twigs: Young ones green and hairy, older ones reddish-brown and smooth.

Trunk: Bark gray-brown with shallow fissures and short, thin plates; wood pale brown, with sapwood paler, heavy, hard, strong, durable, close-grained.

Habitat: Occurs in dry or rocky woods, thickets, old fields, limestone and dolomite glades, prairies, bluff escarpments, occasionally low wet ground, along ponds, streams and at the base of bluffs. Probably in every county.

Range: From Mississippi to the eastern half of Texas, north to Ontario, Ohio, Indiana, Illinois, Iowa and Nebraska.

Wildlife Uses: Although seldom planted in windbreaks or around farmsteads, its dense thickets are excellent cover for birds and small mammals. Many birds, including Bell's vireo, nest in the thickets. The fruit is eaten by at least 40 species of birds, including bobwhite quail, wild turkey and greater prairie chicken.

Medicinal Uses: This species and flowering dogwood are known to contain a highly active antibiotic substance that is effective in preventing toothy decay and treating other aliments. Chew-sticks are made by cutting off a small stem several inches long, removing the outer bark, and chewing on the tip to soften the fibers, which can then be used to massage the gums.

Remarks: The leaves of rough-leaved dogwood emit a faint odor which resembles sour milk. This dogwood is one of the hardiest of Missouri shrubs, and will withstand drought or extreme cold. It spreads by underground stems, sending up sprouts at the margin of the thicket. By virtue of its tenacity, it is difficult to manage in prairies, especially hill prairies in northwestern Missouri. It has been in cultivation since 1836. The wood is used for small woodenware articles, especially shuttleblocks and charcoal.

Cornus is from the Latin word *cornu*, "a horn," in reference to the hard wood; *drummondii* is in honor of Thomas Drummond (1780-1835), a Scottish botanical explorer.

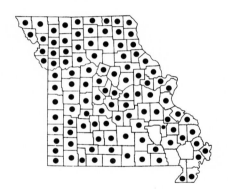

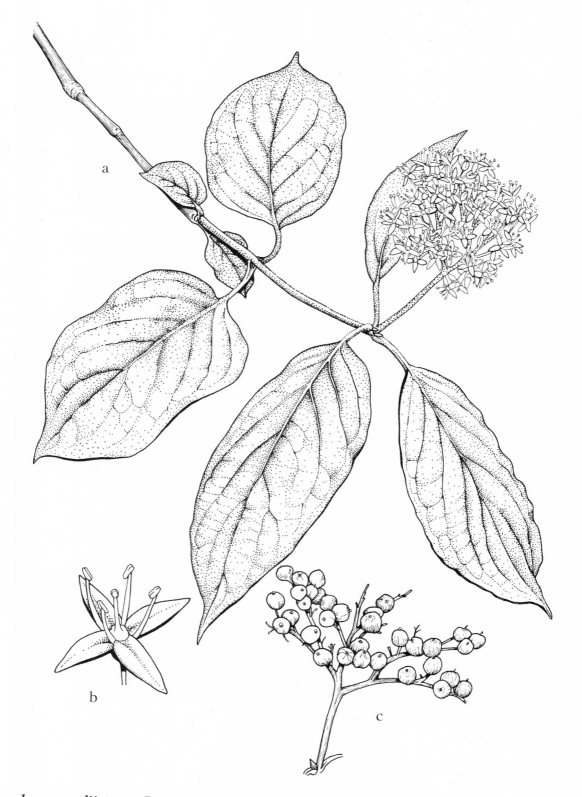

Cornus drummondii ☘ a. Growth form with flower cluster, b. Flower, c. Fruit

Flowering Dogwood

Cornus florida L.

Dogwood family (Cornaceae)

Field Identification: Shrub to small tree to 40 feet with a straggling, spreading crown.

Flowers: Mid-April to mid-May, in terminal clusters with buds formed the previous year; flowers perfect with four stamens and a pistil, small, with four light- to greenish-yellow petals, about 1/8 inch wide **in clusters of 25 to 30 located above four white bracts (often mistaken for flower petals)**, the bracts are 1 1/4 to 2 1/2 inches long, notched at the tip; flower buds developed the previous year.

Fruit: August-November, **brilliant red drupe** (a seed covered by fleshy pulp), oval, shiny, in clusters of 2 to 6, 1/4 to 1/2 inch long; seeds 1 to 2, cream-colored with 5 to 7 shallow longitudinal grooves.

Leaves: Simple, opposite, margins entire, sometimes barely toothed, leaves 3 to 5 inches long, 1 1/2 to 2 1/2 inches wide, oval to egg-shaped, tip pointed, base wedge-shaped and often unequal; shiny-green and somewhat hairy above; much paler and hairy below, heavily veined; petioles stout, grooved, about 3/4 inch long.

Twigs: Flexible, slender, reddish-gray to purplish, or greenish with red dots, hairy. Flower buds terminal. Leaf buds compressed and oval.

Trunk: Bark dark gray to brown with thin, squarish plates; wood brownish, strong, hard, not easily dented.

Habitat: Found along wooded slopes, ravines, along bluffs, upland ridges, successional fields; less common on glades, valleys and low ground; prefers well-drained, acid-based soils.

Range: From Florida to Texas and northeastern Mexico, north to Maine, Ontario, and south to Michigan, Illinois, Missouri, Kansas and Oklahoma.

Wildlife Uses: The fruit of flowering dogwood is eaten by squirrels and white-tailed deer. It is a preferred food for wild turkey and at least 28 other species of birds, including quail.

Medicinal Uses: Native Americans used the dried bark of the root to treat malaria, and the early European settlers fought chills and fevers with it; at one time it also was used as a quinine substitute.

Remarks: Missouri's official state tree, flowering dogwood blooms in April shortly after, but sometimes overlapping, redbud.

A rare pink-flowered form has been found in Jasper, Jefferson, McDonald, Newton, Reynolds and Taney counties. The deep red-colored form commonly sold at nurseries is reported to have originated earlier in this century from a single cutting from a tree growing wild in Tennessee.

The name dogwood comes from the old word "dag," meaning skewer. As the name suggests, this hard, tough, splinter-free wood was used in making skewers to hold meat together while cooking. Other dogwood products include weaving shuttles, spindles, knitting needles, sled runners, roller skates, golf club heads, engraver's blocks, mallet heads, chisel handles and pulleys. North American Indians prepared a scarlet dye from the roots to color their quills and feathers.

Cornus is from the Latin word *cornu*, "a horn," in reference to the hard wood; *florida* means "flowering," indicating the large "flowers."

Cornus florida ❀ a. Branch with flowers, b. Flower, c. Twig with leaves and fruit cluster

Stiff dogwood

Cornus foemina Miller

Dogwood family (Cornaceae)

Field Identification: Shrub with stiff, upright irregular branches, or sometimes a small tree to 15 feet.

Flowers: May-June, in round-topped, rather open clusters 1 1/4 to 2 inches broad; stalk below flower cluster smooth, 1 to 2 3/4 inches long; petals 4, small, white, longer than broad; stamens 4.

Fruit: August-October, drupe (a seed covered by fleshy pulp) almost spherical, 1/4 inch in diameter, **pale blue**; single seed, longer than broad, slightly furrowed.

Leaves: Simple, opposite, margins entire, leaves 1 to 3 inches long, 1 to 1 3/4 inches wide, blade lance-shaped to widest at the middle, tip pointed, green on both sides, lower surface slightly paler, smooth or slightly hairy; petioles 1/4 to 1 inch, smooth or slightly hairy.

Twigs: Young ones reddish, later greenish to brown or gray; older ones gray and smooth; pith white.

Habitat: Occurs in **swamps and low, wet woodlands and wet open ground in the low-land counties of southeastern Missouri.**

Range: From Florida to eastern Texas, north to Virginia, Delaware, Indiana, Illinois and Missouri.

Remarks: Commonly found with bald cypress (*Taxodium distichum*), swamp tupelo (*Nyssa aquatica*), swamp red maple (*Acer rubrum* var. *drummondii*), and pin oak (*Quercus velutina*), and basket oak (*Quercus michauxii*).
  Cornus is from the Latin word *cornu,* "a horn," in reference to the hard wood; *foemina* means "female," a name that 1730s herbalists chose to distinguish it from what they considered to be the "male" flowering dogwood.

Cornus foemina ❦ a. Growth form with fruit cluster, b. Branch with flower cluster

Swamp dogwood

Cornus obliqua Raf.

Dogwood family (Cornaceae)

Also known as pale dogwood, silky dogwood, kinnikinnik

Field Identification: Open, irregularly branched shrub to 9 feet.

Flowers: May-July, **in flat or sometimes indented**, to round-topped clusters, stalks 1 to 2 inches long, very hairy, **yellowish-brown**; petals 4, white, 1/8 to 3/16 inch long, stamens 4.

Fruit: June-October, a drupe (a seed covered by fleshy pulp), blue, globe-shaped, 3/16 to 1/4 inch, style (small stalk) on end of drupe persistent.

Leaves: Simple, opposite, leaves 1 1/2 to 3 1/4 inches long, 1/2 to 1 1/2 inches wide, egg- to lance-shaped or longer than broad, tip pointed, base terminating with a sharp angle or narrow wedge shape, margin entire; upper surface smooth and green, lower surface whitish and smooth or with minute appressed, white hairs, lateral veins 3 to 5 on each side; petioles 1/8 to 1/3 inch, hairy.

Twigs: Slender, light to dark brown, smooth; when young whitish with dense appressed hairs, when older lacking hairs.

Trunk: Bark tight on most stems, red, with tan horizontal lenticels (pores); some stems with longitudinal splits in the outer bark; wood hard, fine-grained, white.

Habitat: Occurs along rocky banks of streams, spring branches, wet places in prairies, fens, wet thickets, swamps and low woodland. Absent from the lowlands of southeastern Missouri.

Range: New Brunswick to North Dakota south to New Jersey, Pennsylvania, West Virginia, Kentucky, Missouri, eastern Kansas, Arkansas and Oklahoma.

Wildlife Uses: The fruit is used by at least 10 species of birds (including ruffed grouse, bob-white quail and wild turkey), cottontail rabbit, woodchuck, raccoon and squirrels. Wood ducks are known to eat the fruits in late summer and fall, before and after ripening. They have been seen reaching as far as they can from the water to strip the shrubs of fruit. The swamp dogwood on streambanks provides escape for wood ducks and cover for their broods. The thicket-forming swamp dogwood also provides cover for woodcock.

Remarks: The reddish-brown or dark brown young branchlets and blue fruit, conspicuous in late fall, are characteristic of this dogwood. The Native American name for tobacco, kinnikinnik, is applied to this and several other species of dogwood. Native Americans removed the outer bark, and scraped and dried the inner bark for smoking. It is fragrant, and many tribes were fond of it.

Cornus is from the Latin word *cornu*, "a horn," in reference to the hard wood; *obliqua* indicates the leaf base is often uneven.

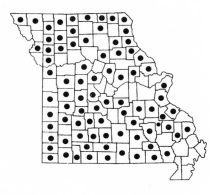

Cornus obliqua ✿ a. Growth form, b. Flower cluster, c. Fruit cluster

Gray dogwood

Cornus racemosa Lam.

Dogwood family (Cornaceae)

Field Identification: Thicket-forming shrub to 7 feet. Stems many-branched, ascending, smooth and light gray to brown.

Flowers: May-July, clusters dome- or globe-shaped, in open, branching pattern 1 1/4 to 2 1/2 inches high or broad; stalk below flower cluster 1/3 to 1 1/2 inches long, **conspicuously red**; individual flowers small, white; petals 4, 1/8 to 1/6 inch long, spreading and recurved; stamens 4.

Fruit: July-October, drupe (a seed covered by fleshy pulp) **white to gray or greenish on red stalks**, rather persistent, resembling a depressed globe, 1/5 to 1/3 inch high, 1 to 2 seeded sometimes shallowly furrowed, about 1/6 inch long and wide.

Leaves: Simple, opposite, lance-shaped, widest at the middle, tip pointed, base ending at a sharp angle to occasionally rounded, margins entire, blade length 1 to 4 inches, width 1/2 to 1 1/2 inches, veins in 3 to 4 pairs on each side, upper surface olive-green, lower surface somewhat whitened; petioles 1/8 to 3/5 inch smooth or with flattened hairs.

Twigs: Older branches gray and smooth or somewhat angled, **younger ones lacking hairs**, brown to red; pith white to brown.

Trunk: Bark gray or gray-brown, tight, roughened by pores called lenticels; old bark with small, squarish, thin flakes; wood hard, fine-grained, white.

Habitat: Occurs in moist or rocky soil along streams, ponds, fens, glades and prairies, thickets along fence rows and roadsides and along bluffs.

Range: Maine to Ontario and Manitoba, south to Florida, Alabama, Kentucky, Illinois, Missouri, Arkansas and Oklahoma.

Wildlife Uses: The fruit of gray dogwood is eaten by at least 25 species of birds, including ruffed grouse and bobwhite quail. It is an important cover plant for woodcock and ruffed grouse. Unlike the sprawling branches of other dogwoods, the fine upper twigs of gray dogwood provide excellent support for the woven grass nests of various sparrows and the bulky nests of catbirds, mockingbirds and red-wing blackbirds.

Remarks: This species of dogwood forms thickets from new shoots that emerge from the spreading roots. Gray dogwood is persistent on unfavorable sites and endures city smoke. It has been cultivated as an ornamental since 1758. The leaves turn a purplish-red to rose-red or purplish-brown in autumn.

The wood of gray dogwood is hard, heavy and durable, but does not get large enough for commercial use. Some of the tips of the upper branches may have an enlarged or swollen portion the size of a marble. This is the dogwood bud gall, caused by a gall gnat, and it occurs only on this species.

Cornus is from the Latin word *cornu*, "a horn," in reference to the hard wood; *racemosa* is for the racemelike (cluster) of flowers.

Cornus racemosa ❀ a. Growth form with fruit cluster, b. Flower cluster

Hazelnut

Corylus americana Walter

Birch family (Betulaceae)

Also called American hazelnut

Field Identification: Thicket-forming, spreading shrub, attaining a height of 3 to 10 feet.

Flowers: Late February-April, staminate (male) catkins mostly solitary, 3 to 4 inches long, cylindrical, brown, petals lacking; stamens 4; pistillate (female) catkins much shorter, clustered at the ends of short branches of the previous year's growth as are the staminate catkins, petals lacking, stigmas red.

Fruit: Maturing July-August, in clusters of 2 to 6, rarely solitary, **encased in large bracts (modified leaves)**, reddish-brown, hairy, 1/2 to 1 1/2 inches long; nut 3/8 to 5/8 inch long, egg- to globe-shaped, usually wider than long, light brown, sweet, edible.

Leaves: Simple, alternate, length 3 to 6 inches, width 2 to 4 inches; egg-shaped to oval, tip pointed, base broadly rounded or heart-shaped, margin finely double-toothed, thin; upper surface dark green, somewhat rough and smooth or nearly so; lower surface paler with matted hairs to more or less hairy; **leaf blade with 5 to 8 veins on each side of the central vein**; petioles 1/6 to 1/3 inch long, often with reddish, gland-tipped hairs, or long white hairs.

Twigs: Slender, angled upwards, reddish-brown at first with gland-tipped hairs, gray and smooth later.

Trunk: Bark brown to gray-brown, fairly smooth, the outer, thin layer slightly grooved; wood nearly white, medium hard, fine-grained.

Habitat: Occurs in dry or moist thickets, woodlands and border of woodlands, in valleys and uplands. Occurs on prairies and loess hill prairies, and once formed large thickets in savannas that have largely disappeared. Throughout Missouri and doubtless in every county.

Range: Florida to Georgia, Arkansas and Oklahoma, north to Maine, and west to Saskatchewan.

Wildlife Uses: It is known to be eaten by bobwhite quail, ruffed grouse, blue jays, squirrels and white-tailed deer. Squirrels and other small mammals will take the nuts as soon as they loosen from the bracts. Hazelnut catkins provide important winter food for ruffed grouse and white-tailed deer, which also browse on the twigs.

Remarks: The leaves are very colorful in autumn, from orange to brick-red or purple-red, or with combinations of rose, orange, yellow and pale green. Hazelnut has been grown as an ornamental since 1798, and is used for shelter-belt planting and as wildlife food and cover. The sweet nuts are sold on the market, and are prized by cooks throughout Europe and the United States.

Corylus is the classical Greek name, probably from *kopus*, a helmet, in reference to the bract covering the top of the nut; *americana* denotes its origin.

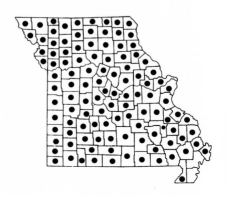

Corylus americana ❀ a. Growth form, b. Twig with drooping male catkins and budlike female catkins, c. Fruit with bracts, d. Nut

Smoke tree

Cotinus obovatus Raf.

Cashew family (Anacardiaceae)

Also called American smoke tree, yellow-wood

Field Identification: Tall shrub to small tree with slender, spreading branches attaining a height of 35 feet.

Flowers: May, greenish-yellow, borne in loose, few-flowered clusters at the end of stems, clusters 5 to 6 inches long, 2 1/2 to 3 inches broad; **flower stalks with gland-tipped hairs and purplish**, flowers about 1/8 inch across, petals 5; stamens 5.

Fruit: June-July, small, hard-cased drupes (a seed covered by fleshy pulp) 1/8 to 1/4 inch long, kidney-shaped, flattened, smooth, pale brown; **fruit stalk slender, conspicuously purple or brown with gland-tipped hairs**.

Leaves: Simple, alternate, most abundant toward the tip of twigs, 1 1/2 to 6 inches long, 2 to 3 1/2 inches wide, broadest in the middle and tapering at both ends to oval, **tip round to blunt**, base broadly wedge-shaped or rounded, margin entire or somewhat wavy; **upper surface bluish- or olive-green** and smooth to hairy; paler and hairy below, veins conspicuous; petioles 1/4 to 2 inches, yellowish-green to reddish, smooth or hairy.

Twigs: Slender, young ones green to reddish or purple, lenticels (pores) small, abundant, pale; older twigs gray, smooth.

Trunk: Bark gray to black, roughly breaking into thin, longer than broad scales; wood orange to yellow, sapwood cream-white, coarse-grained, soft, light.

Habitat: Occurs on dolomite glades and wooded, rocky dolomite bluffs along what was once the White River and its tributaries.

Range: From Alabama, Kentucky, Tennessee, southwestern Missouri, northwestern Arkansas, eastern Oklahoma, to central Texas. Nowhere is it abundant or widespread.

Remarks: The brilliant orange and red colors of the leaves in autumn make it a worthwhile ornamental. Most smoke trees sold at nurseries are the European smoke tree and not the native. The European species is typically a smaller tree with smaller leaves, which are purplish in at least one variety. The "smoke" from smoke tree is often mistaken for a spray of flowers but are actually the hairy, colorful stalks of the flowers after the blossoms have fallen away. The tree is called "yellowwood" by some, although that name is more correctly applied to another tree, *Cladrastis kentuckea*. The wood yields a yellow dye, and was used during the Civil War period. The wood is also very durable in contact with the soil and has been used for fence posts.

Cotinus is the Latin name for European wild olive; *obovatus* refers to the leaf shape, which is described as an inverted egg shape.

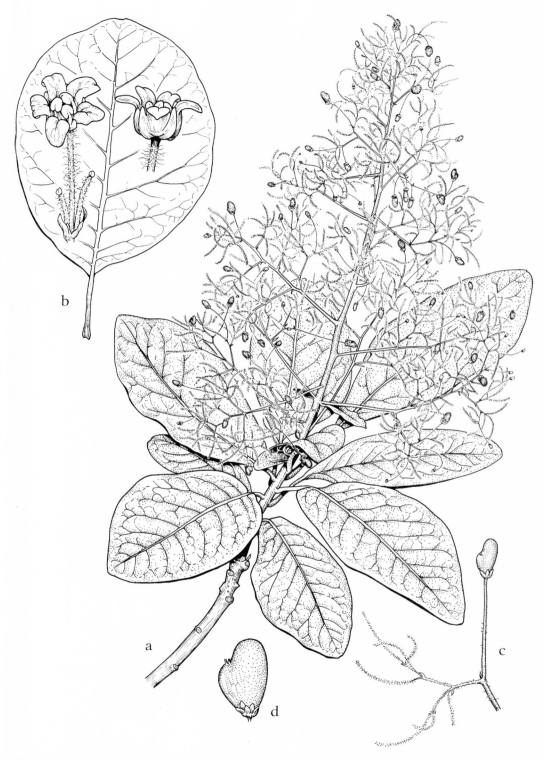

Cotinus obovatus ❧ a. Growth form with fruit, b. Flowers and leaf, c. Hairy stalks with one bearing a fruit, d. Fruit

Frosty hawthorn

Crataegus pruinosa (Wendl.) K. Koch

Rose family (Rosaceae)

Identification: Thorny shrub or small tree, attaining a height of 20 feet and a diameter of 4 to 8 inches.

Flowers: Late April-May, cluster smooth and few-flowered, stalks slender, bearing white, 5-petaled flowers 3/4 to 1 inch across, rounded, showy; stamens 20.

Fruit: September-October, few-fruited, stalks green or red; fruit globe-shaped, 1/2 to 5/8 inch broad, dark red at maturity, smooth, shiny, with white waxy coating, often dotted, pulp yellow; nutlets (seeds with bony covering) 5, about 1/4 inch long.

Leaves: Simple, alternate, blade length 1 to 1 1/2 inches, width 3/4 to 1 inch; broadest in the middle, tip pointed, base wedge-shaped, **margin doubly toothed and also short-lobed**; mature leaves firm and leathery, dark green above, lower surface paler; petioles slender green or reddish, somewhat winged by the leaf base, 1/2 to 1 inch long.

Twigs: Slender, smooth, reddish-brown, with **stout, straight, brown thorns 1/2 to 1 1/2 inches long.**

Trunk: Bark dark gray and scaly.

Habitat: Rocky open woods and thickets.

Range: North Carolina, Kentucky and northern Arkansas, north to New England and Newfoundland, and west to Wisconsin.

Wildlife Uses: The thorniness and dense branching make hawthorns favorite nesting sites for many birds. The small applelike fruits are not used by wildlife to nearly so great an extent as might be expected. Fox sparrows and cedar waxwings are the principal songbird users. Other birds include wild turkey, ruffed grouse and American robin. Coyote, gray fox, cottontail rabbit, raccoon and smaller mammals eat the fruit. White-tailed deer eat the foliage, twigs and fruit.

Remarks: The hawthorn group is complicated, with many variations and hybrids. Estimates as to the number of Missouri species vary from 17 to 50. Only two are considered as shrubs to small trees. Some hawthorn species are used as ornamentals, but most are subject to infection by cedar apple rust, a fungus that produces rusty-orange spots on the leaves and deforms the fruits.

   Crataegus is Greek for "flowering thorn"; *pruinosa* means "frosty" and refers to the waxy, whitish coating of the fruit.

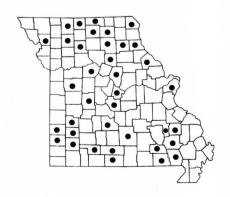

Crataegus pruinosa ❀ a. Growth form with thorns and flower clusters, b. Flower, c. Fruit

One-Flower hawthorn

Crataegus uniflora Muenchh.

Rose family (Rosaceae)

Also called dwarf hawthorn

Field Identification: Slender shrub 3 to 12 feet, with crooked, thorny, small branches. Usually each small branch with a single flower or fruit.

Flowers: May, **flower stalk short, densely hairy with matted wool; flower single or rarely 2 to 3 together**, 3/8 to 5/8 inch wide, petals 5, white, rounded; stamens 20 or more.

Fruit: October, tip with 5 small leafy lobes, fruit body 3/8 to 1/2 inch thick, pubescent, globe-shaped, hairy, greenish yellow to dull red, pulp firm, dry and mealy; nutlets (seeds with bony coverings) 3 to 5, about 1/3 inch long.

Leaves: Simple, alternate, somewhat leathery, leaf varying in shape from egg-shaped to gradually narrowed downward from a rounded summit, tip rounded to somewhat pointed, base wedge-shaped, margin toothed, unlobed, upper leaf surface dark green and shiny, lower leaf surface hairy, especially along the veins, **3/4 to 1 1/4 inches long, 1/2 to 1 inch wide or larger**; petioles very short, hairy.

Twigs: Slender, reddish-brown to gray and very hairy when young, gray and smooth later; **twigs bearing one thorn at the base of a leaf stalk**, thorns slender, straight or slightly curved, gray to black, 1/2 to 2 1/4 inches long.

Trunk: Bark gray or dark brown.

Habitat: Thickets and open woods, usually in sandy or rocky ground.

Range: Florida, Georgia to Texas, north to New York and Pennsylvania, west to the Ozark region of Missouri and Arkansas.

Wildlife Uses: The small applelike fruits are eaten by fox sparrows, cedar waxwings, American robin, wild turkey and ruffed grouse. Coyote, gray fox, cottontail rabbit and smaller mammals eat the fruit. White-tailed deer eat the foliage, twigs and fruit.

Remarks: The hawthorn group is complicated, with many variations and hybrids. Estimates as to the number of Missouri species vary from 17 to 50. Only two are considered as shrubs to small trees. This is the smallest hawthorn in Missouri, both in leaf size and overall height. It is frequently found without flowers or fruit, probably due to growing in too much shade. Its small leaves and hairy young twigs are useful characters for identification.

Crataegus is Greek for "flowering thorn"; *uniflora* means "one-flowered."

Crataegus uniflora 🌼 a. Growth form with thorns and fruit, b. Twig with leaves and flower, c. Fruit

Leatherwood

Dirca palustris L.

Mezereum family (Thymeleaceae)

Field Identification: Widely branching shrub to 7 feet, with a trunk to 4 inches in diameter. Sometimes miniature and treelike.

Flowers: Late March-April, **flowering before the leaves, flowers falling when the leaves expand,** fairly abundant, from leaf axils, clusters of 2 to 4 flowers, stalks very short; flower tube to 1/3 inch long, yellow; petals absent; stamens 8.

Fruit: May-June, sometimes hidden by the dense foliage, stalks 1/8 to 2/5 inch long; fruit dropping early, red to orange, oval to egg-shaped, length 1/4 to 2/5 inch long; 1-seeded, dark brown.

Leaves: Numerous, simple, alternate, inverted egg-shape to oval, tip blunt to somewhat pointed, base narrowed or rounded, margin entire, blade 2 to 4 inches long, width to 2 3/4 inches, surface hairy when immature, light green and smooth later, lower surface with a whitish coat and somewhat hairy; petioles short to 1/5 inch long, hollow; **next year's leaf buds hidden and covered by base of leaf stalk.**

Twigs: Yellow to green and smooth, stems ringed by circular scars at the beginning of the new growth. **Twigs very flexible and capable of being tied into knots without breaking; enlarged at the joints.**

Trunk: Bark mostly smooth and gray on old stems and roughened at the base of old trunks, very tough; wood soft, white, and brittle when dried.

Habitat: Occurs in either low bottom woods on terraces above streams or on rich, wooded lower slopes, usually on north- or east-facing exposures.

Range: Florida to Louisiana and Oklahoma, north to Quebec, west to Ontario and Minnesota.

Medicinal Uses: A small amount of the bark, if taken internally, produces vomiting and has purgative properties. Some people are sensitive to the bark, with their skin becoming irritated or blistered after contact. The fruit is reported to be narcotic.

Remarks: Leatherwood was introduced into cultivation around 1750. A good ornamental plant, it grows slowly and is adjustable to many soil types. It is relatively free from insects and diseases, and when grown in the open develops a well-rounded crown. Because of its flexibility and toughness, Native Americans used the bark and branches for making baskets and for tying purposes. The twigs also were used for thongs.

Dirca is from Dirke, a mythological name of a spring near Thebes; *palustris* refers to the plant's habitat in low, wet soil.

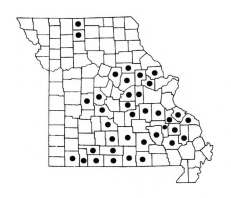

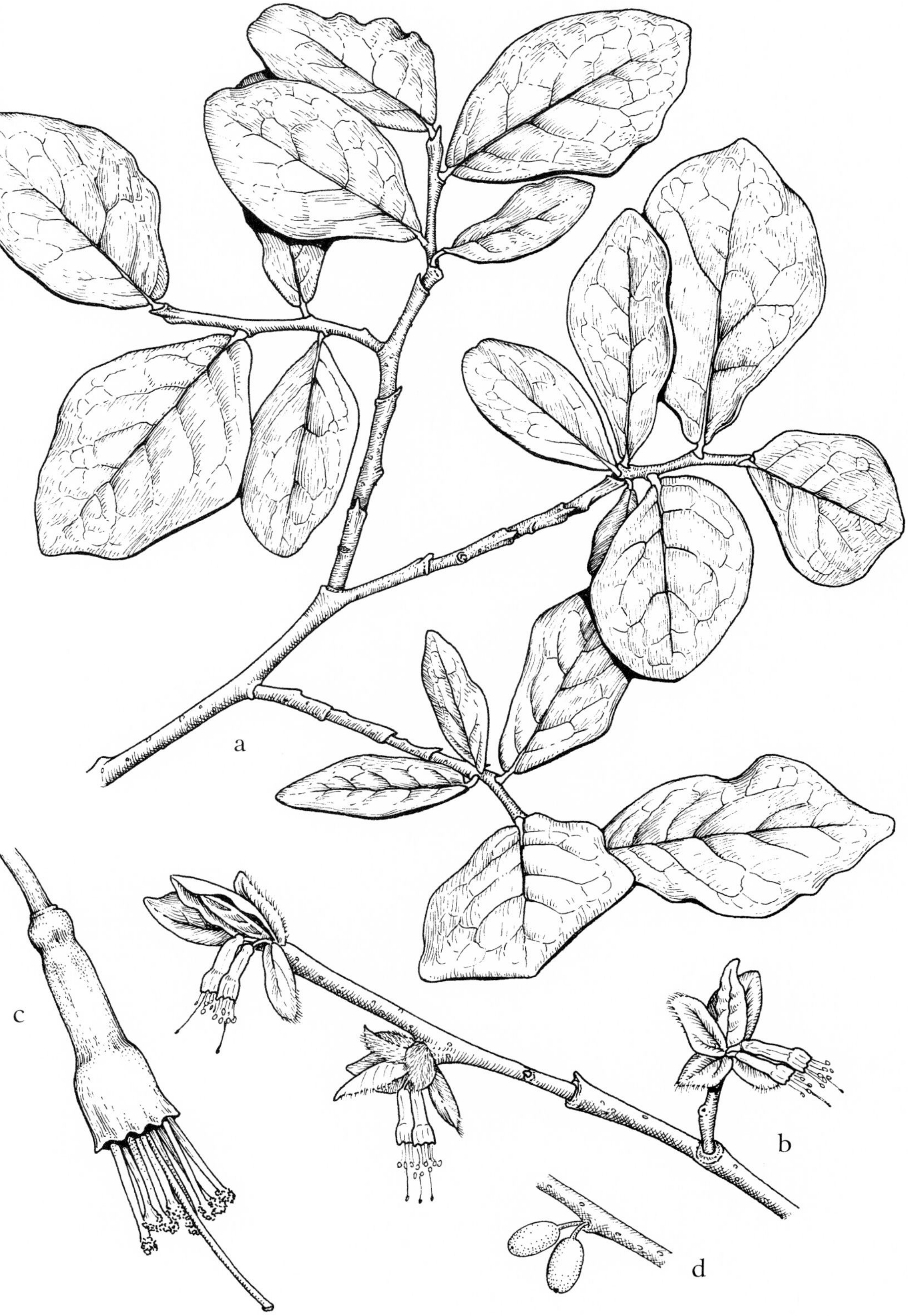

Dirca palustris ❧ a. Growth form, b. Twig with flower clusters, c. Flower, d. Fruit

Autumn olive

Elaeagnus umbellata Thunb.

Oleaster family (Elaeagnaceae)

Field Identification: A large, multi-stemmed shrub reaching 18 feet high and 25 feet across.

Flowers: Late April-May, in clusters emerging at the leaf axils with 1 to 8 flowers; flowers cream to light yellow, fragrant, about 1/2 inch long, 1/4 inch wide, **outside of flowers silvery -scaly**; petals 4, spreading, tip pointed; stamens 4.

Fruit: September-October, speckled red, about 1/4 inch in diameter, globe-shaped to inverted egg-shaped, bitter to semi-sweet, withering after frost; seed solitary.

Leaves: Simple, alternate, 1 1/2 to 3 inches long, 1 to 1 1/4 inches wide, longer than broad and tapering toward the tip; tip pointed, base wedge-shaped, margin entire with some irregular bumps, wavy; upper surface bright green, **lower surface silver green with silver scales, producing a shimmering appearance when wind blown**; petioles about 1/8 inch long, with brown and silver scales.

Twigs: Irregularly armed on older twigs with strong, sharp thorns up to 2 inches long; light brown to grayish-brown with silver and brown scales.

Trunk: Bark smooth, brown; on older shrubs grayish-brown, lightly furrowed.

Habitat: Escapes along roadsides, fence rows, idle fields, pastures, edges of woods, woodlands and edges of streams.

Range: Escaped mostly in the eastern half of the United States. Its native home includes streambanks and thickets up to 9000 feet in elevation, from Afghanistan to China, Korea and Japan.

Wildlife Uses: The flowers are a source of nectar for honeybees. One report indicates that the fruit is used by at least 15 species of birds; however, bird use doubles and triples with such natives as dogwoods, crab apples, elderberries and cherries. Of 17 species of shrubs listed in the report, autumn olive ranks 15th in bird use. However, the fruit is mostly available in fall, when other wildlife food is more abundant. Plantings of dogwoods, small-fruited hawthorns and other plants with more durable fruit are more useful to wildlife during critical periods in winter.

Remarks: Autumn olive has been grown in cultivation since 1830. It was first collected from its native range, and has been commercially available in the United States since 1917. The fruit is used for human consumption in Japan.

This exotic shrub, as with so many other non-native introductions, was made available without adequate knowledge of its effect on native species. For many years following introduction, no reproduction is apparent and the shrubs appear self-contained; then the species suddenly explodes, becoming epidemic in a few years. Control measures often prove time-consuming and costly. Its cultivation as an ornamental, or for wildife use, is not recommended.

The tree, Russian olive *(Elaeagnus angustifolia)*, is another exotic that should not be planted. More silvery in appearance, it is a scourge of streamside habitat in many Southwestern states.

Elaeagnus is from the Greek words *elaia* ("olive") and *agnus* ("sacred"), which refer to its olivelike fruit; *umbellatus* refers to the umbrella-shaped clusters of flowers.

Escapes from cultivation

Elaeagnus umbellata ❀ a. Growth form with flower clusters, b. Flowers, c. Fruit clusters

Winged euonymus

Euonymus alatus (Thunb.) Sieb.

Staff-tree family (Celastraceae)

Also called burning bush

Field Identification: A shrub growing to a height of 15 to 20 feet, with corky wings on the twigs.

Flowers: May-June, in clusters of 3 to 8, from axils of leaves or nodes, stalks slender, 1 to 2 inches long; flowers **yellowish-green**, about 1/2 inch across; petals 4, spreading, oval to inverted egg-shaped, margin wavy; stamens 4, alternating with the petals and arising from the edge of the disk.

Fruit: September-October, capsule deeply 4-lobed, about 1/4 inch long, red, splitting open to expose an **orange to red** seed coating, the seeds often dropping with the leaves in autumn.

Leaves: Opposite, simple, 1 to 3 inches long, 1/2 to 1 1/4 inches wide, tip pointed, base wedge-shaped, margin finely and sharply toothed, upper surface medium to dark green, smooth; lower surface paler, smooth to somewhat hairy; petioles short.

Twigs: Green to brown with 2 to 4 **ridges of corky wings**; wings 1/4 to 1/2 inch wide, generally the more vigorous shoots have the largest wings, twigs smooth.

Trunk: Bark gray, tight; lenticels (pores) raised, narrow, light tan.

Habitat: Introduced from Asia and escaped from cultivation. Found mostly in open woods and thickets near old homesites.

Range: Northeastern Asia to Central China; introduced into eastern North America.

Wildlife Uses: Like other species of *euonymus*, the fruit is probably eaten by a number of species of birds, including wild turkey. The leaves and stems are likely eaten by white-tailed deer and cottontail rabbits.

Remarks: Although not native, winged euonymus — with its striking red foliage in autumn — is an attractive ornamental. It is not considered as aggressive as the shrub honeysuckles. It is used for hedging along borders and for screening. It was introduced into North America about 1860.

Euonymus is the Greek name meaning "true name"; *alatus* means "winged," referring to the corky wings on the stems.

Escapes
from
cultivation

Euonymus alatus ❀ a. Growth form with flower clusters, b. Flowers, c. Fruit, d. Twig with corky wings

Strawberry bush

Euonymus americanus L.

Staff-tree family (Celastraceae)

Also called bursting heart

Field Identification: Shrub to 6 feet, erect or sometimes creeping or trailing.

Flowers: May-June, in clusters mostly 1- to 3-flowered, stalks 1/4 to 3/4 inch long; flowers 1/4 to 1/2 inch broad, petals 5, spreading, greenish- to greenish-purple or reddish; stamens 5, alternating with the petals and arising from the edge of the disk.

Fruit: September-October, capsule globe-shaped, flattened at the base, **bearing a warty surface, pink**, about 1/2 inch thick, splitting to expose 1 to 2 seeds; seeds about 1/4 inch long, flattened with a conspicuous orange-red seed coating.

Leaves: Simple, opposite, petioles short to 1/8 inch long; egg- to lance-shaped to broadly oval, **broadest at middle to lower half**, tip pointed, base narrowed to rounded or heart-shaped, margin toothed, upper surface smooth and dark green, lower surface smooth or slightly hairy on the veins, blade length 3/4 to 4 inches, width 1/2 to 1 inch.

Twigs: Widely spreading, and sometimes horizontal, green to brown or gray, smooth, somewhat 4-angled, sometimes rooting at the nodes if in contact with the soil.

Trunk: Wood light-colored, close-grained, tough.

Habitat: Occurs in low, sandy woods along spring branches, low moist woods, moist wooded slopes of Crowleys Ridge, and moist stream banks.

Range: From Florida to east Texas, north to New York and west through Pennsylvania, Indiana, and Illinois to Nebraska.

Wildlife Uses: The fruit is eaten by a number of species of birds, including wild turkeys. The leaves and stems are eaten by white-tailed deer and cottontail rabbits.

Medicinal Uses: The powdered bark has been used as a remedy for dandruff and scalp irritation. The bark of the root has been prepared for internal use as a laxative, to reduce fever and to increase urine flow. The bark has been taken to treat uterine troubles, venereal diseases, skin ailments and to induce vomiting. The seeds have been used as a strong laxative.

Remarks: Strawberry bush is classified as rare in Missouri, partly because of where it prefers to grow, but also because much of its habitat has been destroyed. It was introduced into cultivation in 1697. It is an attractive shrub because of the dark green leaves, which remain on the branches long into autumn. The unusual pink, warty fruit opens to display colorful orange-red seeds.

Euonymus is the Greek name meaning "true name"; *americanus* denotes it origin.

Euonymus americanus ❧ a. Growth form with flowers, b. Flower, c. Capsule with fruit

Wahoo

Euonymus atropurpureus Jacq.

Staff-tree family (Celastraceae)

Also called burning bush

Field Identification: Usually a shrub, but sometimes a small tree to 25 feet, with spreading branches and an irregular crown.

Flowers: Late April-June, in clusters of 7 to 15, from axils of leaves, stalks slender, 1 to 2 inches long; flowers about 1/2 inch broad, petals 4, spreading, **purple**; stamens 4, alternating with the petals and arising from the edge of the disk.

Fruit: September-October, capsule deeply 4-lobed, smooth, about 1/2 inch across, persistent into winter on long stalks, purple to rose-colored, splitting open to expose brown seeds about 1/4 inch long enclosed by a **scarlet seed covering**.

Leaves: Opposite, simple, 2 to 5 inches long, 1 to 2 inches wide, egg-shaped to broadest in the middle and tapering at both ends, tip pointed, base tapering sharply, margin finely toothed; bright green above; pale and **hairy beneath**; petioles 1/2 to 1 inch long.

Twigs: Slender, somewhat 4-angled, purplish-green turning brownish later; lenticels (pores) pale and prominent.

Trunk: Bark smooth, thin, gray, minute scales; wood almost white, tinged with yellow or orange, close-grained, heavy, hard, tough.

Habitat: Occurs on wooded slopes, bluffs, open woods, alluvial soils along streams, and in thickets. Throughout Missouri, doubtless in every county.

Range: From northern Alabama to east Texas, north to New York, and west to Ontario, Montana, Nebraska and Oklahoma.

Wildlife Uses: The fruit is eaten by a number of species of birds, including wild turkey. The leaves and stems are eaten by white-tailed deer and cottontail rabbits.

Medicinal Uses: Native American women drank a solution of the inner bark for uterine discomfort and used the same preparation as an eye lotion. Pounded stem bark or root bark was applied to facial sores. Settlers used the bark as a liver stimulant and a laxative, and for fever and indigestion. An oil from the seed was used, both in Europe and the United States, to destroy head lice.

Remarks: The shrub has been cultivated since 1756. It is sometimes used as an ornamental because of its beautiful scarlet fruit in autumn. The Native Americans used the powdered bark for tobacco and the wood for arrows.

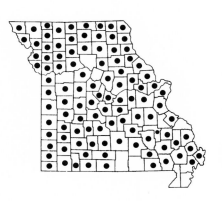

Euonymus atropurpureus ❦ a. Growth form with flowers, b. Flower, c. Capsule with fruit

Running strawberry bush

Euonymus obovatus Nutt.

Staff-tree family (Celastraceae)

Field Identification: A very small shrub less than 18 inches tall, with trailing stems up to 3 feet long.

Flowers: Late April-June, in clusters mostly 1- to 3-flowered, on stalks 1 to 2 inches long; flowers small, about 1/4 inch across; petals 5, greenish to purple, spreading; stamens 5, alternating with the petals and arising from the edge of the disk.

Fruit: September-October, a drooping globe- to heart-shaped capsule, flattened at the base, bearing a warty surface, pale orange to scarlet red, about 3/4 inch across, splitting to expose 1 to 2 seeds; **seeds with a conspicuous scarlet red coating.**

Leaves: Opposite, simple, 1 to 2 1/2 inches long, 3/4 to 1 3/4 inches wide, **inverted egg-shaped at upper end of twig**, remaining leaves broadest above the middle to lance-shaped or oval, tip blunt to slightly pointed, base wedge-shaped, margin finely toothed; upper surface medium to dark green, dull, smooth; lower surface paler, smooth; petioles very short, sometimes winged.

Twigs: Bright green to purple, smooth, slender, with broad ridges or angled; **stems trailing and rooting when in contact with the ground.**

Trunk: Green to brownish, smooth.

Habitat: Occurs on mostly **north-facing, moist, wooded dolomite slopes** or at the base of dolomite bluffs.

Range: Tennessee to Illinois and Missouri, north to New York and Ontario, and west to Michigan.

Wildlife Uses: Like strawberry bush, the fruit is probably eaten by a number of species of birds, including wild turkeys. The leaves and stems are eaten by white-tailed deer and cottontail rabbits.

Remarks: This is a very small shrub that creeps along the ground and forms dense mats. The foliage holds its green color well into December. The plant is sometimes used as a ground cover on bare, shaded slopes. The fruits and leaves are considered poisonous.

Euonymus is the Greek name meaning "true name"; *obovatus* is for the leaf shape, which is obovate or inverted egg-shaped.

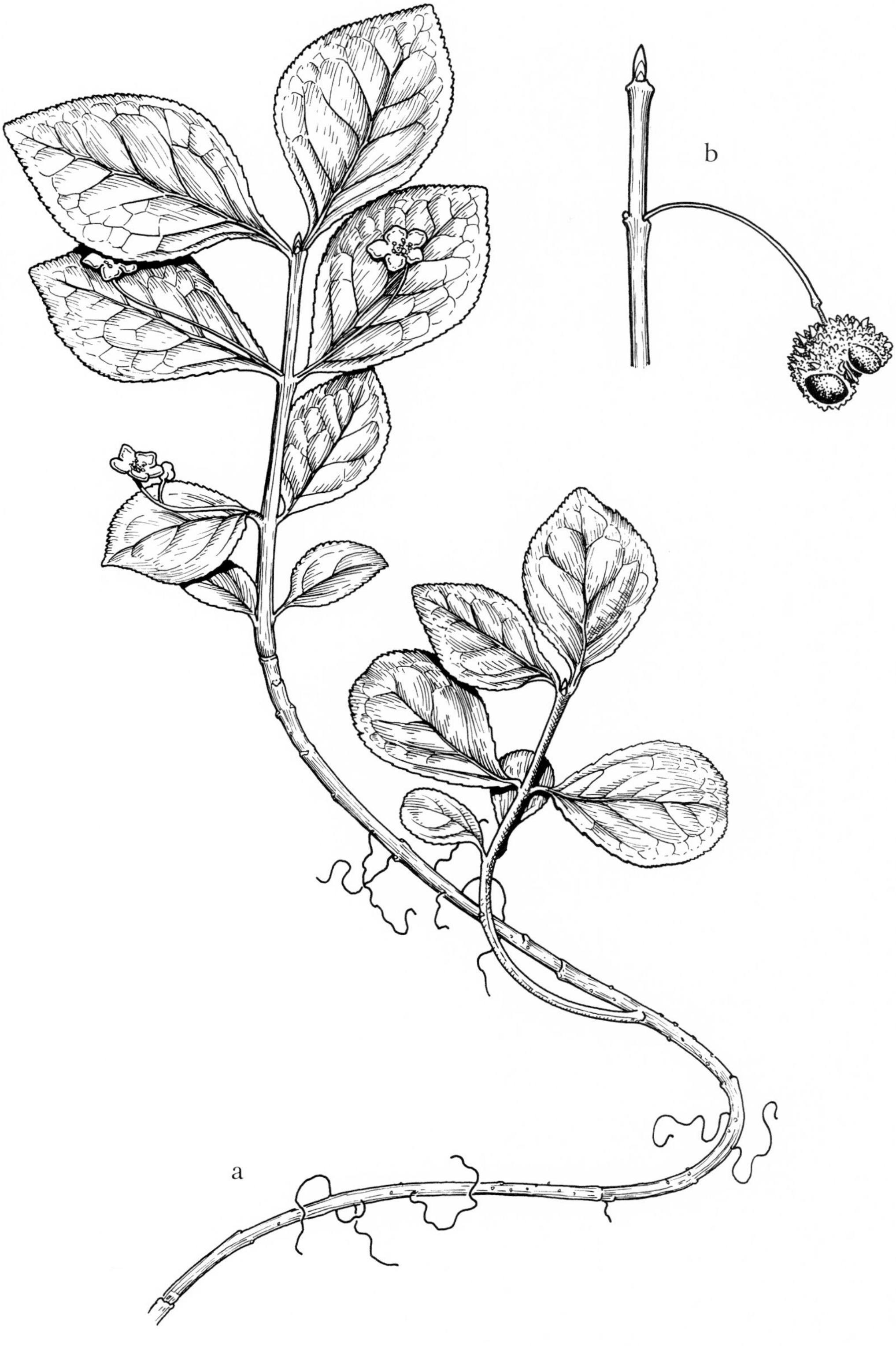

Euonymus obovatus ✤ a. Growth form with flowers, b. Capsule with fruit

Swamp privet

Forestiera acuminata (Michaux) Poiret

Olive family (Oleaceae)

Field Identification: Straggly shrub or small tree to 30 feet, growing in wet to swampy ground.

Flowers: Late March-April, **appearing before the leaves on stem of previous year**, the staminate (male) flowers in dense green clusters above yellow bracts (modified leaves), petals lacking; stamens 4; pistillate (female) flowers in clusters 3/4 to 1 1/4 inches long.

Fruit: June, purplish, sometimes curved, longer than broad, tip pointed, about 1 inch long; single seed, light brown, about 1/3 inch long, one side flatter than the other.

Leaves: Simple, opposite, 2 to 4 1/2 inches long, 1 to 2 inches wide, longer than broad to egg-shaped, tip pointed, **base narrowly wedge-shaped**, margin with few teeth, leaf blade smooth, yellowish-green above, paler with occasional hairs on veins beneath; petioles slender, 1/4 to 1/2 inch long, slightly winged by leaf bases.

Twigs: Light brown to gray, glabrous, slender, warty, with numerous lenticels (pores); twigs sometimes rooting on contact with the mud.

Trunk: Bark dark brown, thin, close, slightly ridged; wood yellowish to reddish-brown, close-grained, light, weak, soft.

Habitat: Occurs in swamps, low wet woods, alluvial and rocky borders of streams, ponds, sloughs and bayous. In Missouri, mainly along the Mississippi River and in the Bootheel.

Range: Florida to Texas, north to South Carolina, Tennessee, Illinois, Missouri, Kansas and Oklahoma.

Wildlife Uses: The fruit is considered to be a good wild duck food.

Remarks: Swamp privet often occurs in small stands. It is quite noticeable in early spring, with the clusters of yellow flowers and bracts appearing along the gray branches before the leaves come out.

Forestiera is in honor of the French physician and botanist, Charles Le Forestier; *acuminata* refers to the pointed leaves.

Forestiera acuminata ❧ a. Growth form with fruit clusters, b. Fruit, c. Branch with flowers

Black huckleberry

Gaylussacia baccata (Wangenh.) K. Koch

Heath family (Ericaceae)

Field Identification: Rigid, upright, much-branched shrub attaining a height of 1 to 4 feet.

Flowers: April-May, short clusters emerging from the previous year's stem; stalks hairy, 1/4 to 1 inch long; flowers pink or reddish, hanging down, about 1/4 inch long, cone-shaped to round, lobes 5, short, curved outward; stamens 10.

Fruit: June-September, berrylike, about 1/4 inch long, black, shining, sweet; seeds 10, flattened.

Leaves: Simple, alternate, firm, 3/4 to 1 3/4 inches long, longer than broad and oval or egg-shaped, tip blunt to pointed, base broadly tapering, margin entire; upper surface yellowish-green, smooth; **lower surface with sticky resinous dots**, paler, hairy or smooth; petioles short.

Twigs: Green and hairy when young; gray and smooth when older; **winter twigs predominantly black.**

Trunk: Bark smooth, dark-colored.

Habitat: Occurs on rocky wooded ridges above bluffs, usually in cherty soils. Known only in two Missouri sites.

Range: Florida to Louisiana, north to Maine, Newfoundland, Quebec, and west to Manitoba, Saskatchewan, Iowa and Missouri.

Wildlife Uses: The fruit is eaten by at least six species of birds, including ruffed grouse, bob-white quail, wild turkey and mourning dove.

Remarks: Endangered in Missouri, it may be overlooked because of its similarity to the common low-bush blueberry, *Vaccinium pallidum*. The resinous dots on the under surface of black huckleberry help to distinguish it from the former species. Also, low-bush blueberry bark is reddish to green, and cracked and split on the older stems. In Canada and the northeastern and eastern United States, where this plant is more abundant, the fruit is eaten for its sweet, spicy flavor.

   Gaylussacia is in honor of J.L. Gay-Lussac (1778-1850), a French chemist; *baccata* refers to the baccate or berrylike fruit.

Gaylussacia baccata ❧ a. Growth form with flowers, b. Flowers, c. Fruit

Ozark witch hazel

Hamamelis vernalis Sarg.

Witch hazel family (Hamamelidaceae)

Also called vernal witch hazel

Field Identification: Shrub attaining a height of 9 feet, and often sending up sprouts from the base.

Flowers: **January-April**, fragrant, stalks short to absent, flowers clustered or solitary; petals 4, **yellow to dark red**, 1/4 to 1/2 inch long, narrow; stamens usually 8.

Fruit: September-October, capsule hard, woody, about 1/2 inch long, splitting down a two-parted tip; seeds 1 or 2, large, hard, black, forcibly discharged to a distance of up to 30 feet.

Leaves: Simple, alternate, blade length 2 to 5 inches, width about 3 inches on the average, inverted egg-shaped to oval, tip rounded to blunt, base wedge-shaped to rounded, margin strongly wavy; upper surface dull green with veins lying below the general surface; lower surface paler green, smooth to hairy, veins prominent beneath. Some forms with lower surface densely velvety-hairy.

Twigs: Rather stout, light brown to reddish-brown or gray, **densely velvety-hairy**, later smooth and light or dark gray.

Trunk: Bark tight not peeling, gray to brown, often with gray blotches, lenticels (pores) narrow, cream-colored.

Habitat: In gravel and rocky streambeds, at the base of rocky slopes along streams, and rarely on wooded hillsides in rocky draws.

Range: From Missouri and Arkansas to Oklahoma

Wildlife Uses: The leaves and shoots are browsed in varying degrees by white-tailed deer. The bark is occasionally eaten by beaver, squirrels and cottontail rabbits. The seeds and flowers are eaten by wild turkey and ruffed grouse.

Medicinal Uses: Like the Eastern witch hazel, the twigs, leaves and bark are the basis of witch hazel extract, which is included in shaving lotions and in many medicinal lotions for bruises and sprains.

Remarks: Ozark witch hazel differs noticeably from Eastern witch hazel in that the flowers are produced in late winter or early spring. The latter produces flowers in late autumn to early winter. Both witch hazels make attractive shrubs in cultivation. The Ozark witch hazel is the first woody species to be found in bloom in Missouri, often blooming while snow is on the ground.

Hamamelis is from the Greek words *hama* ("at the same time") and *melon* ("apple"), possibly because of the presence of both fruit and flower simultaneously; *vernalis* ("spring") refers to its early-blooming habit from midwinter to spring.

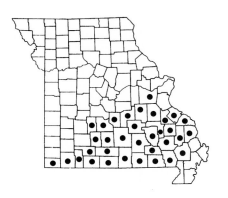

Hamamelis vernalis ✿ a. Growth form, b. Twig with flower clusters, c. Flower, d. Twig with seed capsules and next year's flower buds

Eastern witch hazel

Hamamelis virginiana L.

Witch hazel family (Hamamelidaceae)

Field Identification: Tall shrub or small tree to 30 feet.

Flowers: October-December, fragrant, stalks short to absent, flowers clustered, petals 4, **bright yellow**, 1/2 to 3/4 inches long, narrow; stamens 8.

Fruit: Ripens the following September-October, capsule hard, woody, about 1/2 inch long, splitting down a two-parted tip; seeds 1 or 2, large, hard, black, forcibly discharged to a distance of up to 30 feet.

Leaves: Simple, alternate, blade length 6 inches, width 3 inches on the average, or on older branches much smaller, inverted egg-shaped to oval, tip pointed, base wedge-shaped, margin wavy, sometimes toothed; usually smooth above; somewhat hairy beneath; petiole hairy, about inch long.

Twigs: Slender, zigzag, reddish or orange, **smooth or slightly hairy**.

Trunk: Brown, thin, smooth when immature, and scaly when mature; wood reddish-brown, hard, close-grained, sapwood almost white.

Habitat: Occurs in moist woods on north- or east-facing slopes or in wooded valleys along streams. Uncommon in Missouri and restricted to the extreme southeastern part of the Ozarks.

Range: Florida to east Texas, north to Nova Scotia and west to Minnesota.

Wildlife Uses: The leaves and shoots are browsed in varying degrees by white-tailed deer. The bark is occasionally eaten by beaver, squirrels and cottontail rabbits. The seeds and flowers are eaten by wild turkey and ruffed grouse.

Medicinal Uses: The twigs, leaves and bark are the basis of witch hazel extract, which is included in shaving lotions and in many medicinal lotions for bruises and sprains. Native Americans used this plant profusely. They applied the bark to skin tumors and skin inflammations, used the inner bark as a treatment for irritated eyes, and chewed the bark to freshen their mouths. A boiled solution was rubbed on the legs of young athletes to keep them limber; it also was used to treat a lame back.

Remarks: Eastern witch hazel differs noticeably from Ozark witch hazel in that the flowers are produced in late autumn or early winter. The latter produces flowers in late winter or early spring. Both witch hazels make attractive shrubs in cultivation. The Eastern witch hazel is the last woody species to bloom in Missouri. In superstitious lore, the twigs are used as divining rods or witching sticks to locate water or mineral deposits.

Hamamelis is from the Greek words *hama* ("at the same time") and *melon* ("apple"), possibly because of the presence of both fruit and flower simultaneously; *virginiana* refers to the state of Virginia, where the plant was first described.

Hamamelis virginiana ❧ a. Growth form, b. Flowers, c. Seed capsules, d. Winter twig

Rose of Sharon

Hibiscus syriacus L.

Mallow family (Malvaceae)

Also called shrubby althaea

Field Identification: Many-branched shrub or small tree 3 to 18 feet. Not native, sometimes spreads from plantings.

Flowers: July-September, showy, emerging from axils of leaves, flower stalk variable in length; **flowers large, showy**, 2 to 4 inches across, solitary on new year's growth; petals 5, variable in color in the many horticultural forms — white, pink, lavender, rose, with a crimson or purplish blotch at the base, 1 3/4 inches long, rounded to inverted egg-shaped, margins wavy; **central column prominent with stamens along it and a 5-parted tip (stigma).**

Fruit: September-October, capsule egg- to oval-shaped, **persisting into winter, splitting into five-parts**, 3/4 to 1 inch long, hairy.

Leaves: Alternate, triangular to broadest in the middle, usually more or less 3-lobed, 1 1/2 to 4 3/4 inches long, margin with rounded or pointed teeth; upper surface medium green, often shiny; lower surface smooth except for a few hairs on the veins; young leaves hairy, becoming smooth later; petioles 1/4 to 1 inch long, generally shorter than the blades.

Twigs: Smooth, gray to brown, somewhat roughened, broadened at the tip.

Habitat: Commonly planted as an ornamental shrub, known to spread along roadsides, railroads, thickets and woods.

Range: Florida to Louisiana and Texas, north to Massachusetts, and west to Ohio, Missouri, Arkansas and Oklahoma. Also in coastal regions of Canada. Native of Asia.

Remarks: Rose of Sharon was introduced into cultivation about 1600. This is one of the less aggressive shrubs, rarely competing with native vegetation; although, in one instance, it has spread into the woods at Castlewood State Park, St. Louis County. There are two native hibiscus in Missouri, *Hibiscus lasiocarpos* and *H. militaris*, but neither are considered woody. They occur along borders of streams, ponds, sloughs, ditches in wet soil or shallow water.

Hibiscus is the ancient name of the European Marsh-mallow; *syriacus* is for Syria, where it was once supposed to be native; however, more recent investigations prove it to be originally from China and India.

Hibiscus syriacus ❀ a. Growth form with flower, b. Twig with seed capsules

Wild hydrangea

Hydrangea arborescens L.

Hydrangea family (Hydrangeaceae)

Also called seven-bark

Field Identification: Widely-branched, straggly shrub growing in clumps and attaining a height of 2 to 10 feet.

Flowers: Late May-July, borne in rather flat, hairy clusters, 2 to 6 inches broad; petals white, minute; stamens 8 to 10; **flowers along the margin much larger, more conspicuous, often sterile**.

Fruit: October-November, capsules small, about 1/8 inch long, or wide, prominently 8 to 10 ribbed with two horns at the tip; seeds numerous, reddish-brown, flattened, minute.

Leaves: Opposite, 2 to 6 inches long, 3 to 5 inches wide, broadly egg-shaped to circular, tip pointed, base heart-shaped or broadly tapering, margin sharply toothed; dark green above; smooth, paler and more or less hairy beneath; **petioles 1 to 4 1/2 inches long**, slender, somewhat hairy.

Twigs: Slender, light brown, smooth to hairy, lenticels (pores) large, pith white.

Trunk: Outer layer of bark on branches red to brown, often with small splits; bark of older stems pale tan to brown, peeling into thin sheets; wood soft, greenish-white, open-grained; pith white.

Habitat: Occurs in moist or rocky wooded slopes, talus, at the base of bluffs, along streams and in ravines.

Range: Florida to Louisiana, Arkansas and Oklahoma, north to New York, and west to Iowa and Missouri.

Wildlife Uses: Browsed by white-tailed deer during the growing season. After continued browsing shrubs lose vigor and eventually die. Wild turkey eat the leaves in summer and fall.

Medicinal Uses: Native Americans boiled the roots, along with other plant materials, and gave the liquid to women who had unusual dreams during their menstrual periods. The roots and rhizomes have been used to increase urine flow and as a tonic and laxative. In colonial times, the roots were used to treat kidney stones.

Remarks: The leaves turn from pale green to yellow in autumn. Wild hydrangea was introduced into cultivation in 1736. There are several horticultural varieties commercially available. It blooms well in sun or partial shade. It should be pruned back rather severely in fall or early spring to avoid a straggly appearance.

    Hydrangea is from *hydor* ("water") and *aggeion* ("a vessel") for the cuplike form of the capsular fruit; *arborescens* refers to its likeness to a small tree. The name seven-bark is given because the bark peels off in layers of different colors.

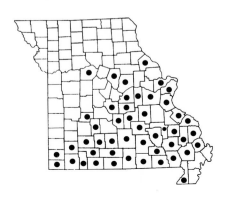

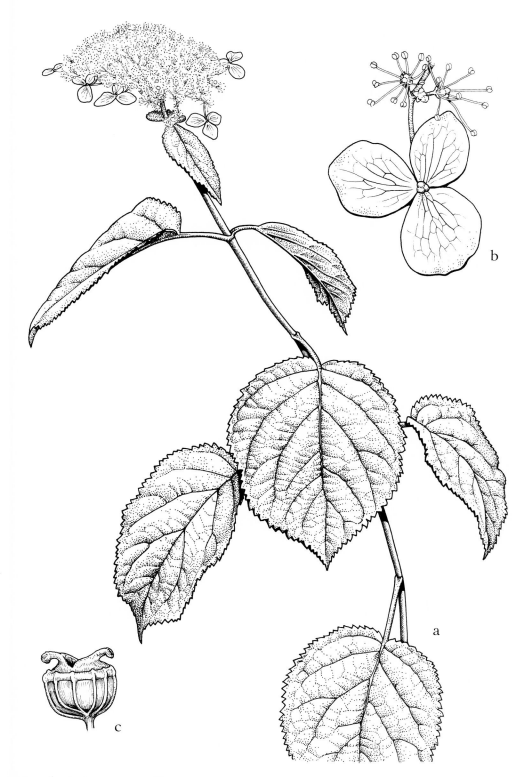

Hydrangea arborescens ✿ a. Growth form with flower cluster, b. Minute- and large-petaled flowers, c. Seed capsule

St. Andrew's cross

Hypericum hypericoides (L.) Crantz

St. John's-wort family (Hypericaceae)

Field Identification: Small, **sprawling shrub** to 3 feet.

Flowers: July-October, at the tip or along the stem/leaf axil, on rather short, lateral leafy stems; petals 4, bright yellow, long and narrow, spreading, tip ending at a sharp angle; stamens numerous, distinct, yellow.

Fruits: September-October, capsule about 1/3 inch long, egg-shaped to oval, flattened, short stalk on tip persistent, splits into two sides when mature, seeds numerous.

Leaves: Opposite, simple, evergreen, the larger leaves often above smaller ones, long and narrow but broadest above the middle, blade 1/2 to 1 1/2 inches long, about 1/4 inch wide, tip rounded to ending at a sharp angle, base narrowed, margin entire; leaves thin, surface bright green and smooth, **dotted with small spots or glands; petioles absent**.

Twigs: Many-branched, slender, brown to red-brown, flattened when young, shredding along the thin ridges; too small to be called true wood. Sprawling twigs root to form a multi-stemmed mat.

Habitat: Occurs in dry, rocky open woods on upland slopes and ridges, or in wooded valleys and ravines, in acid soils associated with chert, sandstone or igneous-based soils.

Range: From Georgia to Texas, north to Massachusetts, west to Pennsylvania, Ohio, Kansas and Oklahoma.

Wildlife Uses: The plant is browsed occasionally by white-tailed deer.

Medicinal Uses: An extract of the leaves is used in home medicine for a contracting or constrictive effect on bodily tissues; it also reduces swelling or inflammation. The seeds are reported to have cleansing or purging properties, usually in reference to the bowels.

Remarks: The former genus name is *Ascyrum*. There are two varieties found in Missouri. The above description is for var. *muticaule,* which is common throughout its range in the Ozarks. The less common one, var. *hypericoides* is upright, usually with a single main stem from 1 to 3 feet tall, many-branched with linear leaves, growing on sandy low wooded knolls, low wet woodland areas, swampy ground and along streams in southeastern Missouri's Bootheel region; it also grows in the Ozark counties of Carter, Douglas and Ozark, where it occurs in sandy soils along streams or on upper slopes of sandstone bluffs in oak-pine woodland.

St. Andrew's cross is sometimes cultivated as an ornamental. It often is used as a rock garden plant, flowering throughout a long period, but never densely flowered.

Hypericum is from the ancient Greek word huperikon, referring to a species of St. John's-wort; *hypericoides* is for its resemblance to certain species of *Hypericum*. The common name comes from the shape of the petals, which approach each other in pairs in the form of St. Andrew's cross.

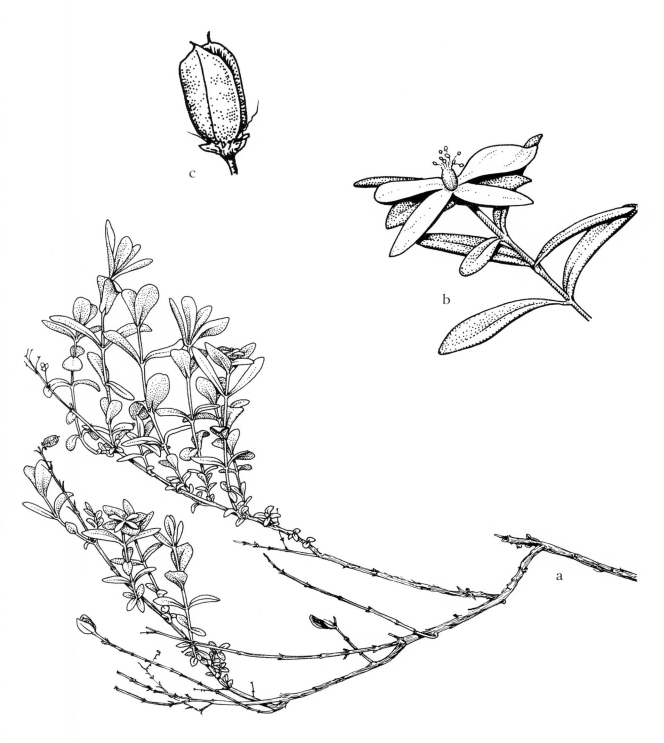

Hypericum hypericoides ❧ a. Growth form, b. Stem with flower, c. Seed capsule

Shrubby St. John's-wort

Hypericum prolificum L.

St. John's-wort family (Hypericaceae)

Field Identification: Shrub 1 to 6 feet tall, usually many-branched above the base, with the stems erect or ascending.

Flowers: June-September, solitary or in twos or threes; flower stalks short; petals 5, 1/4 to 3/4 inch long, flower 3/4 to 1 inch across, bright yellow; stamens numerous.

Fruit: September-October, capsule cone- to egg-shaped, tip pointed, splitting to release numerous black seeds.

Leaves: Opposite, simple, **often with smaller ones in their axils**, 1 to 3 inches long, 1/4 to inch wide, narrow throughout to slightly broader in the middle, tip blunt, base gradually narrowed into a short and often-winged petioles; margin entire and slightly curved under; dull green above, paler beneath.

Twigs: Slender, smooth, reddish-brown at first and sharply 2-edged, older twigs gray to straw-colored and less angled.

Trunk: Bark gray, **with a thin outer layer that sheds to reveal a pale orange surface**.

Habitat: Occurs in rocky ground and gravel bars along streams, dry wooded slopes, bluff escarpments, old fields, and sometimes low moist ground in valleys.

Range: Georgia to Louisiana and Arkansas, north to New York and west to Ontario and Minnesota.

Wildlife Uses: The flowers are a nectar source for bees.

Remarks: This species is known also as *Hypericum spathulatum* (Spach) Steudel. This is an attractive shrub and well-suited for using in native plantings. The dark green leaves, showy yellow flowers, and pale orange bark make it an interesting ornamental shrub. Interestingly, the numerous golden-yellow stamens are the most conspicuous parts of the showy flowers, somewhat hiding the yellow petals.

Hypericum is from the ancient Greek word *huperikon*, referring to a species of St. John's-wort; *prolificum* means abundant in number, referring to the stamens.

Another woody species, dense St. John's-wort, *Hypericum densiflorum*, has been reported from Dunklin and Ripley counties growing in sandy woodlands. Specimens have not been located to verify this, but the shrub is one to be on the lookout for. It ranges from Florida to Texas, north to New York, and west to West Virginia, Indiana and Missouri. It differs from shrubby St. John's-wort in having winged stems and a smaller seed capsule.

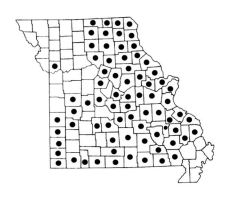

Hypericum prolificum ❀ a. Growth form with flowers, b. Twig with new growth at base of last year's fruit stalk bearing seed capsules

Possum haw

Ilex decidua Walter

Holly family (Aquifoliaceae)

Also called deciduous holly

Field Identification: Usually a shrub with a spreading open crown, but sometimes a small tree to 30 feet.

Flowers: April-May, flowering when leaves are about half grown, single or in clusters, some plants may be male, others female, or flowers may be perfect (see illustration); petals 4 to 6, white, egg-shaped, about 1/4 inch long; stamens 4 to 6.

Fruit: September-October, persistent on branches most of the winter after leaves are shed, berry globe-shaped, orange to red, 1/4 inch across, solitary or 2 to 3 together; seeds usually 4, pale yellow.

Leaves: Simple, alternate or often in clusters on short lateral spurs; 2 to 3 inches long, 1/2 to 1 1/2 inches wide, inverted egg-shaped or rounded at the tip and tapering at the base, **tip rounded or blunt**, base wedge-shaped or narrowly tapering, **margin mostly with round or blunt teeth**; upper surface dark green, smooth or with a few hairs, main vein lying below the general surface; lower surface paler, smooth or hairy on the veins; petioles slender, grooved, smooth to densely hairy, length up to inch.

Twigs: Drawn out, slender, often with many short spurlike lateral twigs, light to dark gray, smooth or slightly hairy.

Trunk: Bark smooth, thin, mottled gray to brown, sometimes with numerous warty protuberances; wood pale yellow to white, heavy, hard, close-grained.

Habitat: Occurs on dolomite glades, rocky upland open woods, fencerows, borders of upland and lowland ponds, swamps, sloughs, valleys and low wet woods along streams.

Range: Florida to East Texas, north to Oklahoma, Kansas, Missouri, Illinois, Indiana and Maryland.

Wildlife Uses: Small mammals, opossums and several species of birds feed upon the fruit, including the bobwhite quail. The female shrub is a heavy producer of fruits, most of which persist until late winter. Often in a particularly hard winter, or when the regular food supply is scarce, birds will clean the fruits from the branches in a short period. On warm, early spring days, intoxicated robins and mockingbirds are sometimes seen after they have eaten the fermenting fruits. White-tailed deer are known to browse the branches.

Remarks: Possum haw is occasionally planted as an ornamental, and is attractive in winter because of its orange to red berries. Some shrubs will have all male flowers, which lack the showy berries. It is best to plant more than one plant to ensure that some will be female. The foliage turns dull purplish and green in autumn.

Ilex is the ancient Latin name of the holly oak rather than of the holly; *decidua* refers to the autumn-shed leaves; many hollies are evergreen.

Ilex decidua ❧ a. Growth form, b. Twig with flowers, c. Flower, d. Winter twig with fruit, e. Stem

Winterberry

Ilex verticillata (L.) A. Gray

Holly family (Aquifoliaceae)

Also called black alder

Field Identification: A shrub or small, rounded tree to 25 feet.

Flowers: April-May, small, staminate (male) flowers in clusters of 2 to 10, pistillate (female) flowers in clusters of 1 to 3; some plants may be male, others female, or flowers may contain both sexes (see illustration); petals 4 to 8, greenish-white, egg-shaped or rounded, 1/4 inch across; stamens usually the same number as the petals and alternating with them.

Fruit: September-October, persistent in winter, globe-shaped, about 1/4 inch in diameter, shiny red to orange or yellow; seeds usually 3 to 6.

Leaves: Simple, alternate, thin to leathery in texture, length 1 1/2 to 4 inches, width about 1 inch, egg-shaped to broadest in the middle and tapering at both ends to lance-shaped, **tip tapering to a point**, base tapering to sometimes rounded, **margin with sharp-pointed teeth;** upper surface smooth; lower surface downy; petioles about 1/4 inch long, somewhat hairy. Leaves turning black in autumn.

Twigs: Gray to reddish-brown, smooth at first but usually roughened by warty lenticels (pores) later.

Habitat: Occurs along igneous shut-ins, rocky stream beds and sandstone bluffs of the St. Francois Mountains.

Range: From Georgia to Missouri, north to Nova Scotia, and west to Minnesota.

Wildlife Uses: The fruit is eaten by small mammals and at least 48 species of birds including bluebirds, American robin, cedar waxwing, bob-white quail and ruffed grouse.

Medicinal Uses: The fruit and bark were used as an astringent internally for diarrhea and locally in ulcerated skin lesions.

Remarks: Winterberry is the most popular of the red-fruited, deciduous hollies. There are many varieties and horticultural forms. It has been cultivated since 1736, and is used for ornamental planting in moist places. It is rather free of insects and disease.

The native winterberry found in Missouri is *Ilex verticillata* var. *padifolia* (Willd.) Torrey & Asa Gray. *Padifolia* is Greek for "leaves like Padus," in reference to *Padus*, a European genus of cherry trees.

Ilex is the ancient Latin name of the holly oak rather than of the holly; *verticillata*, meaning whorled, refers to the axillary clusters of flowers.

Ilex verticillata ❦ a. Twig with flowers, b. Flower, c. Twig with fruit

Virginia willow

Itea virginica L.

Currant family (Grossulariaceae)

Also called sweet-spire, tassel-white

Field Identification: Slender-branched shrub to 10 feet, sometimes almost reclining.

Flowers: May-June, **in terminal, somewhat drooping clusters** that are narrow, lengthened, 2 to 5 inches long; flowers fragrant, white or pink, linear or lance-shaped, about 1/6 inch long; stamens 5.

Fruit: September-October, **fruit a dry 2-celled capsule** longer than broad, about 1/4 inch long, tip pointed; seeds small.

Leaves: Simple, alternate, 1 to 3 inches long, to 1 1/3 inches wide, blade widest in the middle, tapering at the ends, tip pointed, base wedge-shaped, margin sharply toothed; rather thin; upper surface dull green, smooth; lower surface hairy to smooth, red in autumn; petioles hairy, about 1/4 inch long.

Twigs: Slender, smooth, hairy at first, smooth later, green to brown, leaves mostly borne toward the end; **pith of branches chambered.**

Trunk: Bark brown to gray, smooth or broken into small, thin scales on older stems.

Habitat: Occurs in swamps, low wet woods, and along sandy spring branches. **Restricted to the lowlands and base of Crowleys Ridge in southeastern Missouri.**

Range: Florida to Louisiana and east Texas, north to New Jersey and west to southeastern Missouri and Oklahoma.

Remarks: Virginia willow has ornamental possibilities because of the long, tassellike white flower clusters. Because individual plants are straggly in shape, group plantings would bring the best results. This is the only species occurring in North America; the other species are natives of Asia.

Itea is the Greek name for willow; *virginica* refers to the state of Virginia, where it was first described.

Itea virginica ❀ a. Reclining growth form, b. Branch with flower, c. Stalk with fruit, d. Seed capsule

Ashe's juniper

Juniperus ashei Buchholz

Cypress family (Cupressaceae)

Also called Ozark white cedar

Field Identification: Shrub to small evergreen tree rarely more than 30 feet. Usually irregular, leaning, **main branches emerging at the base**, with a fluted and twisted trunk.

Flowers: Minute, solitary staminate (male) and pistillate (female) cones at the tips of scalelike leaves on small branches.

Fruit: August-September, fleshy, berrylike cone about 1/4 inch long, bluish-green, covered with a white, waxy coating, globe-shaped; single seed, egg-shaped, tip pointed, base rounded, shiny, light to dark brown, about 1/8 inch diameter.

Leaves: Usually at the ends of the twigs, minute, scalelike, opposite in 2 to 4 ranks, flatly pressed against the small stem, egg-shaped, tip pointed, margin minutely toothed, lacking glands but resinous, aromatic. The green leaves retain their color in winter.

Twigs: Gray to reddish, scaly, aromatic, rather stiff.

Trunk: Bark gray to reddish-brown beneath, shredding into shaggy, lengthwise strips, **white blotches ringing the stems**; wood streaked reddish-brown, sapwood lighter colored, close-grained, hard, light, not strong, but rot resistent, somewhat aromatic.

Habitat: On dolomite bluffs and glades, and limestone glades on knobs along the reservoirs of the former White River and its tributaries in southwestern Missouri.

Range: Southwestern Missouri, north Arkansas, Arbuckle Mountains and bluffs of Pryor Creek in Oklahoma and in parts of Texas, especially the Edwards Plateau. Southward and westward into Mexico and Guatemala.

Wildlife Uses: The foliage is browsed occasionally by white-tailed deer. The sweet female cones are eaten by several species of birds and mammals, including the bobwhite quail, American robin, bluebird, cedar waxwing, gray fox and raccoon.

Remarks: The best example of a stand of old growth Ashe's juniper in Missouri is protected at Ozark White Cedar Natural Area, Stone County. Mostly in Texas, where it is abundant on the Edwards Plateau, the wood is used for fuel, poles, posts, crossties and small wooden-ware articles. Ashe's Juniper is occasionally cultivated as an ornamental, and is apparently resistant to the cedar-apple rust. Refer to key to distinguish Ashe's juniper from eastern red cedar, *Juniperus virginiana* L.

Juniperus is the classical name; *ashei* is in honor of William Willard Ashe (1872-1932) a pioneer forester who collected botanical specimens in Arkansas.

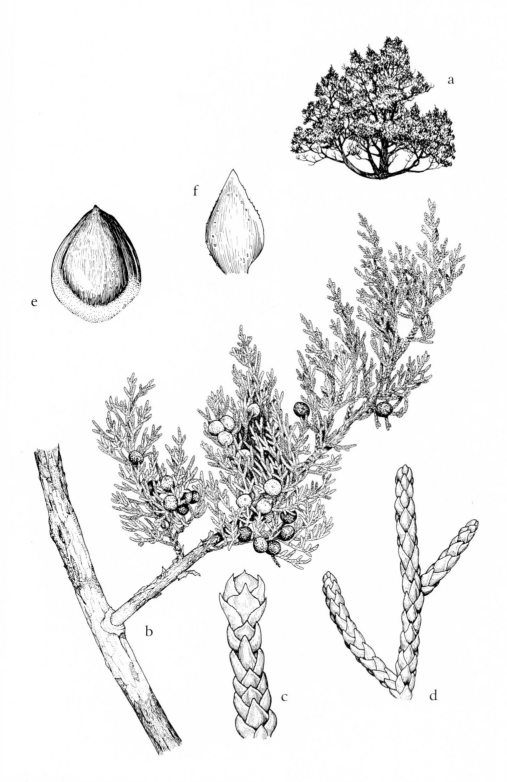

Juniperus ashei ❀ a. Growth form, b. Branch with fruit, c. Male cone at tip of small branch, d. Small female cones at tip of small branches, e. Seed, f. Scalelike leaf

Corkwood

Leitneria floridana Chapman

Corkwood family (Leitneriaceae)

Field Identification: Shrub or small tree attaining a height of 20 feet and often forming thickets by root suckers.

Flowers: March-April, sexes on separate plants, staminate (male) catkins many flowered, each catkin 1 to 2 inches long; stamens 3 to 12; pistillate (female) catkins few-flowered, shorter than the staminate; **catkins flowering before leaves emerge.**

Fruits: June-July, in clusters of 2 to 4, flattened, about 3/4 inch long, 1/4 to 1/3 inch wide, longer than broad, tip pointed to blunt, brown; seed light brown, flattened.

Leaves: Alternate, in terminal clusters, 3 to 6 inches long, 1 to 3 inches wide, longer than broad, tip pointed or rounded, base narrowed; blade hairy above when young and with densely matted hairs beneath, when mature rather leathery, dark olive to dull green; smooth or hairy above; bearing long, soft hairs beneath; petioles 1/4 to 1 1/4 inches long with long, soft hairs.

Twigs: Reddish-brown to gray, smooth, finely furrowed, lenticels (pores) numerous.

Trunk: Bark gray to brown, ridges narrow, cracks shallow; wood pale yellow, soft, close-grained and light weight.

Habitat: Occurs in wooded or open swamps and wet ditches along roadsides in the lowlands of southeastern Missouri.

Range: Florida to east Texas, north to Georgia, east Arkansas and southeastern Missouri.

Remarks: Corkwood is classified as rare in Missouri. Once more widespread in the swamps of the Bootheel, only remnant populations remain due to destruction of habitat. Corkwood Conservation Area, in Butler County, was purchased to protect the largest population of corkwood left in Missouri, along with excellent dune and swale forest.

The wood, lighter than cork and second only to balsawood, is sometimes used for fishing-net floats, bobbers and bottle stoppers.

Leitneria is in honor of the German naturalist E. F. Leitner; *floridana* refers to the early so-called "Floridian Provinces" of the southeastern states.

Leitneria floridana ❧ a. Growth form with fruit, b. Male catkins, c. Female catkins

California privet

Ligustrum ovalifolium Hassk.

Olive family (Oleaceae)

Field Identification: A vigorous shrub forming a dense thicket to a height of 15 feet.

Flowers: May-July, in crowded, stiff clusters of 2 to 8 flowers; clusters 2 to 4 inches long and wide on the tips of stems; flowers small, **tubular-shaped**, dull white, **very fragrant**; petals 4, spreading, egg-shaped, tip blunt; stamens 2, slightly exceeding the flower.

Fruit: August-September, in clusters of 2 to 6 berries on the ends of stems; berry stalk about 1/8 inch long, **fruit shiny black**, globe-shaped, about 1/4 inch long; seed brown to black, solitary.

Leaves: Opposite, simple, 2 to 2 1/2 inches long, 3/4 to 1 inch wide; oval to egg-shaped or broadest in the middle and tapering at both ends, tip blunt to slightly pointed, base wedge-shaped to rounded, margin entire; upper surface medium green, smooth; lower surface paler, smooth; petioles up to 1/8 inch long.

Twigs: Young twigs grayish- to brownish-green; older stems grayish-brown; lenticels (pores) raised.

Trunk: Gray, tight, smooth; lenticels raised.

Habitat: Planted and sometimes escaped into thickets, edges of woods and borders of limestone glades; mostly in urban areas.

Range: Native of Japan; introduced and naturalized in the United States.

Wildlife Uses: The fruit is eaten by cedar waxwing and other birds.

Remarks: This shrub is not as aggressive as autumn olive and the shrub honeysuckles, but its planting is not recommended. There are several species of privet from China and Japan available from nurseries that may escape from cultivation into unwanted areas. These exotics compete with native vegetation, altering native ecosystems that have evolved on Missouri's landscape.

Ligustrum is the ancient name; *ovalifolium* refers to its oval-shaped leaves. It is not known why the common name is California privet, since it is not native to the United States.

Ligustrum ovalifolium ❦ a. Growth form with flowers, b. Twig with flowers, c. Flower,
d. Twig with fruit

Spice bush

Lindera benzoin (L.) Blume

Laurel family (Lauraceae)

Field Identification: Stout, smooth, aromatic shrub of damp woods. Attaining a height of 18 feet, usually with several stems from the base.

Flowers: March-May, appearing before the leaves, yellow, fragrant, about 1/4 inch broad, in clusters of 3 to 6 along the stem, with staminate (male) and pistillate (female) flowers on separate plants, petals absent; stamens 9.

Fruit: September-October, solitary or in small clusters on short stalks about 1/4 inch long, circular to an inverted egg shape, about 3/8 inch long, glossy-red, fleshy, spicy; 1-seeded, seeds light brown, speckled darker brown, hard.

Leaves: Not drooping, aromatic when crushed, simple, alternate, 2 to 6 inches long, 1 to 3 inches wide, inverted egg-shaped to oval, tip pointed, base narrowing at a sharp angle, margin entire, thin; **bright green above; whitish below**; petioles about 3/4 inch long. **Twigs often with 2 leaf sizes, much smaller ones sometimes at base of larger ones.**

Twigs: Slender, smooth, brittle, greenish-brown to brown.

Trunk: Bark light brown to gray, flaking into thin strips; prominent corky lenticels (pores), cream-colored; spicy to the taste.

Habitat: Occurs in low or moist woodland and thickets along streams, in valleys, ravine bottoms, base of bluffs, along spring branches and seepage of wooded slopes.

Range: Florida to Louisiana to Central Texas, north to Maine, and west to Ontario, Michigan, Illinois, Iowa, Missouri, Kansas and Oklahoma.

Wildlife Uses: At least 24 species of birds feed upon the fruit, including the wood thrush and veery; rabbits and white-tailed deer nibble the leaves. The caterpillar of the colorful spicebush swallowtail depends upon the leaves for food.

Medicinal Uses: A tea made from the bark, twigs or fruit was used to stimulate blood circulation, increase perspiration and treat intestinal worms, dysentery, coughs and colds. In the Revolutionary War, the fruit was used as a substitute for allspice. In the South, during the Civil War, the leaves were used as a substitute for tea.

Remarks: The bright red fruits, the showy masses of staminate flowers, and the aromatic nature of the plant adds to its ornamental value. It does well in full to partial shade. Spicebush has been in cultivation since 1683. The foliage persists as dark green well into autumn, eventually turning greenish-yellow.

Lindera is for John Linder, a Swedish botanist and physician (1676-1723); *benzoin* denotes its similarity, in odor, to the true balsamic resin of *Styrax benzoin*, an Asiatic tree.

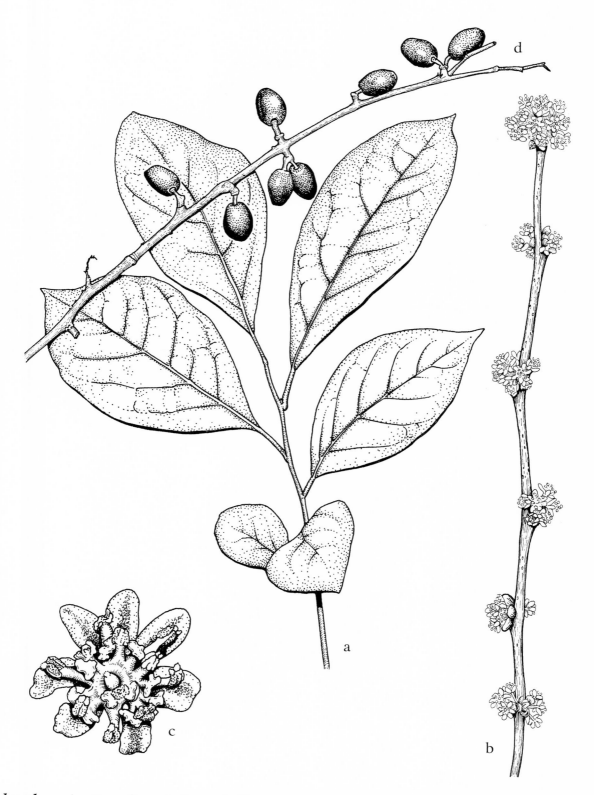

Lindera benzoin ❀ a. Growth form, b. Twig with flower clusters, c. Flower, d. Twig with fruit

Pond berry

Lindera melissaefolia (Walter) Blume

Laurel family (Lauraceae)

Field Identification: Strong-scented colonial shrub 2 to 6 feet tall, growing in low wet woods.

Flowers: Late March-early April, appearing before the leaves, yellow, fragrant, about 1/4 inch broad, in clusters of 4 to 6 along the stem, with staminate (male) and pistillate (female) flowers on separate plants, petals absent; stamens 9.

Fruit: September-October, solitary or in small clusters on stalks about 1/2 inch long, somewhat elongated to an inverted egg shape, about 1/4 to inch long, spicy; 1-seeded, light brown.

Leaves: Simple, alternate, **drooping**, aromatic when crushed, simple, alternate, 2 to 6 inches long, 3/4 to 2 1/4 inches wide, tapering at each end and broadest in the middle to oval or egg-shaped, tip pointed, base narrowing at a sharp angle, margin entire, leaf thin and more or less translucent; **both surfaces dark green**, more or less densely hairy becoming smooth later, veins prominent below; petioles stout, about 1/4 inch long, hairy.

Twigs: Slender, reddish-brown to gray, hairy at first, smooth later.

Trunk: Bark brown to dark gray, aromatic when bruised.

Habitat: Occurs in low, wet sandy woods in Ripley County.

Range: Florida to Louisiana, north to North Carolina, and in the Mississippi River lowlands of Arkansas and Missouri.

Wildlife Uses: The fruit is eaten by several species of birds, and the stems and leaves are sometimes nibbled by swamp rabbits.

Medicinal Uses: The twigs were sometimes brewed into tea and used as a spring tonic.

Remarks: Pond berry is state and federally endangered. Destruction of habitat has caused its decline. In Missouri, a forest-covered dune and swale complex was purchased by the Missouri Conservation Department and The Nature Conservancy to protect this rare landscape and to provide habitat for pond berry and other interesting lowland plants and animals. Originally discovered by Dr. Julian Steyermark, it is called Sand Ponds Natural Area and Conservation Area.

Lindera is for John Linder, a Swedish botanist and physician (1676-1723); *melissaefolia* means melissalike leaves. *Melissa* is from the Greek word meaning "bee," in reference to flowers yielding honey.

Lindera melissaefolia ❀ a. Growth form, b. Flower cluster, c. Fruit, d. Stem

Bush honeysuckle

Lonicera maackii (Rupr.) Maxim.

Honeysuckle family (Caprifoliaceae)

Also called amur honeysuckle

Field Identification: A large, upright spreading shrub reaching up to 15 feet in height.

Flowers: May-June, in clusters from the axils of leaves; flowers white changing to yellow, about 1 inch long, tubular, slender, distinctly 2-lipped; petals 2, upper lip with 4 lobes, lower lip with 1 lobe, both lobes recurved; stamens 5, extending beyond the lips.

Fruit: June-July, in clusters of 1 to 2 in axils of leaves; stalks very short or absent; berries red, about 1/4 inch across.

Leaves: Opposite, simple, 2 to 3 inches long, 1/2 to 1 1/2 inches wide, inverted egg-shaped to broadest in the middle and tapering at both ends, **tip abruptly pointed**, base broadly wedge-shaped, **margin fringed with fine hairs**, entire; upper surface dark green; lower surface paler, usually hairy only on the veins; petioles about 1/8 inch long, hairy.

Twigs: Grayish-brown, with short hairs on current year's growth; older stems gray to grayish-brown, striped, smooth.

Trunk: Bark grayish-brown, tight, with broad ridges and grooves.

Habitat: Escaped from cultivation and naturalized as an understory shrub in woodlands, especially in urban areas.

Range: Introduced from Manchuria and Korea in 1855. It is found in the eastern half of the United States in urban areas and other sites where it escapes from cultivation.

Wildlife Uses: Several species of birds eat the berries, but will pass over them if other food is available. The plants are spread from seed by bird droppings.

Remarks: Bush honeysuckle is probably the most aggressive exotic plant that has escaped and naturalized in urban areas. When driving the interstate highways and beltways around cities such as St. Louis, the understory along the wooded corridors appears as a solid layer of green from bush honeysuckle. It leafs out in April before trees and native shrubs and casts shade over spring wildflowers before they have a chance to flower, fruit, and store energy from the sun for next year. Bush honeysuckle also keeps young seedlings of native trees and shrubs from getting established. It is truly a noxious weed and should not be planted.

    Lonicera honors Adam Lonitzer (1528-1586), a German herbalist; *maackii* is named for its discoverer, Richard Maack (1825-1886), a Russian naturalist.

Escapes from cultivation

Lonicera maackii ❀ a. Growth form with flowers, b. Flowers, c. Twig with fruit

Matrimony-vine

Lycium halimifolium Miller

Nightshade family (Solanaceae)

Field Identification: Spiny or spineless shrub, growing erect or with recurved and drooping branches, sometimes trailing or vinelike, attaining a length of 3 to 10 feet. Rarely more than 3 to 5 feet when erect.

Flowers: May-September, solitary or in clusters of 2 to 4 emerging from the axils of leaves; flower stalks about 1/2 inch long; **flower greenish to purplish, bell-shaped with the tube about 1/4 inch long**; lobes 4 to 5; stamens 5.

Fruit: July-October, **berry orange-red or scarlet**, oval, about 1/4 inch long; seeds 10 to 20.

Leaves: Alternate, simple, 1/2 to 2 1/4 inches long, 1/4 to 1 inch wide; shape various from oval to egg- or lance-shaped, tip blunt or pointed, base tapering to a leaf stalk, margin smooth; upper and lower surfaces grayish-green and smooth; petioles 1/4 inch long.

Twigs: Slender, flexible, arching or recurved, somewhat angled, smooth, gray to tan, spiny or spineless; spines slender, sharp, about 1/2 inch long.

Habitat: Occurs about old dwellings, old fields, waste ground, roadsides and along railroads.

Range: A native of Europe and Asia, cultivated in the United States where it sometimes escapes. From Virginia to Missouri, Kansas and Oklahoma, north to Ontario and west to Minnesota.

Medicinal Uses: An extract of the leaves has been used as an antispasmodic for whooping cough.

Remarks: Matrimony-vine easily escapes from cultivation, becoming a nuisance, so its planting is not recommended. In Europe, the young leaves are cooked and eaten. It is reported that the young shoots and leaves, when eaten, may poison sheep and cattle.

A related species, Chinese matrimony-vine, *Lycium chinense* Miller, also escapes from cultivation and can be differentiated from *Lycium halimifolium* by its more rounded leaves, shorter flower stalks and flower lobes, which are longer than the flower tube.

Lycium refers to Lycia, an ancient country in Asia Minor; *halimifolium* is for the leaves, which resemble those of the plant *Halimus*.

Lycium halimifolium ❦ a. Growth form with flowers, b. Flower, c. Fruit

Stagger bush

Lyonia mariana (L.) D. Don

Heath family (Ericaceae)

Field Identification: Shrub 3 to 6 feet tall, with erect, mostly smooth, black-dotted branches.

Flowers: May-June, flowers clustered on the end of twigs from the previous year, cluster 1 1/4 to 4 inches long, one-sided; petals nodding, white or pink, cylinder-shaped, about 1/2 inch long, lobes 5, mostly spreading; stamens 10.

Fruit: September-October, **capsule pyramid-shaped with a flattened base**, about 1/4 inch long; seeds numerous, club-shaped.

Leaves: Simple, alternate, blade 3/4 to 3 inches long, longer than broad, widest above the middle, tip blunt to pointed, base narrowed; upper surface smooth; lower surface slightly hairy and sometimes black-dotted, margin entire, slightly curved under; petioles about 1/4 inch long.

Twigs: Erect or nearly so, when young hairy, when older smooth, sometimes black-dotted.

Habitat: Occurs in sandy pine-oak woodland. **Known only from the eastern section of the Ozarks in Dent County.**

Range: Florida to east Texas, north to Rhode Island, Connecticut, New York, New Jersey, Pennsylvania, Tennessee, Arkansas, Missouri and Oklahoma.

Remarks: Stagger bush is classified as state endangered. It has not been reported in recent years and may be eliminated from the state. The foliage is said to be poisonous to lambs and calves. The plant was introduced into cultivation about 1736.

 Lyonia honors John Lyon (died 1818), an American botanical explorer; *mariana* means "of Maryland," where it was first described.

Lyonia mariana ❧ a. Growth form with flowers, b. Seed capsules, c. Winter twig

Narrow-leaved crab apple

Malus angustifolia (Aiton) Michaux

Rose family (Rosaceae)

Also called wild crab, southern crab-apple

Field Identification: A large shrub to small tree with rigid, thorny branches forming a broad, open crown; sometimes thicket-forming.

Flowers: April-May, very fragrant, in clusters of 3 to 5 flowers; flower stalks 3/4 to 1 inch long, slender, hairy at first, smooth later; flowers about 1 inch across, white to pink; petals 5, about 1/4 inch wide, inverted egg-shaped; stamens about 40 to 60, shorter than the petals.

Fruit: August-September, a kind of fleshy fruit, applelike, small, about 3/4 to 1 inch across, often broader than long, waxy, pale yellowish-green, fragrant, flesh bitter, sour.

Leaves: Simple, alternate, 1 to 3 inches long, 1/2 to 2 inches wide, **narrow, broadest in the middle and tapering at both ends to lance-shaped**, tip pointed to rounded, base wedge-shaped, margin with rounded teeth; late in the season's growth, tips of twigs with leaves round to inverted egg-shaped and with lobes as well as sharp teeth on the margins; blade firm and leathery; dull green above; lower surface hairy when young, smooth later, main vein sometimes remaining hairy; petioles slender, about 3/4 to 1 inch long, green to reddish, hairy at first, smooth later.

Twigs: Stout, light brown to reddish-brown, hairy at first, smooth later; lenticels (pores) scattered, orange-colored; spurs (short, thick, slow-growing, reduced branches) present.

Trunk: Bark dark reddish-brown to gray, with deep grooves, ridges narrow, separating into small, platelike scales; wood with yellow sapwood and reddish-brown heartwood, close-grained, hard, heavy.

Habitat: Occurs in sandy soil in upland or lowland woods and thickets on Sikeston Ridge and Crowleys Ridge in southeastern Missouri.

Range: Florida to Louisiana, Arkansas, Oklahoma, Missouri, Kentucky and north to New Jersey.

Wildlife Uses: The fruit is eaten by many species of birds and mammals including the bobwhite quail, blue jay, cardinal, ruffed grouse, skunk, opossum, raccoon, cottontail rabbit, and red and gray fox.

Remarks: The narrow-leaved crab apple is classified as state endangered. Before the destruction of much of its habitat in the Bootheel, this plant — like so many others — probably was more common.

The wood, because of its fine grain and hardness, has been used for levers, tools and small woodenware objects. The bitter, sour fruit is made into preserves and cider.

Malus is the classical Latin name of the apple; *angustifolia* is Latin ("angust" for narrow and "folia" for leaf) and refers to the narrow leaves. Some authors place this species in the genus *Pyrus*.

Malus angustifolia ❀ a. Growth form with flowers, b. Flower, c. Fruit

Sweet crab apple

Malus coronaria (L.) Miller

Rose family (Rosaceae)

Also called wild crab

Field Identification: A large shrub to small bushy tree to 26 feet, stiffly-branched with a broadly rounded crown.

Flowers: April-May, fragrant, produced in clusters of 2 to 5 flowers; flower stalks smooth, slender, about 1 inch long; flowers pink at first, maturing to white, about 1 inch across; petals 5, egg-shaped; **green cup-shaped receptacle at the base of the petals smooth**; stamens numerous.

Fruit: August-September, a fleshy fruit, apple-like, small, about 1 to 1 1/4 inches long, rounded to globe-shaped, yellowish-green when mature, with a waxy coating, flesh firm, bitter.

Leaves: Simple, alternate, 1 1/4 to 3 inches long, 1/2 to 1 1/2 inches wide, egg-shaped to sometimes triangular-shaped, tip pointed, base rounded to heart-shaped, margin occasionally with shallow lobes, coarsely toothed; upper surface bright green, hairy when young; **lower surface paler, hairy when young, smooth later**; petioles stout, 1 1/2 to 2 inches long.

Twigs: Slender, spreading, often with angles in cross section, reddish brown to light brown, smooth; twigs often with numerous short lateral shoots or spurs, some of the spurs ending in a thorn.

Trunk: Bark about 1/4 inch thick, reddish-brown, with lengthwise furrows and ridges that separate in long scales; wood heavy, close-grained, not strong, light red, with a yellow sapwood.

Habitat: Occurs in low open or upland woods, thickets along streams and prairie openings.

Range: North Carolina, Georgia, Tennessee and Missouri, north to New York, Ontario, and west to Wisconsin and Illinois.

Wildlife Uses: The fruit is of considerable value as wildlife food, eaten by at least 25 species of birds and mammals, including bobwhite quail, ruffed grouse, gray and red fox, skunk, opossum, raccoon, cottontail rabbit, woodchuck, fox squirrel and white-tailed deer. Songbirds use the dense thickets for cover.

Remarks: The sweet crab apple is slow-growing and short-lived. The fragrant, attractive flowers, dense form and spicy odor makes this plant a popular ornamental for cultivation. The wood has been used for levers, tool handles, and many small domestic articles. The fruits are used to make cider and tart jelly or marmalade.

Malus is the classical Latin name of the apple; *coronaria* means suitable for a wreath, probably referring to its showy clusters of flowers. Some authors place this species in the genus *Pyrus*.

Malus coronaria ❀ a. Twig with flowers and thorns, b. Twig with fruit

Prairie crab apple

Malus ioensis (Alph. Wood) Britton

Rose family (Rosaceae)

Also called wild crab

Field Identification: A large shrub to small tree to 20 feet tall with low, crooked branches and thicket forming from sucker shoots.

Flowers: April-May, fragrant, in clusters of 2 to 5 flowers; flowers stalks very hairy, 1 to 1 1/2 inches long; petals 5, white or pink, about 1/2 inch wide, inverted egg-shaped, base narrowed, margin wavy; **green cup-shaped receptacle at the base of the petals densely hairy on the outside**; stamens numerous.

Fruit: August-September, a kind of fleshy fruit, applelike, small, about 3/4 to 1 1/4 inches long, 3/4 to 1 1/2 inches wide, globe-shaped, greenish to yellow, sometimes with minute, yellow dots, surface waxy and greasy to the touch; pulp bitter, sour.

Leaves: Simple, alternate, 1 1/2 to 5 inches long, 3/4 to 4 inches wide, variable depending if shoot is weak or vigorous; egg-shaped to widest in the middle and tapering at both ends, tip pointed to blunt, base wedge-shaped to rounded, margin with shallow lobes, toothed; upper surface dark green, shiny, smooth; **lower surface pale with white, densely matted hairs**; petiole slender with white, densely matted hairs early, almost smooth later.

Twigs: Reddish-brown to gray, with densely matted hairs early, less so later; lenticels (pores) small and pale; twigs often with numerous short lateral shoots or spurs, some of the spurs ending in a thorn.

Trunk: Bark thin, reddish-brown to gray, grooves shallow, scales narrow and persistent; wood hard, heavy, reddish-brown, with a yellowish sapwood.

Habitat: Occurs in prairies, open woods, thickets, along streams, borders of woods and pastures.

Range: Alabama to Louisiana, Texas, Arkansas and Oklahoma, north to Wisconsin, Minnesota and South Dakota.

Wildlife Uses: The fruit is of considerable value as wildlife food, eaten by at least 20 species of birds and mammals, including bobwhite quail, ruffed grouse, gray and red fox, skunk, opossum, raccoon, cottontail rabbit, woodchuck, fox squirrel and white-tailed deer. Songbirds use the dense thickets for cover.

Remarks: The prairie crab apple is an attractive plant, occasionally cultivated for ornamental use since 1885. A variety called Bechtels crab apple, a double-flowering form, is often planted in parks and gardens. The hard, bitter fruit is used for making jellies, cider and vinegar.

Malus is the classical Latin name for apple; *ioensis* refers to the state of Iowa where it was first described. Some authors place this species in the genus *Pyrus*.

Malus ioensis 🦋 a. Growth form, b. Twig with flowers, c. Fruit

Snow wreath

Neviusia alabamensis A. Gray

Rose family (Rosaceae)

Also called Alabama snow wreath

Field Identification: A small shrub 3 to 6 feet tall, characterized by arching branches, short lateral branches and stems sprouting by way of root suckers.

Flowers: April, in clusters of 1 to 4 flowers appearing with expanding leaves on current year's twigs, flowers white, about 1 inch across, **petals lacking**, calyx with 5 to 7 lobes, each about 1/2 inch long, green, leaflike, deeply toothed above the middle, persisting; **stamens white, usually more than 100**.

Fruit: September, with 2 to 4, small, hard, 1-seeded fruits.

Leaves: Simple, alternate, 3/4 to 2 1/2 inches long, 1/2 to 1 3/4 inches wide, broadest in the middle and tapering at both ends to egg-shaped, tip pointed, base somewhat rounded to heart-shaped, **margin sharply doubly toothed**; upper surface slightly hairy, **lower surface with gland-tipped hairs**; petioles about 1 inch long.

Twigs: Light brown to grayish-brown; slightly hairy at first, smooth later.

Trunk: Bark gray to grayish-brown, tight, lenticels (pores) raised and prominent.

Habitat: Occurs along wooded slopes below bluffs or ridges on talus or rocky soils; however, in Missouri, it was reported to be growing in sandy loam in Butler County.

Range: From Georgia, Alabama, Mississippi, Arkansas and southeastern Missouri. Rare throughout its range, with only a few sites known from each state. **Last reported in Missouri in 1918, eight miles west of Poplar Bluff.**

Wildlife Uses: The flowers provide a nectar source for butterflies and bees.

Remarks: Snow wreath is one of the rarest shrubs throughout its range in the eastern United States. It is being considered for federal listing as an endangered or threatened species. In Missouri its status is extirpated, which means that it formerly occurred as a regularly reproducing species in the state, but no current populations are known.

This shrub, with its white flowers and arching branches, would make an attractive ornamental. It can grow in rich loamy, well-drained soil in shaded or woodland situations. The foliage remains green well into late November, long after other shrubs and trees have turned their autumnal colors.

Neviusia is named in honor of one of the original collectors, Rev. Reuben Denton Nevius (1827-1913); *alabamensis* refers to the state in which it was first described.

Neviusia alabamensis ❧ a. Growth form with flowers, b. Flower, c. Fruit cluster

Hop hornbeam

Ostrya virginiana (Miller) K. Koch

Birch family (Betulaceae)

Also called ironwood

Field Identification: A small tree to 24 feet with wide, spreading branches.

Flowers: April-May, before the leaves; staminate (male) and pistillate (female) flowers in clusters (catkins) on previous year's growth on the same plant; staminate catkins 1 to 3 at ends of branches, 1 1/2 to 3 inches long; catkin scales triangular, hairy, reddish-brown, drooping; stamens 3 to 14, attached beneath the scale; pistillate catkins small, single, slender, about 1/4 inch long; scales lance-shaped, hairy, red.

Fruit: June-July, **in conelike clusters resembling hops**, 1 1/2 to 2 inches long; stalk hairy, about 1 inch long; each papery sac about 3/4 inch long and wide, hairy; nuts enclosed in the sac, small, egg-shaped, brown, shiny, faintly ribbed, about 1/4 inch long.

Leaves: Alternate, simple, blades 2 1/2 to 4 1/2 inches long, 1 1/2 to 2 1/2 inches wide, egg-shaped, broadly lance-shaped, tip pointed, base rounded to heart-shaped, often unequal; margin sharply and densely toothed; upper surface yellowish green to dark green, dull, smooth; **lower surface paler, hairy with veins and vein axils hairiest**; leaf blade usually with 9 to 15 veins on each side of central vein; leaves turning yellow in autumn; petioles about 1/4 inch long, hairy.

Twigs: Usually slightly zigzag, hairy toward the tip, reddish-brown to dark brown, lenticels (pores) small, not obvious.

Trunk: Bark thin, **reddish-gray, with narrow, platelike, tight scales**; some trees with loose, shreddy scales; wood light to reddish brown, heavy, tough, hard, strong, close-grained, durable; sapwood wide, white.

Habitat: Occurs in fairly dry soil on rocky slopes, along bluffs, in upland woods, and rarely along streams.

Range: Florida, Tennessee, Louisiana, Arkansas, Texas and northern Mexico, north to Nova Scotia, and east to Manitoba and North Dakota.

Wildlife Uses: The fruit is eaten by at least five species of birds, including bobwhite quail and wild turkey. The catkins and buds rank as the most important ruffed grouse food by volume consumed during late autumn, winter and early spring.

Medicinal Uses: The bark has been used both as a laxative and as a tonic. In colonial times, a fluid extract was used to treat malaria. Both bark and inner bark have been used to treat indigestion and fever.

Remarks: The wood of hop hornbeam ranks among the hardest and strongest of woods; harder than oak, hickory, locust, osage orange and persimmon, surpassed only by flowering dogwood. Because of its size, its use is limited to tool and ax handles, mallets and fence posts. The small tree is slow-growing, but has possibilities as an ornamental; it has been cultivated since 1690.

Ostrya is the ancient Greek name; *virginiana* refers to the state of Virginia where it probably was first described.

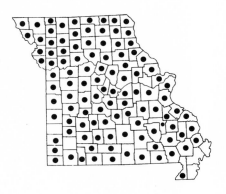

Ostrya virginiana ❀ a. Growth form with fruit, b. Male catkins, c. Female catkins, d. Male catkins in winter, e. Seed, f. Stem with bark

Mock orange

Philadelphus pubescens Lois.

Hydrangea family (Hydrangeaceae)

Field Identification: Vigorous shrub 3 to 15 feet tall, with close gray bark.

Flowers: Late April-May, in **conspicuous clusters of 5 to 9 flowers**, 1 to 1 1/2 inches across; petals 4, white, inverted egg-shaped to oval; stamens numerous.

Fruit: September-October, capsule inverted egg-shaped, splitting at the top; seeds numerous.

Leaves: Simple, opposite, 2 to 3 1/4 inches long, about 1 inch wide, egg-shaped to narrowing at both ends and widest in the middle, tip pointed, base rounded to wedge-shaped, margin entire or sharply and remotely toothed, sometimes with short pointed lobes, **leaf blade with 1 or 2 pairs of side veins originating near the base and curving sharply toward the leaf tip and not toward the immediate margin**; upper surface dark green, smooth; lower surface pale with gray hairs; petioles about 1/2 inch long, hairy.

Twigs: Young ones green to yellowish- or reddish-brown, angled, later gray and smooth the first season.

Trunk: Bark gray, shedding into thin, narrow strips.

Habitat: Occurs on north-facing, steep, wooded limestone bluffs, known in Missouri only from McDonald County.

Range: Alabama, Tennessee, Illinois and Missouri, south to Arkansas and Oklahoma.

Wildlife Uses: The numerous flowers are a good nectar source for bees.

Remarks: Mock orange is classified as state endangered. One population is **found in Missouri near Southwest City**. It is more common in Arkansas and is probably on the edge of its range, just across the state line in Missouri.

It was introduced into cultivation in 1800, and is the most commonly grown of the mock orange species. The leaves turn greenish-yellow in autumn.

Another mock orange, *Philadelphus coronarius*, from southeastern Europe, can be found around old homesites. It has brown bark the first season of growth, which separates into flakes or strips the second year. The native mock orange has gray bark the first season of growth which does not flake or strip the second year.

Philadelphus is in honor of Ptolemy Philadelphus (283-247 B.C.), king of Egypt; *pubescens* is for the short hairs on the foliage.

Philadelphus pubescens ❧ a. Growth form with flowers, b. Seed capsule

Mistletoe

Phoradendron flavescens (Pursh) Nutt.

Mistletoe family (Loranthaceae)

Field Identification: Small shrub to 2 feet, **semiparasitic on branches of deciduous trees.**

Flowers: March-August, in axils of leaves, flowers in spikes 3/8 to 2 inches long, solitary or 2 to 3 together, spikes shorter than the leaves, joints along the spike usually about 4, some joints 6-flowered in pistillate (female) clusters, others 12-flowered when staminate (male), flowers green, petals lacking; stamens 3.

Fruit: September-January, berry without stalk, white or creamy, translucent, globe-shaped and flattened at the base, sticky when crushed, about 1/4 inch long, fleshy, 1-seeded.

Leaves: Opposite, simple, 1 to 2 inches long, to 3/4 inch wide, longer than broad or inverted egg-shaped, flattened, margin entire, apex rounded, base tapering; both surfaces dark green to yellowish-green, smooth, leathery, 3- to 5-nerved; petioles about 1/4 inch long.

Twigs: Yellowish-green to dark green, stout, thick, brittle at base, at first minutely hairy, and then becoming smooth.

Trunk: Bark green with irregular, very shallow fissures, the inner bark brownish; wood soft, white.

Habitat: Occurs in low woods in valleys and along streams in southern Missouri where it is commonly found on sycamore trees. In the lowlands of the Bootheel it can be found on host trees of black gum and river birch.

Range: Florida to Louisiana, Texas and New Mexico, north to New Jersey, Pennsylvania, Ohio, Indiana, Illinois, Missouri, Kansas and Oklahoma.

Wildlife Uses: The berries are eaten by several species of birds that distribute the seeds as they wipe their sticky beaks on branches, or leave droppings on the limbs of future host trees.

Medicinal Uses: The berries are considered poisonous if eaten by humans.

Remarks: The plant is much used for Christmas decorations.
    Phoradendron is from the Greek and means "tree-thief," from its parasitic habit; *flavescens* refers to the yellowish stem and leaves.

Phoradendron flavescens ❀ a. Growth form with fruit clusters on sycamore branch, b. Male flowers, c. Female flower

Ninebark

Physocarpus opulifolius (L.) Maxim.

Rose family (Rosaceae)

Field Identification: Shrub 3 to 10 feet, with wide-spreading, graceful, recurved branches, and bark peeling off in conspicuous thin strips.

Flowers: May-June, **clusters many-flowered at the tips of twigs**, 1 to 2 inches broad; individual flowers about 1/4 inch wide, white, petals 5, rounded; **stamens numerous (30 to 40).**

Fruit: September-October, dried fruit in drooping clusters, each fruit 1/4 to 1/2 inch long, egg-shaped, inflated, papery, smooth, shiny, reddish, splitting along two sides; seeds 2 to 4, rounded, shiny, yellowish to pale brown.

Leaves: Simple, alternate, 2 to 4 inches long, 2 to 3 inches wide, egg-shaped to circular, often 3 to 5 lobed, tip pointed, base broadly narrowing to flat or heart-shaped, margin with teeth pointed to rounded; upper surface dark green, smooth; mostly smooth beneath; petioles 1/2 to 1 inch long.

Twigs: Brown to yellowish, smooth, flexible, **bark peeling off in thin strips**.

Trunk: Bark brown, peeling into long thin strips; on larger trunks, light red-brown and peeling into long, papery sheets, exposing the reddish or pale brown inner bark and giving a shaggy appearance; wood soft, pale brown.

Habitat: Occurs on gravel bars, rocky banks and bluffs along streams and moist thickets.

Range: Georgia to Arkansas and Oklahoma, north to New York and Quebec, west to Minnesota and Colorado.

Wildlife Uses: The flowers are a good nectar source for bees and butterflies. Ninebark has particularly good flowers for beetles, since the flat-topped arrangement provides a large landing platform for these generally clumsy fliers, and its pollen is very accessible to their chewing mouthparts. The seeds are eaten by several bird species.

Remarks: The shrub is a good ornamental plant through the season, first with its emerging leaves, then its blooms and insects, then its ripening reddish fruits, and finally, in winter, its interesting shredding bark.

Physocarpus is from the Greek words *physa* ("bladder") and *karpos* ("fruit"), referring to the inflated capsules; *opulifolius* means "having leaves of Opulus," referring to *Viburnum opulus*, the Guelder rose, an introduced species from Europe. The common name ninebark is believed to have been acquired when the plants were known for the number of medicinal cures they could produce. Another explanation for the name comes from how many strips of bark can be removed from the trunk.

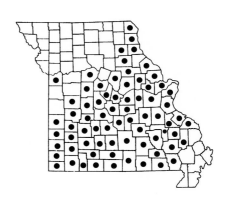

Physocarpus opulifolius ❧ a. Growth form with flowers, b. Flowers, c. Seed capsules

Water elm

Planera aquatica (Walter) J. Gmelin

Elm family (Ulmaceae)

Also called planer tree

Field Identification: A large shrub or small tree to 40 feet, growing in swampy ground.

Flowers: March-April, in separate clusters of staminate (male) and pistillate (female) flowers on last year's twigs; staminate flowers in clusters of 2 to 5; **petals lacking; calyx 4 to 5 lobed, bell-shaped**, greenish-yellow, lobes egg-shaped, tips blunt; stamens 4 to 5, extending beyond the flower; pistillate flowers 1 to 3, greenish-yellow, on short stalks.

Fruit: August-September, about 3/8 inch long, **covered with an irregular warty surface**, leathery, egg-shaped, flattened, ridged, on a short stalk; seed egg-shaped, shiny black.

Leaves: Alternate, simple, **similar to elm leaves, which are lopsided (asymmetrical), with one-half of the blade longer or broader than the other half**; blades 2 to 4 inches long, 1/2 to 1 inch wide, egg- to lance-shaped, tip pointed, **base uneven**, heart-shaped or flattened, margin toothed; upper surface dark green, paler beneath; petioles about 1/4 inch long, stout, hairy.

Twigs: Slender, reddish.

Trunk: Bark on young trunk thin, smooth, light reddish-brown or gray; when older gray, dividing into large shreddy scales, inner bark reddish.

Habitat: Occurs in swamps and low, wet bottomland forests in southeastern Missouri's Bootheel. Base of trunk frequently inundated during wet seasons.

Range: Florida, Louisiana, Texas, Arkansas and Oklahoma, north to North Carolina, and west to Kentucky, Illinois and Missouri.

Wildlife Uses: The peculiar little warty fruit is considered to be an important food for waterfowl, especially mallards and wood ducks. Squirrels also eat the fruit.

Remarks: Water elm is a small understory tree often found in swamps in association with bald-cypress *(Taxodium distichum)*, water tupelo *(Nyssa aquatica)*, pin oak *(Quercus palustris)*, Nuttall's oak *(Quercus texana* formerly *Q. nuttallii)*, pumpkin ash *(Fraxinus tomentosa)*, and water locust *(Gleditsia aquatica)*.

   Planera is in honor of the German botanist Johann Jakob Planer (1743-1789), a professor at the University of Erfurt in Germany; *aquatica* refers to the swampy habitat in which the small tree occurs.

Planera aquatica ❀ a. Growth form, b. Branch with flower, c. Male flower, d. Female flower, e. Fruit

Jointweed

Polygonella americana (Fischer & C. Meyer) Small

Smartweed family (Polygonaceae)

Field Identification: A somewhat branched, half-evergreen, stout perennial to 4 feet.

Flowers: July-October, in clusters 1 to 3 inches long, flowers white or pink, petallike segments 5, the three inner are rounded, the two outer are pointed; stamens 8.

Fruit: September-November, small, dry, hard, rounded or narrowing at both ends and broadest in the middle, 3-angled, about 1/8 inch long, chestnut brown, smooth, shiny; 1-seeded.

Leaves: Numerous, alternate, **needlelike**, often in clusters, persistent, fleshy, 1/4 to 1 1/2 inches long, long and narrow to broadest at the tip, tip blunt, leaves gray-green; petioles absent.

Twigs: Bark light to dark brown, erect and sometimes zigzag, jointed, ridged and scaly. Lower portion of stem considered woody.

Habitat: Occurs in **dry sandy soil, mainly on Crowleys Ridge** in the southeastern portion of the state known as the Bootheel.

Range: Georgia to Texas and New Mexico, north to South Carolina, and westward to southeast Missouri, east Arkansas and Oklahoma.

Wildlife Uses: The flowers are a good nectar source for bees.

Remarks: The wiry, needlelike appearance of this small shrub is similar to heather or juniper. This plant, with its attractive pinkish bloom, would do well in a rock garden if provided with sandy, well-drained soil. An early colonizer of disturbed sands, jointweed occurs in abandoned sand pits, natural "blowouts" (erosional features) and along roadsides in areas where loose sands occur.

Polygonella is a diminutive of *polygonum*, a Greek word meaning "many-knees," and referring to the swollen joints of some species; *americana* refers to the country in which it was discovered.

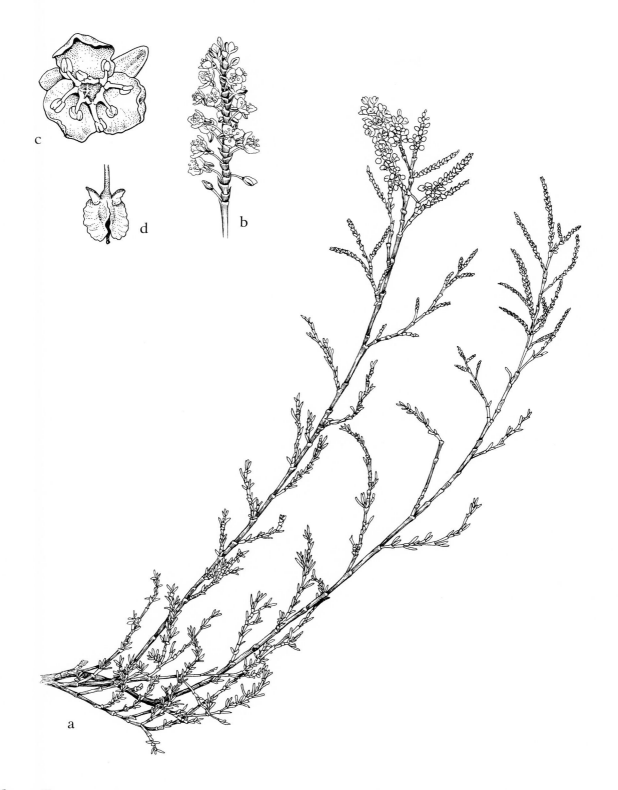

Polygonella americana ❦ a. Growth form with flowers, b. Flower cluster, c. Flower, d. Fruit

Wild plum

Prunus americana Marshall

Rose family (Rosaceae)

Also called American plum

Field Identification: Shrub propagates by root sprouts to form thickets or a small tree to 20 feet with spreading, more or less hanging, branches.

Flowers: April-May, in clusters of 2 to 5, stalks 1/4 to 3/4 inch long, smooth; flowers 3/4 to 1 1/4 inches broad, white, fragrant; petals 5, inverted egg-shaped and narrow, tip rounded; stamens about 20.

Fruit: July-September, variable in size, usually 3/4 to 1 inch long, globe-shaped, **red or sometimes yellow, conspicuously marked with pale dots**; skin tough; flesh yellow and juicy, varying in flavor; stone oval, rounded at the tip, grooved on one side.

Leaves: Simple, alternate, 2 1/2 to 4 inches long, 1 1/2 to 2 inches wide, egg-shaped to broadest in the middle and narrowing at both ends, tip pointed, base rounded or wedge-shaped, margin sharply toothed, blade thick, firm; dark green, smooth above; paler and net-veined beneath; **petioles smooth** 1/2 to 3/4 inch long, slender, sometimes with glands at the tip where it meets the leaf blade.

Twigs: Slender, **smooth**, green to orange to reddish-brown; lateral branches spurlike, or sometimes thorny; lenticels (pores) circular, raised, minute.

Trunk: Bark dark brown to reddish, breaking into thin, long, scaly plates, lenticels (pores) horizontal and prominent; wood dark brown, with lighter colored sapwood, close-grained, strong, hard.

Habitat: Occurs in woodlands, pastures and thickets throughout Missouri.

Range: Florida to Arizona and New Mexico, north to Massachusetts, New York, Ontario, Michigan, Wisconsin, Minnesota, Manitoba, Wyoming and Utah.

Wildlife Uses: The fruit is eaten by many species of birds, including bobwhite quail. White-tailed deer, raccoons and squirrels also eat the fruits.

Remarks: There are many horticultural forms and hybrids of this popular shrub; one source lists 76 hybrids. The fruit makes excellent jellies and preserves, or may be eaten raw or cooked. It is rated as the best fruit plum in the Midwest and North regions.

Wild plum is one of the first shrubs to bloom in woodlands. Its showy white flowers appear before the leaves have unfolded and while the woods are mostly bare of foliage.

Prunus is the classical name for a European plum; *americana* refers to the country in which it was discovered.

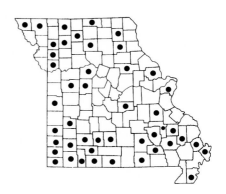

Prunus americana ❧ a. Growth form, b. Branch with flowers, c. Flower, d. Fruit

Chickasaw plum

Prunus angustifolia Marshall

Rose family (Rosaceae)

Field Identification: A twiggy shrub forming dense thickets, or a short-trunked, irregularly branched small tree to 25 feet.

Flowers: March-April, in 2- to 4-flowered clusters along the stem before the leaves emerge, flower stalks smooth, 1/4 to 1/2 inch long; petals 5, about 1/4 inch across, white, inverted egg-shaped, tip rounded; stamens usually 15 to 20.

Fruit: June-July, globe-shaped, 1/2 to 3/4 inch in diameter, **red or yellow with yellow dots**, shiny, skin thin with juicy, edible pulp; stone (hard seed casing) egg-shaped to longer than broad, about 1/2 inch long.

Leaves: Simple, alternate, 3/4 to 2 inches long, 1/4 to 3/4 inch wide, mostly lance-shaped, tip pointed, **base rounded to wedge-shaped and folded, margin sharply toothed and bearing a gland between the two teeth**; upper surface bright yellowish-green, smooth, shiny; lower surface paler, smooth; **blade usually slightly folded lengthwise and the tip curled down**; petioles slender, smooth to slightly hairy, 1/4 to 1/2 inch long, sometimes reddish, often with two red glands near the base of leaf.

Twigs: Reddish-brown, shiny, hairy at first but smooth later, slender, zigzag, often with thorn-like spurs; lenticels (pores) horizontal and prominent.

Trunk: Bark reddish-brown to dark gray, scales thin and flattened; lenticels horizontal and prominent; wood reddish-brown, sapwood lighter, rather soft, not strong, fairly heavy.

Habitat: Occurs in thickets, pastures, fields, along fence rows, roadsides and prairie streams.

Range: From Florida to Texas, north to Kansas, Missouri, Indiana, West Virginia and New Jersey.

Wildlife Uses: Dense thickets of this shrub provide excellent cover for small birds and also produce a quantity of fruit for a variety of birds and mammals. Rodents often open the hard stones by gnawing and then eating the kernel inside.

Remarks: The Chickasaw plum is sometimes used in shelter-belt plantings. There have been several ornamental varieties developed including big chickasaw, transparent, Emerson, Coletta, Clark, and Caddo Chief plum. The Comanche Indians ate the fresh fruits or they pitted and dried them for winter use. Early European settlers in the prairie region of western Missouri and Kansas made extensive use of the Chickasaw plum. They gathered the fruit by the bushel and wagonload, and used it for sauces, pies, puddings, jellies and preserves.

Prunus is the classical name for a European plum; *angustifolia* refers to the narrow leaves.

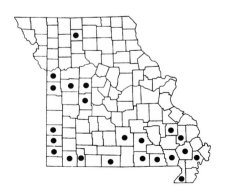

Prunus angustifolia ❧ a. Growth form with fruit, b. Stem with flowers, c. Gland-tipped leaf margin

Wild goose plum

Prunus hortulana Bailey

Rose family (Rosaceae)

Also called Hortulan plum

Field Identification: Many-stemmed shrub or small tree to 30 feet, with a broad, round-topped crown.

Flowers: March-May, in clusters of 2 to 3 flowers on slender, smooth to slightly hairy stalks about 1/2 inch long, flowers white, 3/4 to 1 inch across; petals 5, oval to broad in the middle and narrowing at both ends, tip rounded; stamens numerous.

Fruit: July-October, globe-shaped, 3/4 to 1 inch long, red or yellow-red, white-dotted, shiny, thin-skinned; stone net-veined, about 3/4 inch long, tip round or short-pointed, grooved on one edge.

Leaves: Simple, alternate, blades 4 to 6 inches long, 1 to 1 1/2 inches wide, egg-shaped to somewhat lance-shaped, tip pointed, base heart-shaped or rounded, **margin finely toothed with a gland arising from the very tip of each tooth, teeth conspicuous, spreading away from the margin**; upper surface smooth, dark green, shiny; lower surface paler, smooth or slightly hairy; petioles slender, 1 to 1 1/2 inches long, orange to reddish-colored, grooved, usually two glands just below the base of leaf.

Twigs: Dark reddish-brown, stout, rigid, smooth or hairy, occasionally with thorns.

Trunk: Bark dark or light brown, separating into large, thin plates; wood reddish-brown, hard, heavy, with a wide, white sapwood.

Habitat: Occurs in open woodlands, borders of woods, along streams and thickets. Scattered in Missouri.

Range: From Alabama, Texas, Arkansas, Oklahoma, north to Kentucky, Iowa and Kansas.

Wildlife Uses: The fruit is eaten by many species of birds, including bobwhite quail. White-tailed deer, raccoons, opossum, fox, squirrels and other mammals also eat the fruit.

Remarks: Wild goose plum is considered by some to be the most beautiful American plum. It is known mostly in horticultural forms, being rather rare in a wild state. About 34 forms are known, including Miner Hortulan plum and Missouri Hortuland plum.

In Missouri, wild goose plum is often a small tree and rarely forms thickets. When thickets are present they are created from seedlings, since this plum does not form sucker sprouts from the roots. The fruit is hard and firm until fully ripe, then becomes soft, juicy and edible. It may be eaten raw or cooked in pies or made into jams or jellies.

Prunus is the classical name for a European plum; *hortulana* means "of gardens" and refers to its value in horticulture.

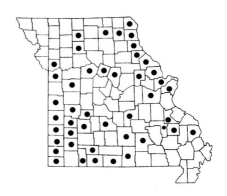

Prunus hortulana ✿ a. Growth form, b. Twig with flower clusters, c. Flower, d. Fruit, e. Gland-tipped leaf margin

Perfumed cherry

Prunus mahaleb L.

Rose family (Rosaceae)

Also called Mahaleb cherry

Field Identification: A large shrub to small tree up to 26 feet, with low branches, often forming small thickets around the parent plant.

Flowers: April-May, fragrant, opening with the leaves on short lateral branches of the current year's growth; clusters with 4 to 10 flowers; flowers white, about 3/4 inch across; petals 5, oval to inverted egg-shaped, about 3/8 inch long, narrowed to the base, tip rounded; stamens 20, extending beyond the flower.

Fruit: July, about 3/8 inch long, about 1/4 inch across, globe- to egg-shaped, dark reddish-purple, flesh thin, bitter; stone egg-shaped, slightly flattened, pinkish, smooth, tip pointed, a ridge on one side, a groove on the other.

Leaves: Alternate, simple, 1 to 3 inches long, 3/4 to 1 inch wide, **egg-shaped to broadly heart-shaped or circular, tip abruptly pointed to blunt**, base rounded or slightly heart-shaped, margin with rounded teeth; **upper surface dark green, shiny, smooth;** lower surface paler, with a few hairs on the central vein; petioles 1/4 to 3/4 inch long, hairy at first, smooth later, flattened or grooved on the upper side, with 1 to 2 greenish or red glands at the upper summit.

Twigs: Reddish- to grayish-brown, hairy at first, smooth later, covered with a white, waxy coating; lenticels (pores) prominent.

Trunk: Bark on young trees not fissured, grayish-brown, with large crosswise lenticels; on old trees, dark gray and scaly; wood aromatic, hard, light, reddish-brown, with a light sapwood.

Habitat: Escapes from cultivation and forms thickets along roadsides, fence rows, and into wooded areas and borders of limestone glades.

Range: Native of Europe; introduced and naturalized in North America from Delaware to Indiana, Missouri, Arkansas and Kansas, north to New England and west to Ontario. Also cultivated in the Pacific Northwest.

Wildlife Uses: Several species of birds readily eat the bitter fruits.

Remarks: Perfumed cherry has the potential to become aggressive; it has been found invading at least one natural area and other sites where it is unwelcomed. Its planting is discouraged.

Because of its hardiness, perfumed cherry has been used as a root base for grafting other cherries. It is used for making cabinets, smoking pipes and walking sticks. Oil from the seeds has been used in making perfume and by the Arabs as a remedy for bladder disorders. The fruit yields a violet dye and also a fermented liquor which is used in Eurasia.

Prunus is the ancient Latin name of a European plum; *mahaleb* is a Persian name.

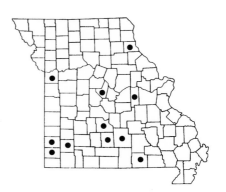

Prunus mahaleb ✻ a. Growth form with flower clusters, b. Flower, c. Twig with fruit

Big tree plum

Prunus mexicana S. Watson

Rose family (Rosaceae)

Also called wild plum, Mexican plum

Field Identification: Shrub or small tree to 25 feet, with an irregular open crown.

Flowers: April-May, in clusters of 2 to 4 flowers on slender, smooth stalks; flowers white, 3/4 to 1 inch in diameter; petals 5, inverted egg-shaped, tip rounded, hairy; stamens 15 to 20.

Fruit: July-September, globe-shaped, **eventually turning grayish-blue or grayish-lavender with a whitish coating,** 1 1/4 to 1 1/2 inches across; flesh thick, juicy with a tendency to stick to the stone; stone oval to egg-shaped, one edge grooved, the other ridged.

Leaves: Simple, alternate, thickish, blades 1 3/4 to 3 1/2 inches long, 1 to 2 inches wide, egg-shaped to broad in the middle and tapering at both ends, tip pointed, base heart-shaped or rounded, margin toothed; upper surface yellowish-green, smooth, shiny; **lower surface hairy,** especially on the veins; prominently net-veined both above and below; **petioles stout, hairy,** about 3/4 inch long, with glands near the base of leaf.

Twigs: Slender, stiff, smooth or pubescent early, shiny, grayish-brown.

Trunk: Bark gray to black, separating into plate-like scales when young, when older rough and deeply furrowed; upper branches tight and with large lenticels (pores); wood hard, heavy, brown, with a narrow, light sapwood.

Habitat: Occurs in rocky or open woodlands and thickets throughout Missouri.

Range: Alabama to Texas and northeastern Mexico, north to Kentucky, Missouri, Arkansas, Kansas and Nebraska.

Wildlife Uses: The fruit is eaten by many species of birds, including wild turkey and bob-white quail. White-tailed deer, raccoons, opossum, fox, squirrels and other mammals also eat the fruit.

Remarks: The common name refers to its tendency to form small trees, since it does not usually form sucker sprouts from the roots. Big tree plum is somewhat drought resistent and it has been used as grafting stock. Several varieties have been described across its range. Horticultural varieties include Quaker, Van Buren and Wolf.

The fruit is sweet and juicy, but, too often, is assumed to be ripe when it turns red. At that time it is still somewhat bitter and not really edible.

Prunus is the classical name for a European plum; *mexicana* refers to this species' Southwestern distribution. Some authors consider this species to be a variety of *Prunus american*, i.e. *Prunus americana* var. *lanata*.

Prunus mexicana ❀ a. Growth form with fruit, b. Twig with flowers, c. Flower

Wild goose plum

Prunus munsoniana Wight & Hedrick

Rose family (Rosaceae)

Field Identification: Shrub or small tree to 25 feet, with an irregular open crown.

Flowers: March-May, in clusters of 2 to 4 flowers, white, about 1/2 to 3/4 inch across, appearing before the leaves expand; stalks slender, smooth, 3/4 to 1 inch long; petals 5, about 1/4 inch long, egg-shaped, tip pointed or blunt, with glands on the margins, smooth or hairy; stamens usually 15 to 20.

Fruit: June-August, globe-shaped to oval, about 3/4 inch long, **red or yellow, white-dotted, with thin whitish coating**, skin thin, flesh yellow and juicy; stone oval, tip pointed, a wide groove on one side, narrow on the other.

Leaves: Simple, alternate, blades 2 1/2 to 4 inches long, 3/4 to 1 1/4 inches wide, lance-shaped, tip pointed, base heart-shaped or rounded, **margin finely toothed to rounded with a gland on the incurved face**; bright shiny green above; sparingly hairy, especially along the veins beneath; **fully grown leaves more or less folded lengthwise, troughlike**; petioles slender, smooth or hairy, with two glands near the base of the leaves.

Twigs: Flexible, reddish-brown, shiny, smooth becoming gray in the second year, lenticels (pores) pale and numerous.

Trunk: Bark reddish- or chestnut-brown, thin, smooth, usually with horizontal white patches; the lenticels horizontal; old trunks gray to gray-brown, flaky; wood hard, heavy, pale red-brown, with a light sapwood.

Habitat: Occurs in thickets, prairies, borders of streams and woodlands, and idle ground. Scattered throughout Missouri except for the extreme northwestern and southeastern parts of the state.

Range: Louisiana, Oklahoma, Texas and northeastern Mexico, north to Kentucky and Ohio, and west to Missouri and southeastern Kansas.

Wildlife Uses: The fruit is eaten by many species of birds, including wild turkey and bobwhite quail. White-tailed deer, raccoons, opossum, fox, squirrels and other mammals also eat the fruit. The dense thickets provide cover for small birds.

Remarks: This is a shrub to small tree that sends up sucker sprouts from the roots, forming rather dense thickets. The name wild goose plum comes from the discovery of a seed of this species in the craw of a wild goose, which had been shot by a Captain Means of Nashville, Tenn. From this seed, which was planted, grew a plum which was later developed by nurserymen into a superior strain.

The fruit is somewhat bitter and firm even after falling to the ground, but because of its abundance is often gathered in quantities to be made into jelly. Most wild plums have a tendency to be infected by insects and should be carefully examined before using.

Prunus comes from the classical name of a European plum; *munsoniana* refers to T. V. Munson (1823-1913), an American botanist.

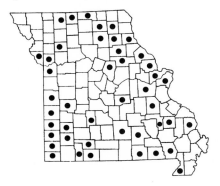

Prunus munsoniana ❀ a. Growth form, b. Twig with flower clusters, c. Flowers, d. Fruit, e. Gland-tipped leaf margin

Peach

Prunus persica (L.) Batsch

Rose family (Rosaceae)

Field Identification: A small tree to a height of 24 feet, with a rounded crown and spreading branches.

Flowers: March-April, opening before the leaves on the previous year's growth; flowers single or 2 together, fragrant, pink to rose-colored, 1 to 2 inches across; petals 5, spreading, rounded; stamens 20 to 30, extending beyond the flower.

Fruit: July-October, 2 to 3 1/4 inches across, globe-shaped, grooved on one side, **velvety to densely hairy with matted wool,** fleshy, separating in halves along a groove; stone rounded in the middle and rounded toward the end, deeply pitted, very hard; fruit of escaped trees usually harder and smaller.

Leaves: Alternate, simple, some appearing clustered, often more than one leaf emerging from the same bud, almond-scented, impregnated with prussic acid; blades 3 to 6 inches long, lance-shaped, the edges often turned upward, tip pointed, base tapering to broadly wedge-shaped, margin finely toothed; both surfaces bright green, smooth, shiny, thin; **leaves troughlike, the halves more or less folded lengthwise, conspicuously drooping;** petioles about 1/2 inch long, with 1 or 2 glands at the upper summit.

Twigs: Upper portion often reddish, while the lower part is greenish, smooth.

Trunk: Bark rough, scaly, grayish-brown, lenticels (pores) prominent.

Habitat: Commonly planted and escaped from cultivation to thickets, fence rows and along roadsides.

Range: Native of China; introduced and naturalized in the United States from Florida to Texas, north to New England and west to Michigan, Illinois, Iowa and Missouri.

Wildlife Uses: The fruit is eaten by several species of birds and small mammals.

Remarks: Although it escapes from cultivation, peach does not seem to be aggressive, and appears to limit its naturalizing to disturbed areas. There are many forms, varieties and hybrids that have been developed for ornamental and fruit-bearing qualities. Peaches are notoriously susceptible to insect and disease pests. The flowers are often injured in cold winters or by late frosts.

Prunus is the ancient Latin name of a plum of Europe; *persica* means "Persian," and is also an old name for peach.

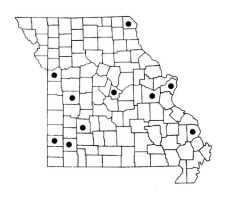

Prunus persica ❀ a. Growth form, b. Twig with flowers, c. Fruit

Choke cherry

Prunus virginiana L.

Rose family (Rosaceae)

Field Identification: Large shrub or small tree to 30 feet, with erect or horizontal branches, sometimes forming thickets from root sprouts.

Flowers: April-May, in short, dense cylinderlike clusters 3 to 6 inches long, many-flowered; flowers white, 1/4 to 1/2 inch in diameter, on slender, smooth stalks; petals 5, small, rounded; stamens 15 to 20.

Fruit: August-September, cherry 1/4 to 3/8 inch across, dark red, scarlet or nearly black, globe-shaped, shiny; skin thick, flesh juicy, bitter, barely edible; stone egg-shaped to oval, one edge ridged, the other with a sharp angle. Good crops are produced almost annually.

Leaves: Simple, alternate, **thin,** blades 3/4 to 4 inches long, 1/2 to 2 inches wide, oval to longer than broad and tapering at both ends, **tip abrupt and sharp-pointed,** base rounded to wedge-shaped or heart-shaped, margin sharply toothed; dark green and shiny above; paler on the lower surface, sometimes hairy on the veins, turning yellow in autumn, strong odor when crushed; petioles slender, 1/2 to 1 inches, smooth, grooved above, 2 glands near the base of leaf.

Twigs: Shiny reddish-brown to orange-brown, smooth, slender, flexible, lenticels (pores) prominent, pale.

Trunk: Bark thin, reddish-brown; lenticels prominent on young trees; fissured and scaly on old trees; wood heavy, hard, reddish-brown, with a wide, light sapwood.

Habitat: Occurs on moist, mostly north-facing wooded slopes and bluffs, and ravines, rarely on borders of woods, thickets, fence rows, ditches or roadsides. More frequent north of the Missouri River.

Range: Georgia to Texas, Oklahoma and New Mexico, north to Maine and Newfoundland, west to Saskatchewan and North Dakota.

Wildlife Uses: There are about 14 native species of wild cherries widely distributed throughout the country. They are considered to be some of the most important wildlife food plants. The wild cherries are eaten by a wide variety of songbirds, game birds, and mammals from black bear to white-footed mouse.

Medicinal Uses: Native Americans used a warm drink made from the bark to ease the pains of childbirth, and a tea made of the root bark as a sedative and stomach remedy. Early settlers used root bark to treat malaria, worms, tuberculosis, indigestion and fever. A tea made from the bark, leaves and dried root has been used for lung ailments and colds. The bark is sometimes used as a flavoring agent in cough syrup.

Remarks: The small tree is sometimes planted for ornament and for erosion control. It has been in cultivation since 1724. The fruit is used to make jellies and jams.

Prunus is the classical name for a European plum; *virginiana* refers to the state of Virginia.

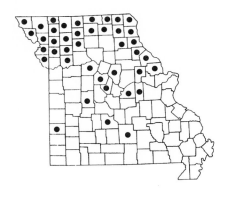

Prunus virginiana ❧ a. Growth form with fruit, b. Twig with flower cluster

Hop tree

Ptelea trifoliata L.

Citrus family (Rutaceae)

Also called common hop tree, wafer ash, stinking ash

Field Identification: Usually a rounded shrub, but occasionally a small tree to 25 feet. Leaves are divided into 3 leaflets that are unpleasantly scented.

Flowers: April-June, arising from the leaf axils in both staminate (male) and (pistillate) flower clusters on slender stalks 1/4 to 1 1/2 inches long; flowers small, greenish-white; petals 4 to 5, longer than broad, somewhat hairy; stamens 4 to 5, alternating with the petals; pistillate flowers with a raised central pistil and stamens absent.

Fruit: August-September, **samaras (winged fruits) in drooping clusters on slender stalks**; yellowish-green, later turning brown when dry, persistent into winter; net-veined, compressed, thin, waferlike or somewhat circular, 3/4 to 1 inch across, persistent in winter, unpleasantly scented; seeds 2 to 3, oval, leathery, reddish-brown, about 1/4 inch long.

Leaves: Alternate, **compound with 3 leaflets; leaflets stalkless**, blades 4 to 6 inches long, 2 to 4 inches wide, longer than broad and tapering at both ends, tip pointed, base wedge-shaped, **margin entire or finely toothed**; upper surface dark green, shiny; lower surface paler, slightly hairy; **unpleasantly scented**; petioles stout, base slightly swollen, 2 to 3 inches long, hairy.

Twigs: Slender, green to yellow or reddish-brown, hairy, unpleasantly scented when bruised.

Trunk: Bark thin, smooth except for the prominent lenticels (pores), light to dark gray or brown, older bark slightly cracked, bitter to the taste; wood heavy, hard, yellowish-brown, with a narrow light sapwood.

Habitat: Occurs on limestone and dolomite glades, prairies, rocky open woods and edge of woods, low woods in ravines, and valleys, thickets and along fence rows.

Range: Florida to Texas, New Mexico and Mexico, north to New York and Ontario, west to Quebec, around Lake Michigan to Nebraska, Kansas and Oklahoma.

Wildlife Uses: The flowers are a nectar source for bees.

Medicinal Uses: Early European settlers used the root as a tonic or invigorating drink. It also was thought that it might be a substitute for quinine because of its bitter flavor. The name hop tree came about not because the fruits looked like hops, but because they were thought to be a possible replacement for the hops that were put into beer. Most of these promises of medicinal or economic value faded throughout the years.

Remarks: Hop tree is occasionally planted for ornament. It was first introduced into cultivation in 1724, and eventually became widespread in European gardens. All parts of the plant emit a disagreeable odor, with some comparing the smell to that of a bobcat.
 Ptelea is the classical Greek name for the elm, here applied to a plant with similar fruit; *trifoliata* (three-leaved) refers to the three leaflets.

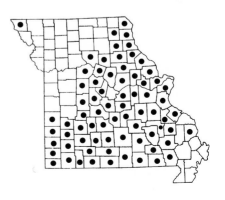

Ptelea trifoliata ❧ a. Growth form with flower cluster, b. Flower, c. Fruit

Dwarf chinquapin oak

Quercus prinoides Willd.

Oak family (Fagaceae)

Also called dwarf chestnut oak, scrub oak

Field Identification: A shrub to 8 feet high, usually growing in clumps or thickets.

Flowers: April-May, **with staminate (male) and pistillate (female) flower in separate clusters (catkins) on the same plant**; staminate catkins near the base of new growth, 1 to 2 1/2 inches long, drooping, cylindrical-shaped, loosely flowered; flowers small, green, densely hairy; stamens 4 to 6; pistillate catkins near the tip of new growth, short, 1 to 4 flowered in axils of leaves; flowers small, green, densely hairy.

Fruit: September-October, **fruit an acorn, maturing the first season**, cap enclosing 1/3 of the acorn; cup 3/8 to 1/2 inch high, about 3/4 inch wide, grayish-brown; scales on the cup small, densely hairy; acorn about 1/2 to 3/4 inch long, about 3/4 inch thick, egg-shaped, dark reddish-brown; nut sweet, edible.

Leaves: Alternate, simple, blade leathery, 1 1/2 to 4 inches long, 1 to 2 1/2 inches wide, inverted egg-shaped to broadest in the middle and narrowing at both ends, tip pointed, base wedge-shaped, margin wavy, widely toothed, **teeth 4 to 8 on each side**, a vein running to each tooth; upper surface olive-green to bright green, shiny, smooth; lower surface much paler, velvety hairy; petioles slender, grooved, 1/4 to 3/4 inches long, hairy; leaves red in autumn.

Twigs: Young reddish-brown and hairy, older ones gray and smooth.

Trunk: Bark on young trunks gray, smooth, except for noticeable, horizontal lenticels (pores); old trunks gray with flat, scaly, checkered ridges and shallow furrows; wood hard, yellowish.

Habitat: Occurs in dry soils in open woods, glades, prairies, along bluffs and thickets.

Range: Tennessee, Arkansas, Oklahoma and Texas, north to Virginia and Maine, and west to Minnesota, southeastern Nebraska and Kansas.

Wildlife Uses: The acorns are eaten by several birds and mammals, including ruffed grouse and gray squirrel, and the foliage is browsed by cottontail rabbit.

Remarks: Dwarf chinquapin oak easily can be confused with the taller chinquapin oak. The former has leaves 1 1/2 to 4 inches long, with 4 to 8 teeth on each side; the latter with leaves 4 to 8 inches long and 8 to 13 teeth on each side.

Dwarf chinquapin oak can sometimes be difficult to manage in prairies, having a tendency to form thickets. Periodic burning (a natural process) or haying helps to keep it and other woody plants from dominating prairies. The dwarf nature of this oak makes for an interesting planting for borders. It was introduced into cultivation about 1730.

Quercus is the classical name; *prinoides* refers to its resemblance, especially in the leaves, to Rock chestnut oak, *Quercus prinus.*

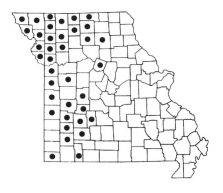

Quercus prinoides ❧ a. Growth form, b. Twig with catkins, c. Acorns, d. Winter twig

Carolina buckthorn

Rhamnus caroliniana Walter

Buckthorn family (Rhamnaceae)

Also called Indian cherry

Field Identification: Shrub or small tree attaining a height of 35 feet, with a diameter of up to 8 inches.

Flowers: May-June, single or in clusters of 2 to 10, arising from leaf axils; flowers small, greenish-yellow; petals 5, minute, tip broad and notched; stamens 5, alternating with the petals.

Fruit: August-October, berry persistent, sweet, round, about 1/4 inch in diameter, red at first, at maturity black and shiny, usually 3-seeded; seeds reddish-brown.

Leaves: Simple, alternate, scattered along the branches; blade 2 to 6 inches long, 1 to 2 inches wide, narrow at the ends and broadest in the middle, tip pointed, base wedge-shaped to rounded, **margin slightly toothed**, rather thin; **upper surface bright green, smooth, shiny**, sometimes hairy; lower surface velvety hairy to only slightly hairy or smooth; leaf blades usually 4 to 10 veins on each side of the central vein; leaves turning yellow in autumn; petioles slender, about 1/4 to 1/2 inch long, widened at base, smooth or hairy.

Twigs: Slender, young ones green to reddish, later gray; hairy at first, smooth later; sometimes terminating in a cluster of very small folded leaves; **buds naked, not covered by scales, densely hairy, slender and elongated.**

Trunk: Bark gray to brown, sometimes blotched, smooth, furrows shallow; wood light brown, sapwood yellow, close-grained, fairly hard, rather weak.

Habitat: Occurs in low woodlands in valleys along streams, rocky open wooded slopes, upland ridges, thickets and glades.

Range: Florida, Louisiana to the Pecos River in Texas, north to North Carolina and Virginia, and west to Ohio, Illinois, Missouri, Arkansas and Oklahoma.

Wildlife Uses: The fruit is eaten by several species of birds, especially the catbird and pileated woodpecker. White-tailed deer browse the twigs in winter.

Remarks: The attractive leaves and fruit make Carolina buckthorn a good candidate for woodland plantings. The foliage turns yellow to orange-yellow in autumn and often lasts into winter.

The fruit is sweet and edible, accounting for the plant's other name, Indian cherry.

Rhamnus is an ancient Greek name; *caroliniana* refers to the state of South Carolina where it was first named.

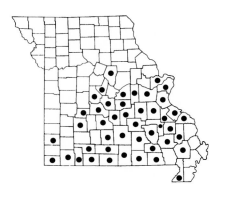

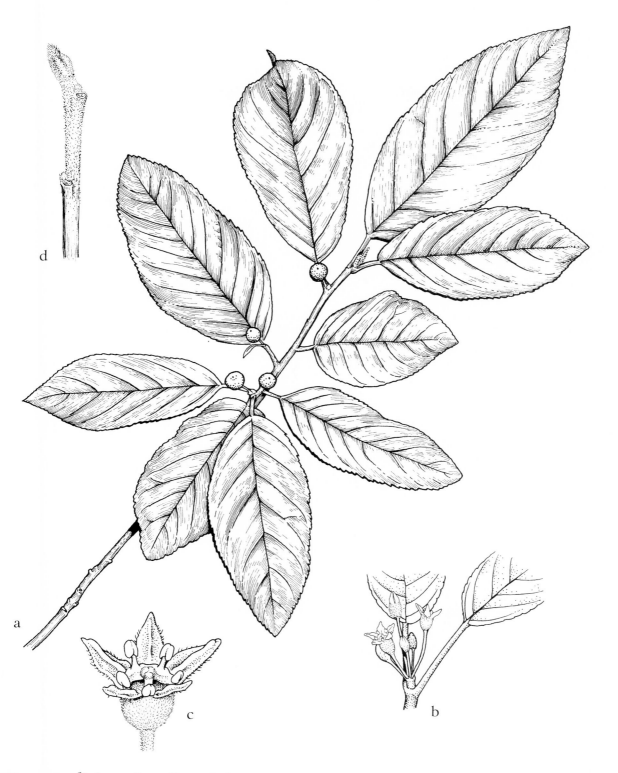

Rhamnus caroliniana ✤ a. Growth form with fruit, b. Twig with flowers, c. Flower, d. Winter twig

Common buckthorn

Rhamnus cathartica L.

Buckthorn family (Rhamnaceae)

Field Identification: A profusely branched shrub or small tree to 25 feet high.

Flowers: April-June, staminate (male) flowers on a short branch of the new year's growth, clusters of 2 to 6; flowers small, smooth, yellowish-green; petals 4, spreading, sometimes recurved; stamens 4; pistillate flowers 2 to 15 on a short spur (thick, slow-growing, reduced branch) of the new year's growth; calyx lobes 4, green; usually no petals, but 4 if present, linear, yellowish-brown; stamens absent.

Fruit: August-September, often remains until December; single or clustered along short spur branches; fruit black, globe-shaped, 1/4 to 3/8 inch across, smooth, semiglossy, juicy, 4 seeds per fruit, but usually only 1 to 2 mature; seeds round, slate gray, smooth, dull, a ridge along one side.

Leaves: Simple, **some leaves appearing alternate but most are opposite**, 1 1/4 to 3 inches long, 1 to 2 1/4 inches wide, longer than broad and tapering at both ends to oval or inverted egg-shaped, **tip abruptly pointed** or sometimes rounded, base rounded to wedge-shaped, margin toothed with the tip usually turned in and bearing a gland; dark green above; paler below; both surfaces smooth; **leaf blades with mostly 3 to 4 veins on each side of the central vein**; petiole 1/2 to 1 1/4 inches long, slightly grooved, hairy above.

Twigs: Slightly flattened, gray to yellowish-brown, dull, smooth, lenticels (pores) are narrow vertical slits, numerous; **twigs often ending in a thorn.**

Trunk: Bark of young trunks gray, smooth; older trunks with somewhat scaly bark and with long, horizontal lenticels, trunk usually blotched with light and dark gray; wood hard, fine-grained, light brown, sapwood wide, white.

Habitat: Escaping occasionally from cultivation and invading wooded thickets, along roadsides and abandoned fields. Can invade tallgrass prairie and woodland habitats.

Range: Introduced from Europe and escaping in North America, from Virginia, Ohio, Illinois and Missouri, north to Nova Scotia, Saskatchewan, and Minnesota.

Wildlife Uses: The fruits are eaten by several bird species, which help to spread this nuisance shrub.

Medicinal Uses: The fruits are a strong laxative.

Remarks: This is an invasive shrub and should not be planted. Once established it is difficult to eradicate. Common buckthorns and other exotic buckthorns are sold as ornamentals by nurseries, and are used as hedges in many urban areas.

Rhamnus cathartica ❦ a. Growth form, b. Flower, c. Twig with fruit and thorns

Lance-leaved buckthorn

Rhamnus lanceolata Pursh

Buckthorn family (Rhamnaceae)

Field Identification: Small to large shrub to 9 feet, with an erect and widely branched habit.

Flowers: Mid-April to June, single or in clusters arising from leaf axils; flowers greenish-yellow, about 1/8 inch broad; petals 4; staminate (male) flowers on short branches from wood of the previous year, 1 to 3 flowers per leaf axil, stamens 4; pistillate (female) flowers on short, new branches — some of which continue to grow during the summer — others lose their leaves at fruiting and remain short; 1 to 3 flowers per leaf axil, smaller and not as showy as the staminate flowers; petals 4, greenish; stamens absent.

Fruit: June-August, berry about 1/4 inch thick, globe-shaped, black, with a thin white coating that does not rub off easily, 2-seeded; seeds about 1/4 inch long, deeply grooved along one edge, light brown, smooth, glossy.

Leaves: Simple, alternate, **blades 1 to 3 1/2 inches long, 1/2 to 1 inch wide**, longer than broad and tapering at both ends to lance-shaped, tip pointed to blunt, base wedge-shaped to rounded, **margin finely toothed with incurved glandular teeth;** upper surface smooth or nearly so; lower surface lighter green and more or less hairy especially on the veins; leaf blades usually 4 to 10 veins on each side of the central vein; petiole about 1/4 inch long, sometimes reddish, hairy to smooth.

Twigs: Slender, flexible, reddish-brown and hairy at first, later gray and smooth; **buds for next year covered with scales**.

Trunk: Bark smooth, gray, often with light blotches, the lenticels (pores) horizontal, dark; occasionally the bark of an old trunk peels and curls parallel to the trunk; wood medium-hard, light, reddish-brown, with a narrow, pale sapwood.

Habitat: Occurs on open wooded slopes, in thickets and on glades; usually on rocky limestone or dolomite surfaces. Absent from the lowland counties of southeastern Missouri.

Range: Alabama to Arkansas and east Texas, north to Pennsylvania, and west to Illinois, Missouri, Kansas, Nebraska, and southeastern South Dakota.

Wildlife Uses: The fruit is eaten by at least five species of birds. White-tailed deer browse the twigs in winter. The branches are low to the ground and the shrub has many small branchlets. It is excellent for song- and game-bird protection.

Remarks: Lance-leaf buckthorn is a solitary plant, only occasionally forming thickets. Easy to grow, it is sometimes used as an ornamental.

Rhamnus is an ancient Greek name; *lanceolata* refers to the lance-shaped leaves.

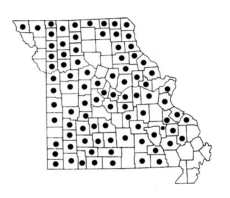

Rhamnus lanceolata ❀ a. Growth form with fruit, b. Branch with flowers, c. Flower bud, d. Flower

Wild azalea

Rhododendron roseum (Loisel.) Rehd.

Heath family (Ericaceae)

Also called azalea, wild honeysuckle, mountain azalea, election pink

Field Identification: Erect shrub to 9 feet tall, with picturesque ascending branches, often sending up new stems from roots.

Flowers: Late April-May, in clusters of mostly 6 to 8 flowers arranged more or less in a circular fashion; flower stalk with gland-tipped hairs, **flowers pink, showy, very fragrant**, 1 1/2 to 2 inches wide, tubular, densely hairy with hairs gland-tipped; petals 5, spreading; stamens 5, extending much beyond the flower.

Fruit: September-October, capsule brown, cylindrical, densely hairy, about 1/2 inch long, peeling back from the top; seeds minute, numerous.

Leaves: Simple, alternate, **usually clustered at or near the tip of the twigs**, 1 1/2 to 3 1/2 inches long, 3/4 to 1 1/2 inches wide, longer than broad and tapering at the ends or broadest towards the end, tip pointed to blunt, base wedge-shaped, margin entire, fringed with hairs; upper surface green, finely hairy, **lower surface densely hairy**; petiole about 1/4 inch long, hairy.

Twigs: Young twigs of the year reddish- to grayish-brown, densely hairy; brown to dark grey and smooth when older.

Trunk: Bark dark gray with thin squarish scaly plates or sometimes smooth.

Habitat: Occurs in acid soils overlying sandstone, chert or igneous bedrock, north-facing steep wooded slopes of ravines, small bluffs, slopes along streams, upland ridges and shallow draws.

Range: Virginia, Tennessee, Kentucky, southern Illinois and Missouri, north to Maine and Quebec.

Wildlife Uses: The leaves and twigs are browsed by white-tailed deer. Ruffed grouse are reported to eat the leaves, buds, twigs, and seeds. The leaves are eaten by several small mammals, including the white-footed mouse.

Remarks: This azalea also is known as *Rhododendron prinophyllum* (Small) Millais. The flowers are very attractive and fragrant, making it a good candidate as an ornamental shrub. The leaves turn purplish in autumn. The plants need acid, well-drained soil and can be grown in either shade or full sun. A white-flowered form was discovered in 1933 by Dr. Julian Steyermark in Ste. Genevieve County.

    Rhododendron is an ancient Greek name meaning "rose-tree"; *roseum* refers to the color of the flowers.

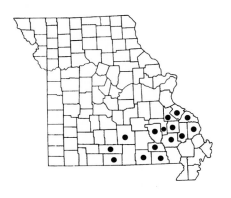

Rhododendron roseum ❀ a. Growth form with flowers, b. Twig with seed capsules

Fragrant sumac

Rhus aromatica Aiton

Cashew family (Anacardiaceae)

Also called aromatic sumac, pole-cat bush

Field Identification: Thicket-forming shrub to 8 feet, branches vary from ascending to lying on the ground.

Flowers: Late March-April, **flowers usually appearing before leaves at the ends of twigs in clusters**, 1 1/2 inches long, 3/4 to 1 1/4 inches wide; flowers small, yellowish-green; petals 5, egg-shaped, tip blunt; stamens 5, shorter than the petals. Catkins form on the tips of twigs in the summer and overwinter to flower the following spring.

Fruit: May-July, globe-shaped, **red, hairy with simple or gland-tipped hairs**, about 1/4 inch long; stone light reddish- or yellowish-brown, somewhat spherical.

Leaves: Alternate, three-leaved, **fragrant when crushed, leaflets without stalks**; terminal leaflet 2 to 2 1/2 inches long, 3/4 to 1 1/2 inches wide, short stalked, egg-shaped, tip pointed to rounded, base wedge-shaped, margin lobed or coarsly toothed, lower edge entire; lateral leaflets 3/4 to 1 3/4 inches long, 3/4 to 1 1/4 inches wide, oval to egg-shaped, tip pointed to rounded, base terminating at a sharp angle, margin lobed or coarsely toothed, lower edge entire; upper surface dark yellow-green, dull or shiny, with or without hairs; lower surface pale, smooth to densely hairy; petioles about 1 inch long.

Twigs: Slender, flexible, brown, hairy to smooth later.

Trunk: Bark dark brown, smooth on young stems, lenticels (pores) prominent; cracked on old stems; wood brown with a light sapwood.

Habitat: Occurs in rocky or open woods, thickets, glades and along ledges.

Range: Florida, Louisiana, east Texas and Oklahoma, north to Vermont, and west to Michigan, Minnesota, North Dakota.

Wildlife Uses: The fruit is eaten by many species of birds, including wild turkey, ruffed grouse and flicker; it's also eaten by raccoon, opossum, chipmunk and white-tailed deer. Cottontail rabbits eat the bark during severe winter weather with heavy snow.

Remarks: There is some debate over the status of certain varieties in Missouri, so this treatment does not address any further distinction. Fragrant sumac does well as a border planting along woods. The often brilliant, multicolored leaves in autumn add to its small shrub value. Spreading branches often root when in contact with the soil.

The Kiowa Indians ate the berries of fragrant sumac, which was recognized as one of their "ancient" foods. The berries were mixed with corn meal, beaten with sugar (after exposure to the ways of European settlers) or boiled into a tea. Today, some prepare a drink with the sourish fruit, made with sugar and served cold.

Although superficially resembling the related poison ivy, fragrant sumac does not cause dermatitis. It is readily distinguished by a shorter or absent stalk on the middle leaflet and by its hairy, reddish fruits.

Rhus is the ancient Latin name for a bushy sumac; *aromatica* refers to the *aromatic* leaves.

Rhus aromatica ❧ a. Growth form with fruit clusters, b. Twig with flower clusters, c. Flower

Winged Sumac

Rhus copallina L.

Cashew family (Anacardiaceae)

Also called dwarf sumac, shining sumac, flame-leaf sumac

Field Identification: Slender-branched shrub to 10 feet and forming thickets from root sprouting.

Flowers: Late May-July, in dense clusters at the end of new growth, 6 to 8 inches long, 5 to 7 inches wide; flowers numerous, both staminate (male) and pistillate (female) flowers about 1/8 inch across; petals 5, greenish-white; stamens 5.

Fruit: September, compact clusters, erect or drooping, persistent; fruit globe-shaped, flattened, red, hairy, about 1/8 inch in diameter; seeds solitary, smooth, oval to bean-shaped, olive-brown.

Leaves: Pinnately compound, alternate, 5 to 12 inches long, **central stem hairy, broadly winged**; leaflets 7 to 17, sides of leaflets unequal, longer than broad to lance-shaped, tip pointed, base ending at a sharp angle, **margin entire or remotely toothed**; upper surface dark green, shiny, smooth to hairy; lower surface paler, hairy; petioles about 3 inches long, hairy.

Twigs: Brittle, green to reddish-brown, **hairy at first**, smooth later; lenticels (pores) dark. Part of the previous year's twig-growth often dies back over winter. This process is called indeterminate growth, where the twig continues to grow and does not harden off before winter arrives, causing the upper part of the stem to die back.

Trunk: Bark thick, greenish-brown to gray, some shallow fissures, lenticels red and prominent; wood soft, brittle, brown, with a white sapwood.

Habitat: Occurs in prairies, thickets, open woods, rocky sandstone, chert and igneous glades, borders of woodland generally in acid soils, abandoned fields, roadsides and along railroads.

Range: Georgia, Alabama, Louisiana and Texas, north to New Hampshire, and west to Michigan, Missouri, Kansas and Oklahoma.

Wildlife Uses: The fruit is eaten by at least 20 species of birds, and white-tailed deer occasionally browse it, as well as the stems and foliage.

Remarks: Winged sumac makes a desirable ornamental shrub due to its glossy, dark green leaves and brilliant red leaves in autumn. The bark and leaves contain tannin and are used in the tanning industry. The crushed, somewhat bitter, fruit was added to drinking water by Native Americans to make it more palatable.

Rhus is the ancient Latin name for a bushy sumac; *copallina* means "copal gum," which refers to a hard resin characteristic of some tropical trees. Winged sumac is somewhat smaller than smooth sumac, hence the common name, dwarf sumac, is sometimes used.

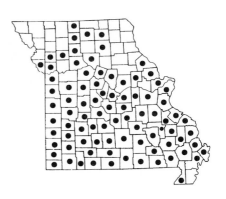

Rhus copallina ✿ a. Growth form with flower clusters, b. Male flower, c. Female flower, d. Twig with fruit cluster

Smooth sumac

Rhus glabra L.

Cashew family (Anacardiaceae)

Field Identification: Thicket-forming shrub or small tree attaining a height of 20 feet.

Flowers: Late May-July, in dense clusters at the end of new growth, 5 to 9 inches long, 3 to 5 inches wide; flowers numerous, both staminate (male) and pistillate (female) flowers, about 1/8 inch across; petals 5, white; stamens 5.

Fruit: August-September, compact clusters, erect, persistent; fruit globe-shaped, dark red with red velvety hairs; 1-seeded, stone smooth, oval, straw-colored.

Leaves: Pinnately compound, alternate, 12 to 16 inches long, **central stem smooth, lacking wings**; leaflets 15 to 23, longest leaflets near middle of the leaf; leaflets longer than broad to lance-shaped, tip pointed, base rounded or wedge-shaped, **margin coarsely toothed; upper surface dark green, shiny**; lower surface lighter to conspicuously white, smooth; **petioles smooth**, about 3 inches long.

Twigs: Rigid, **smooth, with white coating**, reddish-brown to purplish, with prominent gray lenticels (pores). Part of the previous year's twig-growth often dies back during winter. This process is called indeterminate growth where the twig continues to grow and does not harden off before winter arrives, causing the upper part of the stem to die back.

Trunk: Bark grayish-brown, roughened with raised lenticels; old trunks with shallow fissures; wood soft, brittle, yellowish-brown, with a white sapwood.

Habitat: Occurs in upland prairies, thickets, idle fields, borders and openings of woods, roadsides and along railroads. Throughout Missouri in every county.

Range: Florida, Louisiana, Texas, New Mexico and Mexico, north to Maine and Quebec, west to British Columbia.

Wildlife Uses: The fruit is eaten by at least 32 species of birds, including wild turkey and bob-white quail. Cottontail rabbit and white-tailed deer eat the leaves and twigs.

Medicinal Uses: Native Americans used the plant in many ways. The somewhat bitter fruits were crushed and added to water to freshen it. Various concoctions of the bark, twigs, leaves and flowers were used medicinally as astringents, to stop bleeding, and for renal disorders. In Appalachia, the leaves are rolled and smoked as a treatment for asthma. The fruits in infusion (boiling water poured over them) have been used as a treatment for fever. The bark, boiled in milk, has been used to treat burns.

Remarks: Smooth sumac, with its bright red clusters of fruit and brilliant autumn foliage, makes a good ornamental shrub. It has been in cultivation since 1620. The leaves are reported to have been mixed with tobacco and smoked. The twigs, leaves and roots contain tannin and were used for staining and dyeing.

Rhus is the ancient Latin name for a bushy sumac; *glabra* refers to the plant's smoothness.

Rhus glabra ❀ a. Growth form with fruit cluster, b. Male flower, c. Female flower, d. Fruit, e. Winter twig

Wild Black Currant

Ribes americanum Mill.

Currant family (Grossulariaceae)

Field Identification: An erect or spreading spineless shrub attaining a height of 5 feet.

Flowers: April-May, from 2 to 12 flowers in drooping clusters from 1 to 3 inches long emerging from axils of leaves; flowers greenish-white or yellowish, 3/8 to 1/2 inch long; petals 5, shorter than the 5 sepals; stamens 5, not extending beyond the flower.

Fruit: August-September, in drooping clusters 1 1/2 to 2 1/2 inches long; fruits 1/4 to 1/2 inch across, globe-shaped, black, smooth; seeds numerous, minute, reddish-purple, the surface rough or pitted.

Leaves: Alternate or in clusters, simple, blades 1 to 3 inches long or wide, outline is circular; lobes 3 to 5, sharply pointed to blunt, base flattened to somewhat heart-shaped, margins irregularly toothed; upper surface dull green, smooth; lower surface somewhat hairy and **dotted with an abundance of minute orange glands**; petioles slender, 1 1/2 to 2 1/2 inches long, hairy.

Twigs: Upright to spreading, yellowish-brown to grayish-brown, with three ridges extending below each leaf axil; lacking **spines**, hairy at first, smooth later, **occasionally dotted with orange glands**.

Trunk: Bark reddish-brown, smooth, tight; lenticels (pores) small, oval, light-colored; wood soft, fine-grained, white, with a brown pith.

Habitat: Moist, wooded hillsides and margins of fens. **Recently discovered in Missouri from Schuyler County. An 1897 record from near Allenton, St. Louis County, has not been relocated.**

Range: Delaware to northern Illinois, northern Missouri, Iowa, Nebraska, and at altitudes of 3,000 to 5,500 feet in Colorado and New Mexico, north to New Brunswick, and west to Manitoba, Montana, Wyoming and California.

Wildlife Uses: The fruits, which are eaten by several species of birds and small mammals, mature during a long period, making the food last for some time. The bushes are too thin to supply wildlife cover or nesting.

Medicinal Uses: Native Americans made a strong tea from the root as a remedy for kidney trouble and to expel intestinal worms.

Remarks: Wild black currant is classified as endangered in Missouri. It is found along the southern edge of its range, where it grows at the base of a north-facing wooded slope. Additional searches in similar habitat along the state line may yield additional locations.

The plant was first cultivated in 1727. The berries can be eaten fresh, dried or made into jelly or wine. Like other species of *Ribes*, wild black currant has been eradicated from parts of its range because it is the alternate host of blister rust that attacks White Pine forests.

Ribes is from the old Danish word "ribs," the word for "red currant"; *americanum* refers to its native home.

Ribes americanum ❧ a. Growth form, b. Twig with flower clusters, c. Flower, d. Fruit

Prickly gooseberry

Ribes cynosbati L.

Currant family (Grossulariaceae)

Also called dogberry, pasture gooseberry

Field Identification: Low, straggly shrub with rigid, spreading or trailing branches. Generally armed with simple reddish or black slender spines along the stem.

Flowers: April-June, single or in clusters of 2 to 4 flowers; stalk bearing flower clusters 1/4 to 1 1/4 inches long, hairs present, sometimes gland-tipped; petals 5, yellowish-green; stamens 5, barely showing beyond the petals; ovary (swollen base of flower) spiny.

Fruit: July-September, reddish-purple, globe-shaped, 1/4 to 1/2 inch in diameter, **armed with long stiff prickles**; seeds 10 to 20, dark brown.

Leaves: Simple, alternate or clustered, 1 to 2 inches long or wide, round to broadly egg-shaped, base cut back sharply to slightly rounded, margin 3 to 5 lobed, lobes with teeth rounded to pointed; **both surfaces hairy;** under surface more densely so and paler green than above; petioles slender, 1/2 to 1 inch long, hairy.

Twigs: Slender, at first tan to brown and hairy, later gray to almost black and smooth; spines slender, solitary or 2 to 3 together, straight, to 3/4 inch long; young twigs often with numerous, slender reddish or black spines.

Trunk: Outer bark thin, papery, tan to brown with spines (modified petiole) and few to many recurved prickles (outgrowth of the bark); inner layer of bark reddish-brown or purplish, smooth, with numerous light-colored lenticels (pores); wood hard, fine-grained, white, with a dark pith.

Habitat: Occurs on north-facing, shaded bluffs and wooded ledges; often seen dangling its stems over the face of rocks.

Range: North Carolina, Alabama, Kentucky, Arkansas, Missouri and Oklahoma, north to Maine, New Brunswick, and west to Quebec and Manitoba.

Wildlife Uses: The fruit is eaten by several bird species and by squirrels and chipmunks.

Remarks: Prickly gooseberry has been in cultivation since 1759. There are spineless varieties, but they have not been reported in Missouri. Since gooseberries and currants are an alternate host of the white pine blister rust, there have been active campaigns to eradicate these shrubs within the natural range of white pine, which is north of Missouri. The fruits may be cooked and eaten or put up as preserves or jelly.

Ribes is from the old Danish word "ribs," the word for "red currant"; *cynosbati* means "dogberry."

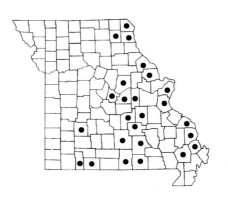

Ribes cynosbati ❀ a. Growth form with flowers, b. Flower, c. Fruit, d. Stem with spines

Missouri gooseberry

Ribes missouriense Nutt. ex Torrey & A. Gray

Currant family (Grossulariaceae)

Also called wild gooseberry

Field Identification: A thorny shrub to 3 feet tall, spreading to 6 feet wide, with clustered trunks and arching branches.

Flowers: April-May, single or in clusters of 2 to 4 flowers; stalk bearing flower clusters 1/4 to 3/4 inch long, drooping, slender, smooth to hairy; petals 5, whitish-green, longer than broad; stamens 5, much extended and about as long or longer than the length of the flower.

Fruit: June-September, berry smooth, **without prickles**, blackish-purple, globe-shaped, about 1/4 inch across; seeds 8 to 25, oval, flattened, black.

Leaves: Simple, alternate, 3/4 to 2 1/2 inches long or wide, outline rounded, cut into 3 to 5 lobes that, in turn, are coarsely toothed or bluntly lobed, base cut back sharply to somewhat rounded; **upper surface green, smooth; lower surface soft hairy or smooth later**; petioles 1/2 to 1 1/2 inches long, smooth to sparsely hairy.

Twigs: Slender, pale to dark brown, often reddish; young shoots light tan, with many dark reddish-brown spines, lateral twigs short and spurlike; spines solitary or 2 to 3 together, sometimes 1/4 to 3/4 inch long.

Trunk: Bark dark gray or reddish-brown, separating into thin, papery scales curling along the trunk; wood hard, heavy, nearly white.

Habitat: Occurs in rocky or open dry woods, thickets, upland or lowland woodland borders, and grazed or cut-over areas. **Plants common throughout Missouri except in the southeastern lowlands**.

Range: Tennessee, Arkansas, Missouri and Kansas, north to Connecticut, and west to Minnesota and North Dakota.

Wildlife Uses: The shrub furnishes excellent cover for small mammals and birds, some of which eat the fruits. Dead leaves are caught and held by the low-lying branches in the autumn, giving good cover for the soil.

Remarks: Missouri gooseberry has been in cultivation since 1907.

Many species of gooseberries and currants have been the subject of an aggressive eradication campaign in parts of the country where white pine grows and is used for lumber. The shrubs are an alternate host of the blister rust, which was unintentionally brought in from Europe around 1900. This fungus attacks and kills white pine. Like many other rusts, it needs two hosts to complete its life cycle; its alternate host is various species of *Ribes*. Since Missouri is not in the range of white pine, other than as ornamental plantings, the blister rust has not been considered a threat.

The fruits are commonly gathered for pies and jellies.

Ribes is from the old Danish word "ribs," the word for "red currant"; *missouriense* is for the state of Missouri.

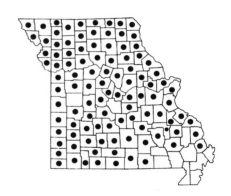

Ribes missouriense ❦ a. Growth form with fruit, b. Growth form with flowers, c. Flowers

Golden currant

Ribes odoratum Wendland f.

Currant family (Grossulariaceae)

Also called flowering currant, Missouri currant, buffalo currant, clove currant

Field Identification: Erect spineless shrub attaining a height of 6 feet.

Flowers: April-June, in clusters of 4 to 10 flowers, nodding, **golden yellow, fragrant**, cylinder-shaped; petals 5, spreading or reflexed, tip broadly rounded; stamens 5, short.

Fruit: June-August, berries smooth, black, globe-shaped, about 1/4 inch across; many seeds, reddish-brown, irregular-shaped, pitted.

Leaves: Simple, alternate, 1 1/4 to 3 1/4 inches long or wide, circular, 3 to 5 lobed, lobes entire or toothed toward the tip, usually entire toward the base, margin often fringed with hairs, green on both sides, smooth, hairy on the veins above and below; petioles 1/4 to 1 inch long.

Twigs: Flexible, reddish-brown, hairy; spurs on stem bearing fruit; older twigs grayish-brown; **no spines**.

Trunk: Bark reddish-brown to gray, often splits, and the thin sheets curl along the trunk; lenticels (pores) prominent; wood white, soft.

Habitat: Occurs on exposed, high rocky limestone or dolomite bluffs often on narrow ledges of nearly sheer rock faces along the White River drainage and locally along the Jacks Fork River.

Range: Louisiana, Arkansas, east Texas and Oklahoma, north to Missouri, Kansas, Nebraska, North Dakota, and Minnesota; also, to the east side of the Rocky Mountains in Colorado. Escaping cultivation in the Eastern states.

Wildlife Uses: The fruit is eaten by several bird species and by squirrels and chipmunks.

Remarks: Golden Currant is not abundant in any place where it grows in Missouri. It once was classified as rare, but recent surveys have found enough populations to drop it from the listing.

The shrub commonly is used as an ornamental, and was introduced into cultivation in 1812. The fruit is considered a sweet and flavorful fruit of the Great Plains' prairies. It was used by many of the Indian tribes and early settlers, as it is today. The fruit is full of seeds, but makes good jams and jellies and sometimes is used in pies.

Ribes is from the old Danish word "ribs," the word for "red currant"; *odoratum* refers to the fragrant flowers. The common name, clove currant, is in reference to the aromatic clovelike smell of the flowers.

Ribes odoratum ❀ a. Growth form, b. Twig with flowers, c. Twig with short spur shoot and fruit

Bristly locust

Robinia hispida L.

Bean family (Fabaceae)

Also called rose acacia

Field Identification: Shrub 3 to 10 feet tall, spreading by suckering of the roots; branches numerous, covered by bristly reddish hairs.

Flowers: May-June, in clusters of 3 to 9 flowers, flower stalks 1/4 to 1/2 inches long, bristly-hairy; base of flower (calyx) with short bristly hairs; **flower pink, rose or rose-purple**, bonnet-shaped, 3/4 to 1 1/4 inches long; petals 5, composed of a banner petal (upright) and two wing (side) petals that clasp two keel (central) petals; stamens are within keel petals.

Fruit: September, pod 2 to 3 1/4 inch long, linear, flattened, with conspicuous and densely reddish-brown bristles; seeds several.

Leaves: Pinnately compound, alternate, 5 to 9 inches long; leaflets 7 to 15, length 3/4 to 2 inches, width 3/4 to 1 3/4 inches circular to egg-shaped or longer than broad, tip rounded to abruptly pointed, base rounded, margin entire; upper surface light to dark green, smooth; lower surface smooth or with occasional scattered hairs.

Twigs: Young ones brown with dense reddish bristles; older ones gray to brown with fine grooves, smooth.

Habitat: Escaped from cultivation. Native in the Southeastern states.

Range: Native in Georgia and Alabama, north to Virginia and Kentucky. Escaped from cultivation and naturalized (reproducing on its own) north to New York and Minnesota, and west to Missouri, Kansas, Oklahoma and Texas.

Wildlife Uses: The flowers are a good nectar source for bees. The leaves host the caterpillar of the silver-spotted skipper.

Remarks: Bristly locust has been known to hybridize with black locust *(Robinia pseudo-acacia)*. Bristly locust, a showy ornamental, often is grown along the edge of yards as a border. In the Southern states it has been planted along roadsides on steep fills and road cuts to stabilize banks. Like many other legumes, the shrub has the ability to fix atmospheric nitrogen through certain bacteria living in nodules on its roots, and, therefore, tends to enrich any soil in which it grows.

    Robinia honors Jean Robin (1550-1629) and his son, Vespasian Robin (1579-1662), who first cultivated the locust tree in Europe; *hispida* refers to the dense bristly hairs of the foliage and flowers.

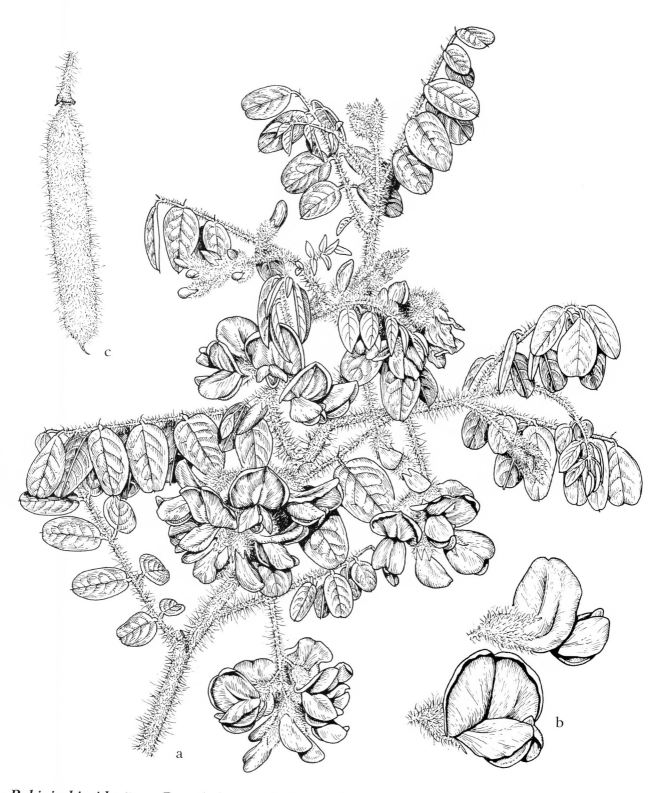

Robinia hispida ❦ a. Growth form with flower clusters, b. Flowers, c. Fruit

Prairie wild rose

Rosa arkansana Porter

Rose family (Rosaceae)

Field Identification: A small shrub with erect stems, attaining a height of 1 1/2 feet.

Flowers: May-July, single or in clusters of 2 to 4 on the tips of new growth, **flower stalks smooth**, 1/4 to 3/4 inch long; petals 5, pink, broadly inverted egg-shaped, 3/4 to 1 inch long; stamens numerous, attached to the rim of the hypanthium (upward, cuplike extension of the receptacle).

Fruit: Late August, single or in clusters of 2 to 4, central stalk 1/2 to 1 inch long, shorter and stouter than the laterals, smooth, glossy; fruit, which is called "hips," 1/2 to 3/4 inch broad, globe-shaped to sometimes longer than broad, bright red, **tip of rose hips with persistent lobes**; seeds flattened on the sides, straw-colored to light reddish-brown, smooth, often with a tuft of hairs at both ends.

Leaves: Pinnately compound, alternate, 3 to 4 inches long, **5 to 9 leaflets**, longer than broad, 1/2 to 1 inch long, 1/4 to 1/2 inch wide, tip round to pointed, base wedge-shaped, margin sharply toothed nearly to the base; upper surface dark green, smooth; lower surface paler, soft hairy; petioles 3/4 to 1 inch long, hairy.

Twigs: Flexible, usually simple and erect, red to reddish-brown; very bristly and prickly.

Trunk: Prickles abundant, up to 1/4 inch long, some flexible; bark green to reddish-brown, smooth except for the numerous prickles; wood hard, pale reddish-brown, large pith.

Habitat: Occurs in prairies, open banks, loess hills, bluffs, thickets, along roads and railroads.

Range: New York to Alberta, south to District of Columbia, and west to Indiana, Wisconsin, North Dakota, and south to Kansas, Missouri, Texas and New Mexico.

Wildlife Uses: The flowers are a nectar source for bumblebees, one of the rose's main pollinators. The rose hips are eaten by several species of birds, including greater prairie chicken and bobwhite quail.

Medicinal Uses: The Great Plains Indians used this rose as a medicine and, in some cases, as an emergency food. The Omahas steeped the rose hips or roots to make a wash to treat inflammation of the eyes. The Pawnees collected insect galls from the lower parts of the stems. The galls were charred and crushed to make a dressing for burns. The Chippewas of the Great Lakes region used the inner bark of the roots to treat cataracts. Rose hips are an excellent source of vitamin C; three fresh rose hips may contain as much vitamin C as a whole orange.

Remarks: Prairie wild rose is referred to as *Rosa suffulta* in some references, but authors in Missouri use the name *Rosa arkansana* var. *suffulta*.

Rosa is the ancient Latin name; *arkansana* refers to the Arkansas River, on the banks of which — near Canon City, Colo. — the plant was first found.

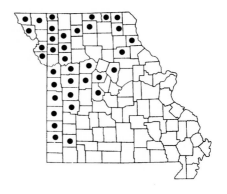

Rosa arkansana ❀ a. Growth form with fruit, b. Stem with flower

Smooth wild rose

Rosa blanda Aiton

Rose family (Rosaceae)

Field Identification: A straight, upright, colony-forming shrub up to 3 feet tall, usually lacking thorns except at the base.

Flowers: May-July, mostly single to few-flowered in clusters on new growth arising from leaf axils; the central flower opening first, its stalk shorter and stouter than the others; flower stalks 3/4 to 1 1/2 inches long, smooth; petals 5, about 1 inch long and wide, inverted egg- to heart-shaped, outer end notched, pink, often streaked with red; stamens numerous, many lying flat against the petals until petals fall, then becoming upright.

Fruit: August-September, rose hips bright red, about 1/2 inch across, globe-shaped, smooth; seeds egg-shaped, about 1/8 inch long, yellow to dark brown, hairy near the tip on one side.

Leaves: Pinnately compound, alternate, 2 1/4 to 3 inches long, 5 to 7 leaflets; leaflets oval to inverted egg-shaped, 1/2 to 1 inch long, 3/8 to 3/4 inch wide, tip and base rounded, margin toothed; upper surface dull, yellowish-green; lower surface paler, hairy; petioles about 1/2 inch long, hairy.

Twigs: Red for first 1 to 2 years, smooth, prickles few or absent. Sprouts from the roots to form new shoots.

Trunk: Bark grayish-brown, smooth, tight; prickles only at the base of the stem, small, straight, often lacking entirely; wood white, soft, with a large white pith.

Habitat: Occurs in open woods, dry hillsides, thickets and roadsides; **found in northeastern Missouri.**

Range: Pennsylvania, Ohio, Indiana, Illinois, Missouri and Kansas, north to New York and Quebec, and west to Manitoba and North Dakota.

Wildlife Uses: The flowers are a nectar source for bumblebees, one of the rose's main pollinators. The rose hips persist into winter and are eaten by several species of birds, including greater prairie chicken and bobwhite quail.

Medicinal Uses: The Mesquakie Indians, whose territory was what is now Minnesota and Wisconsin, ate the skin of the rose hip to help alleviate stomach trouble. They also boiled the whole fruits down to make a syrup that was used to relieve itching anywhere on the body, especially hemorrhoids.

Remarks: Smooth wild rose is uncommon in Missouri, but often may be overlooked for its similarity to other species of rose. **It is a sturdy rose; the stems are stout and the fruits are much larger than those of most other rose**s. It was introduced into cultivation in 1773.

Rosa is the ancient Latin name; *blanda* means "mild" and refers to its lack of prickles.

Rosa blanda 🌼 a. Growth form with fruit, b. Branch with flower

Pasture rose

Rosa carolina L.

Rose family (Rosaceae)

Also called Carolina rose

Field Identification: Slender, simple or little-branched stems, attaining a height from 6 inches to 3 feet.

Flowers: May-June, mostly single, 1 1/2 to 2 1/2 inches across; flower stalks 1/2 to 1 1/4 inches long, with gland-tipped bristly hairs; petals 5, pink, spreading, inverted egg-shaped, tip often notched; stamens many, attached to the rim of the hypanthium (upward, cuplike extension of the receptacle).

Fruit: Late August, rose hips red, about 1/4 inch broad, globe-shaped, with scattered gland-tipped hairs, stalk about 1/2 inch long; seeds 2 to 12, staw-colored to dark reddish-brown, white hairs toward the tip.

Leaves: Pinnately compound, alternate, 3 to 4 inches long, leaflets 5 to 7, longer than broad, 3/4 to 1 1/2 inches long, 1/4 to 3/4 inches wide, the lower ones smaller, tip pointed, base ending at a sharp angle, **margin coarsely toothed, often fringed with hairs**; upper surface dark green, smooth; lower surface paler, a few hairs on the veins; **petioles with flat stipules (leafy growth) not fringed**, about 1/2 inch long.

Twigs: Flexible, smooth, green to greenish-brown, covered with short prickles.

Trunk: The stem prickles up to 1/4 inch long, straight; bark green to reddish-brown; wood soft, white, with a large, white pith.

Habitat: Occurs mainly in dry, rocky ground of open woods, glades, prairies, thickets, clearings, and along railroads and roadsides.

Range: Florida to Louisiana, Arkansas and Texas, north to Nova Scotia, Ontario, Michigan, Wisconsin, Minnesota and Nebraska.

Wildlife Uses: The flowers are a nectar source for bumblebees, one of the rose's main pollinators. The rose hips are eaten by several species of birds, including greater prairie chicken and bobwhite quail.

Remarks: Some botanists have considered pasture rose as a complex and variable species that consists of numerous minor forms and variations. However, they are all lumped together in this treatment for the purpose of simplicity.

Rose hips, for comparable weights, contain about one hundred times more vitamin C than oranges.

Rosa is the ancient Latin name; *carolina* refers to the Carolinas, where the plant is found.

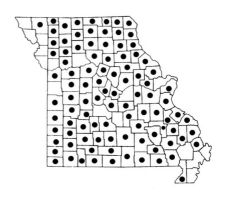

Rosa carolina ❀ a. Growth form with flowers, b. Flower, c. Fruit

Damask rose

Rosa X damascena Miller

Rose family (Rosaceae)

Field Identification: A shrub to 8 feet tall with many hooked prickles; commonly **found around old homesites and along fence rows.**

Flowers: May-July, in clusters; flowers fragrant, **white to pink or red; petals 6 to 9**; stamens numerous.

Fruit: Typically no fruit is developed, which is common among hybrids.

Leaves: Alternate, pinnately compound; leaflets commonly 5, about 2 1/2 inches long, egg-shaped, tip pointed, margin toothed; upper surface dark green, smooth; lower surface paler, hairy.

Stems: Arching to 8 feet, **with many hooked prickles.**

Habitat: Planted as an "old-fashioned" rose, it can escape and establish itself along roads, fence rows and thickets.

Range: Originated in Asia and escaped from cultivation in the United States.

Remarks: Damask rose, *Rosa X damascena*, is a hybrid, which is signified by an "X" before the species name. It is probably derived from crossing the French rose, *Rosa gallica* L. with another species. The damask rose has been in cultivation since the 16th century, and probably long before that. An ancient selection of this rose, with flowers varying from white to pink, was designated as a symbol of unity of the red (House of Lancaster) and white (House of York) rose factions at the end of the War of the Roses in the 15th century.

The damask rose is one of the sources for the "Otto (attar) of roses," the perfume obtained through steam distillation from the blossoms of this rose and *Rosa X alba*, produced in Bulgaria.

Rosa is the ancient Latin name; *damascena* refers to Damascas, Syria.

Rosa X damascena 🌼 a. Growth form with flower clusters, b. Flower, c. Aborted fruit

Multiflora rose

Rosa multiflora Thunb. ex Murray

Rose family (Rosaceae)

Field Identification: A diffusely branched shrub with branches up to 12 feet long and arching or sprawling.

Flowers: May-June, **in rounded or pyramid-shaped clusters 3 to 6 inches long with 6 to 30 flowers**; flower stalks about 1/2 inch long, green, hairs gland-tipped; **flowers small for a rose, 3/4 to 1 1/2 inches across**; petals 5, pale pink to white, inverted egg-shaped; stamens numerous.

Fruits: Late September-October, in drooping or erect clusters; developing into hard fruits called rose hips, red, 1/4 to 3/8 inch long, oval to inverted egg-shaped, glossy, smooth; seeds several, yellow, flattened on two sides.

Leaves: Alternate, pinnately compound, 3 to 4 1/2 inches long, leaflets 7 to 9; leaflets narrow or broad, tip pointed, base wedge-shaped, margin with numerous sharp teeth; upper surface dark green, smooth; lower surface pale, finely hairy; mature leaves often thick and leathery; petioles about 1/2 inch long, **with a deeply dissected, fringed and comblike stipule (a leaflike growth) along the base of the petioles**, hairy.

Twigs: Flexible, smooth, red to green, armed with stout, recurved prickles.

Trunk: Bark of young stems red or greenish, prickles about 1/4 inch long, sharp, brown, flattened, broad-based; bark of old trunks grayish-brown, smooth; wood hard, nearly white, with a large pith.

Habitat: Introduced and planted around farmsteads, fields, and pastures; escaped in many places, including woodlands and along streambanks; long persistent.

Range: Native of Japan; introduced and naturalized in New England and New York south and west to Missouri, Oklahoma and Texas.

Wildlife Uses: The fruit may remain on the plant well into winter; it is eaten, to some extent, by birds. The shrub is used for cover by a variety of birds and small mammals during both summer and winter.

Remarks: Multiflora rose was designated a noxious weed by Missouri state law in 1983. As such, Missouri counties may adopt a law that requires mandatory control of this shrub. Although it originally was introduced with the intention of providing habitat for wildlife and "living fences" for livestock, it was found to form almost impenetrable thickets and smother out other vegetation in natural habitats and in pastures.

Multiflora rose spreads when its seeds drop to the soil nearby, and when birds and small mammals disperse seeds greater distances. It also spreads by layering (where tips of canes touch the ground and form roots), and by plants that arise from shallow roots.

Rosa is the ancient Latin name; *multiflora* refers to the numerous flowers produced.

Rosa multiflora ❀ a. Growth form with flowers, b. Flower, c. Twig with fruit

Swamp rose

Rosa palustris Marshall

Rose family (Rosaceae)

Field Identification: Large shrub of swamps or wet ground with erect stems sometimes attaining a height of 8 1/2 feet.

Flowers: Late May-July, solitary or 2 to 3 flowers in a cluster; flower stalk 1/2 to 3/4 inch long, **stalk with rigid gland-tipped hairs**; petals 5, rose-colored, inverted heart-shaped, 1/2 to 3/4 inch long; stamens numerous.

Fruit: July-October, rose hips red, globe-shaped to inverted egg-shaped, with rigid gland-tipped hairs but sometimes smooth, 1/4 to 1/2 inch broad.

Leaves: Alternate, pinnately compound, stem bearing hairy, rarely prickly, leaflets; **leaflets 5 to 7, rarely 9**, 3/4 to 2 1/2 inches long, lance-shaped to broadest in the middle and tapering at both ends, tip pointed, base tapering, **margin with numerous fine teeth; upper surface dark green, smooth; lower surface paler** with scattered fine hairs, at least on the veins; **petioles above the leafy base about 1/4 inch long, leafy lower portion 3/4 to 1 1/4 inches long, usually narrow and rolled-up, only the upper portion somewhat expanded and spreading.**

Twigs: Rather erect, sometimes reddish, smooth, armed with strong but rather short, curved prickles that are usually paired, flattened at the base, about 1/4 inch long.

Habitat: Occurs in swamps, low wet woods, borders of upland wooded sinkhole ponds, along streams, bayous, and drainage ditches; found in southeastern Missouri.

Range: Florida to Louisiana and Arkansas, north to Nova Scotia, and west to Quebec, Ontario, Michigan, Wisconsin and Minnesota.

Wildlife Uses: Rose hips are eaten by several species of birds and small mammals.

Remarks: Swamp rose is restricted to southeast Missouri where it usually is associated with swamps and low, wet woods. It sometimes can be found growing on the trunks of bald cypress trees in depressions, especially above the waterline where debris has accumulated.

Swamp rose is worthy of cultivation because of its attractive stems and flowers. It is easily cultivated, grows rather tall, and is a great plant for gardens with drainage problems. It grows well in moderate shade.

Rosa is the ancient Latin name; *palustris* refers to the occurrence of the plant in marshy ground.

Rosa palustris ❀ a. Growth form with flowers, b. Twig with compound leaf and prickles, c. Fruit

Prairie rose

Rosa setigera Michaux

Rose family (Rosaceae)

Also called climbing rose

Field Identification: Shrub with high-climbing, trailing or leaning stems reaching a length of 6 to 15 feet when supported by other shrubs or small trees; in the open, a dense shrub to 4 feet high.

Flowers: Late May-June, in many-flowered clusters on new stem growth, flower stalks with gland-tipped hairs; **flowers large, 1 1/2 to 3 1/4 inches across**; petals 5, pink, inverted egg- to heart-shaped, about 1 1/2 inches long and wide; stamens numerous.

Fruit: September, red, about 3/8 inch long, fleshy, globe-shaped to inverted egg-shaped, usually with gland-tipped hairs; seeds yellow, smooth.

Leaves: Alternate, pinnately compound, axis bearing leaflets with gland-tipped hairs and often with a few prickles; **leaflets commonly 3 on old stems, on new stems 3 or 5**; end leaflet with petiole about 1/4 inch long; leaflets 1 1/2 to 4 inches long, about 1 inch wide, lance- to egg-shaped, tip pointed, base ending at a sharp angle or sometimes heart-shaped, margin sharply toothed; upper surface dark green, shiny; lower surface paler, smooth; petioles often with gland-tipped hairs and prickles, leafy lower portion (stipule) 3/8 to 3/4 inch long, smooth, margin entire with fine hairs, end portion spreading.

Twigs: Flexible, smooth, green or reddish-green; prickles straw-colored or pale brown, base expanded, recurved, about 1/4 inch long, often in pairs at the nodes.

Trunk: Bark on young stems green to reddish-brown, smooth, glossy; prickles (thorns) scattered along the whole length; bark of old stems grayish-brown, split with narrow, long slits; wood soft, pale brown, with a large, brown pith.

Habitat: Occurs in moist ground and rocky places along streams and spring branches, moist thickets, low open woodland, pastures, prairie thickets, clearings, fence rows and along roadsides.

Range: Florida, Louisiana, Arkansas and Texas, north to New York, and west to Indiana, Missouri and Kansas. Naturalized in New England.

Wildlife Uses: White-tailed deer browse the twigs and fruits throughout the year. A variety of song birds — as well as greater prairie chicken, ruffed grouse and quail — eat the fruits or rose hips. When forming dense thickets, it makes good cover for small birds and mammals.

Remarks: Prairie rose should more appropriately be named climbing rose, since it is less commonly found in prairie and more often climbing into tall bushes and low trees. Planted, prairie rose does well in open sun to shady areas and borders. It flowers a little later than most other rose species. The leaves turn a deep rose-red in late fall.

Rosa is the ancient Latin name; *setigera* in Latin means "bristle-bearing," which probably refers to the prickles.

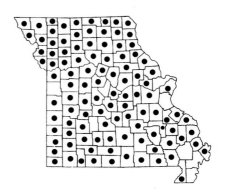

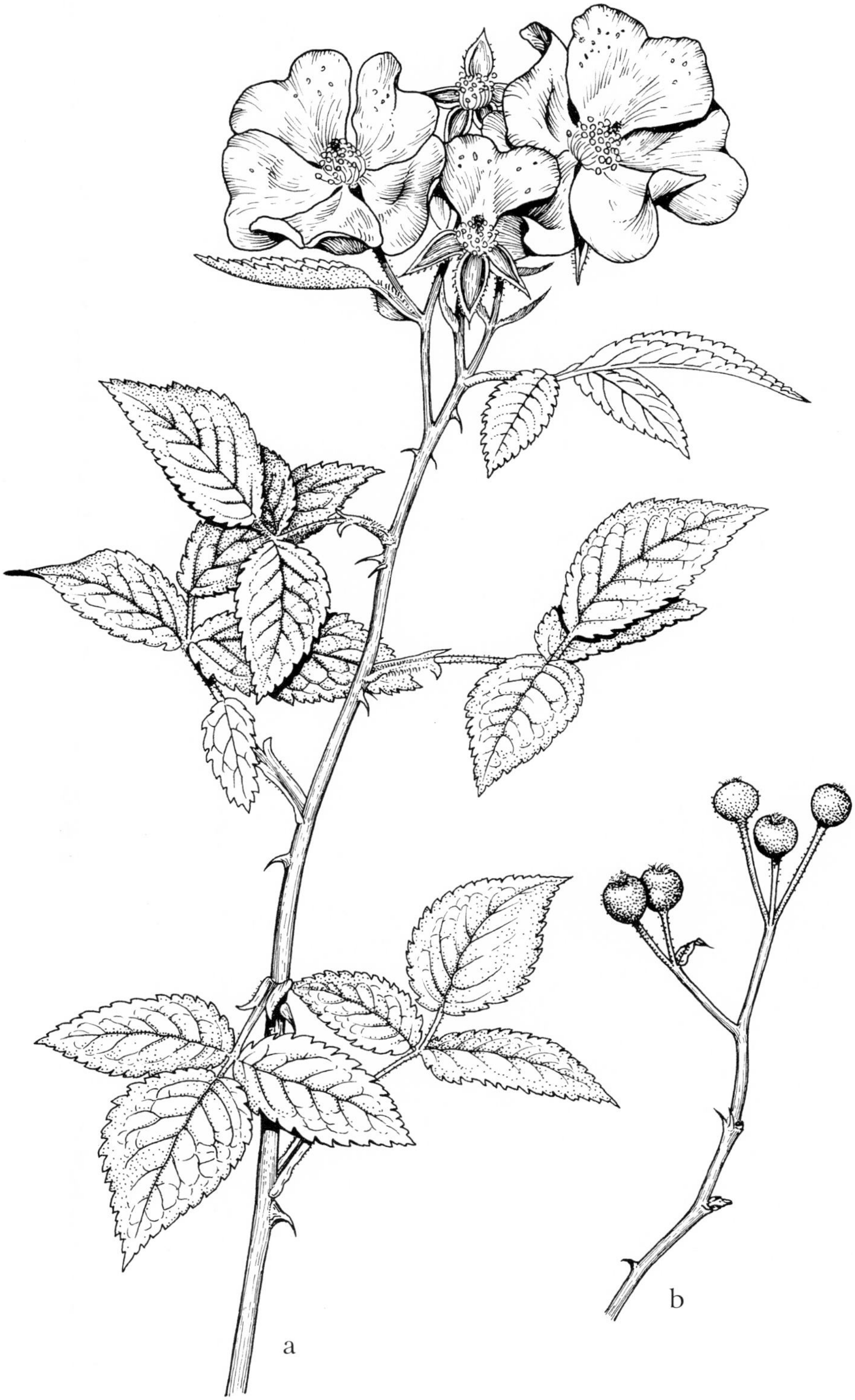

Rosa setigera a. Growth form with flowers, b. Twig with fruit

Highbush Blackberry

Rubus allegheniensis Porter

Rose family (Rosaceae)

Also called common blackberry, Allegheny blackberry

Field Identification: An erect shrub, the branches occasionally to 8 feet and arching high or being supported by surrounding trees or shrubs.

Flowers: April-June, in clusters 4 to 5 inches long, or **2 to 4 times as long as broad, rather elongated and cylinder-shaped**, extending beyond the foliage, but provided with small leaves at the base; flower stalks with gland-tipped hairs; flowers 6 to 12 and sometimes to 30, 3/4 inch across; petals 5, white, oval; stamens numerous.

Fruit: June-August, abundant; fruit stalks 1/2 to 1 inch long, with gland-tipped hairs; fruit deep violet to black, glossy, juicy, sweet, globe- or cylinder-shaped, about 3/4 inch long; seeds straw-colored with the surface net-veined.

Leaves: Alternate, leaflets on flower canes 3, on primary canes 5; middle leaflet stalked; **end leaflet on primary canes 3 1/4 to 5 inches long, or 2 or 3 times longer than broad**, the lower pairs smaller, egg-shaped to broadest in the middle and tapering at both ends, tip pointed, base rounded to flattened, margin sharply toothed; upper surface dark, dull green, smooth; lower surface paler, hairy with a few gland-tipped hairs on the veins; thick and often wrinkled.

Twigs: Greenish- to reddish-brown; prickles broad-based, recurved, about 1/8 inch long, red at the base, yellowish tip; twig hairy with some gland-tipped.

Trunk: Primary canes (first year) green to reddish, ribbed; prickles numerous, straight or recurved, flat, reddish; flower canes (second year) brown.

Habitat: Occurs in rocky open woods, along bluffs, thickets and open valleys.

Range: North Carolina to Tennessee and Missouri, north to New Brunswick and Quebec, and west to Minnesota.

Wildlife Uses: Brambles provide food and cover for many species of birds and small mammals. White-tailed deer eat the fruit and browse the tender primary canes in spring and summer. Much of the summer diet of wild turkeys is composed of blackberries.

Remarks: A similar species — high-bush blackberry, *Rubus orarius* Blanchard — differs by having its flower clusters as long as broad, with the flowers mostly crowded at the tip; topmost leaflet of leaves of the first year's canes broadly egg-shaped to nearly round in shape; scattered throughout Missouri.

The shrub is widely variable; growing only to a height of 2 feet in hard, dry pastures or up to 8 feet in close colonies in areas with better soils. The blackberries as a group are difficult to identify. They vary within the species and integrade with other species, and the description of any one species is difficult. No attempt is made here to determine varieties.

Highbush blackberry is the original wild form from which many of the cultivated blackberries have been selected.

Rubus is the old Roman name similar to *ruber* or red, possibly in reference to the red fruit of raspberries; *allegheniensis* refers to its distribution in the Allegheny region.

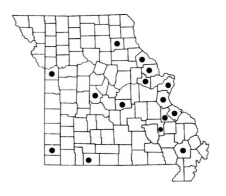

Rubus allegheniensis ❧ a. Growth form with flowers, b. Twig with leaves and fruit

Highbush blackberry

Rubus argutus Link

Rose family (Rosaceae)

Also called sharp-tooth blackberry

Field Identification: Usually a low, thicket-forming shrub to 6 feet tall. The canes with scattered straight, but not very large, prickles.

Flowers: April-June, in short clusters of 1 to 7 flowers on the ends of short branches of stems; flower stalk 3/4 to 1 1/2 inches long, green, hairy with an occasional recurved prickle, **flower about 1 inch across**; petals 5, white, **narrow, about 3/8 inch broad**, rounded; stamens numerous.

Fruit: June-August, about 1/4 to 3/4 inch long, cylinder- or globe-shaped, black, glossy; seeds straw-colored, flattened, surface net-veined.

Leaves: Alternate, 3 to 5 leaflets; **upper 3 leaflets of primary cane (without flowers) 2 1/4 to 4 inches long, 1 1/2 to 2 inches wide, or 2 to 3 times as long as broad, widest near the middle**, tip pointed, base rounded to heart-shaped, margin with large, sharp, doubly-toothed teeth; upper surface dark green, smooth; lower surface paler, soft hairy, hooked prickles on the midrib of the end leaflet; petioles 1 1/2 to 2 1/2 inches long, hairy, recurved prickles on the lower side.

Twigs: Semi-rigid, reddish-brown or blotched red and green, ridged, hairy; prickles broad-based, recurved, red near the base, yellow at the tip.

Trunk: Second year canes green, blotched with reddish-brown, 5-ridged and with a few nearly straight prickles; flower canes reddish-brown, slightly ridged and with straight or hooked prickles; wood soft with a large, brown pith.

Habitat: Occurs in low wet woods, thickets, open woods, margins of woods, fence rows, gullies, roadsides and pastures.

Range: Georgia and Alabama to Arkansas, north to Massachusetts, Pennsylvania, Kentucky, Illinois and Missouri.

Wildlife Uses: Brambles provide food and cover for many species of birds and small mammals. White-tailed deer eat the fruit and browse the tender primary canes in spring and summer. Much of the summer diet of wild turkeys is composed of blackberries.

Remarks: The fruits of this species are smaller and less desirable, having a more seedy and more bitter quality than most other blackberries in Missouri. The blackberries as a group are difficult to identify, and it may be difficult to separate this species from *Rubus ostryifolius* and *Rubus pensilvanicus*.

Another similar species — highbush blackberry, *Rubus mollior* Bailey — differs by having short, cylinder-shaped flower clusters, not broadened across the top and with an elongated cluster stalk. It is found in shallow draws in upland thickets and dry open woods in a few scattered counties across southern Missouri.

Rubus is the old Roman name similar to *ruber* or red, possibly referring to the red fruit of raspberries; *argutus* means "sharp-toothed," in reference to the margin of the leaves.

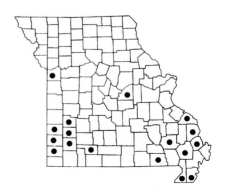

Rubus argutus ❀ a. Growth form with fruit, b. Flowers, c. Primary cane with prickles and compound leaf

Twice-leafed blackberry

Rubus bifrons Vest ex Tratt.

Rose family (Rosaceae)

Field Identification: A strong, low-arching bramble, making canes 6 to 9 feet or more long with the tips lying or creeping on the ground, and sometimes rooting at the tip, the clump or colony standing 3 to 4 1/2 feet.

Flowers: May-June, **in narrow and long pyramid-shaped clusters**; flower stalks with densely matted hairs; bearing straight conspicuous prickles; flowers white or rose, 3/4 to 2 inches across; petals 5, narrow; stamens numerous.

Fruit: July-August, **in narrow and long pyramid-shaped clusters**; black, juicy, about 1/2 inch thick; **fruit remaining attached to the central green receptacle, even when ripe.**

Leaves: Alternate, flower-bearing canes with 3 leaflets, primary canes with 5 leaflets; all leaflets about 3 to 3 1/2 inches long, 2 to 2 1/2 inches wide, oval to egg-shaped, tip pointed, base rounded to abruptly narrowing or heart-shaped, margin finely and sharply toothed; upper surface green, smooth to slightly hairy; **lower surface with brownish to grayish woolly hairs; petioles hairy with stout prickles.**

Twigs: Primary canes with fine lines, ridges or grooves, scantly hairy, prickles irregularly scattered and of different lengths, averaging about 1/4 inch long, moderately broad-based, nearly straight to somewhat hooked.

Habitat: Occurs along rocky stream beds, banks and pastures.

Range: Native of Europe; introduced and naturalized in the United States from Florida to Louisiana, north to Rhode Island, Tennessee, Missouri and Oklahoma.

Wildlife Uses: Brambles provide food and cover for many species of birds and small mammals.

Remarks: This species has been confused with the Himalaya berry *(Rubus procerus)* in Missouri and elsewhere. Refer to the key to make the distinction.

Neither species is native, and planting them should be discouraged. Native blackberry shrubs are better adapted to living in balance with other plants, and are less likely to overwhelm and dominate a habitat.

Rubus is the old Roman name similar to *ruber* or red, possibly referring to the red fruit of raspberries; *bifrons* refers to the leaves, which often appear in two forms.

Rubus bifrons ✺ a. Growth form with fruit, b. Flowers, c. End leaflet, d. Cane with prickles, e. Primary cane

Dewberry

Rubus flagellaris Willd.

Rose family (Rosaceae)

Also called northern dewberry, whiplash dewberry

Field Identification: A trailing vinelike plant, the branches up to 10 feet.

Flowers: April-June, solitary or in clusters of 2 to 6 flowers that stand up well above the foliage; flower stalks lacking gland-tipped hairs, 3/4 to 2 inches long; flowers 3/4 to 1 1/4 inch across; petals 5, white, rounded, tip blunt; stamens many.

Fruit: June-August, red then turning black at maturity, shiny, about 1/4 inch thick, globe-shaped, sweet, juicy, very edible when ripe; seeds straw-colored, egg-shaped, strongly net-veined.

Leaves: Alternate, leaflets 3 to 5, **end leaflet on primary cane 2 1/4 to 3 1/4 inches long, 1 3/4 to 2 1/2 inches wide, broadly egg-shaped, widest below the middle**, tip pointed, base rounded, margin coarsely toothed; upper surface dark green, slightly rough, a few long hairs; lower surface paler with soft hairs; petioles 1 1/2 to 2 1/2 inches long, often with long prickles. Leaflets on flower canes smaller.

Twigs: Flexible, green or reddish, angled or round, smooth, armed with recurved prickles with wide bases; twigs very thin and almost leafless toward the ends of primary canes and whip-like in appearance.

Trunk: Bark of primary cane green, usually brown on the flower canes; wood soft, white, a large pith; branches often root when covered with dirt.

Habitat: Occurs in rocky open woods, thickets, prairies, along roadsides and railroad embankments.

Range: Florida, Louisiana, Arkansas and Texas, north to New Brunswick and west to Minnesota and Kansas.

Wildlife Uses: The fruit is widely used by a variety of species of birds and small mammals.

Remarks: There are two other species similar to *Rubus flagellaris* Willd. The first dewberry, *Rubus invisus* (L. Bailey) Britton, has flower stalks with gland-tipped hairs. The plant, which is rare, is found in dry rocky woods and on open rocky exposures. The other, southern dewberry, *Rubus enslenii* Tratt., has no gland-tipped hairs. The topmost one of 3 leaflets of the flowering cane is broadly lance-shaped or inverse egg-shaped, and is narrowed toward the base. The plant is scattered throughout Missouri in old fields, prairies, open banks and along roadsides.

The fruits of dewberry are large and of good quality. The flavor is excellent, and the berries are gathered often for sauce, pies or jams, or eaten raw with a bit of sugar. The plants bear less prolifically than the highbush blackberries. The dewberries have long been a popular food of Native Americans. Seeds have been recovered from excavations of the Seven Acres and Maybrook sites of villages dating to the 12th and 13th centuries A.D. in Jackson County, Mo., near Kansas City.

Rubus is the old Roman name similar to *ruber* or red, possibly referring to the red fruit of raspberries; *flagellaris* refers to the whiplashlike habit of the stems.

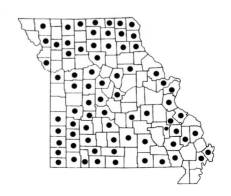

Rubus flagellaris ❀ a. Growth form with flowers, b. Fruit

Black raspberry

Rubus occidentalis L.

Rose family (Rosaceae)

Also called blackcap raspberry

Field Identification: An arching shrub, the canes attaining a height of 3 to 7 1/2 feet with tip-rooting stems.

Flowers: April-June, in tight clusters of 3 to 7 flowers on the end of shoots; **flower stalks bearing stout-hooked prickles**, hairy; flowers 1/2 to 3/4 inch across; petals 5, white, narrow; stamens numerous.

Fruit: June-July, firm and compact, center hollow and thimblelike, **purple-black**, aromatic, mostly globe-shaped with a flattened base, about 1/2 inch across, **becoming detached as a unit from the receptacle**; seeds straw-colored, egg- to crescent-shaped, surface net-veined.

Leaves: Alternate, leaflets 3, and sometimes 5, all leaflets broadly egg-shaped to lance-shaped; end leaflet commonly 2 3/4 to 3 1/4 inches long, tapering to a narrow point, margin sharply and unequally double-toothed; side leaflets smaller and narrower, more or less lobed; leaflets on flower canes smaller, perhaps 2 1/2 to 3 1/4 inches long, 1 1/2 to 2 1/2 inches wide; upper surface on all leaflets dark green, slightly hairy; lower surface densely white with matted hairs; petioles 2 to 2 1/2 inches long, smooth and usually bearing short, stout, curved prickles.

Twigs: Flexible, smooth, **first-year canes with whitish coating that rubs off**, light reddish-purple, prickles broad-based, recurved.

Trunk: Bark smooth, **reddish-purple with a whitish coating, prickles or thorns recurved, stout**; wood soft, white, large pith. Tip of cane often rooting when in contact with the soil.

Habitat: Occurs in open woods, along bluffs and in thickets. Throughout Missouri except for the southeastern lowland counties.

Range: Georgia to Louisiana, Arkansas and Oklahoma, north New Brunswick, and west to Minnesota, North Dakota and Colorado.

Wildlife Uses: Brambles provide food and cover for many species of birds and small mammals. White-tailed deer eat the fruit and browse the tender primary canes in spring and summer. Much of the summer diet of wild turkeys is composed of raspberries and blackberries.

Remarks: A similar, but rare species — red raspberry, *Rubus strigosus* Michaux — differs by having stems that lack a whitish coating; fruit red when ripe; and stalks of flowers and fruits and stems bearing bristles but no thorns or prickles. This species occurs on wooded slopes of loess hills in northwestern Missouri.

Black raspberry has long been cultivated in many commercial varieties. The fruits are gathered and eaten raw or made into jam and jelly, or put in pies, muffins and ice cream. The mass of canes catches and holds the leaves in autumn and makes a good soil cover against erosion and water evaporation.

The leaflets of raspberries are whitish beneath; those of blackberries and dewberries are green or grayish-green. Raspberries also are distinguished by the hollow thimblelike fruit, whereas the fruit of blackberries and dewberries is solid.

Rubus is the old Roman name similar to *ruber* or red, possibly referring to the red fruit of raspberries; *occidentalis* means "western."

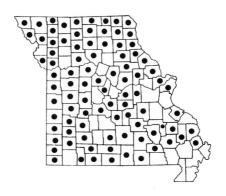

Rubus occidentalis ❧ a. Primary cane, b. Flowers, c. Cane with fruit

Highbush blackberry

Rubus pensilvanicus Poiret

Rose family (Rosaceae)

Field Identification: A shrub with arching canes to 10 feet long, forming open thickets.

Flowers: April-June, **in clusters short and rather hidden in the leaves attached just below; leaflike bracts 7 to 12 in the flower cluster**; flower stalks 3/4 to 1 1/2 inches long, densely soft hairy, **a large bract at the base of each or nearly each flower stalk**; petals 5, white, egg- to inverted egg-shaped, about 3/4 inch long; stamens numerous.

Fruit: June-August, cluster 2 1/2 to 4 inches long, 1 1/2 to 2 1/2 inches wide; fruit red before ripening, black at maturity, glossy, 3/8 to 3/4 inch long, juicy, sweet; seeds straw-colored, surface net-veined.

Leaves: Alternate, 5 leaflets on primary cane, 3 leaflets on flower cane; **end leaflet on primary cane widest toward the base**, 3 1/4 to 4 inches long, 2 1/2 to 3 1/4 inches wide, **broadly egg-shaped**, tip pointed, base rounded or heart-shaped, terminal leaf stalk 1 1/2 to 2 inches long, hairy with few prickles; side leaflets smaller, middle leaflets with leaf stalk 3/4 to 1 1/4 inches long, lowest pair stalkless; leaflets on flower canes smaller, more variable in shape; upper surface of leaflets sparingly hairy; densely hairy below; margin irregularly toothed with some large teeth; petioles 3 1/4 to 5 1/2 inches long, sharply grooved above, densely hairy, prickles few.

Twigs: Primary canes with ridges and valleys; red, reddish-brown or greenish; hairy, with some gland-tipped hairs, prickles broad-based, recurved.

Trunk: Primary canes nearly erect, fruiting canes arched and with longer lateral branches. Canes with ridges and valleys, bark tight, reddish-brown or greenish, the broad-based, recurved prickles mainly on the ridges; wood hard, greenish-white, porous, pith tawny.

Habitat: Occurs in open, rich or rocky wooded hills, thickets, meadows, pastures, prairie openings, and along fence rows and roadsides. Common throughout Missouri.

Range: Alabama to Arkansas and Oklahoma, north to Newfoundland, and west to Ontario, Minnesota, and eastern Kansas.

Wildlife Uses: Brambles provide food and cover for many birds and small mammals. White-tailed deer eat the fruit and browse the tender primary canes in spring and summer. Much of the summer diet of wild turkeys is composed of blackberries. In winter, the canes provide food and potective cover for cottontail rabbits.

Remarks: A similar species of highbush blackberry, *Rubus ostryifolius* Rybd., differs by having fewer leaflike bracts in the flower cluster; topmost leaflet of the 5 leaflets of the first year's vegetative canes widest near the middle; main flower clusters standing above the leaves attached just below. It shares habitat and locations similar to *Rubus pensilvanicus*.

This highbush blackberry is considered to have one of the best-tasting fruits of the blackberries. As with other members of this genus, the abundance of local rains in late spring to early summer often determines the fruit size and quality.

Rubus is the old Roman name similar to *ruber* or red, possibly referring to the red fruit of raspberries; *pensilvanicus* means "of Pennsylvania," probably indicating where it was first discovered.

Rubus pensilvanicus a. Primary cane, b. Flowers, c. Fruit

Southern dewberry

Rubus trivialis Michaux

Rose family (Rosaceae)

Field Identification: With trailing stems more than 3 feet long, rooting at the tip and along the stem (cane). Canes with reddish, gland-tipped hairs and prickles (small, pointed outgrowth of skin tissue).

Flowers: April-May, flowers usually solitary, variable in size, commonly 1/2 to 3/4 inch across, but sometimes twice these dimensions, on solitary, erect stalks bearing prickles; petals 5, white to pinkish, broad, overlapping, tip blunt; stamens numerous.

Fruit: Late May-June, black, large seeded, about 1/4 to 3/8 inch long, but sometimes 3/4 to 1 1/4 inches long; usually longer than broad; sweet, juicy, showy.

Leaves: Alternate, leaflets 5 on primary cane, firm, 1 3/4 to 2 3/4 inches long, usually twice or more longer than broad, tip pointed, base more or less narrowed, not heart-shaped, margin sharply toothed; flower-bearing canes usually with 3 leaflets; leaflets widely variable in size and shape, smooth, margins strongly toothed; upper surface green, shiny; lower surface dull; **petioles on both canes stout, bearing prickles and often with reddish, gland-tipped hairs.** The leaves are more or less evergreen.

Twigs: Primary canes at first ascending but soon prostrate, becoming woody, branching, bearing many short, broad-based, often hooked reddish prickles and reddish gland-tipped hairs.

Habitat: Occurs in low or bottomland woods, moist thickets and wooded banks of streams.

Range: Florida to Louisiana, Texas, Arkansas and Oklahoma, north to Maryland, and west to Pennsylvania, Illinois and Missouri.

Wildlife Uses: The fruit is used by a variety of species of birds and small mammals.

Remarks: Southern dewberry is variable as to size of flower, leaf and amount of gland-tipped hairs. **This species, however, is easily recognized by the slender reddish-purple gland-tipped hairs and bristles on the trailing stems.**

In general, the growth habit of blackberries and raspberries is unusual: they never have a true bark. Although their roots are perennial, their stems are biennial; that is, they have a life cycle of only two years. The first year, the root system produces long unbranched canes, which grow leaves but no flowers. The second year, these same canes grow smaller side branches, which produce flowers that later mature into fruits. After producing fruits, the canes die back, but the roots remain living and send up new shoots the following year. That is why, in gardening, it is best to cut away the old, second-year canes at the end of the season to allow for new canes to grow and spread their leaves the following year.

Rubus is the old Roman name similar to *ruber* or red, possibly referring to the red fruit of raspberries; *trivialis* means "ordinary."

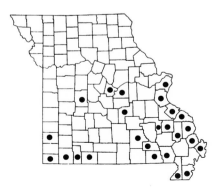

Rubus trivialis ❀ a. Primary cane, b. Cane with flowers and fruit, c. Flower, d. Fruit

Carolina willow

Salix caroliniana Michaux

Willow family (Salicaceae)

Also called ward's willow, coastal plain willow

Field Identification: Shrub or small tree to 30 feet. Branches spreading or drooping to form an open, irregular crown.

Flowers: April-May, male and female flowers in separate catkins on the tips of twigs, borne on separate plants; catkins slender, narrowly cylindrical, up to 4 inches long; staminate (male) catkins with 4 to 7 stamens; pistillate (female) catkins not as full or as showy as the yellow staminate catkins.

Fruit: June-July, capsule about 1/4 inch long, egg- to cone-shaped, abruptly long-pointed, brown at maturity, stalk of capsule very short, almost absent; seeds minute with long, silky hairs at the base, which are 2 to 3 times as long as the seed.

Leaves: Alternate, simple, **2 to 7 inches long**, 3/8 to 3/4 inch wide, **narrowly lance-shaped**, tip pointed, base gradually narrowed on young leaves, on older ones often rounded; upper surface bright green, smooth; lower surface white to silvery-white, smooth, young leaves with matted hairs; margin finely toothed; petioles 1/4 to 1/2 inch long, densely hairy, lacking glands; **stipules up to 3/4 inch across, conspicuous, margin toothed.**

Twigs: Slender, yellowish- to reddish-brown or grayish, more or less hairy, eventually smooth.

Trunk: Bark reddish-brown to gray, ridges thin to broad, fissures shallow to deep, conspicuously checkered, breaking into closely flattened scales; wood dark reddish-brown, sapwood nearly white, light, soft, not strong.

Habitat: Occurs along gravel bars, sandy gravel beds and rocky banks of streams. The most common willow along gravel bars in Ozark streams.

Range: Florida to Texas and western Arkansas and eastern Oklahoma, north to Maryland, West Virginia, Pennsylvania, Indiana, Illinois, Missouri and eastern Kansas.

Wildlife Uses: Willow twigs and leaves are browsed by white-tailed deer. The shoots and buds are eaten by many rodents (including muskrat and beaver), as well as cottontail rabbits. Some ducks and water birds feed on willow catkins and leaves. Bees use willow nectar to produce high-grade honey. Dense thickets also provide cover for wildlife.

Remarks: Carolina willow is a pioneer species invading and stabilizing newly formed gravel bars. The common phrase "bend like a willow" comes from the shrub's ability to withstand the force of floods and storms by bending and being flexible.

It is one of the willow species used in the Ozarks for making wickerwork for baskets, furniture and ornamental pieces.

Salix is the classical Latin name; *caroliniana* refers to the states of Carolina, where the plant was first described.

Salix caroliniana ❋ a. Growth form, b. Catkin, c. Seed capsules

Pussy willow

Salix discolor Muhlenb.

Willow family (Salicaceae)

Field Identification: A large shrub to small tree to 16 feet high, the trunks single or clustered, the branches high.

Flowers: February-April, before the leaves, male and female flowers in separate catkins and on separate plants in axils on twigs of previous year; staminate (male) catkins 3/4 to 1 1/2 inches long, 1/2 to 1 1/4 inches wide, densely flowered, showy; stamens 2; pistillate (female) catkins 3/4 to 1 1/4 inches long, about 1/2 inch wide, numerous flowers.

Fruit: June, catkins drooping, 2 1/2 to 3 1/4 inches long; capsules wide spreading, about 1/2 inch long, egg-shaped with a long neck; seeds dark green, cylindrical, blunt-tipped, a ring of short, stiff hairs and an outer ring of long, silky hairs around the base more than twice the length of the seed.

Leaves: Simple, alternate, 1 1/2 to 3 1/4 inches long, 3/4 to 1 1/4 inches wide, longer than broad, the width about 1/2 the length, tip pointed, base wedge-shaped to narrowly rounded, margin irregularly toothed and wavy; upper surface dark green, semi-shiny, smooth; **lower surface with a light, whitish coating**; petioles about 3/8 inch long, hairy, the blade slightly pointing down.

Twigs: Flexible, reddish-purple to reddish-brown, dull, **smooth**; lenticels (pores) oval, small, yellow.

Trunk: Bark grayish-brown, tight with fine ridges along the stem, slightly grooved and ridged on old trunks; wood soft, brownish, with a wide, white sapwood.

Habitat: Along creeks and rivers in open or wooded areas; **collected only from Clark County**.

Range: Maryland, Kentucky and Missouri, north to Labrador to North Dakota, Montana and Alberta.

Wildlife Uses: Willow twigs and leaves are browsed by white-tailed deer. The shoots and buds are eaten by many rodents (including muskrat and beaver), as well as cottontail rabbits. Some ducks and water birds feed on willow catkins and leaves. Bees use willow nectar to produce high-grade honey. Dense thickets also provide cover for wildlife.

Remarks: Pussy willow hasn't been seen in Missouri growing in the wild since 1892. The only location was in Clark County, 3 to 4 miles north of Dumas on the Des Moines River bank. In Iowa, it is common in the northern third of the state and infrequent to rare elsewhere. Since pussy willow is more northern in its distribution, its occurrence in Missouri probably always was extremely rare. Other possible sites for this willow may be found along the Des Moines River.

The soft, silky hairs clothing the bracts of the catkins before they open give this species the name of "pussy willow," because of their similarity to the pads of cats' feet. The pussy willow sold in florists shops is a species from Europe and Asia known as goat willow (*Salix caprea L.*). It has much larger fuzzy catkins, but rarely escapes from cultivation and has not been recorded to do so in Missouri.

Salix is the classical Latin name; *discolor* means "of two different colors," probably referring to the yellow male and greenish female catkins.

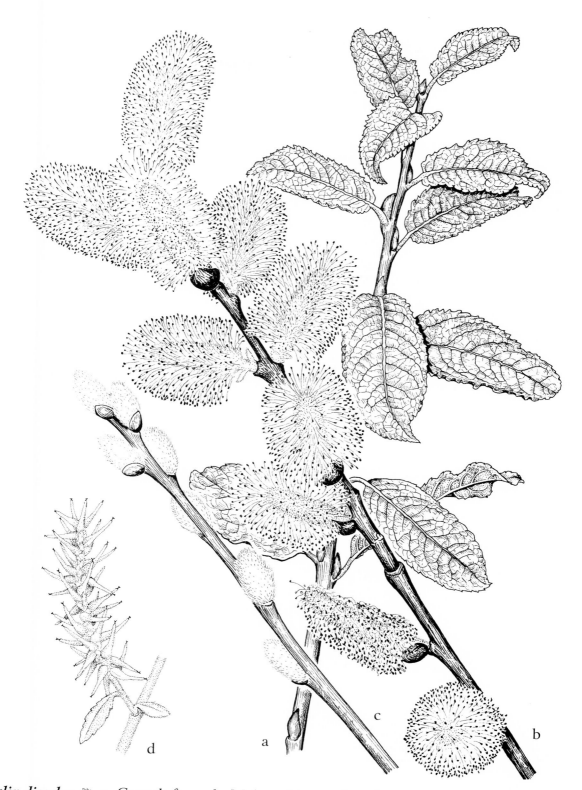

Salix discolor ❀ a. Growth form, b. Male catkins, c. Female catkins, d. Seed capsules

Prairie willow

Salix humilis Marshall

Willow family (Salicaceae)

Field Identification: Shrub from 3 to 9 feet tall with wandlike branches.

Flowers: March-May, flowering before the leaves, male and female flowers in separate catkins and on separate plants in axils on twigs of previous year; staminate (male) catkins 1/4 to 1 1/4 inches long, 1/4 to 3/4 inch wide, oval to inverted egg-shaped; flowers numerous; stamens 2; pistillate (female) catkins at maturity 1/2 to 3 1/4 inches long; flowers numerous.

Fruit: June, catkins 3/4 to 1 1/4 inches long; capsule about 1/4 inch long, narrowly lanceolate with a beaklike point, yellowish-brown, hairy, a tuft of long silky hairs at the base; seeds cylindrical, surrounded by a ring of long white, silky hairs at the base.

Leaves: Simple, alternate, 1 1/4 to 4 inches long, 1/4 to 3/4 inch wide, blade lance-shaped to narrowly inverted egg-shaped, tip blunt to pointed, base tapering, margin entire or wavy with rounded teeth; upper surface grayish-green, slightly hairy; **lower surface silvery white with hairs**; petioles 1/4 to 1/2 inch long, hairy; stipules lance-shaped, very short, dropping early.

Twigs: Slender, wandlike, **young twigs hairy**, later smooth, yellowish to brown; usually crowded toward the end of the trunk.

Trunk: Bark grayish-brown, rough, with crooked lines of cracked bark; wood white, soft.

Habitat: Occurs in prairies, hill prairies, open woods, rocky draws or washes, rocky slopes, thickets, roadsides and railroad prairies.

Range: Florida to east Texas, Arkansas and Oklahoma, north to Newfoundland and Quebec, and west to Minnesota and North Dakota.

Wildlife Uses: Willow twigs and leaves are browsed by white-tailed deer. The shoots and buds are eaten by cottontail rabbits, and the buds and catkins are eaten by greater prairie chickens. Bees use willow nectar to produce high-grade honey. Dense thickets also provide cover for wildlife.

Remarks: Unlike the wet habitats most willows occupy, prairie willow prefers drier ground. It is easily recognized in prairies by its low, shrubby appearance. Dense thickets of prairie willow can form in unmanaged prairies. In presettlement conditions, elk and American bison, as well as white-tailed deer, browsed the twigs. Also, lightning-started fires, and those set by Native Americans to green-up the prairie grasses in spring, helped to keep this willow in check.

Today, unless prescribed fire or fire in combination with haying is practiced, prairie willow can spread and compete with other prairie plants and diminish diversity.

Salix is the classical Latin name; *humilis* refers to its low stature.

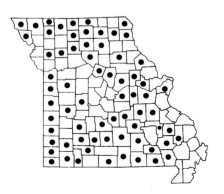

Salix humilis ✿ a. Growth form, b. Male catkins, c. Female catkins, d. Seed capsule

Sandbar willow

Salix interior Rowlee

Willow family (Salicaceae)

Field Identification: A slender, upright shrub forming thickets by spreading roots, or a small tree to 30 feet.

Flowers: May-June, flowering with leaves present, male and female flowers in separate catkins in axils on twigs, borne on separate plants; catkins slender, cylinder-shaped; staminate (male) catkins 3/4 to 2 inches long, about 1/4 to 3/4 inch broad; many-flowered, stamens 2; pistillate (female) catkins loosely flowered, 2 to 3 inches long, about 1/4 inch broad.

Fruit: June-July, catkins 1 1/2 to 2 inches long; capsules about 1/4 inch long, oval with a beaklike point, pale brown, smooth; seeds minute, attached to long white silky hairs at the base 2 to 3 times the length of the seed.

Leaves: Simple, alternate, 2 to 6 inches long, 1/8 to 3/8 inch wide, narrow lance-shaped, thin, tip pointed, base gradually narrowed to a short petiole, **margin with scattered and unevenly spaced, gland-tipped teeth, only 3 to 12 to an inch**; upper surface dark green, smooth or hairy along the main vein; lower surface paler, hairy; **petioles 1/8 inch or less,** hairy; stipules small or absent. Young leaves silky hairy beneath.

Twigs: Slender, erect, green to brown or red, smooth or hairy and sometimes with a white, waxy coating.

Trunk: Slender, straight, with small branches; bark green to gray or brown, smooth; on older trunks furrowed and broken into closely flattened scales; lenticels (pores) sometimes large and abundant; wood soft, light-weight, close-grained, weak, brittle, light brown, with a pale brown sapwood.

Habitat: Occurs on sand bars, mud flats and alluvial muddy banks of streams, oxbow lakes, ponds and ditches of river bottoms and floodplains throughout Missouri; absent from four counties of the southeastern lowlands.

Range: Virginia to West Virginia, Louisiana, Mississippi, Arkansas, Texas and Oklahoma, north to Quebec and west to North Dakota and Alaska.

Wildlife Uses: Willow twigs and leaves are browsed by white-tailed deer. The shoots and buds are eaten by many rodents (including muskrat and beaver), as well as cottontail rabbits. Some ducks and water birds feed on willow catkins and leaves. Bees use willow nectar to produce high-grade honey. Dense thickets also provide cover for wildlife.

Remarks: Sandbar willow often forms dense thickets that can be hard to penetrate. It is one of the first woody plants to inhabit a newly made sandbar in a river. It is associated with silver maple *(Acer saccharinum)* and cottonwood *(Populus deltoides)* on the river flats of the Missouri and Mississippi rivers. Sandbar willow is a good soil binder and bank stabilizer, and prevents washing and erosion of alluvial soil.

Salix is the classical Latin name; *interior* refers to the plant's inland distribution along water courses.

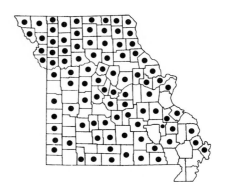

Salix interior ❧ a. Growth form, b. Twig with seed capsules, c. Open capsule

Meadow willow

Salix petiolaris Smith

Willow family (Salicaceae)

Field Identification: A low-growing shrub to a height of 8 feet.

Flowers: April-June, flowering with leaves about 1/4 grown, staminate (male) and pistillate (female) flowers in separate catkins in axils of leaves, borne on separate plants; catkins on a short stalk with 1 to 4 small leaves; staminate catkins 3/4 to 1 inch long, about 1/2 inch wide, many flowered; stamens 2; pistillate catkins 1/2 to 3/4 inch long, about 1/4 inch wide, with silky hairs.

Fruit: June-July, catkins erect, 3/4 to 1 inch long, about 1/2 inch wide; capsules cone-shaped, with short, silky hairs; seeds cylindrical with long, silky hairs at base.

Leaves: Alternate, simple, 1 1/4 to 3 inch long, 1/2 to 3/4 inch wide, lance-shaped, tip pointed, base narrowly wedge-shaped or slightly rounded, margin finely toothed, **teeth do not occur at base of leaf, and teeth that are present are tipped with glands**; upper surface dark green, semiglossy, smooth; lower surface smooth or with a few hairs; **stipules absent, or if present, small and quickly disappearing**; petioles 1/4 to 1/2 inch long, smooth to hairy, broadly grooved above.

Twigs: Reddish-brown or yellowish-brown, nearly smooth or with whitish hairs; lenticels (pores) small, barely noticeable, yellowish-orange; pith greenish.

Trunk: Bark of young branches grayish-green or reddish-brown; bark of old trunks brown, either smooth or flaky; wood fine-grained, soft, white, with no distinct heartwood or sapwood.

Habitat: Occurs in low, wet ground in mud or sandy gravel along streams associated with other species of willows. **Found only in the northeastern part of the state.**

Range: From New Jersey, Pennsylvania, Ohio, Indiana, Illinois, Iowa, Missouri and Nebraska, north to Quebec, and west to Manitoba and North Dakota.

Wildlife Uses: Willow twigs and leaves are browsed by white-tailed deer. The shoots and buds are eaten by many rodents (including muskrat and beaver), as well as cottontail rabbits. Some ducks and water birds feed on willow catkins and leaves. Bees use willow nectar to produce high-grade honey. Dense thickets also provide cover for wildlife.

Remarks: Meadow willow is also known as *Salix gracilis* var. *textoris*. Meadow willow is classified as endangered in Missouri probably because the plant is at the southern edge of its range in Missouri. This willow probably is overlooked and often mistaken for small sandbar willows.

    Salix is the classical Latin name; *petiolaris* is in reference to the petiole.

Salix petiolaris ❀ a. Growth form, b. Male catkins, c. Female catkins, d. Seed capsule, e. Open capsule

Heart-leaved willow

Salix rigida Muhl.

Willow family (Salicaceae)

Also called diamond willow

Field Identification: Shrub or small tree to 22 feet tall with one main trunk, rarely clustered.

Flowers: April-May, flowering with or prior to the leaves, male and female flowers in separate catkins and on separate plants in axils on twigs of previous year; staminate (male) catkins 1 1/2 to 2 3/4 inches, cylindrical; flowers clustered; stamens 2; pistillate (female) catkins 1 to 3 inches long.

Fruit: May-June, catkins 2 to 3 inches long; capsules about 3/8 inch long, egg-shaped with a long neck, yellowish-brown; seeds cylindrical, surrounded by a ring of long, white, silky hairs at the base.

Leaves: Simple, alternate, 1 1/2 to 3 inches long, 1/4 to 3/4 inch wide, blade lance-shaped, tip pointed, base rounded or heart-shaped, **margin finely toothed, equally and closely spaced, 13 to 25 to an inch**; upper surface dark green to yellowish-green, smooth; lower surface pale to lightly covered with a white, waxy coating, smooth to hairy; **petioles 1/8 to 3/4 inch long; stipules persistent on vigorous shoots, heart- to kidney-shaped surrounding the stem.**

Twigs: Gray-brown to dark brown, somewhat hairy, branchlets reddish-brown with gray hairs.

Trunk: Bark thin, smooth, light gray with a slight tinge of red, lenticels (pores) large; older bark shallowly fissured, the ridges wide, flat and tightly flattened; wood durable, dark brown, with a narrow, pale sapwood.

Habitat: Occurs in wet ground along streams, spring branches and in fens.

Range: North Carolina to Mississippi, Arkansas and Kansas, north to Newfoundland and Ontario.

Wildlife Uses: Willow twigs and leaves are browsed by white-tailed deer. The shoots and buds are eaten by many rodents (including muskrat and beaver), as well as cottontail rabbits. Some ducks and water birds feed on willow catkins and leaves. Bees use willow nectar to produce high-grade honey. Dense thickets also provide cover for wildlife.

Remarks: Some authors refer to larger plants of heart-leaved willow as *Salix eriocephala*, which occur in bottomland soils of silt and mud along the Missouri and Mississippi and other large rivers mainly north of the Missouri River. Prized among craftsmen for its straight limbs, this willow is used to make walking sticks.

Salix is the classical Latin name; *rigida*, which means "stiff," refers to the upright position of the leaves and catkins; *eriocephala* is from *erios* ("woolly") and *cephala* ("head"), possibly referring to the fuzzy male catkins.

Salix rigida ❧ a. Growth form, b. Male catkins, c. Female catkin

Silky willow

Salix sericea Marshall

Willow family (Salicaceae)

Field Identification: A shrub to small tree to 12 feet, with clustered stems and dark green leaves that are brightly silvered beneath with close, silky hairs.

Flowers: March-May, numerous catkins appear in the spring before the leaves, male and female flowers in separate catkins and on separate plants in axils on twigs of previous year; staminate (male) catkins are 1/4 to 3/4 inch long, oval to egg-shaped; flowers several; stamens 2; pistillate (female) catkins are 1/2 to 1 inch long; flowers several.

Fruit: June, catkins up to 1 1/4 inches long, narrow, cylindrical; capsules about 1/8 inch long, egg-shaped, tip blunt, with silvery hairs.

Leaves: Simple, alternate, 2 to 3 inches long, 1/2 to 3/4 inch wide, narrowly lance-shaped, tip pointed, base narrowing sharply to rounded, margin finely toothed; upper surface dark green, hairy to smooth; lower surface with dense shiny-silvery hairs; the small veins becoming finely netted with age; petioles slender, 1/4 to 3/4 inch long, light to dark brown, hairy to smooth; **stipules linear- to lance-shaped, dropping early.**

Twigs: Slender, **easy to break, brittle**; light to dark brown, hairy to smooth.

Habitat: Occurs in fens, swampy ground around springs, and spring branches in the eastern part of the Ozarks.

Range: South Carolina to Tennessee and Missouri, north to Quebec, and west to Wisconsin and Iowa.

Wildlife Uses: Willow twigs and leaves are browsed by white-tailed deer. The shoots and buds are eaten by many rodents (including muskrat and beaver), as well as cottontail rabbits. Bees use willow nectar to produce high-grade honey. Dense thickets also provide cover for wildlife.

Remarks: A characteristic inhabitant of Ozark fens, silky willow can be found growing with other unique plants, many of which are found more commonly in northern states. These plants migrated south with glacial advances and found refuge in the unglaciated Ozarks. As the climate warmed, some populations died because of changing habitat, others migrated north, and some remained in pockets of cool, moist soils.

These special areas, called Ozark fens, provide continuous moisture as water percolates down through ancient broken-down rocks in nearby hills. At some point, the water meets an impenetrable bedrock deep in the hill and seeps out, usually at the base of a slope. This seepage is continuous, even during drought years, because of the water working its way through the hills. This concentration of fens in the Ozarks is found nowhere else in unglaciated North America.

Salix is the classical Latin name; *sericea* means "silky," and refers to the underside of the leaves.

Salix sericea ❀ a. Growth form, b. Male catkins, c. Female catkins with open seed capsules, d. Seed capsule

Common elderberry

Sambucus canadensis L.

Honeysuckle family (Caprifoliaceae)

Field Identification: A shrub to 8 feet, forming colonies from root sprouts, with branches near the top.

Flowers: Late May-July, in conspicuous large, **flattened flower clusters sometimes up to 10 inches across at the tip of twigs**; flower stalks with fine lines, green at first, reddish later; flowers white, sweet-scented, about 1/4 inch across; petals 5, about 1/8 inch long, egg-shaped, tip rounded; stamens 5, extending beyond the petals.

Fruit: August-October, **clusters in flat-topped heads**; fruit berrylike, **purple or black**, smooth, glossy, about 1/4 inch across, globe-shaped, bittersweet; seeds 4, yellow, surface rough.

Leaves: Opposite, pinnately compound, 4 to 12 inches long; leaflets 5 to 11 (usually 5 to 7), blades 2 to 6 inches long, 1 to 2 inches wide, lance-shaped to sometimes egg-shaped, tip pointed, base rounded or broadly wedge-shaped, margin sharply toothed; upper surface shiny, bright green, smooth; lower surface paler, barely or densely hairy; petioles 2 to 3 inches long, grooved above. Occasionally the lower leaflets are 2- or 3-parted.

Twigs: Rigid, round but sometimes angular or grooved, smooth, light yellowish-brown or grayish-brown; lenticels (pores) prominent.

Trunk: Bark yellowish-brown, lacking grooves; lenticels large and raised, causing a rough bark; wood white, soft, with a large pith.

Habitat: Occurs throughout Missouri in open woods, thickets, along streams, fence rows, roadsides and railroads.

Range: Florida and Georgia, to Louisiana, Texas, Arkansas and Oklahoma, north to Nova Scotia, and west to Quebec, North Dakota and Manitoba.

Wildlife Uses: The plant has considerable value as a wildlife food. The fruit is eaten by raccoons and squirrels, and by approximately 45 species of birds, including bobwhite quail and prairie chicken. The leaves, twigs and fruit also are browsed by white-tailed deer.

Medicinal Uses: The leaves have been used to treat sores and tumors. The berries, bark and leaves have been used as a laxative.

Remarks: There are several varieties and horticultural forms. Common elderberry is a fast grower, with seeds being produced from the shrub after three years. Native Americans used the fruits for food, and made a pleasant drink by dipping the flowers into hot water. Today we use the fruit to make pies, wines and jellies, and the flowers to flavor candies and jellies. The dried leaves have been used as an insecticide, and to keep mice away from garden plants. A black dye has been made from the bark. The stems, with the pith removed, once were used as drains in tapping maple sugar. Children still make flutes, whistles and popguns from them.

Sambucus is the classical Latin name; *canadensis* refers to Canada, where the plant grows at its most northern limit.

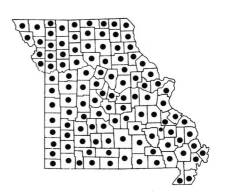

Sambucus canadensis ❀ a. Growth form with flower cluster, b. Flower, c. Fruit cluster

Red-berried elder

Sambucus racemosa L.

Honeysuckle family (Caprifoliaceae)

Also called red-berried elderberry, stinking elder, scarlet elder

Field Identification: A shrub or small tree to 24 feet, not forming colonies.

Flowers: April-May, **in pyramidal clusters**, longer than broad, on new growth, clusters 2 to 4 inches long, 1 1/4 to 2 inches wide; cluster stalk 3/4 to 2 1/2 inches long; flowers white, about 1/8 inch across; petals 5, rounded, spreading; stamens 5, extending beyond the flower.

Fruit: June-August, **in pyramidal clusters** at the ends of branches, berrylike fruit about 1/8 inch diameter, egg-shaped, **red**, semi-glossy, juice yellowish; seeds 3, yellow, less than 1/8 inch long, flattened on the sides, minutely roughened.

Leaves: Opposite, pinnately compound, 3 to 7 inches long; leaflets 5 to 7, blades 2 to 4 inches long, 3/4 to 1 1/4 inches wide, broadly lance-shaped to egg-shaped, tip pointed, base narrowed or rounded, blade often with uneven sides, margin sharply toothed; upper surface dark green, smooth; lower surface paler, hairy but smooth later; end leaflet stalk 1/4 to 1 inch long, side leaflet stalks short or absent, hairy.

Twigs: Young ones hairy, gray to reddish- or yellowish-brown, smooth later; lenticels (pores) prominent.

Trunk: Bark tight, greenish-brown or grayish-brown, smooth; lenticels raised; wood a narrow ring of soft, greenish-white material around the brown pith.

Habitat: Occurs on shaded, north- to northeast-facing wooded limestone bluffs and ledges; found only in Marion County in Missouri.

Range: Georgia and Tennessee, north to Newfoundland, and west to Ohio, Indiana, Illinois, Missouri, South Dakota, Colorado, Oregon and Alaska.

Wildlife Uses: The fruit is eaten by at least 23 species of birds, and by raccoons and squirrels. The leaves, twigs and fruit also are browsed by white-tailed deer.

Medicinal Uses: The leaves have been used to treat sores and tumors. The berries, bark and leaves have been used as a laxative.

Results: Red-berried elder also is known as *Sambucus pubens* Michx., an older reference. There are several varieties that occur across its range. Once established, it is known as a fast grower. The striking, large purple buds stand out in the winter against a background of snow.

Sambucus is the classical Latin name; *racemosa* is for the racemelike (cluster) of flowers and fruits.

Sambucus racemosa ❦ a. Growth form with flower cluster, b. Flower, c. Growth form with fruit cluster

Meadow-sweet

Spiraea alba Du Roi

Rose family (Rosaceae)

Field Identification: A shrub to 4 feet high, finely branched; often forming small colonies.

Flowers: June-August, in clusters cone- to pyramid-shaped, 3 to 4 inches long, 1 1/2 to 2 1/2 inches wide, open or compact, the flower stalks hairy; **flowers white**, small, about 1/8 inch across, petals 5, egg-shaped, ends cupped, margin wavy; stamens 20 to 40.

Fruit: September, dried fruit with 5 pod-shaped follicles (a dried casing that splits down one side to release its seeds), reddish-brown, smooth, 3 to 10 seeds in each follicle; seeds narrowly spindle-shaped, golden-brown, surface rough.

Leaves: Alternate, simple, 1 1/4 to 2 inches long, about 1/2 inch wide, narrowly egg- to lance-shaped, tip pointed, base long tapered, margin with fine hairs, sharply toothed except on the lower portion; **both surfaces green, smooth or slightly hairy**; petioles about 1/8 inch long, winged, trough-shaped, somewhat keeled below.

Twigs: Erect, reddish-brown to grayish-brown, somewhat lined and angular instead of round, smooth; lenticels (pores) conspicuous.

Trunk: Bark thin, reddish-brown, covered with a white, waxy coating, smooth, tight; wood soft, fine-grained, pale yellow, often slightly greenish, the pith dark brown.

Habitat: Occurs in wet river bottom prairies, wet prairies along railroads, alluvial soils bordering oxbow lakes of rivers and open ground along streams.

Range: North Carolina, Virginia, Ohio, Indiana, Illinois, Missouri and South Dakota, north to Vermont, and west to Quebec and Saskatchewan.

Wildlife Uses: White-tailed deer browse the leaves and twigs, but the plants are low in preference. Cottontail rabbits eat the twigs and bark; greater prairie chickens favor the seeds, buds and leaves. In clones the shrub is cover for cottontail rabbit and woodcocks. The flowers are a source of nectar for bees.

Remarks: Meadow-sweet is classified as endangered in Missouri. **One small population exists in Grundy County**; previously it was recorded from five counties. Habitat loss due to draining and farming the bottoms accounts for its endangered status.

Native Americans and European settlers used the stems of meadow-sweet for pipe stems; hence the common name, "pipestem," used in the eastern United States.

Spiraea is from the Greek word *speira* ("wreath"), possibly referring to the showy cluster of flowers; *alba*, which is Latin for "white," describes the color of the flowers.

Spiraea alba ❀ a. Growth form with flower clusters, b. Flower, c. Twig with seed capsules, d. Seed capsule

Hardhack

Spiraea tomentosa L.

Rose family (Rosaceae)

Also called steeple bush

Field Identification: A shrub, simple or sparingly branched, attaining a height of 4 feet.

Flowers: June-August, in spirelike clusters 2 to 8 inches long, flower stalks densely hairy with matted wool; flowers white or more commonly pink, small, 1/8 to 1/4 inch across; petals 5, wide-spreading, round to egg-shaped, ends cupped, margin wavy; stamens numerous.

Fruit: September, dried fruit with 5 pod-shaped follicles (a dried casing that splits down one side to release its seeds), densely hairy with matted wool; seeds 4 to 7, longer than broad.

Leaves: Alternate, simple, blade 1 1/4 to 2 1/2 inches long, 3/8 to 1 1/4 inches wide, apex pointed to blunt, base wedge-shaped to rounded, margin unequally toothed, leathery; upper surface dark green and hairy; **lower surface white or rusty with densely hairy matted wool**; petioles about 1/8 inch long, with densely hairy matted wool.

Habitat: Occurred only at the base of Crowleys Ridge in the Bootheel of southeastern Missouri. Similar habitat in Arkansas is in a seepy meadow at the base of a slope.

Range: Georgia to Tennessee, eastern Arkansas and southeastern Missouri, north to Virginia and Ontario, west to Minnesota and Manitoba.

Wildlife Uses: White-tailed deer browse the leaves and twigs, but the plants are low in preference. Cottontail rabbits eat the twigs and bark. In clones, the shrub is cover for cottontail rabbit and woodcocks. The flowers are a source of nectar for bees.

Medicinal Uses: The leaves and bark, when boiled in water, produce a tea for treating diarrhea. An application of the leaves and bark has been applied to tumors and skin ulcers. Native Americans made a tea from flowers and leaves for use during pregnancy to ease childbirth.

Remarks: Hardhack is classified as extirpated from the state. This means it no longer exists in the wild. Probably never common due to its habitat preference, maybe someday new populations will be found at the base of Crowleys Ridge.

A showy plant, it was introduced into cultivation in 1736. This shrub is used for ornamental planting for mass effects in low, moist ground.

Spiraea is from the Greek word *speira* (wreath), possibly referring to the showy cluster of flowers; *tomentosa* refers to the dense, woolly hairs of the leaves and stems. The common name "hardhack" refers to the difficulty early farmers had with cutting them in meadows. The plants are persistent: even after they are cut they can send up new stems from their spreading roots. Its other name, "steeple bush," is for the cluster of flowers shaped like the spire of a church steeple.

Spiraea tomentosa ❀ a. Growth form with flower clusters, b. Flower, c. Twig with seed capsules, d. Seed capsule

American Bladdernut

Staphylea trifoliata L.

Bladdernut family (Staphyleaceae)

Field Identification: A thicket-forming shrub or small tree to 25 feet, the branches near the top.

Flowers: April-May, in **drooping clusters** 2 to 4 inches long from twigs of the previous year; flowers small, white, about 1/4 inch long; petals 5, about 1/4 inch long, tip blunt; stamens 5, extending beyond the petals.

Fruit: August, **persistent until midwinter**, fruits solitary or in drooping clusters of 2 to 5; **capsule bladderlike**, 1 1/4 to 2 1/2 inches long, 3-lobed, inverted egg-shaped, net-veined, green to brown, opening at the tip; seeds 1 to 4, about 1/4 inch long, rounded, somewhat flattened, yellowish- to grayish-brown, hard, shiny.

Leaves: Opposite, **compound with 3 leaflets**, the 3 leaflets 1 1/2 to 4 inches long, 1 1/4 to 2 inches wide, egg-shaped to inverted egg-shaped, tip pointed, base tapering, margin sharply toothed; upper surface bright green, hairy on the veins; lower surface slightly paler, hairy; end leaflet petioles 1/2 to 1 1/2 inches long, much longer than side leaflet petioles, hairy; main petioles 2 to 4 inch long, hairy.

Twigs: Flexible, smooth, reddish-brown to greenish-brown, often striped, curved, ascending.

Trunk: Bark grayish-brown, smooth on young shrubs and slightly fissured and flaky on older trunks; wood hard, nearly white, with no definite line of sapwood.

Habitat: Occurs in rich wooded valleys, and north- or east-facing wooded slopes — especially of limestone or dolomite, along streams, and in thickets.

Range: Georgia, Tennessee, Alabama, Mississippi, Arkansas, Missouri and Oklahoma, north to Quebec and west to Ontario and Minnesota.

Remarks: American bladdernut sometimes is cultivated for ornament. Its attractive drooping flower clusters, dark green leaves, and interesting pods are worthy of planting in partial shade, especially along a border. It has a habit of suckering from the roots, so allow plenty of room.

The foliage remains green late into autumn, but eventually turns a yellowish-green. The fruit, which becomes inflated and bladderlike at maturity, makes a popping sound when crushed between the fingers. It is reported that the seeds from an Old World species taste like pistachio nuts, and that American bladdernut is similar in taste.

Staphylea is from the Greek word meaning "cluster of grapes," in reference to the drooping clusters of flowers; *trifolia* denotes the 3 leaflets.

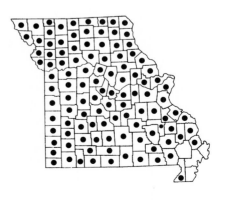

Staphylea trifoliata ❧ a. Growth form with seed capsules, b. Twig with flower cluster

Snowbell

Styrax americanum Lam.

Styrax family (Styracaceae)

Also called American snowbell, mock orange

Field Identification: Widely branched shrub attaining a height of 3 to 9 feet.

Flowers: May, solitary or in clusters of 2 to 7 along side branches; flower stalks about 1/4 inch long, drooping, with some gland-tipped hairs when young, smooth when older; **flowers white, fragrant, about 1/4 inch long, drooping**; petals 5, narrow, slightly hairy to smooth; stamens 10, extending beyond the flower.

Fruit: September, persistent, dry, brittle, globe-shaped, about 1/4 inch across, with fine, dense hairs, splitting into three parts; seed solitary, rarely 2 to 3, globe-shaped, hard-coated.

Leaves: Alternate, simple, blades 3/4 to 4 inches long, 1/2 to 1 1/2 inches wide, oval or at least twice as long as broad, tip pointed, base usually abruptly tapering to wedge-shaped, margin varying from entire to toothed to remotely toothed; upper surface dark green, smooth; lower surface paler, slightly hairy to smooth; petioles about 1/4 inch long, with gland-tipped hairs.

Twigs: Slender, with star-shaped hairs when young, but smooth later; bark thin, smooth, reddish-brown to gray.

Habitat: Occurs in bald cypress and tupelo swamps, and low wet woods of the south-eastern Missouri counties known as the Bootheel.

Range: Florida, Georgia, Louisiana, east Texas, Arkansas and Oklahoma, north to Virginia, and west to Ohio, southern Indiana, southern Illinois and southeastern Missouri.

Remarks: This is a showy shrub, with its fragrant white flowers and dark green leaves. It occurs in the swamps and bottomland forests of the Bootheel, a habitat that has become uncommon due to intensive agriculture in the region.

A related species, bigleaf snowbell (*Styrax grandifolia* Aiton.), is found in low, wet, sandy woods as far north as Arkansas. As the species name suggests, the leaves are large, up to 6 inches long and 3 inches wide. The broad, spreading shrub or small tree to 25 feet (in its southern range) might possibly be found someday in southern Ripley County or at the base of Crowleys Ridge near Dexter. Both locations have low, wet, sandy woods.

Styrax is the Greek name of the Old World tree which produced storax, an expectorant (decongestant) and a weak antiseptic used for treating scabies; *americanum* refers to its North American habitat.

Styrax americanum ❀ a. Growth form, b. Branch with flowers, c. Flowers, d. Fruit

Wolfberry

Symphoricarpos occidentalis Hook.

Honeysuckle family (Caprifoliaceae)

Also called western snowberry

Field Identification: A shrub 1 to 4 feet, with shoots arising from the roots and forming thickets.

Flowers: June-August, in clusters of 10 to 20 flowers at the tip or along the axils of stems, clusters 3/8 to 1 inch long; **flowers about 1/4 inch long**, bell-shaped, white or pink, densely hairy inside with long white hairs; petals 5, egg-shaped; stamens 5.

Fruit: August-September, in clusters up to 2 inches long, **fruits white**, berrylike, persistent in winter, globe-shaped, about 1/4 inch in diameter; seeds 2, small, hard, oval, flattened, light tan.

Leaves: Simple, opposite, blades 1 to 4 1/4 inches long, 3/4 to 2 3/4 inches wide, oval to egg-shaped, tip blunt to pointed, base wedge-shaped or rounded, margin entire or with coarse round teeth; upper surface dull, yellowish-green or grayish-green, smooth or with short hairs along the veins; lower surface grayish-green, finely hairy or almost smooth; petioles about 1/8 inch long, hairy.

Twigs: Slender, flexible, upright, reddish-brown and hairy at first, later gray.

Trunk: Bark grayish-brown, peeling into wide, often rigid sheets attached at one edge and curling outward, appears shaggy; wood hard, white, often brown around the small pith.

Habitat: Occurs on loess hills along woods and prairies, open banks, thickets, and, in one instance, on a prairie remnant along a railroad track.

Range: Illinois, Missouri, Kansas, Oklahoma and New Mexico, north to Ontario, and west to Michigan, North Dakota, Montana, and British Columbia.

Wildlife Uses: The flowers are used as a nectar source for bees. The fruit is eaten by at least 15 species of birds, including the greater prairie chicken. Small thickets furnish good cover and nesting sites for small birds and mammals.

Medicinal Uses: The Omaha, Dakota and Ponca Indians made a tea from the leaves for weak or inflamed eyes. The Flatheads applied the crushed leaves, fruits and bark as a bandage on sores, cuts, chapped or injured skin, or used it to cover scabs and burns to promote rapid healing, without scarring.

Remarks: Wolfberry is classified as endangered in Missouri. Known from only one site in Nodaway County, but in the past has been found in Atchison and Adair counties.

Wolfberry has been in cultivation since 1880. Its short stature and persistent white berries make an interesting border plant for ornamental use. It also has been used for erosion control in Western states.

Symphoricarpos is from the Greek, and means "fruit borne together," with reference to the clustered berrylike fruit; *occidentalis* refers to the westerly distribution of the plant.

Symphoricarpos occidentalis ❀ a. Growth form with fruit, b. Twig with flowers, c. Flower

Buckbrush

Symphoricarpos orbiculatus Moench

Honeysuckle family (Caprifoliaceae)

Also called coral berry, Indian currant

Field Identification: Slender, erect or ascending, thicket-forming shrub spread by roots. Usually 2 to 4 feet tall.

Flowers: July-August, in clusters of 10 to 20 flowers at the tip or along the axils of stems; flowers greenish-white, sometimes purplish, **about 1/8 inch long**, bell-shaped, somewhat hairy within; petals 5, blunt; stamens 5.

Fruit: September-October, often prolific, persistent through most of the winter, in dense clusters; **fruit pink to coral-red**, globe-shaped, about 1/4 inch thick; seeds 2, hard, egg-shaped, flattened on one side, white, smooth.

Leaves: Simple, opposite, blades 1 1/2 to 2 inches long, 1/2 to 1 1/2 inches wide, egg-shaped to oval, tip rounded to blunt, base rounded or wedge-shaped, margin entire, sometimes with a few large, rounded teeth; upper surface dull green, smooth or slightly hairy; lower surface paler, smooth to hairy; petioles very short, less than 1/8 inch long, hairy.

Twigs: Flexible, slender, brown, young twigs with curved white hairs, becoming smooth.

Trunk: Bark brown, peeling into small, short flakes that are easily rubbed off or shredded into long, thin strips; wood soft, nearly white, with a small pith.

Habitat: Occurs in grazed and second-growth dry or rocky woodland, old fields, pastures, thickets, rocky bluffs and along railroads. In every county throughout Missouri.

Range: Florida to Texas, Arkansas, Oklahoma and Mexico, north to Pennsylvania, Ohio, Indiana, Illinois, Minnesota, Nebraska and Colorado; escaped from cultivation north to Connecticut and New York.

Wildlife Uses: Buckbrush thickets provide good cover for birds and small mammals. Sometimes smaller bird species build their nests in the dense thickets. The fruits are persistent into winter, but apparently are not eaten to any extent by birds, except in harsh winter weather when preferred foods are unavailable. One Southwestern reference, however, credits the fruit to be eaten by 12 species of birds, including the cardinal, bobwhite quail, wild turkey, greater prairie chicken and ruffed grouse, in addition to being browsed by white-tailed deer. Small mammals also will eat the fruits during severe winter conditions.

Remarks: The presence of large populations of buckbrush in woodlands and open land is indicative of past or current grazing. Cattle seem to avoid this plant. Most stems are upright to arching, but some creep almost vinelike along the ground, where they send out runners for several feet and root to form new thickets.

The plant, although common in Missouri, has been cultivated elsewhere for its attractive red fruit and autumn leaves. It was first introduced into horticulture in 1727.

Symphoricarpos is from the Greek and means "fruit borne together," with reference to the clustered berrylike fruit; *orbiculatus* refers to the rounded leaf.

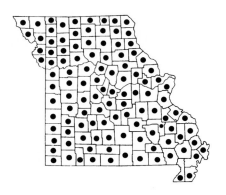

Symphoricarpos orbiculatis ❧ a. Growth form with flowers, b. Twig with fruit, c. Flowers

Poison oak

Toxicodendron toxicarium (Salisb.) Gillis

Cashew family (Anacardiaceae)

Also called Eastern poison oak

Field Identification: Poisonous, a low-branching shrub to 3 feet, with leaves divided into 3 leaflets.

Flowers: May-June, in clusters 1 to 3 inches long on old stem; flowers small, greenish-yellow, petals 5, about 1/8 inch long, lance-shaped, tip blunt, smooth; stamens 5, extending beyond the flower.

Fruit: August-November, in small grapelike clusters, creamy white, about 1/4 inch across, globe-shaped, **hairy when immature, smooth and bearing small warty projections when ripe**; seeds about 1/8 inch long.

Leaves: Alternate, 3 leaflets, end leaflet 2 to 3 1/2 inches long, 1 1/2 to 2 3/4 inches wide, leaflet stalk about 3/4 inch long, with slanting equal sides and egg-shaped, **lobes usually 3 to 4 (oaklike)**, blunt, **tip rounded to blunt, rarely pointed**, base blunt or wedge-shaped, leathery, firm; upper surface dark green, smooth to hairy; lower surface pale green, densely velvety hairy; side leaflets smaller, asymmetrical, 3- to 7-lobed, leaflet stalk short or absent.

Stems: Slender, densely hairy, green to brown, **aerial roots lacking, upright, not climbing, leaves clustered near the top**; the plant spreads by underground stems.

Habitat: Occurs at edges of dolomite glades, and sandy or rocky open woods; **uncommon, known only from extreme southern Missouri.**

Range: Florida, Louisiana, Texas, Arkansas and Oklahoma, north to New Jersey and Maryland, and west to Tennessee and Missouri.

Wildlife Uses: The fruit is eaten by a variety of songbirds, in addition to wild turkey, bobwhite quail and ruffed grouse. The plants are browsed by white-tailed deer.

Remarks: The name of this species is synonymous with *Rhus toxicodendron* L. Like poison ivy, poison oak is not recommended for planting. An oil called toxicodendrol or urushiol, found in all parts of the plant, is poisonous and produces an intense skin irritation. Upon contact with the skin, this oil produces blisters that are accompanied by intense itching and burning. Some people are immune to poison oak, but this does not appear to be a constant factor. Some have been known to become suddenly affected who previously had come into contact with it for years with no harmful results. Washing immediately with cold, soapy water after contact is the best treatment; warm water opens the skin pores and allows the oil to enter. Various lotions and injections also are helpful.

Many people in Missouri use the names poison ivy and poison oak synonymously. They are, of course, different species; most Missourians never have seen poison oak because of its limited range and habitat in the state.

Toxicodendron is from the ancient Greek and means "poison tree"; *toxicarium* refers to the poisonous nature of the plant.

Toxicodendron toxicarium ❧ a. Growth form with fruit, b. Twig with flower clusters, c. Flower

Farkleberry

Vaccinium arboreum Marshall

Heath family (Ericaceae)

Also called highbush blueberry, sparkleberry

Field Identification: Stiff branched shrub or small crooked tree attaining a height of 10 feet.

Flowers: May-June, in loose clusters in the axils of leaves; flowers hanging, about 1/2 inch long, white or pinkish, bell-shaped, 5-lobed, curled at the tip; stamens 10, not extending beyond the flower.

Fruit: July-October, about 3/8 inch across, globe-shaped, black, shiny, sweet, mealy, dry, persistent; seeds many, of various shapes, flattened sides, golden-brown, glossy, deeply pitted.

Leaves: Alternate, simple, **sometimes evergreen**, 1 to 3 inches long, about 1 inch wide, oval to inverted egg-shaped, **tip mostly rounded or blunt, or with a short abrupt point**, base wedge-shaped, margin entire or slightly toothed; **leathery, glossy above**; duller green and slightly hairy below; petioles almost absent, hairy.

Twigs: Slender, light brown to dark or reddish-brown, spreading apart, smooth or hairy.

Trunk: Bark dark brown or grayish-brown, with fine fissures exposing the reddish inner bark; younger branches reddish, with brown outer bark peeling off in flat, thin plates; wood hard, fine-grained, light reddish-brown.

Habitat: Occurs in acid soils overlying sandstone, chert or igneous bedrock, rocky open woods on dry slopes and ridges, along bluffs and glades, occasionally in low woods along creeks and near swamps.

Range: Florida to east Texas, north to Virginia, and west to Illinois, Missouri and Oklahoma.

Wildlife Uses: The edible fruit is eaten by several bird species.

Medicinal Uses: The leaves and the bark of the root have been used to treat sore throat and diarrhea. The fruit has been used to make a drink for treating chronic dysentery.

Remarks: The dark green foliage, which is partially evergreen, together with the white flowers, give this shrub a very ornamental appearance. It does well in full sun, but, like the azalea, needs acid soil.

Some of the plants are tall, with rounded crowns, and others are somewhat flat-topped and have crooked, zigzag branches. Cut or burned stems will produce uncharacteristic straight shoots the first year with thinner, less glossy leaves. It flowers abundantly, but is sparsely fruited; the fruits ripen throughout a long period. Fruits are edible, but their dryish, mealy texture makes them less palatable than deerberry or lowbush blueberry. The plant usually is found in loose thickets.

Vaccinium is the classical Latin name for an Old World species; *arboreum* refers to the treelike habit.

Vaccinium arboreum ✿ a. Growth form with fruit and lichens, b. Twig with flowers, c. Stem with bark and lichens

Lowbush blueberry

Vaccinium pallidum Aiton

Heath family (Ericaceae)

Also called lowbush huckleberry, hillside blueberry

Field Identification: Low, stiffly branching shrub, 1/2 to 3 feet high, often in extensive colonies.

Flowers: April-May, flowering when leaves are partly expanded, at the end of branches or from the old axils; flowers white, pink, or red, about 1/4 inch long, **cylinder-shaped, longer than broad**; lobes 5, short, spreading to reflexed; stamens 10, **not exceeding the petals**.

Fruit: Late June-August, berry about 1/4 inch across, dull dark blue to almost black with a faint whitish coating, globe-shaped, sweet, palatable, ripening throughout a long period; seeds many, glossy, red-brown, pitted.

Leaves: Alternate, simple, blade length 3/4 to 1 3/4 inch, width 1/2 to 1 inch wide, shape variable from oval to egg- or inverted egg-shaped, tip blunt to pointed, base tapering, margin entire or finely toothed especially near the tip; upper surface pale green, glossy, somewhat more net-veined above than below, smooth; lower surface pale green, hairy or smooth; **small leaves (bracts) absent at the base of flowers or fruit**; petioles very short.

Twigs: Rather loosely arranged, stiff, green to brown, rough with minute dots, hairy or smooth.

Trunk: Bark greenish-brown or red, smooth, often slightly ridged; wood soft, white.

Habitat: Occurs in dry rocky open woods, ledges of bluffs, glades, and upland level flats, ridges or slopes, in acid soils overlying sandstone, chert or igneous bedrock.

Range: Georgia, Alabama, Mississippi to Arkansas and Oklahoma, north to Maine and Nova Scotia, and west to Ontario, Michigan, Illinois and Iowa.

Wildlife Uses: The cottontail rabbit, gray fox and white-tailed deer eat the fruit, as do bluebirds, scarlet tanagers, bobwhite quail, wild turkey and ruffed grouse. White-tailed deer also favor the leaves and stems.

Remarks: This is a variable species with differences in leaf size and degrees of hairiness on the leaves and twigs. Three varieties have been differentiated for Missouri. *Vaccinium vacillans* is considered by many botanists to be the same as *Vaccinium pallidum*.

Lowbush blueberry has been in cultivation since 1884. The berries ripen on the branches throughout a long period, making it more difficult to collect in quantity at any one time. This is, however, more advantageous to birds and small mammals. The berries are eaten raw or cooked in pies, muffins, jelly, preserves and jams.

Vaccinium is the classical Latin name for an Old World species; *vacillans* refers to the variable or inconsistent nature of the plant's characters.

Vaccinium pallidum ❧ a. Growth form with flowers, b. Twig with flowers, c. Twig with fruit

Deerberry

Vaccinium stamineum L.

Heath family (Ericaceae)

Also called highbush huckleberry, squaw huckleberry

Field Identification: Irregularly branched shrub, rarely more than 6 feet.

Flowers: April-June, in loose, hanging clusters with 3 to 10 flowers, flowers white to pinkish, **broadly bell-shaped, wider than long**, about 1/4 inch across, 5-lobed, spreading; **stamens 10, extending beyond the flower.**

Fruit: July-September, about 1/4 inch in diameter, globe-shaped, reddish- to dark purple, somewhat sweet, seeds egg-shaped, golden brown, finely pitted.

Leaves: Alternate, simple, 3/4 to 2 3/4 inches long, 1/2 to 1 inch wide, slightly broader above the middle, tip pointed, base narrow, rounded; margin entire, fringed with hairs; upper surface dull, light- to yellow-green, mostly smooth; lower surface duller and hairy, veins conspicuous, hairy; **small leaves (bracts) present at the base of flower and fruit stalks;** petioles very short.

Twigs: Slender, growth of current year green to reddish, hairy; later green to brown and smooth.

Trunk: Bark gray to brown, rather smooth, split into long, narrow, papery strips with loose margins, inner bark reddish-brown; wood soft, fine-grained, white to pale brown.

Habitat: Occurs in acid soils over sandstone, chert and igneous bedrock, rocky open dry woods, ridges, upland slopes and glades.

Range: Georgia, Tennessee and Florida to east Texas, Arkansas, and Oklahoma, north to New Jersey and west to Pennsylvania, West Virginia, Ohio, Indiana, Missouri and Kansas.

Wildlife Uses: The fruit is eaten by gray fox, white-tailed deer and at least 14 species of birds, including bluebirds, scarlet tanagers, bobwhite quail, wild turkey and ruffed grouse. White-tailed deer favor the leaves and stems.

Remarks: The fruit is used in pies and jellies or eaten fresh. Deerberry frequently grows in association with lowbush blueberry, the former typically being the larger shrub with larger leaves and larger fruits.

Vaccinium is the classical Latin name for an Old World species; *stamineum* refers to the prominent stamen structure.

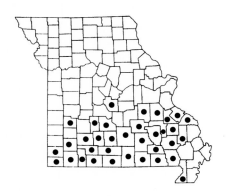

Vaccinium stamineum ✿ a. Growth form with flowers, b. Flowers, c. Fruit

Southern arrow wood

Viburnum dentatum L.

Honeysuckle family (Caprifoliaceae)

Field Identification: Shrub attaining a height of up to 15 feet with slender, elongate and ascending branches.

Flowers: May-June, in clusters at the ends of branches or on short side branches, clusters 1 1/4 to 4 1/2 inches broad; flowers white, small, numerous; lobes 5, spreading; stamens 5, extending beyond the petals.

Fruit: August-November, bluish-black, about 1/4 inch across, globe- to egg-shaped, pulp soft; single-seeded, seed encased in a hard covering that is deeply grooved on one side.

Leaves: Opposite, simple, blade length and width from 1 to 4 1/2 inches, circular to broadly egg-shaped tip pointed or rounded, base rounded to near heart-shaped, margin with teeth pointed to rounded; upper surface smooth or nearly so or with star-shaped hairs; **lower surface with star-shaped hairs**; veins 5 to 11 pairs, straight or nearly so, conspicuous beneath the leaf blade; petioles very slender, 1/4 to 1 1/4 inches long, smooth to star-shaped hairy.

Twigs: Slender, elongate, straight or arching, young ones hairy, older ones smooth.

Trunk: Bark tight, smooth, gray to grayish-brown or reddish-brown; lenticels (pores) cream-colored, prominent.

Habitat: Occurs in low alluvial woods on terraces and wooded slopes. In Missouri, **known only from along the Salt River**.

Range: Florida to Louisiana and east Texas, north to Massachusetts, Pennsylvania, Tennessee and Missouri.

Wildlife Uses: Viburnums form a minor, but important, segment of the diet of many birds and mammals. The fruits are eaten by many species of birds including cardinal, cedar waxwing, robin, ruffed grouse and wild turkey, and mammals such as white-tailed deer, cottontail rabbit, chipmunk, squirrel, skunk and mice. The twigs, bark and leaves are eaten by white-tailed deer and beaver.

Medicinal Uses: The bark of viburnums has been used to treat uterine infections and malaria. Native Americans made a tea from the bark to increase urine flow.

Remarks: In Missouri, southern arrow wood is classified as state endangered. This is an attractive shrub with its showy clusters of white flowers and strongly veined leaves. It grows best in partial shade to full sun. Native Americans were known to have made arrows from the straight stems. They also used the inner bark as tobacco for smoking in pipes.

Viburnum is the classical Latin name of the Wayfaring-tree, *Viburnum lantana* L., of Eurasia, which is often cultivated; *dentatum* refers to the coarsely toothed margins of the leaf.

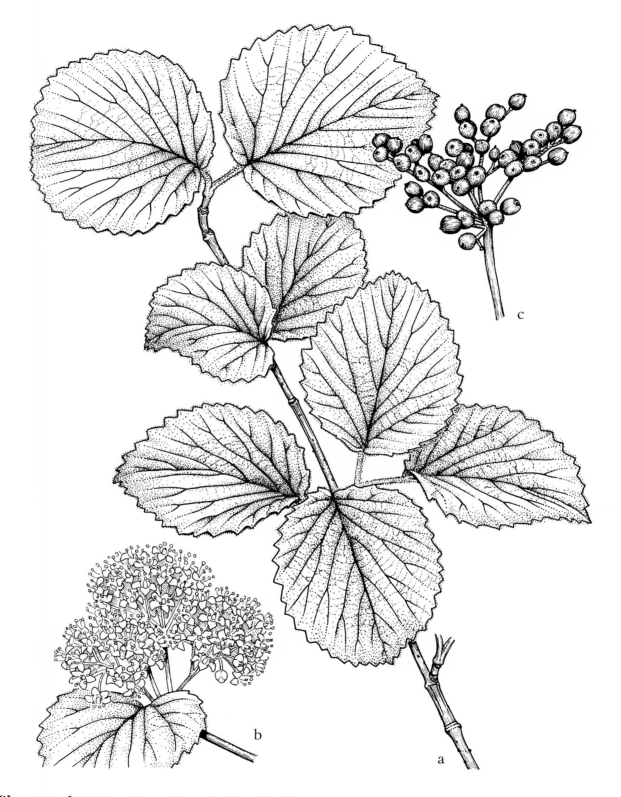

Viburnum dentatum ❀ a. Growth form, b. Twig with flower cluster, c. Twig with fruit

Nannyberry

Viburnum lentago L.

Honeysuckle family (Caprifoliaceae)

Also called sheepberry, wild raisin

Field Identification: A shrub to 18 feet high; often in small open colonies.

Flowers: May-June, in round-topped clusters 2 to 5 inches across; flower stalks with reddish scales; flowers numerous, small, white; petals 5, spreading; stamens 5, extending beyond the flower.

Fruit: September-October, in drooping to upright clusters of 15 to 30 fruits; fruits 3/8 to 1/2 inch long, about 3/8 inch across, dark blue with a whitish coating, glossy when the coating is removed, smooth, 1-seeded; seeds broadly oval, often nearly circular, about 3/8 inch long and wide, sides slightly rounded, with warty surface.

Leaves: Opposite, simple, 2 1/4 to 3 inches long, 1 to 1 1/2 inches wide, **tip abruptly slender and long pointed**, base wedge-shaped to rounded, margin sharply and finely toothed, **teeth conspicuously pointing outward**; upper surface dark green, smooth; lower surface slightly paler with reddish, star-shaped hairs especially on the central vein; petioles about 1/2 inch long, grooved above, **winged or wavy** at least part way, with some reddish, star-shaped hairs.

Twigs: Yellow to reddish-brown early, grayish-green later, covered with a white, waxy coating, smooth; lenticels (pores) nearly circular, pale orange.

Trunk: Bark of branches gray, smooth except for the raised lenticels; bark of the trunk grayish- to reddish-brown, with thin, somewhat squarish plates; wood hard, fine-grained, nearly white, sapwood white.

Habitat: Occurs in low woods, wooded slopes, and moist valleys bordering or near streams; **known only from Schuyler County.**

Range: New Jersey and in the mountains of Georgia, to Ohio, Indiana, Illinois, northern Missouri and eastern Nebraska, north to Quebec and west to Manitoba and North Dakota.

Wildlife Uses: Viburnums form a minor, but important, segment of the diet of many birds and mammals. The fruits are eaten by many species of birds including cardinal, cedar waxwing, robin, ruffed grouse and wild turkey, and mammals such as white-tailed deer, cottontail rabbit, chipmunk, squirrel, skunk and mice. The twigs, bark and leaves are eaten by white-tailed deer and beaver.

Medicinal Uses: The bark of viburnums has been used to treat uterine infections and malaria. Native Americans made a tea from the bark to increase urine flow.

Remarks: Nannyberry is classified as endangered in Missouri, but its rarity may simply be because it is on the southern edge of its range. Although sometimes mistaken for other viburnums, its abruptly pointed leaves is a key character.

Viburnum is the classical Latin name of the Wayfaring-tree, *Viburnum lantana* L., of Eurasia, which is often cultivated; *lentago* is an old name meaning flexible or bending, its reference is uncertain.

Viburnum lentago ❧ a. Growth form with fruit, b. Twig with flower cluster, c. Flower, d. Bud and leaf

Arrow Wood

Viburnum molle Michaux

Honeysuckle family (Caprifoliaceae)

Also called Kentucky viburnum

Field Identification: A shrub 9 to 12 feet tall, with gray shredding bark.

Flowers: May-June, in clusters on short end or side branches, clusters 2 to 3 1/2 inches broad, cluster stalk 1 1/4 to 2 inches long, hairy, often with gland-tipped hairs; flowers white, numerous, about 1/4 inch across; petals 5, spreading; stamens 5, extending beyond the petals.

Fruit: August-October, about 3/8 inch long, bluish-black, about half as broad as long, flattened, ends blunt; pulp soft; single seeded, seed encased in a hard covering that is grooved on one side.

Leaves: Opposite, simple, blade 2 to 5 inch long and about as wide, round to broadly egg-shaped, tip pointed, **base deeply heart-shaped**, margin coarsely toothed, **usually 16 to 30 teeth along the margin on each side of the leaf blade**; upper surface dark green, smooth or slightly hairy; lower surface pale, soft hairy; petioles 3/4 to 2 inch long, slender, smooth or with gland-tipped hairs.

Twigs: Young ones smooth or sparingly soft hairy, older ones gray to black, or reddish-brown after the outer bark shreds.

Trunk: Bark grayish, **loose and peeling off**.

Habitat: Occurs at the base of and on steep wooded slopes of bluffs, talus slopes, and rocky woods along streams.

Range: Kentucky to Arkansas and Oklahoma, north to Kentucky, and west to Indiana, Illinois, Missouri and Iowa.

Wildlife Uses: Viburnums form a minor, but important, segment of the diet of many birds and mammals. The fruits are eaten by many species of birds including cardinal, cedar waxwing, robin, ruffed grouse and wild turkey, and mammals such as white-tailed deer, cottontail rabbit, chipmunk, squirrel, skunk and mice. The twigs, bark and leaves are eaten by white-tailed deer and beaver.

Medicinal Uses: The bark of viburnums has been used to treat uterine infections and malaria. Native Americans made a tea from the bark to increase urine flow.

Remarks: This is an attractive shrub with its large, heart-shaped leaves, showy flowers, blue-black fruits, and vaselike habit of growth. It has purple-red and yellow-orange autumn foliage.

Native Americans were known to have used the inner bark as tobacco for smoking in pipes.

Viburnum is the classical Latin name of the Wayfaring-tree, *Viburnum lantana* L., of Eurasia, which is often cultivated; *molle* refers to the soft undersurface of the leaves.

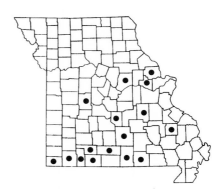

Viburnum molle ❀ a. Growth form with flower cluster, b. Fruit cluster, c. Stem with shedding bark

Black haw

Viburnum prunifolium L.

Honeysuckle family (Caprifoliaceae)

Field Identification: A shrub or small tree to 18 feet, with stiff spreading branches forming an irregular crown near the top.

Flowers: April-May, in round-topped clusters 2 to 4 inches wide; flowers numerous, white, about 1/4 inch wide; petals 5, spreading; stamens 5, extending beyond the petals.

Fruit: September-October, stalks red, bluish-black with a white coating, about 1/2 inch long, globe-shaped to half as broad as long, flesh thin and dry but edible, sweet; seed solitary, encased in a hard covering that is grooved on one side, oval, flat, dark brown.

Leaves: Opposite, simple, blades 1 1/2 to 3 inches long, 1 to 1 3/4 inches wide, oval to egg-shaped or half as broad as long, tip pointed to blunt or rounded, base blunt to rounded, margin finely toothed, **pointing inward or upward**; upper surface dull green, not shiny, smooth; lower surface paler, smooth; petiole green to red, slender, 1/4 to 3/4 inches long, **not winged**, broadly grooved.

Twigs: Slender, rigid, green to reddish or brown, some with short lateral spurs.

Trunk: Bark dark gray to brown, appears checkered with shallow furrows and flat squarish ridges; wood reddish-brown, hard, heavy, with a wide white sapwood.

Habitat: Occurs in low woods along streams, at the base and edge of bluffs, dry upper slopes of ravines and thickets. Throughout Missouri and probably in every county.

Range: Florida, Louisiana, Arkansas, Oklahoma and Texas, north to Connecticut, and west to New York, Ohio, Michigan, Illinois, Iowa and Kansas.

Wildlife Uses: Viburnums form a minor, but important, segment of the diet of many birds and mammals. The fruits are eaten by many species of birds including cardinal, cedar waxwing, robin, ruffed grouse and wild turkey, and mammals such as white-tailed deer, cottontail rabbit, chipmunk, squirrel, skunk and mice. The twigs, bark and leaves are eaten by white-tailed deer and beaver.

Medicinal Uses: The bark of viburnums has been used to treat uterine infections and malaria. The bark also is used as an astringent, nerve tonic and antispasmodic. Native Americans made a tea from the bark to increase urine flow.

Remarks: The plant has been in cultivation as an ornamental since 1727. The fall colors are deep lavender or maroon-purple to finally deep rose-red.

Viburnum is the classical Latin name of the wayfaring-tree, *Viburnum lantana* L., of Eurasia, which is often cultivated; *prunifolium* means "plum-leaved" which refers to its leaves resembling those of plum.

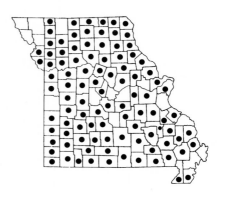

Viburnum prunifolium ❀ a. Growth form with flower cluster, b. Flower, c. Fruit cluster

Downy arrow wood

Viburnum rafinesquianum Schultes

Honeysuckle family (Caprifoliaceae)

Field Identification: Rather loose scraggly shrub to 6 feet.

Flowers: May-June, in clusters on the ends of branches, clusters 3/4 to 2 1/2 inches across, flowers numerous, white, about 1/4 inch across; petals 5, lobes rounded, spreading; stamens 5, extending beyond the petals.

Fruit: September-October, dark purple, glossy, about 1/4 inch across, globe-shaped, pulp soft; seed solitary, with hard outer coating, flattened, dark reddish-brown.

Leaves: Opposite, simple, 1 to 3 inches long, 1 1/4 to 2 inches wide, egg-shaped or half as broad as long, tip pointed, base heart-shaped, margin coarsely toothed, **usually 4 to 10 teeth along the margin on each side of the leaf blade**; upper surface dull green, smooth or slightly hairy; lower surface soft and densely hairy; veins rather straight and conspicuous; petiole about 3/8 inch long or less, **nearly absent on some leaves (particularly those below the flower clusters)**, sharply grooved above, hairy.

Twigs: Rigid, at first light to dark brown and hairy to smooth, eventually gray and smooth; lenticels (pores) circular.

Trunk: Bark gray, sometimes with a purplish cast, tight, smooth, except for the lenticels; wood hard, fine-grained, light brown, with a white pith.

Habitat: Occurs on steep wooded bluffs and rocky open woods generally bordering streams, sometimes in thickets along rocky stream beds.

Range: Georgia to Arkansas and Missouri, north to Quebec, and west to Manitoba and North Dakota.

Wildlife Uses: Viburnums form a minor, but important, segment of the diet of many birds and mammals. The fruits are eaten by many species of birds including cardinal, cedar waxwing, robin, ruffed grouse and wild turkey, and mammals such as white-tailed deer, cotton-tail rabbit, chipmunk, squirrel, skunk and mice. White-tailed deer and beaver eat the twigs, bark and leaves.

Medicinal Uses: The bark of viburnums has been used to treat uterine infections and malaria. Native Americans made a tea from the bark to increase urine flow.

Remarks: The more common variety in the state is *Viburnum rafinesquianum* var. *affine*, which has few to no hairs on the lower surface of the leaves compared to the rarer var. *rafinesquianum*.

The autumn colors vary from dull purplish-red to dull wine-purple. This is an attractive shrub for planting where a smaller woody species is desired.

Viburnum is the classical Latin name of the wayfaring-tree, *Viburnum lantana* L., of Eurasia, which is often cultivated; *rafinesquianum* honors its discoverer, Constantine Samuel Rafinesque (1783-1840).

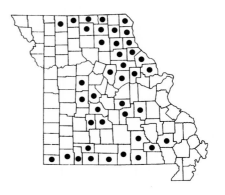

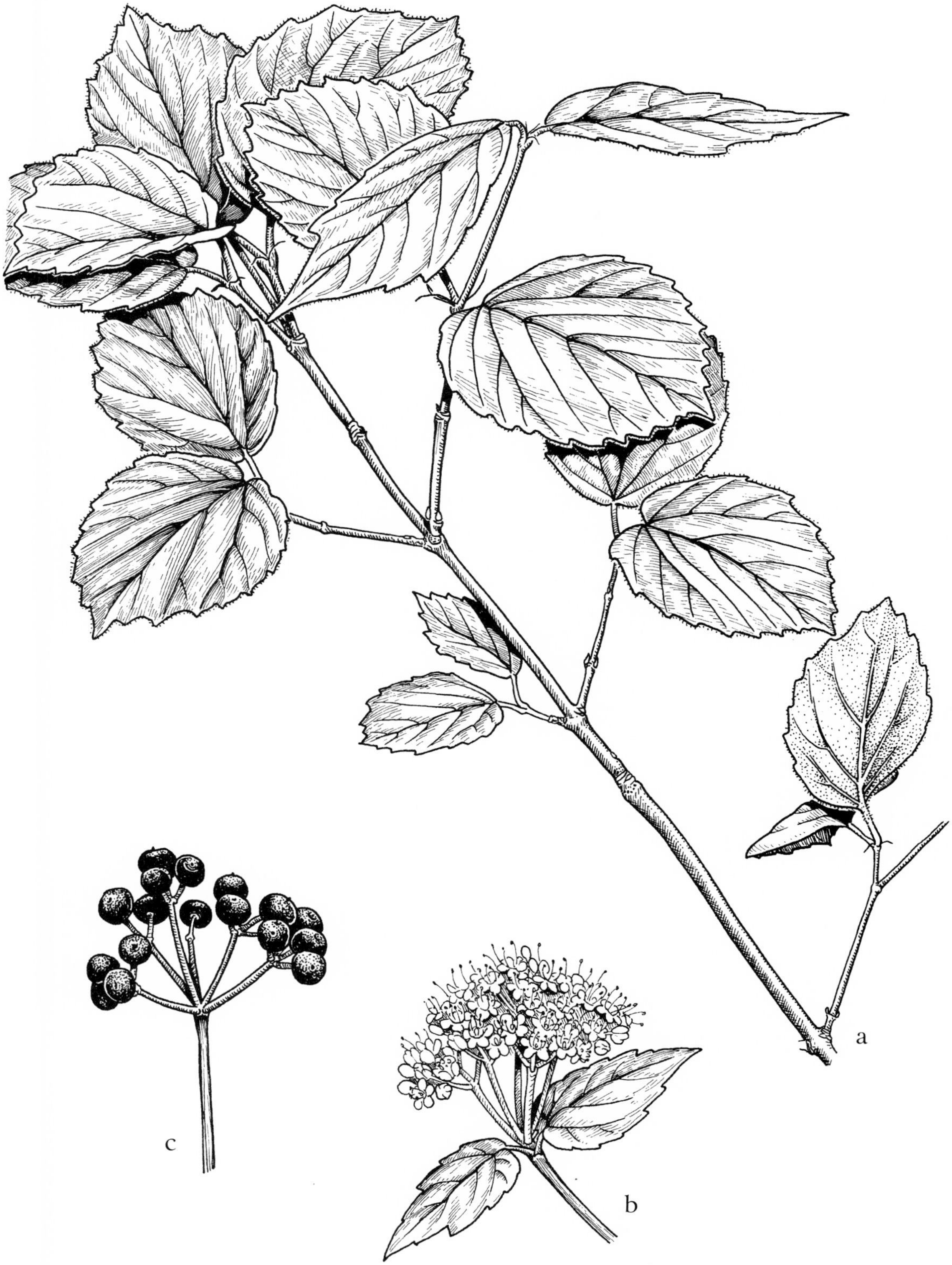

Viburnum rafinesquianum ❧ a. Growth form, b. Twig with flower cluster, c. Fruit cluster

Arrow wood

Viburnum recognitum Fern.

Honeysuckle family (Caprifoliaceae)

Field Identification: Shrub attaining a height of up to 16 feet with slender, elongate and ascending branches.

Flowers: May-June, in clusters at the ends of branches or on short side branches, clusters 1 1/4 to 4 1/2 inches broad; flowers white, small, numerous; lobes 5, spreading; stamens 5, extending beyond the petals.

Fruit: August-November, bluish-black, about 1/4 inch across, globe- to egg-shaped, pulp soft; single seeded, seed encased in a hard covering that is deeply grooved on one side.

Leaves: Opposite, simple, blade length and width from 1 to 4 1/2 inches, circular to broadly egg-shaped tip pointed or rounded, base blunt or rounded or nearly heart-shaped, margin with teeth pointed to rounded; **upper surface smooth; lower surface smooth** with some hairs along the veins; veins 5 to 11 pairs, straight or nearly so, conspicuous beneath the leaf blade; **petioles smooth**, very slender, 1/4 to 1 1/4 inches long.

Twigs: Slender, elongate, straight or arching, young and old branches smooth.

Trunk: Bark tight, smooth, gray to grayish-brown or reddish-brown; lenticels (pores) cream-colored, prominent.

Habitat: Occurs along gravel bars of small streams. In Missouri, **known only from Iron, St. Francois and Oregon counties**.

Range: South Carolina, Ohio, Michigan, Illinois and Missouri, north to Maine and New Brunswick, west to Ontario.

Wildlife Uses: Viburnums form a minor, but important, segment of the diet of many birds and mammals. The fruits are eaten by many species of birds including cardinal, cedar waxwing, robin, ruffed grouse and wild turkey, and mammals such as white-tailed deer, cottontail rabbit, chipmunk, squirrel, skunk and mice. White-tailed deer and beaver eat the twigs, bark and leaves.

Medicinal Uses: The bark of viburnums has been used to treat uterine infections and malaria. Native Americans made a tea from the bark to increase urine flow.

Remarks: In Missouri, arrow wood is classified as state-endangered. This is an attractive shrub, with its showy clusters of white flowers and strongly veined leaves. It grows best in partial shade to full sun. Native Americans were known to have made arrows from the straight stems. They also used the inner bark as tobacco for smoking in pipes.

Viburnum is the classical Latin name of the wayfaring-tree, *Viburnum lantana* L., of Eurasia, which is often cultivated; *recognitum* means "restudied," referring to its review and subsequent splitting from *Viburnum dentatum*.

Viburnum recognitum ❀ a. Growth form with flower cluster, b. Flower, c. Twig with fruit cluster

Southern black haw

Viburnum rufidulum Raf.

Honeysuckle family (Caprifoliaceae)

Also called rusty nannyberry, rusty black haw, wild raisin

Field Identification: An irregularly branched shrub to 18 feet.

Flowers: April-May, in flat clusters 2 to 6 inches across; flowers numerous, white, about 1/4 inch in diameter; petals 5, spreading, tips rounded; stamens 5, extending beyond the petals.

Fruit: September, in drooping clusters, stalks red, fruit about 3/8 inch long, bluish-black, smooth, oval, the skin smooth and tough, the flesh mealy, sweet and edible; seeds solitary, oval, flat, dark brown.

Leaves: Opposite, simple, blades 1 1/2 to 4 inches long, 1 to 2 1/2 inches wide, inverted egg-shaped to half as broad as long, tip rounded to pointed, base heart-shaped or rounded, margin finely toothed; upper surface dark green, leathery, **glossy**, smooth; **lower surface paler with scattered rust colored hairs especially on the veins**; petioles about 1/4 inch long, with or without a wing, smooth, broadly grooved above and often with scattered rust-colored hairs.

Twigs: Fairly rigid, gray-brown, smooth, **lightly to densely matted with rust-colored hairs at first**, becoming nearly smooth later.

Trunk: Bark rather rough, ridges narrow and rounded, fissures narrow, breaking into dark reddish-brown or black squarrish plates; wood hard, heavy, brownish, with a wide white sapwood.

Habitat: Occurs in rocky or dry woods, rich moist valleys and alluvial ground along streams, rocky glades and thickets.

Range: Florida, Mississippi, Louisiana, Texas, Arkansas and Oklahoma, north to Virginia, and west to Ohio, Indiana, Illinois, Missouri and Kansas.

Wildlife Uses: Viburnums form a minor, but important, segment of the diet of many birds and mammals. The fruits are eaten by many species of birds including cardinal, cedar waxwing, robin, ruffed grouse and wild turkey, and mammals such as white-tailed deer, cottontail rabbit, chipmunk, squirrel, skunk and mice. White-tailed deer and beaver eat the twigs, bark and leaves.

Medicinal Uses: The bark of viburnums has been used to treat uterine infections and malaria. Native Americans made a tea from the bark to increase urine flow.

Remarks: The shrub is worthy of cultivation because of the dark green shiny leaves, clusters of white flowers, bluish-black fruit and autumn colors. The foliage turns a deep rose-purple to rose-red or bright red.

Viburnum is the classical Latin name of the wayfaring-tree, *Viburnum lantana* L., of Eurasia, which is often cultivated; *rufidulum* refers to the rusty-red hairs on young leaves, petioles and twigs.

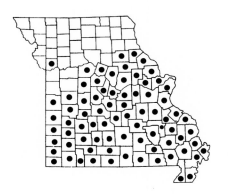

Viburnum rufidulum ❦ a. Growth form with flower cluster, b. Flower, c. Twig with fruit cluster

Soapweed

Yucca glauca Nutt.

Lily family (Liliaceae)

Field Identification: A short stemmed plant to 4 feet high; young plants lacking a stem.

Flowers: May-June, on an **unbranched stalk** 1 to 3 feet high, flowers usually 25 to 30 opening from the base upward, drooping, fragrant; petals 6, greenish-white to white, 1 1/2 to 2 1/2 inches long, 1 to 1 1/2 inches wide, globe- to bell-shaped; stamens 6, not exceeding the petals.

Fruit: September-October, capsules cylindrical, erect, 1 3/4 to 2 3/4 inches long, 3/4 to 2 inches wide, 6-sided, rough, splitting open into three parts with six columns of seeds; seeds black, semi-glossy, flat, roughly triangular, about 1/4 inch long.

Leaves: Simple, widely radiating from the base of stem, evergreen, blades 8 inches to 3 feet long, 1/4 to 1 inch wide, usually straight, occasionally curved, stiff, linear, tapering to a point, tip bearing a spine of varying length, gray-green, covered with a whitish, waxy bloom, smooth, most of the leaf with a narrow white margin from which white threads strip and curl.

Trunk: Short, stocky, up to 2 feet tall and 4 inches thick, not including the dead leaves or their bases; wood soft, fibrous, most of it decaying soon after the plant dies.

Habitat: *Yucca glauca* var. *glauca* occurs only on open, dry exposed slopes of loess hill prairies in Holt and Atchison counties, northwestern Missouri. *Yucca glauca* var. *mollis* occurs on rocky wooded slopes, gravel bars and banks of streams in dolomite soils and on dry dolomite glades. Known only from southernmost Missouri counties and into Arkansas.

Range: Var. *glauca*: northwestern Missouri, Texas, New Mexico and Arizona, north to Iowa, and west to North Dakota and Montana. Var. *mollis*: Texas to Arkansas and southern Missouri to Oklahoma.

Wildlife Uses: Small mammals and birds, as well as reptiles, use the plant for shade and nesting sites; the seeds are a staple food for small mammals.

Medicinal Uses: The Lakota Indians pulverized the roots, mixed them with water, and drank the resulting tea for stomach ache. The Blackfeet placed small roots on cuts to stop bleeding and to reduce inflammation.

Remarks: Var. *glauca* has stiff, rigid leaves up to 1 inch wide; the petals are pointed. Var. *mollis* has leaves rather soft and flexible, mostly 1/2 to 1 inch broad; the petals are mostly blunt at the tip.

Soapweed is an interesting and showy plant, with its tall spike of large flowers and evergreen needlelike leaves. It does best in full sun.

Native Americans used the mashed root like a soap, especially for washing hair. Yucca leaves were macerated until the fibers were cleared, and, with the sharp, hard spine of the leaf attached, were twined into thread, with the sharp point being used as a needle.

For a discussion on pollination by the yucca moth, see remarks under *Yucca smalliana*.

Yucca is from the native Haitian name; *glauca* refers to the white, waxy coating on the leaves; *mollis* means "soft," and refers to the rather soft and flexible leaves.

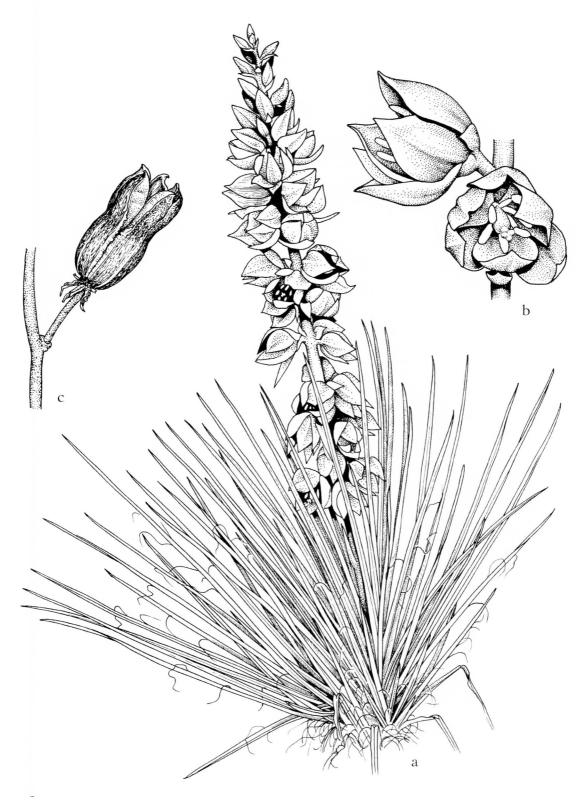

Yucca glauca ❀ a. Growth form with flowers, b. Flowers, c. Seed capsule

Spanish Bayonet

Yucca smalliana Fern.

Lily family (Liliaceae)

Also called Adam's needle

Field Identification: A short-stemmed shrub to 6 feet high, the leaves at the base of the plant.

Flowers: Late May-July, **in branched clusters** at the upper end of a stalk 3 to 6 feet tall, branches 10 to 20, finely hairy, spreading, with 4 to 8 flowers on each branch; flowers white, bell-shaped, 2 to 3 inches long; petals 6, egg-shaped, cupped, tip pointed; stamens 6, not exceeding the petals.

Fruit: September-October, capsules cylindrical, erect, 1 1/2 to 2 1/2 inches long, 3/4 to 1 inch thick, hard, 6-sided, splitting open into three parts with six columns of seeds; seeds black, flat, semi-glossy, roughly triangular, about 1/4 inch long.

Leaves: Simple, widely radiating from the base, evergreen, blades 18 to 22 long, 1 1/2 to 1 1/4 inches wide, usually straight, linear, tapering to a point, tip bearing a spine of varying length, gray-green, surface rough with minute projections, most of the leaf with a narrow white margin from which white threads strip and curl.

Trunk: Short, stout, concealed by the leaves or their old bases.

Habitat: Commonly cultivated in gardens and occasionally escaped to establish in thickets, along roadsides, open banks, railroads, open woods and prairie. Scattered in Missouri.

Range: Native of the United States from Florida to Louisiana, north to North Carolina, and east to Tennessee.

Wildlife Uses: Small mammals and birds, as well as reptiles, use the plant for shade and nesting sites; the seeds are a staple food for small mammals.

Medicinal Uses: Yucca species contain large quantities of saponins. These substances are bitter, generally irritating, and characterized by their ability to foam when shaken with water. Extracts from yuccas are showing some antitumor activity, and also may be useful as an anti-inflammatory. Some claims have been made as to ability to treat rheumatism, but they appear questionable.

Remarks: Spanish bayonet is not native to Missouri. It is often planted for decoration around homes, parks and cemeteries, and has escaped from there. The plant requires little attention and produces a long spike with branches holding many white flowers.

The flowers of this and other species of yucca are used fresh in salads or may be cooked as a vegetable, dipped in eggs and fried. The flower stalk that emerges in the spring can be cooked and eaten like asparagus.

Yucca plants are pollinated exclusively by yucca moths, which are found wherever yucca occurs in Missouri. The yucca moth carries pollen from one flower to another as it lays its egg in the ovary of the flower. The larvae, which develop inside the seed pods, eat the seeds and later pupate in the soil. The moths are found during the flowering period of the yucca plants, usually in June. They can be found upon a careful examination of the insides of the flowers.

Yucca is from the native Haitian name; *smalliana* is in honor of John K. Small (1869-1938).

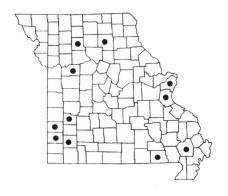

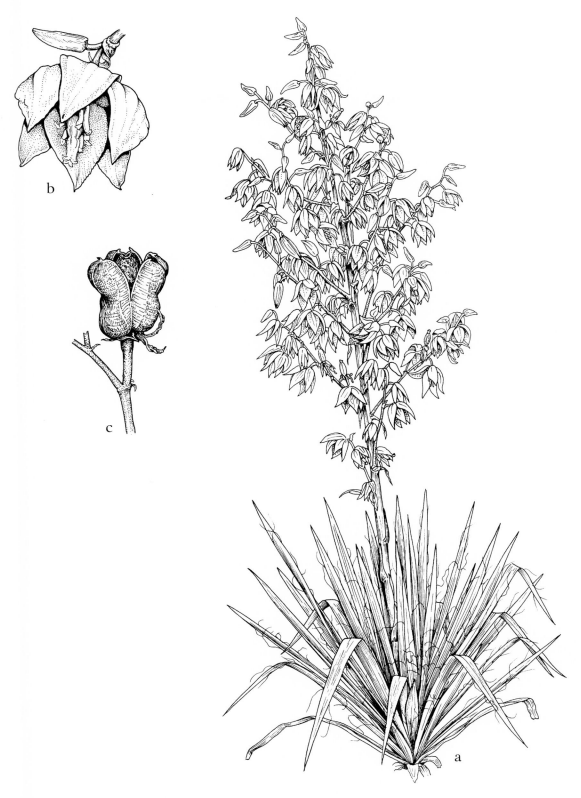

Yucca smalliana ❦ a. Growth form with flowers, b. Flower, c. Seed capsule

Prickly ash

Zanthoxylum americanum Miller

Rue family (Rutaceae)

Also called toothache tree

Field Identification: A thicket-forming shrub to 8 feet high, often densely branched above the middle.

Flowers: April-May, **before the leaves in axillary clusters on twigs of the previous year**; both staminate (male) and pistillate (female) flowers present; staminate flowers in clusters of 2 to 10 on short spurs or from buds of the previous year; petals 5, inverted egg-shaped, minute, yellowish-green, sometimes with minute reddish glands; stamens 5, alternate with the petals; pistillate flowers in clusters of 2 to 10, flowers about 1/4 inch long, longer than the staminate flowers, yellowish-green, sometimes with minute reddish glands.

Fruit: June-August, **in dense clusters**, fruit green to reddish-brown, strongly aromatic, about 1/4 inch long, globe-shaped, firm, fleshy, surface pitted, splitting down one side; seeds 1 or 2, oval, about 1/8 inch long, finely pitted, glossy black; seed coating oily, aromatic.

Leaves: Alternate, pinnately compound, 4 to 12 inches long, leaflets 5 to 11; side leaflets without stalks, end leaflet with short stalk, **aromatic**; leaflets 3/4 to 3 inches long, 3/8 to 1 1/2 inches wide, egg-shaped or half as broad as long, tip pointed to blunt, base rounded, margin entire or with finely rounded teeth; **upper surface dull deep-green, dotted with glands**; lower surface paler, hairy on the veins; petioles about 1 inch long.

Twigs: Rigid, smooth, dark brown to gray; **2 spines at each node, spines about 1/4 inch long, flat, broad-based, recurved.**

Trunk: Bark smooth, gray to brown with light blotches, slightly fissured on old trunks; wood soft, not strong, light brown.

Habitat: Occurs in open and rocky woods, along bluffs, and thickets in low, moist ground or dry upland.

Range: Georgia, Alabama, Arkansas, Missouri, Oklahoma and Kansas, north to Quebec, and west to Minnesota and North Dakota.

Wildlife Uses: The flowers are a nectar source for bees. The fruit is eaten by birds and small mammals including red-eyed vireo, bobwhite quail, cottontail rabbit and eastern chipmunk.

Medicinal Uses: Native Americans chewed the bark for toothache, used a preparation of the bark to treat colic, rheumatism and gonorrhea, and made it into a bandage with bear grease to treat sores and ulcers. The Comanches used the bark as a medicine for fever, sore throat and toothache. The Illinois used the bark to draw out pus.

Remarks: Prickly ash forms thickets by sending up shoots from the underground, creeping stems. It is occasionally planted for ornament, and was introduced into cultivation about 1740.

Zanthoxylum is from the Greek, meaning "yellow" and "wood," referring to the wood color; *americanum* is for the shrub's native home.

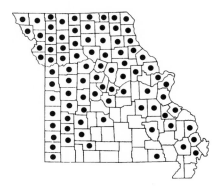

Zanthoxylum americanum ❧ a. Growth form, b. Twig with flower clusters, c. Flower, d. Seed capsules and seed

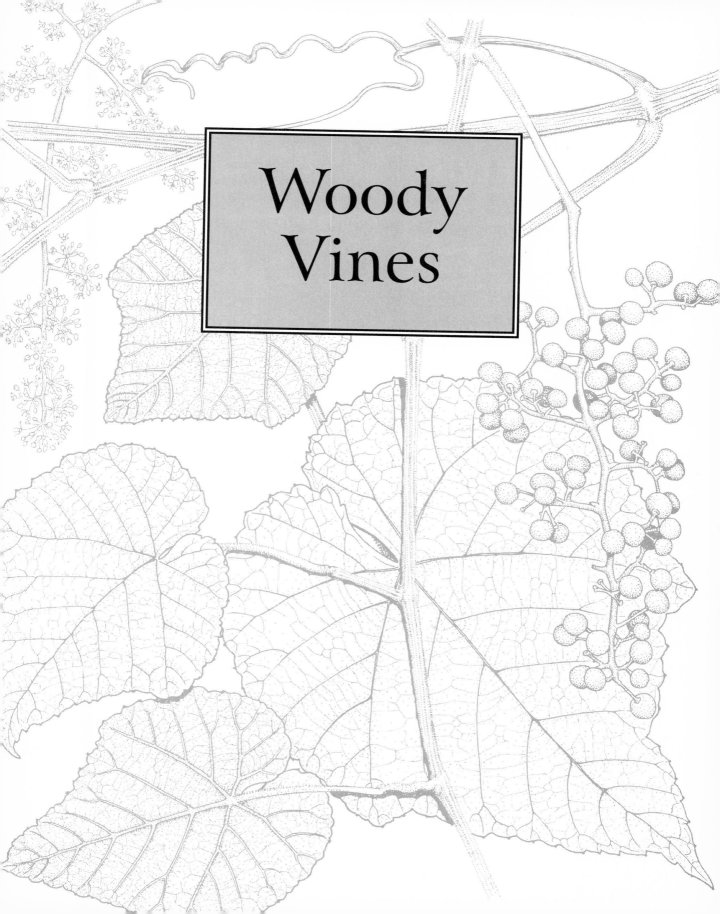

Woody Vines

Pepper Vine

Ampelopsis arborea (L.) Koehne

Grape family (Vitaceae)

Field Identification: Rather slender, upright vine, either high-climbing or bushy.

Flowers: June-August, in clusters 3/4 to 2 1/2 inches across; flowers small, inconspicuous; petals 5, greenish-white, spreading, egg-shaped, tip pointed; stamens 5, extending beyond the flower.

Fruit: September-October, about 1/4 inch long, globe-shaped, slightly flattened, at first green to pink or bluish, at maturity shiny black, often with warty dots, juicy, flesh thin, not edible; seeds 1 to 4, about 1/8 inch long, green to brown.

Leaves: Alternate, **bipinnate (divided twice)**, 3 to 8 inches long; **leaves divided into 9 to 34 leaflets**; leaflets 1/2 to 1 1/2 inches long, egg-shaped, tip pointed, base wedge-shaped, margin coarsely toothed, cut sharply and deeply or lobed; **upper surface dark green, shiny, smooth** or with a few scattered hairs; lower surface lighter green, smooth, or with a few scattered white hairs especially along the veins; young leaves and shoots sometimes conspicuously reddish or bronze; petioles shorter than the blades, hairy, sometimes with reddish blotches at the base.

Stems: Erect, ascending or bushy, tendrils present or absent; young stems green to reddish, smooth or white-hairy; older stems tan to reddish-brown, rounded or angular, sometimes roughened by oval, warty lenticels (pores).

Habitat: Occurs in low, wet thickets and alluvial soils along wooded banks of streams and river forest floodplains and at the base of bluffs along streams. Much of its habitat in southern Missouri has been eliminated with the impoundment of the White River. In southeastern Missouri, it is found in the swampy lowlands and along the Mississippi River to the mouth of the Meramec River. In Boone County is has escaped and naturalized.

Range: Florida to Texas and Mexico, north to Maryland, Illinois, Missouri and Oklahoma.

Wildlife Uses: The fruits are eaten, to some extent, by birds and small mammals.

Remarks: Pepper vine is sometimes confused with poison ivy and poison oak, but these plants have once-pinnate (divided once), trifoliolate leaves.

The lacelike, dark green leaves are very ornamental. The plant is sometimes found sprawling and trailing along the banks of rivers or as a high-climbing vine.

Ampelopsis is from the Greek *ampelos* ("the vine") and *opsis* ("appearance"); *arborea* means "of trees," referring to its high-climbing habit in the trees.

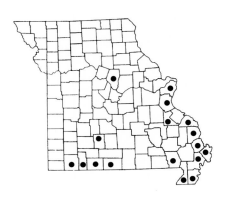

Ampelopsis arborea 🐝 a. Growth form, b. Stem with flower clusters, c. Fruit cluster

Raccoon grape

Ampelopsis cordata Michaux

Grape family (Vitaceae)

Also called false grape, heartleaf ampelopsis

Field Identification: A vine climbing by tendrils to a length of 60 feet, the trunk becoming 3 to 6 inches in diameter.

Flowers: May-July, **in flat-topped loose greenish clusters** at the nodes on new growth, 1 to 3 1/2 inches broad; flower stalks 1 to 1 1/2 inches long, slender and often acting as tendrils; **petals 5, all separate from one another**, egg-shaped, minute, reflexed; stamens 5.

Fruit: August-November, **fruiting clusters much broader than long**; clusters on slender, smooth stalks about 1/2 inch long; **fruit not edible**, about 1/4 inch across, globe-shaped, changing colors several times, causing one cluster to have several different colors at the same time — from green, to orange, to rose-purple, and finally turquoise blue; seeds 1 to 3, about 1/8 inch across, globe-shaped, reddish- to yellow-brown.

Leaves: Alternate, simple, blade 2 to 5 inches long, 2 1/2 to 4 1/2 inches wide, broadly egg-shaped, tip pointed, base flattened or somewhat heart-shaped, margin coarsely toothed; upper surface olive-green, rather dull, smooth or with a few scattered white hairs, palmately veined; lower surface paler and smooth or with a few scattered white hairs especially on the veins; petioles 1/2 to 4 inches, smooth or with a few white hairs.

Stems: Young stems green, flexible, slightly angular, with ridges extending along the stem from the leaf bases, smooth; older stems gray to light brown, numerous oval, warty lenticels (pores); tendrils from some nodes, each opposite a leaf, stout, forked at the end; stems often die back in winter.

Trunk: Bark tight, on older trunks dark brown, deeply fissured, the ridges long, flat-topped and netted; **pith white**.

Habitat: Occurs in rich alluvial soils in valleys, low woods, and slopes near streams, borders of streams, oxbow lakes in river floodplains, lowland thickets, borders of low woods and fence rows.

Range: Florida to Texas, Arkansas, Oklahoma and Mexico, north to Virginia, Ohio, Illinois, Missouri and Nebraska. Naturalized north to Massachusetts.

Wildlife Uses: Several species of birds consume the fruit including the cardinal, bobwhite quail, yellow-shafted flicker, brown thrasher and wood thrush; undoubtedly eaten by some mammals including the raccoon.

Remarks: Raccoon grape is often mistaken for grape vines, but the triangular-shaped leaves differ from the more heart-shaped grape leaves. This vine is fast-growing and can sometimes be seen forming dense matted thickets. It also can pull down small trees from its weight and compete with canopy trees for sunlight. It is not recommended for growing as an ornamental because of its aggressiveness.

Ampelopsis is from the Greek *ampelos* ("the vine") and *opsis* ("appearance"); *cordata* refers to the cordate or heart-shaped leaf.

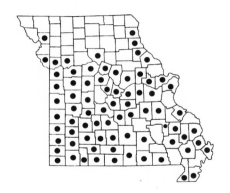

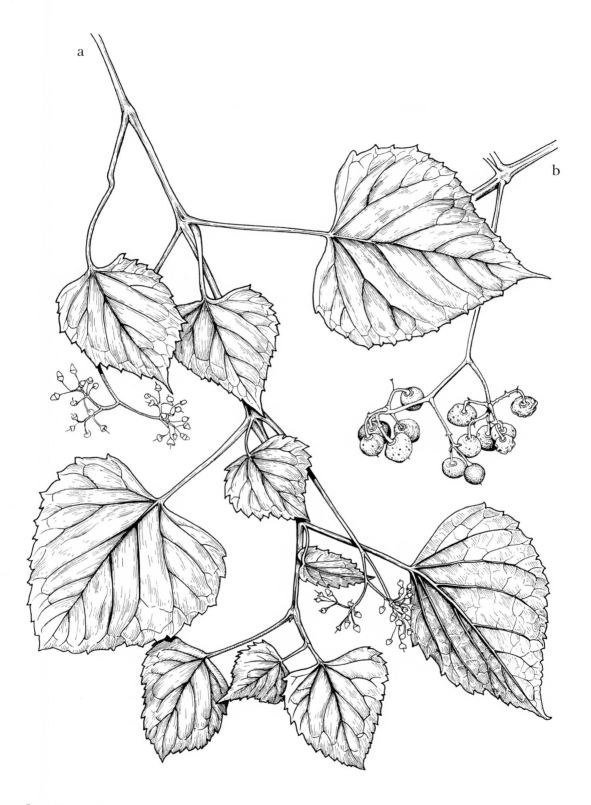

Ampelopsis cordata a. Growth form with flower clusters, b. Fruit cluster

Woolly pipe-vine

Aristolochia tomentosa Sims

Birthwort family (Aristolochiaceae)

Also called Dutchman's pipe-vine

Field Identification: Twining, high climbing vine to 75 feet.

Flowers: May-June, **single, opposite a leaf on new growth**; flower stalk 1 to 1 1/2 inches long, stout, curved, hairy; flower 1 to 2 inches long, cylindrical, yellow or greenish-yellow, densely hairy, **flower tube sharply curved**, throat almost closed; calyx (outer part of flower) with 3 lobes, reflexed, wrinkled, dark purple; petals absent; stamens 6.

Fruit: September, **a dry capsule**, 1 1/2 to 3 inches long, 1 to 1 1/4 inches wide, cylindrical, grayish-brown, hanging, 6-sided with many seeds compressed in vertical columns; seeds about 3/8 inch long, flat, thin, triangular-shaped, grayish-brown.

Leaves: Alternate, simple, blades 3 to 6 inches long, 2 to 3 1/2 inches wide, **heart-shaped**, tip blunt to rounded, base heart-shaped, **margin entire**; upper surface dark green, somewhat densely hairy with matted wool; lower surface pale, densely hairy with matted wool; petioles 2 to 2 1/2 inches long, stout, densely hairy with matted wool.

Stems: Gray to brown or black, downy when young, more smooth and somewhat grooved when older; ends of the vine usually die back a few feet during winter; tendrils absent.

Trunk: Bark grayish-brown, somewhat fissured, ridges narrow, often peeling into strips; wood soft, somewhat pithy, pale brown.

Habitat: Occurs in low alluvial woodlands along streams, often along the stream banks, usually climbing trees or brush, rarely found in open ground.

Range: Florida to east Texas, Arkansas and Oklahoma, and north to North Carolina, and west to southern Illinois, Missouri and southeastern Kansas.

Wildlife Uses: The pipe-vine or blue swallowtail butterfly lays its eggs on the leaves, where the larvae hatch and feed together on the leaf edges. The woolly pipe-vine flower produces a bad odor, similar in smell to rotting flesh, to attract flies and gnats. Once the insect enters the narrow tube, it cannot escape because of the hairs pointing downward. Only when the pollen is developed will the flower wither enough for the fly to escape, carrying pollen on its body. It is then attracted to a new flower by its smell, and pollinates the flower as it becomes trapped again.

Remarks: This vine is often cultivated for ornament in the South. The attractive heart-shaped leaves, interesting flowers and capsules make it one of Missouri's most fascinating vines.

Aristolochia is a combination of two Greek words: *aristos* ("best") and *lochos* ("childbirth"). It refers to an herbaceous member, *Aristolochia serpentaria*, commonly called Virginia snakeroot — which by chewing the roots was thought to ease some of the pains of childbirth; *tomentosa* refers to the tomentose or densely hairy, matted wool of the leaves and stems. The common name, Duchman's pipe, refers to the pipe-shaped flowers.

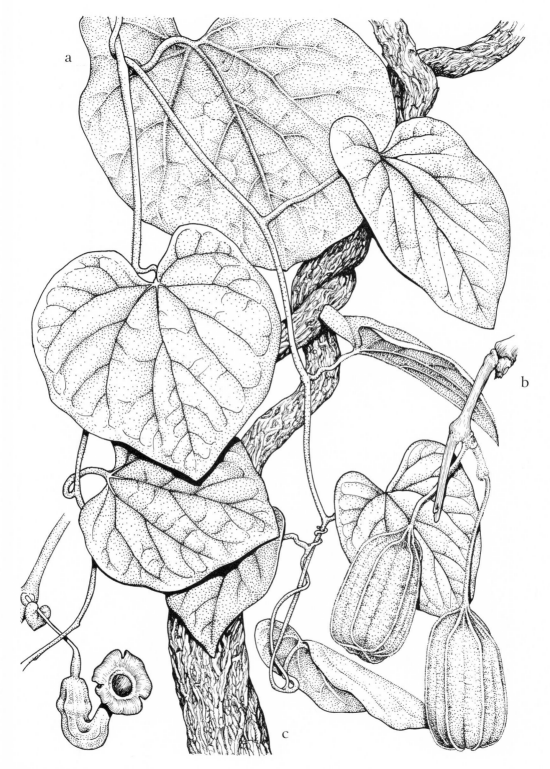

Aristolochia tomentosa 🌿 a. Growth form with flower, b. Stem with seed capsules, c. Stem with bark

Supple-jack

Berchemia scandens (Hill) K. Koch

Buckthorn family (Rhamnaceae)

Also called rattan vine

Field Identification: A high-climbing, large, woody, twining vine in bottomland forests; a smaller, densely matted, sprawling vine on dolomite glades.

Flowers: May-June, in loose clusters at the ends of stems; flowers small, greenish-yellow; petals 5, egg-shaped, tip pointed.

Fruit: August-October, bluish-black, about 1/4 inch long, egg-shaped to half as broad as long, slightly flattened, fleshy; stone with two seeds.

Leaves: Alternate, simple, 1 1/2 to 3 inches long, 3/4 to 1 1/2 inches wide, egg-shaped to longer than broad and tapering at both ends, tip pointed, base wedge-shaped or rounded, margin entire, wavy or slightly toothed; **upper surface dark green, shiny, leathery, smooth; lower surface with side veins conspicuous, nearly straight, evenly spaced and parallel**; petioles about 1/4 inch long, smooth or somewhat hairy.

Stems: Many-branched, smooth, round, slender, green and gray-streaked to brown, finely grooved when young, reddish-brown or black when older, twining, pliant, strong; **tendrils absent**.

Habitat: Occurs in low swampy woods in the southeastern lowland or Bootheel counties; on dolomite glades, rocky dolomite ledges, along bluffs or in rocky ground along stream beds and small draws of ravines in Ozark counties.

Range: Florida to east Texas, Arkansas and Oklahoma, north to Virginia, Kentucky, southern Illinois and Missouri.

Wildlife Uses: At least 17 species of birds feed on the fruit including wild turkey, bobwhite quail, and mallard duck (in bottomland areas). On dolomite glades, the densely woven stems provide shelter for birds, small mammals snakes and lizards in the hot, desertlike conditions of summer.

Remarks: Supple-jack is one of few plant species that can tolerate extremes in habitat conditions. It grows in low, wet woods with its roots sometimes covered with water; it also grows in shallow, dry soil over bedrock on seemingly inhospitable Ozark glades. The strong, twining stems can girdle, and, in time, kill good-sized trees. The bitter fruit produces a purple stain.

Berchemia is in honor of Berthout van Berchem, an 18th-century Dutch botanist; *scandens* refers to the climbing or leaning habit. Another common name, rattan vine, is a reference to the strong, pliant stems that are often used in making wickerware. Supple-jack also refers to the pliant stems.

Berchemia scandens 🌿 a. Growth form, b. Stem with flower cluster, c. Flower, d. Stem with fruit cluster, e. Winter stem

Cross vine

Bignonia capreolata L.

Trumpet creeper family (Bignoniaceae)

Also called quarter vine

Field Identification: A semi-evergreen vine, climbing by forked tendrils and bearing opposite leaves having paired leaflets.

Flowers: April-June, in clusters of 2 to 5 flowers on the axils of leaves, very showy on stalks 1/2 to 2 inches long; flower about 2 inches long, bell-shaped, red to orange externally, yellow internally; petals 5, rounded; stamens 4, not extending beyond the petals.

Fruit: September-October, capsule linear, 4 to 7 inches long, flattened, leathery, splitting down the side; seeds about 1/2 inch long, numerous, flattened, longer than broad, ends rounded.

Leaves: Opposite, compound, 2 leaflets paired; blades 2 to 7 inch long, 3/4 to 1 1/2 inches wide, lance-shaped or longer than broad and tapering at both ends, tip pointed, base heart-shaped, sometimes with earlike flaps; margins entire, wavy; upper surface dark green, smooth to slightly hairy; lower surface paler, veins prominent, hairy or smooth; leaflet stalks about 1/4 inch long. The tendrils, appearing at the base or leaflets, are flattened and used for clinging onto vertical surfaces.

Stems: Young ones green, smooth to hairy, finely grooved, climbing by means of leaf tendrils as high as 70 feet, older stems brown.

Habitat: Occurs in low bottomland woods, swampy ground, thickets along streams, low fields and fence rows.

Range: Florida to Texas, Arkansas and Oklahoma, north to New Jersey and west to Ohio, Indiana, southern Illinois and southeast Missouri.

Wildlife Uses: The brightly-colored tubular flowers attract ruby-throated hummingbirds.

Remarks: This is an attractive vine, with its showy flowers and near evergreen leaves. The vine may be a high-climber or it may sprawl along the ground. It is well-suited for ornamental planting in open sun and good soil.

The sections of stems are smoked like cigars in some localities and given the name smoke-vine.

Cross vine, and a number of other vines, tend to not flower until they have climbed to some height where they receive more light than what is available on the forest floor. For this reason, most observers see only the shorter vines without flowers or fruits.

Bignonia is in honor of Abbe Jean Paul Bignon, court librarian to King Louis XV; *capreolata* means "winding" or "twining," referring to its growth habitat. The common name, cross vine, is derived from a shape resembling a Greek cross, which is visible in the wood when the stem is cross-sectioned. Quarter vine also refers to the four parts or quarters when cut crosswise.

Bignonia capreolata a. Growth form, b. Stem with flowers, c. Seed capsule

Ladies' Eardrops

Brunnichia ovata (Walter) Shinn.

Smartweed family (Polygonaceae)

Also called buckwheat vine

Field Identification: A tendril-climbing woody vine to 40 feet, with green to reddish-brown stems.

Flowers: May-August, in clusters on the end of stems, 2 to 10 inches long; flowers several, minute, composed of a petallike, 5-parted, greenish calyx that is borne on a slender pedicel flattened into a wing; stamens 7 to 10.

Fruit: August-October, on stalks about 1/4 inch long; a fruiting body 3/4 to 1 1/2 inches long, **fruit pink, showy, hardened, drooping, leathery**, upper half with the remains of the 5 sepals, lower half flattened into a wing with a ridge on one side; seed is tightly enclosed, light brown, smooth, triangular.

Leaves: Alternate, simple, blades 1 1/4 to 6 inches long, 1/2 to 3 inches wide, thin, egg- to lance-shaped, tip pointed, base heart-shaped or broadly wedge-shaped, margin entire; upper surface light green, smooth; lower surface smooth or slightly hairy; petioles 1/4 to 1 inch long, smooth or hairy.

Stems: High-climbing, sometimes as long as 40 feet, green to reddish-brown, finely grooved, older stems up to 1 inch across; **tendrils at the axils**, delicate.

Habitat: Occurs in swamps, low wet woods, and moist alluvial thickets in the lowland section of southeastern Missouri. Often best developed at woodland edges or where disturbance has created full sun conditions, and brush or trees are available for support.

Range: Florida to Texas, Arkansas and Oklahoma, north to South Carolina, Kentucky, southern Illinois and southeastern Missouri.

Remarks: Formerly known as *Brunnichia cirrhosa* Gaertner. **The fruit somewhat resembles ear pendants because of the long, narrow, winged fruit; hence the common name, Ladies' Eardrops**. The persistent pendant fruiting structures make this plant an interesting possibility for use as an ornamental vine on an arbor or trellis, although it may be aggressive in moist, fertile sites.

Brunnichia is in honor of M. T. Brunnich, a Norwegian naturalist of the 18th century; *ovata* refers to the egg-shaped leaves.

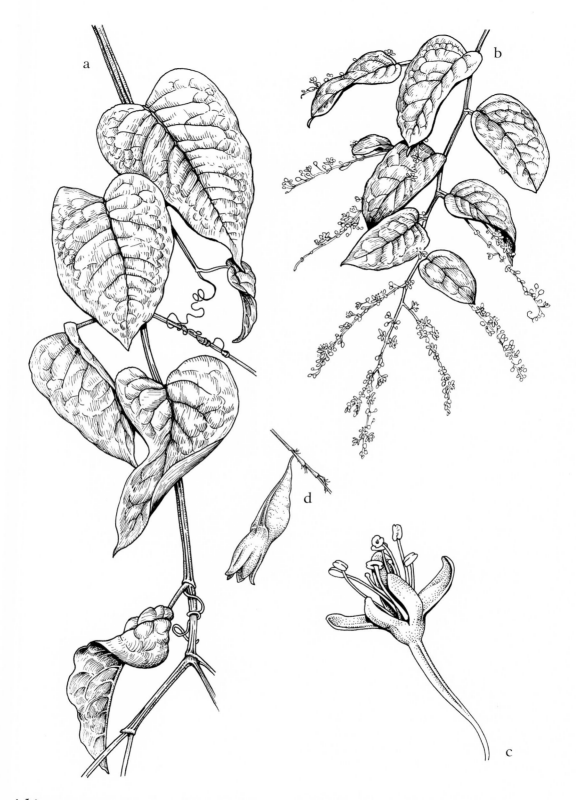

Brunnichia ovata ❧ a. Growth form, b. Stem with flower clusters, c. Flower, d. Fruit

Cupseed

Calycocarpum lyonii (Pursh) A. Gray

Moonseed family (Menispermaceae)

Field Identification: A twining vine to 30 feet that **dies back to the ground in severe winters**.

Flowers: May-June, in drooping clusters at the leaf axils on new growth; staminate (male) and pistillate (female) flowers in separate clusters; staminate flowers in loose many-flowered clusters 3 to 6 inches long, cluster stalk finely hairy; flowers minute; calyx lobes 6, distinct, spreading, white; petals absent; stamens 12; pistillate flowers 15 to 20 in a cluster 3 to 4 inches long; flowers minute; calyx lobes 6, distinct, spreading, white; petals absent; stamens 12, not fully developed.

Fruit: September-October, grapelike clusters, 2 1/2 to 3 1/2 inches long, fruits crowded; fruit stalks finely hairy; fruit oval to globe-shaped, smooth, about 3/4 inch long and wide, usually black, but sometimes green, becoming slightly yellowish and soft before falling; **seed yellowish-brown, in the shape of a hollow bowl or cup, with a keel on the round side**, 1/2 to 3/4 inch long, about 1/2 inch wide, with a 1/4 inch depression, shell thin, hard, the edge of the rim with small, close, sharp teeth.

Leaves: Alternate, simple, **with 5 to 7 veins radiating out from a base**; variable in size, 3 to 8 inches long, 3 to 7 inches wide, rounded to egg-shaped, **margin with 3 to 5 deep lobes**, end lobe usually egg-shaped, sinuses between lobes rounded, tips of lobes pointed, base broadly heart-shaped; **upper surface dark yellow-green, smooth; lower surface slightly paler**, scattered long, straight hairs on the veins; petioles 2 1/2 to 6 inches long, smooth to hairy, with fine grooves and ridges.

Stems: Smooth, flexible, yellowish-brown, **with fine grooves and ridges**, dies back near the ground each winter; tendrils absent.

Trunk: Bark greenish to brown, **finely ridged**; wood white, soft, weak.

Habitat: Occurs in low alluvial ground in wooded valleys and along banks of streams, in thickets, and borders of fields.

Range: South Carolina and Florida to Louisiana, north to Kentucky, and west to Illinois, Missouri, southeast Kansas and Oklahoma.

Remarks: The large grapelike leaves and cup-shaped seeds are the most distinctive characteristics of this vine. This interesting plant would be suitable for planting along borders in partial shade. Although it dies back near to the ground in hard winters, it rebounds in the spring and summer with its vigorous growth.

Calycocarpum is derived from the Greek word *calyx* ("a cup") and *carpos* ("a fruit"), referring to the cup-shaped seeds; *lyonii* is named for its discoverer, John Lyon, an English botanical explorer of North America prior to 1818.

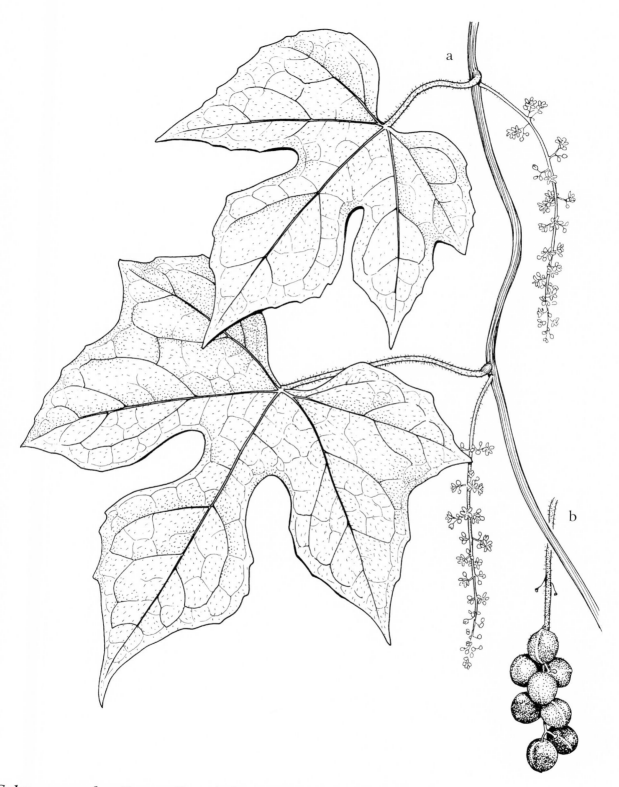

Calycocarpum lyonii 🌿 a. Growth form with flower clusters, b. Fruit

Trumpet creeper

Campsis radicans (L.) Seemann

Trumpet creeper family (Bignoniaceae)

Also called trumpet vine, devil's shoelaces, shoestrings, hell vine, cow itch vine

Field Identification: Woody vine climbing tall trees or structures by means of aerial rootlets to a height of 60 feet but often seen sprawling over fences or low bushes.

Flowers: May-August, in clusters of 2 to 9 flowers at the ends of twigs, flower stalks stout 1/2 to 3/4 inch long; flowers showy, tubular to funnel-shaped, 2 to 3 1/2 inches long; lobes 5, rounded, spreading, red to orange on the outside, yellow on the inside; stamens 4, not extending beyond the petals.

Fruit: August-September, pods 2 to 6 inches long, narrowed toward the ends, slightly flattened, tan to brown, splitting open on each side; seeds dark brown, flattened, about 3/4 inch long, winged on 2 sides.

Leaves: Opposite, pinnately compound, 8 to 15 inches long; leaflets 7 to 13, 3/4 to 3 inches long, 1/2 to 2 inches wide, egg-shaped, oval, or longer than broad, tip pointed, base narrowed and somewhat uneven, margin coarsely toothed; upper surface olive-green, shiny, smooth; lower surface paler, smooth, veins distinct with some hairs; leaflet stalks with wings along the margins, about 1/4 inch long;

Stems: Green to reddish, smooth, rather stiff, climbing by aerial rootlets to great heights or creeping on the ground.

Trunk: Bark yellow and tight on young plants; brown, and stripping into long shreds on old trunks; wood soft, yellow.

Habitat: Occurs in open woods, thickets, cliffs, stream banks, fallow and old fields, and along roadsides and railroads.

Range: Florida to Texas, Arkansas and Oklahoma, north to New Jersey and Pennsylvania, and west to Kentucky, Indiana, Illinois, Iowa, Missouri and southeastern Kansas. Naturalized north to Connecticut, Ohio and Michigan.

Wildlife Uses: Its bright red flowers attract ruby-throated hummingbirds, which seek out the nectar. In turn, they pollinate the flowers with pollen attached to their heads from a previously visited flower. The range of trumpet creeper closely coincides with that of the hummingbird. Ants are frequent visitors to the flowers, as well; presumably, they are attracted to the nectar. The vine, in its creeping habit, is valuable cover for birds and small mammals.

Remarks: The vine can be very aggressive and can resprout from pieces of roots broken off below the ground. It is often cultivated as an ornamental vine, but it is best suited in areas where it will not compete with other plantings.

Some cases of dermatitis are known where susceptible individuals have handled the leaves and flowers.

Campsis is from the Greek name *campsis* ("curvature"), which is in reference to the curved stamens; *radicans* refers to the aerial rooting habit.

Campsis radicans 🐾 a. Growth form with flowers, b. Stem with seed pods

Round-leaved bittersweet

Celastrus orbiculatus Thunb.

Staff tree family (Celastraceae)

Field Identification: A twining woody vine climbing to heights of 20 feet but more commonly found sprawling on bushes or fences.

Flowers: May-June, in clusters along the leaf axils or at the end of new twigs; staminate (male) and pistillate (female) flowers in separate clusters; plants with mostly female or male flowers only; flowers small, inconspicuous, greenish; petals 5; stamens 5, poorly developed on the pistillate flowers.

Fruit: July-October, in hanging clusters; fruit about 1/4 inch across, globe-shaped, **orange-yellow to orange**, leathery, splitting into 3 sections, each section with 1 to 2 globe-shaped seeds; **seeds covered by a red coating**, about 1/4 inch long, persistent into winter.

Leaves: Alternate, simple, blade 2 to 4 inches long and wide, **circular to broadly inverted egg-shaped**, tip pointed or blunt, base wedge-shaped to rounded, **margin with small rounded teeth**; upper surface green, smooth; lower surface paler, smooth; petioles about 1/2 inch long, smooth.

Stems: Spreading to twining, green to gray or brown; tendrils absent.

Trunk: Bark brown, smooth with prominent lenticels (pores); bark of old stems peeling into thin flakes and small sheets; wood soft, porous, white.

Habitat: Edge of woodlands, thickets, disturbed sites and along fence rows.

Range: Native of Asia; occasionally escaped from cultivation in the eastern United States.

Wildlife Uses: Fruits are eaten by birds to some extent.

Remarks: The use of this plant is discouraged. It is very aggressive, and has the potential to invade natural habitats if its use increases. The fruits are not as showy as the native American bittersweet. The fruits are reported to be poisonous if ingested, but no detailed cases of human poisoning have been reported in this country.

Celastrus is from the ancient Greek name *kelastrus*, for an evergreen tree; *orbiculatus* refers to the round leaves.

Escapes from cultivation

Celastrus orbiculatus 🐾 a. Growth form, b. Stem with flowers, c. Stem with fruit, d. Stem with bark, e. Vine twining around a support stem

American bittersweet

Celastrus scandens L.

Staff tree family (Celastraceae)

Field Identification: A twining woody vine, climbing to heights of 20 feet but more commonly found sprawling on bushes or fences.

Flowers: May-June, in clusters along the leaf axils or at the end of new twigs; staminate (male) and pistillate (female) flowers in separate clusters; plants with mostly female or male flowers only; staminate flowers in clusters about 2 inches long; flower stalks about 1 inch long; flowers small, inconspicuous, greenish-white to yellow; petals 5; stamens 5, shorter than the petals; pistillate flowers in clusters 1 to 1 1/2 inches long; flower stalks 1 1/4 to 2 inches long; flowers small, 5 to 25, greenish-white to yellow; petals 5; stamens 5, poorly developed.

Fruit: July-October, in hanging clusters 2 1/2 to 4 inches long; fruits 6 to 20, globe-shaped, about 1/4 inch across, fruit orange to yellow, leathery, splitting into 3 sections, each section with 1 to 2 globe-shaped seeds; seeds covered with a bright red, fleshy coating, persistent and showy in autumn; seeds white at first, then cream-colored and drying to brown, oval, about 1/4 inch long.

Leaves: Alternate, simple, blade 2 to 4 inches long, 1 to 2 inches wide, egg-shaped to oval to lance-shaped, tip pointed, base ending at a sharp angle or rounded, margin entire or with small finely pointed teeth; upper surface dark yellowish-green, smooth; lower surface paler, smooth; petioles about 1/2 inch long, smooth.

Stems: Spreading to twining, green to gray or brown; tendrils absent.

Trunk: Bark light brown, smooth, with prominent lenticels (pores); bark of old stems peeling into thin flakes and small sheets; wood soft, porous, white.

Habitat: Occurs in woodlands, rocky slopes, along bluffs, borders of glades, thickets and along fence rows. Probably in every county in Missouri.

Range: Georgia to Louisiana, Arkansas, Oklahoma, Texas and New Mexico, north to Quebec, and west to Ontario, Manitoba and Wyoming.

Wildlife Uses: Cottontail rabbits and fox squirrels, and at least 15 species of birds (including ruffed grouse and bobwhite quail), eat the fruit.

Medicinal Uses: The bark of the root has been taken internally to induce vomiting, to quiet disturbed people, to treat venereal diseases, and to increase urine flow. As an ointment mixed with grease it has been used to treat skin cancers, tumors, burns and swellings.

Remarks: American bittersweet has been in cultivation since 1736, and is used for covering trellis work, trees, rocks and walls. The twining habit of the strong vines may be loose around small trees, but may form tight constrictions as the tree's diameter increases. The vine spreads when birds distribute the seed, or when root suckers form large colonies on favorable sites.

The fruit is persistent and ornamental in winter because of the scarlet seed coating. It sometimes is used for indoor floral decorations. The fruits are reported to be poisonous if ingested, but no detailed cases of human poisoning have been reported in this country.

Celastrus is from the ancient Greek name, *kelastrus,* for an evergreen tree; *scandens* refers to its climbing habit.

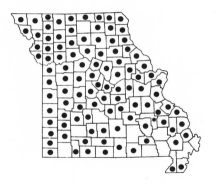

Celastrus scandens 🌿 a. Growth form with flower cluster, b. Flower, c. Stem with fruit cluster, d. Stem with bark

Marine vine

Cissus incisa (Nutt. ex Torrey & A. Gray) Des Moul.

Grape family (Vitaceae)

Also called marine ivy, ivy treevine, possum grape

Field Identification: A climbing or trailing vine to 30 feet high, climbing by tendrils.

Flowers: June-July, in umbrella-shaped clusters with 3 to 5 stalks 1 to 2 inches wide; flowers small, 50 to 80 in the umbrella-shaped cluster; petals 4, green, minute; stamens 4, opposite the petals, extending beyond the petals.

Fruit: October, on curved, green to reddish-brown stalks 1/2 to 1 inch long; berries globe- to egg-shaped, about 1/4 inch long, shiny black, flesh thin, not edible; seed solitary, brownish, about 1/4 inch long, oval, tip pointed, base rounded.

Leaves: Alternate, **3 leaflets or leaves deeply 3-lobed; bad-smelling when crushed**; end leaflet 1 1/2 to 2 inches long, 1 1/4 to 2 inches wide, with equal, slanting sides, commonly 3-lobed; side leaflets 1 1/4 to 1 1/2 inches long and as wide, fan-shaped, commonly 2-lobed; leaflet margins coarsely toothed; both surfaces dull green, smooth or with a few minute white hairs, veins obscure; **leaves very fleshy or succulent (thick)**; petioles about 1/2 inch long, stout, with a narrow groove above; leaflets without stalks or nearly so.

Stems: Green to reddish and angled when young; brown to gray, often warty, when older; lenticels (pores) orange; tip often dying back during the winter; **climbing by coiled tendrils emerging from the nodes.**

Trunk: Bark thin, soft, light tan to gray, with numerous, raised, orange lenticels; inner bark green; wood soft, fibrous, white, with large, white pith.

Habitat: Occurs along upper portions of south- or west-facing rocky ledges of dolomite bluffs and upper slopes of dolomite bluffs bordering streams.

Range: Florida to Louisiana, Texas, Arizona and Mexico, north to Arkansas, southern Missouri, southeastern Kansas and Oklahoma.

Remarks: Marine vine is classified as rare in Missouri. A more southern ranging plant, marine vine in Missouri scrambles over hot, dry, west- and south-facing dolomite exposures. It can be found growing with ashe juniper (*Juniperus ashei*), prairie acacia (*Acacia angustissima*), soapberry tree (*Sapindus drummondii*), golden currant (*Ribes odoratum*), stickleaf (*Mentzelia oligosperma*) and cloak-fern (*Notholaena dealbata*).

Cissus is the Greek name for ivy; *incisa* refers to the incised or sharply cut leaves.

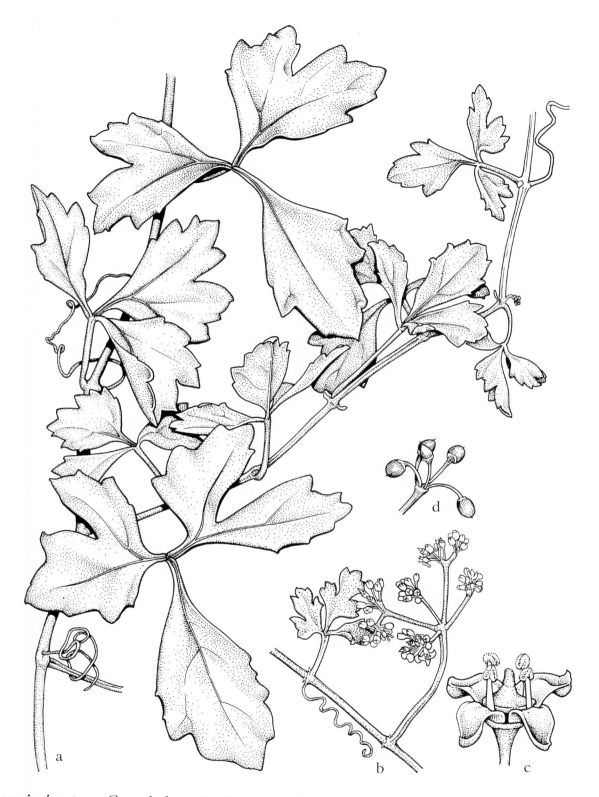

Cissus incisa 🦇 a. Growth form, b. Stem with flower cluster, c. Flower, d. Fruit

Virgin's bower

Clematis virginiana L.

Buttercup family (Ranunculaceae)

Field Identification: Semi-woody vine climbing to a height of 20 feet by twisting leaf petioles.

Flowers: July-September, in clusters on new growth of stems; flowers numerous, creamy-white, 1/2 to 1 1/4 inches wide; petals absent; sepals 4, 1/4 to 1/2 inch long, wide-spreading, thin, long and narrow, hairy; stamens numerous, spreading.

Fruit: August-September, in large fruiting heads; hard, dry one-seeded, about 1/8 inch long, brown, with long hairs, with plumelike projections about 1 inch long.

Leaves: Opposite, compound, mainly with 3 leaflets, lower sometimes with 5 leaflets; length 2 to 3 1/2 inches, thin, broadly rounded, tip pointed, base heart-shaped or rounded, margin entire, or deeply toothed or somewhat lobed; surfaces sparingly hairy to almost smooth when mature; petioles green to brown, twisting on supports to pull the plant upward.

Stems: Slender, green to brown, sparingly hairy or smooth.

Habitat: Occurs in moist or low ground of woodland and thickets bordering streams, ponds, and fence rows; especially common on limestone soils. Scattered throughout Missouri.

Range: Georgia, Alabama, Mississippi, Louisiana, Arkansas and Oklahoma, north to Nova Scotia and Quebec, and west to Manitoba and Kansas.

Remarks: Of the seven species of *clematis* known from Missouri, this is the only one that is semi-woody, especially in the more southern areas of its range.

Virgin's bower — with its showy white flowers and silky seed heads that glisten with backlighting — is suitable in landscape planting, but does best on a trellis. When sprawling, it searches for places to climb, pulling down herbaceous plants in the process. The plant was first introduced into cultivation in 1720.

Clematis is a name given by Dioscorides, a Greek physician, to a slender climbing plant, from *clema*, a shoot; *virginiana* is given for the state of Virginia, or the colonial territory once assigned generally under that name, where the plant was first described.

Clematis virginiana ❧ a. Growth form, b. Stem with flower clusters, c. Fruit

Carolina moonseed

Cocculus carolinus (L.) DC.

Moonseed family (Menispermaceae)

Also called Carolina snailseed, fishberry, coral berry

Field Identification: A slender, twining vine to 40 feet high, bearing clusters of brilliant red, somewhat flattened fruits.

Flowers: July-August, in loose clusters 1 to 6 inches long; flowers minute, yellowish-green; petals 6; stamens 6, not extending beyond the petals; staminate (male) and pistillate (female) flowers are found in separate clusters on the same plant, but in some cases flowers may contain both sexes.

Fruit: September-October, in grapelike clusters 1 to 6 inches long, rarely more than 2 inches wide; **fruit brilliant red, very showy, glossy,** smooth, globe-shaped, about 1/4 inch across, flattened; **seed creamy-white, solitary, flattened, with a spiral pattern.**

Leaves: Simple, alternate, blades 2 to 4 inches long and wide, broadly egg- to heart-shaped or **often triangular**, tip pointed to blunt or rounded, base flattened to heart-shaped, margin entire or 3 to 5 lobed; upper surface dark green, smooth or with scattered hairs; **lower surface paler, densely hairy**; petioles 3/4 to 4 inches long, slender, hairy, occasionally sharply bent near the blade.

Stems: Slender, twining, grayish-green or grayish-brown, hairy; tendrils absent.

Trunk: Bark pale grayish-green to grayish-brown, slightly fissured, the thin edges curled; old vines with ridges and warty spots of corky bark; wood soft, whitish, porous.

Habitat: Occurs in rocky open woods, dolomite and limestone glades, alluvial ground and thickets bordering streams and ponds, fence rows and roadsides. Naturally occurring in southern Missouri; the records for Ralls and Marion counties are probably from cultivated or introduced plants.

Range: Florida, Louisiana, Texas and northeastern Mexico, north to Virginia, Kentucky, Illinois, Missouri and southeastern Kansas.

Wildlife Uses: The fruits are consumed by several species of birds.

Remarks: The vine is sometimes confused with catbrier, but the latter has stiffer and much more leathery foliage and prickly stems. The attractive, brilliant red fruits add to the vine's ornamental value.

Cocculus is an old name and a diminutive of *coccus* ("a berry"); *carolinus* is for Carolina, where the plant was first described; but it is uncertain if the reference is for North or South Carolina or both. The common name, moonseed, refers to the seed's resemblance to a 3/4 moon or a snail; hence, the name snailseed is sometimes used.

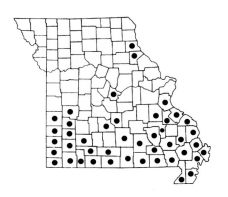

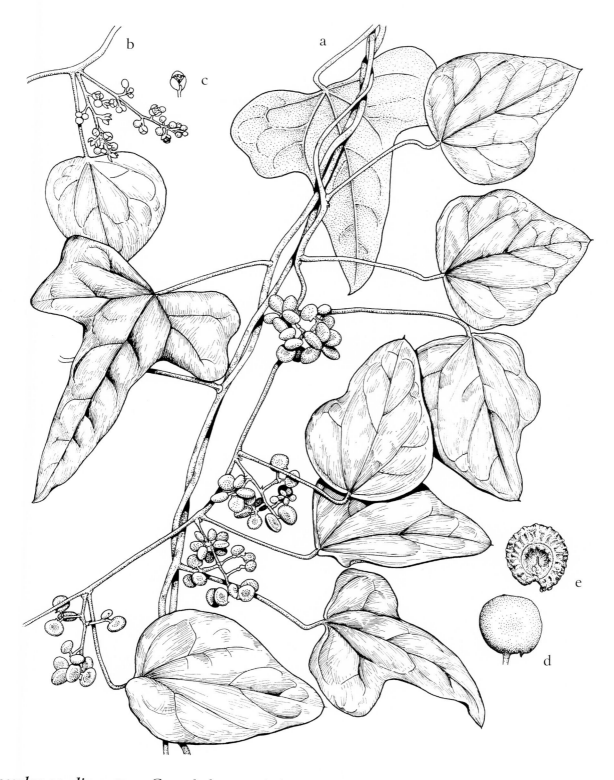

Cocculus carolinus 🌿 a. Growth form with fruit clusters, b. Stem with flowers, c. Flower, d. Fruit, e. Seed

Wintercreeper

Euonymus fortunei (Turcz.) Hand.-Mazz.

Staff-tree family (Celastraceae)

Also called climbing euonymus

Field Identification: An evergreen vine forming a dense ground cover or climbing or trailing to 20 feet.

Flowers: June-August, in clusters with several flowers emerging from leaf axils of new stems; **flowers very small, about 1/8 inch long**, greenish-white; petals 4, oval, spreading, margins curved inward, wavy; stamens 4, alternating with the petals and arising from the edge of the disk.

Fruit: September-October, capsule globe-shaped, flattened at the base, surface not warty, orange, splitting open to expose 1 to 2 seeds.

Leaves: Opposite, simple, **evergreen**, about 1 1/2 inches long, 3/4 inch wide, rounded equally to both ends or egg-shaped, tip pointed, base wedge-shaped, **margin irregularly toothed**; upper surface green, smooth, leathery in texture, veins light green to cream-colored; lower surface paler, smooth.

Stems: Green, smooth; aerial roots present on climbing stems; stem also rooting when in contact with the ground.

Trunk: Bark of young trunk green and smooth with narrow, flat, brown ridges, aerial roots present; older trunks brown with plates peeling into thin strips.

Habitat: Frequently planted as an ornamental or ground cover; it has escaped into moist to dry woods. It can invade natural openings and relatively undisturbed forests.

Range: Native of Asia; brought into the United States as a ground cover, especially in urban areas.

Wildlife Uses: The fruit is eaten by several species of birds and small mammals. The leaves and stems are eaten by white-tailed deer and cottontail rabbits.

Remarks: The planting of this vine as an ornamental ground cover should be avoided. It is very aggressive and can form dense mats that smother other vegetation. The vine maintains a sprawling or creeping habit until it finds an upright support, usually a tree. Wintercreeper then changes to a vigorously climbing vine and ascends to the top of its support tree, anchoring itself along the way with aerial roots.

Once the vine reaches the canopy, it branches and forms dense mats that compete with the tree for sunlight. With sunlight, it has enough energy to produce flowers and fruit; the latter is then eaten by birds that disperse the seeds to new areas by way of their droppings. Once established, wintercreeper is difficult to eliminate.

Euonymus is Greek for "true name"; *fortunei* is for its discoverer, Robert Fortune (1817-1880).

Escapes from cultivation

Euonymus fortunei 🌿 a. Growth form, b. Stem with flower cluster, c. Flower, d. Fruit, e. Stem with leaves

Limber honeysuckle

Lonicera dioica L.

Honeysuckle family (Caprifoliaceae)

Also called wild honeysuckle

Field Identification: A sprawling or climbing vine, the stems often reaching 10 feet long.

Flowers: April-June, in clusters at the end of stems on new growth; **clusters arranged in 1 to 3 crowded whorls or layers on a stalk**, each whorl with 3 flowers; **flowers yellow or greenish-yellow tinged with purple, rose, or a brick-red color**, fragrant, **3/4 to 1 inch long**, tubular, **flower tube noticeably enlarged on one side at the base**, smooth to hairy; tip of tube strongly spreading into two lips, one lip with a single narrow lobe, the other lip with 4 short lobes; stamens 5, extending beyond the flower.

Fruit: July-October, crowded in clusters at the ends of stems; **clusters arranged in 1 to 3 crowded whorls or layers on a stalk**; berries red, globe-shaped, about 3/8 inch across, smooth, glossy; seeds about 1/8 inch long, oval, often irregular, flattened, yellowish-brown, smooth.

Leaves: Opposite, simple, upper pair just below the flowers united throughout to form a disk; **disk longer than broad**, tips blunt; **upper surface of the disk green or barely whitened**; leaves below disk not united, each 1 1/2 to 3 inches long, 1 to 2 inches wide, tip blunt but ending in a slight, abrupt point, base wedge-shaped or rounded, margin entire, often wavy; upper surface yellowish-green, smooth; **lower surface covered with a white waxy coating**, smooth or hairy; petioles lacking or very short and partly clasping.

Stems: Slender, flexible, twining, pale to dark brown, smooth.

Trunk: Bark yellowish-brown, shredding into thin, long strips; wood yellowish.

Habitat: Occurs along wooded bluffs and ledges, upland forests, rocky banks of streams and thickets.

Range: North Carolina, Kentucky, Missouri and Kansas, north to Quebec and west to Manitoba, North Dakota and British Columbia.

Wildlife Uses: The flowers are sought after by ruby-throated hummingbirds for their nectar. Some species of birds and small mammals eat the fruit. The stems and leaves are browsed by white-tailed deer.

Remarks: Limber honeysuckle does well in partial shade to full sun, and can be grown to sprawl over shrubs like sumac or on a trellis. It is often encountered as a sterile vine in heavier shade, preferring more light to flower.

Lonicera honors Adam Lonitzer (1528-1586), a German herbalist; *dioica* means dioecious or separate sexes, in reference to the male and female flowers on separate plants, which is not the situation in this species; a botanist erred when he thought both male and female parts were in the same flower.

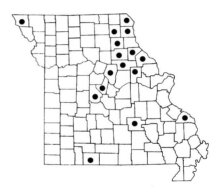

Lonicera dioica ❦ a. Growth form with flower cluster, b. Flower, c. Stem with fruit cluster

Yellow honeysuckle

Lonicera flava Sims

Honeysuckle family (Caprifoliaceae)

Field Identification: A twining or loosely ascending climber.

Flowers: April-May, in clusters at the end of stems on new growth; **clusters arranged in 1 to 3 crowded whorls or layers on a stalk; flowers bright orange to yellow but lacking purple, rose, or brick red along the tube**, fragrant, **3/4 to 1 1/4 inches long**, tube cylindrical, slender, **tube slightly enlarged at the base but not a significant protuberance**, smooth on the outside, slightly hairy on the inside; petals in the shape of 2 lips, lower lip narrow, with a solitary lobe, upper lip with 4 lobes; stamens 5, extending beyond the petals.

Fruit: August-September, crowded in heads at the ends of stems; **clusters arranged in 1 to 3 crowded whorls or layers on a stalk**; berries red to orange-red, globe-shaped, about 1/4 inch across, fleshy, many-seeded.

Leaves: Simple, opposite, upper pair just below the flowers united at the base to form a disk; both sides of disk totaling about 6 inch across, about 2 inches wide, **often longer than broad but sometimes rounded**, tips round to blunt; **upper surface of the disk green or barely whitened**; leaves below the disk 2 to 4 inches long, 2 to 3 inches wide, longer than broad, or circular, tip pointed to blunt, base narrowed or rounded, margin entire; upper surface bright green, smooth, **lower surface grayish-green or pale but not noticeably whitened**; petiole short or absent.

Stems: Slender, twining, smooth, with a white coating that rubs off, reddish-brown above, green below, or tan, or green throughout, finely grooved.

Trunk: Bark gray to brown, shredding into long, papery strips to reveal a reddish-brown inner bark; wood solid with white pith.

Habitat: Occurs in rocky woods, on ledges and upper slopes above bluffs, and rocky ground along streams.

Range: Georgia, Alabama, Arkansas and Oklahoma, north to North Carolina, and west to Kentucky and Missouri.

Wildlife Uses: The flowers are sought after by ruby-throated hummingbirds for their nectar. Some species of birds and small mammals eat the fruit. The stems and leaves are browsed by white-tailed deer.

Remarks: Yellow honeysuckle has been in cultivation since 1810. It is easy to grow and prefers full sun to partial shade. It is not aggressive like Japanese Honeysuckle.

Lonicera honors Adam Lonitzer (1528-1586), a German herbalist; *flava* refers to the yellow color of the flowers. The name honeysuckle applies to the practice of pulling off the flower and sucking the bead of sweet nectar or honey at the back of the flower.

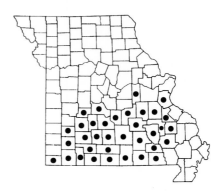

Lonicera flava 🌿 a. Growth form, b. Stem with flower clusters, c. Flower, d. Fruit cluster

Japanese honeysuckle

Lonicera japonica Thunb.

Honeysuckle family (Caprifoliaceae)

Field Identification: A climbing or sprawling vine to 20 feet.

Flowers: May-June, in pairs from leaf axils; flowers 1/2 to 1 1/2 inches long, white or pink, turning yellow with age, tubular, slender, hairy, distinctly 2-lipped; petals 2, upper lip with 4 lobes, the lower lip with 1 lobe, both lips recurved; stamens 5, extending beyond the lips.

Fruit: September-October, berries single or paired on stalks from the leaf axils; fruit about 1/4 inch long, black, glossy, smooth, pulpy, globe-shaped, 4 to 10 seeds; seeds oval, minute, dark brown to black.

Leaves: Opposite, simple, near evergreen, at least until single digit Fahrenheit temperatures arrive in winter; blades 1 to 3 inches long, 3/4 to 1 1/4 inches wide, egg-shaped or half as wide as long, tip pointed or blunt, base rounded or flattened, margin entire, often with fine hairs; upper surface dark green, semishiny, hairy; lower surface pale, smooth, hairy along the central vein; petioles about 1/2 inch long, hairy, **none of the leaves joined at the base.**

Stems: Flexible, hairy, pale reddish-brown, shredding to reveal straw-colored bark beneath.

Trunk: Bark yellowish-brown, shredding into long, papery strips; wood white, soft, fine-grained, pith hollow.

Habitat: Escaped from cultivation into thickets, fence rows, edge of woods, open woods, rocky slopes, ditches, roadsides and along railroads.

Range: Native of Asia; introduced and naturalized in the United States from Florida to Texas, Arkansas and Oklahoma, north to Massachusetts, and west to New York, Ohio, Indiana, Missouri and Kansas.

Wildlife Uses: Ruby-throated hummingbirds frequent the flowers for nectar. Bobwhite quail will use the thickets of this vine for winter cover and will eat the still-green leaves during the winter. Some species of birds eat the fruits, but cultivation of the vine should be discouraged because of its rampant growth and weediness. Native honeysuckles offer a good substitute.

Remarks: Japanese Honeysuckle is very pervasive, climbing over native vegetation and shading it out. It is sometimes planted for its penetrating fragrance, showy flowers, ability to cover unsightly areas and for control of soil erosion. There are several horticultural varieties available at nurseries that do not appear to be as aggressive.

Lonicera honors Adam Lonitzer (1528-1586), a German herbalist; *japonica* denotes the plant's Asiatic origin.

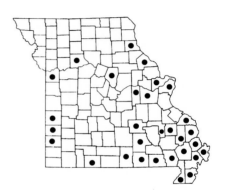

Lonicera japonica 🐛 a. Growth form with flowers, b. Stem with fruit

Grape honeysuckle

Lonicera reticulata Raf.

Honeysuckle family (Caprifoliaceae)

Field Identification: A twining vine to 15 feet, or sometimes semibushy when no support is present.

Flowers: April-June, in clusters at the end of stems on new growth; **clusters arranged in 2 to 6 whorls or layers, which are usually separated along the stalk**; flowers pale yellow, fragrant, 3/4 to 1 inch long, tubular, slender, noticeably enlarged on one side at the base, smooth on the outside, hairy inside; tip of tube strongly spreading into two lips, one lip with a single narrow lobe, the other lip with 4 short lobes; stamens 5, extending beyond the flower.

Fruit: July-October, crowded in heads at the ends of stems; **clusters arranged in 2 to 6 whorls or layers, which are usually separated along the stalk**; berries red to orangish-red, globe-shaped, about 1/4 inch across, fleshy; seeds several, about 1/8 inch long, oval, flat.

Leaves: Simple, opposite, upper pair just below the flowers united throughout to form a disk; both sides of disk totaling about 6 inches long, 2 inches wide, **disk oval-shaped to sometimes nearly circular**, tips rounded and slightly notched, **upper surface of disk with a white coating**, margin entire, smooth; leaves below the disk not united, each 3 to 4 inches long, 1 1/2 to 2 1/2 inches wide, broadly oval to inverted egg-shaped, tip blunt to rounded, sometimes with a notch, base tapering, margin entire; upper surface dark green to yellow-green, smooth; lower surface smooth or somewhat hairy; petioles short or absent.

Stems: Slender, twining, green to tan or reddish-brown, finely grooved.

Trunk: Bark gray, shredding into long, papery strips to reveal a reddish-brown inner bark; wood solid with white pith.

Habitat: Occurs in open woods, wooded slopes, bluff ledges, upper slopes and wooded thickets.

Range: Mississippi, Arkansas and Oklahoma, north to New York and Ontario, and west to Wisconsin and Manitoba.

Wildlife Uses: Ruby-throated hummingbirds frequent the flowers for nectar. Some species of birds and small mammals eat the fruit. The stems and leaves are browsed by white-tailed deer.

Remarks: Some taxonomists refer to this species as *Lonicera prolifera* (Kirchn.) Rehder. Grape honeysuckle has been in cultivation since 1840. It is easy to grow and prefers full sun to partial shade. It is not aggressive like Japanese honeysuckle.

Lonicera honors Adam Lonitzer (1528-1586), a German herbalist; *prolifera* means "abundant growth."

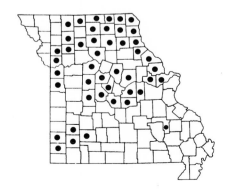

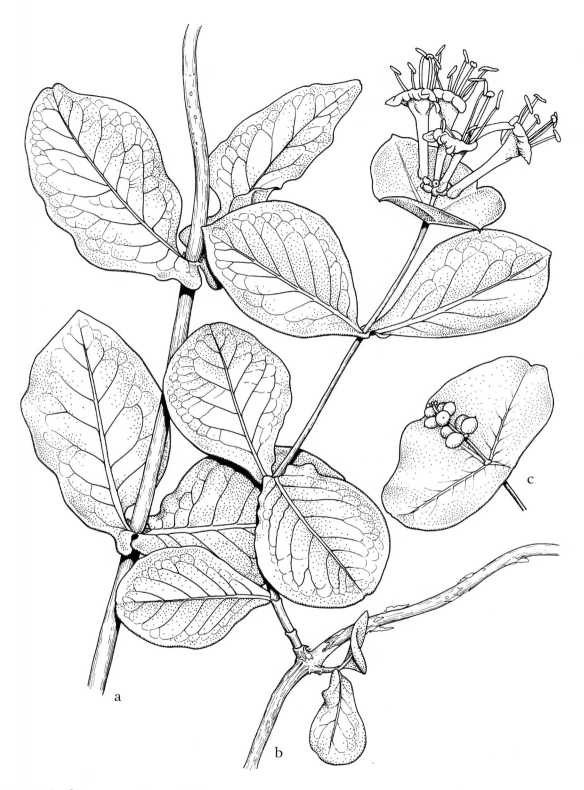

Lonicera reticulata 🦫 a. Growth form, b. Stem with flower cluster, c. Stem with fruit cluster

Trumpet honeysuckle

Lonicera sempervirens L.

Honeysuckle family (Caprifoliaceae)

Also called coral honeysuckle

Field Identification: A twining vine to 18 feet in length, occasionally dense.

Flowers: April-July, in clusters at the end of stems on new growth, in 2 to 4 whorls of 3 to 6 flowers each; **flowers deep red on the outside**, yellow inside, fragrant, **1 1/2 to 2 inches long**, tubular, slender; tip of tube spreading into 5 lobes; lobes egg-shaped, tips rounded; stamens 5, barely extending beyond the flower.

Fruit: August-September, in whorls of 2 to 4; fruit about 3/8 inch long, bright red with a minute black tip, egg-shaped, smooth, 1-seeded; seeds oval, flattened, yellow to brown, finely pitted.

Leaves: Simple, opposite, upper pair just below the flowers united throughout to form a disk; both sides of disk totaling 2 to 2 1/2 inches long, 1 1/2 to 1 3/4 inches wide, each side triangular-shaped, tip rounded or blunt and slightly notched, margin entire, smooth; leaves below the disk not united, each 1 1/2 to 3 inches long, 1 1/4 to 2 inches wide, oval to broadly egg-shaped or inverted egg-shaped, tip pointed to blunt, base tapering, margin entire; upper surface dark yellow-green, semiglossy, smooth; lower surface smooth; petiole short or absent.

Stems: Slender, twining, yellow-brown, shredding in the second year, smooth.

Trunk: Bark yellow-brown, shredding into long fibrous strips; wood soft, yellow.

Habitat: Escaped from cultivation along roadsides, sandy or rocky stream banks, and in thickets.

Range: Florida to Texas, north to Massachusetts and Maine, and west to New York, Ohio, Iowa, Nebraska and Kansas. Native to southeastern United States, escaped elsewhere.

Wildlife Uses: Ruby-throated hummingbirds frequent the flowers for their nectar. Some species of birds and small mammals eat the fruit. The stems and leaves are browsed by white-tailed deer.

Remarks: Although escaped from cultivation in this region, trumpet honeysuckle is not nearly as aggressive as Japanese honeysuckle. The showy, bright red flowers are abundantly produced throughout a long period if given full to partial sun. The vine does well on a trellis or fence. In the southern states the leaves are evergreen.

Lonicera honors Adam Lonitzer (1528-1586), a German herbalist; *sempervirens* means "evergreen," referring to its condition in southern states.

Lonicera sempervirens 🐾 a. Growth form with flower cluster, b. Stem with fruit cluster, c. Stem with bark

Moonseed

Menispermum canadense L.

Moonseed family (Menispermaceae)

Also called yellow sarsaparilla

Field Identification: A twining vine to 25 feet high, climbing or sprawling.

Flowers: May-June, in loose drooping clusters along the leaf axils of new growth; both staminate (male) and pistillate (female) flowers are present in separate clusters; flowers numerous, often 40 to 50, greenish-white to white, smooth; petals 4 to 8, inverted egg-shaped; stamens 18 to 20, slightly extending beyond the flower, stamens not well-developed in the pistillate flowers.

Fruit: September-October, in a grapelike cluster, about 1/4 inch in diameter, **dark blue to black with a whitish coating that can be rubbed off**, globe-shaped, somewhat flattened on the sides; flesh thick, juicy, the skin tough; seeds solitary, yellowish, **circular, crescent-shaped, flattened**; fruit somewhat poisonous.

Leaves: Alternate, simple, nearly circular, 2 to 6 inches long and wide, **with 3 to 7 lobes**, tips of lobes pointed or blunt, base heart-shaped to flattened; **point of petiole attachment not at the margin but just inside on the lower surface of the leaf**; margin entire; upper surface dull green, smooth; **lower surface much paler green, pale gray or silvery gray**, smooth to thinly hairy; **leaf blade firm and thickish**; petioles slender, elongate, about as long as the blades.

Stems: Slender, twining, reddish-brown or greenish-brown, shiny, with fine grooves and ridges, slightly hairy to smooth later; tendrils absent.

Trunk: Bark reddish-brown to greenish-brown, smooth on young stems; brown to grayish-brown, scaly or warty with short ridges of corky bark near the base of old stems; vine herbaceous above, somewhat woody near the base; wood soft, white.

Habitat: Occurs in low moist woods and thickets in ravines and along streams, in valleys, along fence rows and at the base of bluffs. Known throughout Missouri in every county.

Range: Georgia, Alabama, Texas, Arkansas and Oklahoma, north to Quebec, and west to Manitoba and North Dakota.

Wildlife Uses: The fruit is seldom eaten by wildlife. It is considered somewhat poisonous.

Medicinal Uses: An extraction of the fresh roots has been used as a laxative and as a treatment for syphilis, rheumatism, gout and skin infections. The roots have been used as a substitute for sarsaparilla and are said to have tonic properties and to increase urine flow.

Remarks: It is not recommended to plant this vine in a yard because the fruits, which resemble a cluster of grapes, are considered toxic to some people and should be kept from the reach of children.

Menispermum is a combination of Greek words *meni* ("moon") and *spermum* ("seed"), in reference to the moon-shaped seed; *canadense* denotes its growth in Canada where it may have been first found.

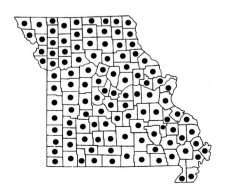

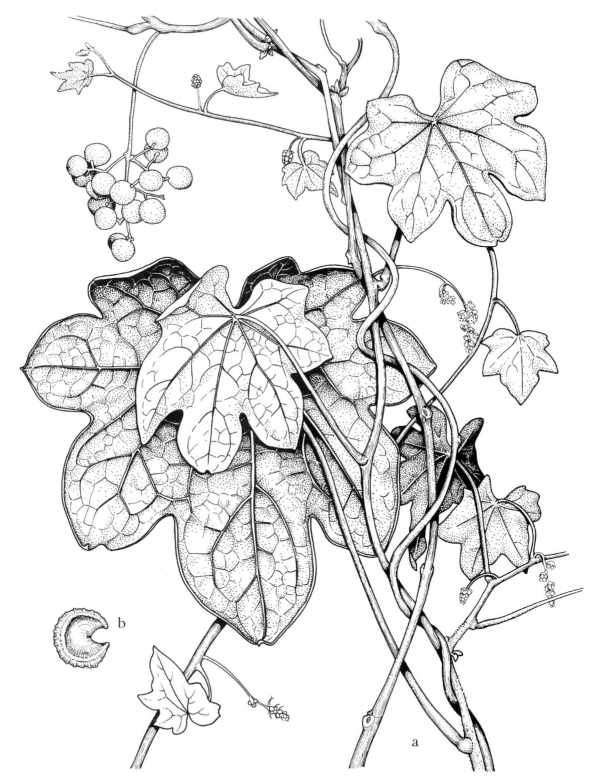

Menispermum canadense ❧ a. Growth form with flowers and fruit, b. Seed

Partridge berry

Mitchella repens L.

Madder family (Rubiaceae)

Also called twin berry

Field Identification: A low-growing, ground-hugging evergreen vine scarcely above the ground and often found trailing over moist shaded sandstone ledges.

Flowers: Late May-July, **usually in pairs at the tips of stems**; flowers white or pinkish, sometimes tinged with purple, very fragrant, about 1/2 inch long, narrow trumpet-shaped; petals 4, spreading, densely hairy inside; stamens 4, exceeding the flower.

Fruit: September through winter, **fruit red, shiny**, about 1/4 inch across, globe-shaped, edible but tasteless; seeds 4 to 8; flowers and fruit sometimes appearing at the same time.

Leaves: Simple, opposite, **evergreen**, 1/4 to 1 inch in length and width, circular to egg-shaped, tip blunt, base heart-shaped to rounded, margin entire; upper surface shiny, smooth, often variegated with whitish lines; petioles 1/8 to 1/4 inch long.

Stems: Bark tight, light green to brown; rooting at the nodes.

Habitat: Occurs in acid soils along moist ledges of sandstone bluffs, sandy banks of small streams, and low moist woodland.

Range: Florida to Texas, Arkansas, Missouri and Oklahoma, north to Newfoundland, and west to Quebec, Ontario and Minnesota. Also in Mexico and Guatemala.

Wildlife Uses: The fruits are eaten by some songbirds, ruffed grouse, bobwhite quail, wild turkey, red fox, eastern skunk and white-footed mouse.

Medicinal Uses: A tea made of the plant has been used for insomnia and excessive water retention, to aid in childbirth and to alleviate diarrhea.

Remarks: This interesting vine is **found in sandstone canyons along moist, shaded cliffs in eastern Missouri and in sandy bogs and hummocks in the southeastern lowlands, including Crowleys Ridge**. In the northeastern United States, where it is more common, partridge berry is collected or grown and sold at Christmas time as part of a terrarium display, usually in a bowl with assorted ferns and mosses.

Mitchella commemorates Dr. John Mitchell (1676-1768), an early correspondent of Linnaeus (father of plant taxonomy) and a botanist who resided in Virginia; *repens* refers to its creeping habit.

Mitchella repens 🌺 a. Growth form, b. Stem with flowers, c. Stems with fruit

Virginia creeper

Parthenocissus quinquefolia (L.) Planchon

Grape family (Vitaceae)

Also called woodbine, five-leaf ivy

Field Identification: Climbing vine with tendrils and aerial roots to 75 feet high.

Flower: Late May-August, in clusters arising opposite the leaves near the end of a short stems of the season; clusters 2 1/2 to 5 inches long; **flowers 25 to 200 per cluster**, greenish; petals 5, spreading; stamens 5, extending beyond the flower.

Fruit: September-October, in clusters 3 to 6 inches long, 1 1/2 to 2 1/2 inches wide, stalk red, smooth; fruit dark purple, **about 1/4 inch across**, globe-shaped, slightly flattened; seeds 2 to 4, about 1/8 inch long, round to egg-shaped, dark chocolate brown, glossy.

Leaves: Alternate, palmately-compound with 5 leaflets (rarely 7) or sometimes 3 leaflets on new growth; leaflets 2 to 6 inches long, 1 to 3 inches wide, egg-shaped to lance-shaped, tip pointed, base gradually narrowing into the leaf stalk, margin coarsely toothed, except near the base; **upper surface dull, dark green**, smooth; lower surface paler green, smooth; petioles slender, 3 to 12 inches long, flattened, grooved, base enlarged and often bent sharply.

Stems: Reddish-brown, finely hairy; **tendrils many branched**, 1 1/2 to 2 inches long, **ending in sucker disks**; older stems with coarse aerial roots used to attach to tree trunks, walls of buildings, and other upright objects. The tendrils and aerial roots do not develop while the vine trails over the ground, forming only when it finds something to climb.

Trunk: Bark of older stems brown, somewhat roughened; old trunks dark brown, deeply fissured, the ridges broad and rounded; inner bark fibrous; wood light, soft, porous, pale brown with a wide, pale sapwood.

Habitat: Occurs in open and moist woods, fence rows, rocky wooded hillsides, ravines and bluffs.

Range: Florida to Texas and Mexico, north to Maine and Quebec, and west to New York, Ohio, Indiana, Illinois, Wisconsin, Minnesota and South Dakota. Also in Guatemala.

Wildlife Uses: The flowers are frequented by honeybees. The fruits are eaten by many species of birds. White-tailed deer browse the leaves and stems during spring and summer, and eat the fruits during autumn. Bobwhite quail consume the fruit, and squirrels eat the bark in winter and leaves and fruit in summer. Wild turkeys eat the young tendrils.

Medicinal Uses: The bark has been used in domestic medicine as a tonic, expectorant and remedy for dropsy.

Remarks: This is an excellent vine for covering fences, walls of buildings, trellises and other objects. The leaves turn a bright crimson to red or purple in autumn. Many people confuse this vine with poison ivy, but it is readily distinguished by its 5 leaflets on a typical leaf.
Parthenocissus is from two Greek words, *parthenos* ("virgin") and *cissos* ("ivy") based on the English Virginia Creeper; *quinquefolia* refers to the 5 leaflets.

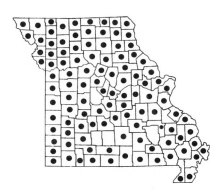

Parthenocissus quinquefolia ❧ a. Growth form, b. Stem with flowers, bark and aerial rootlets, c. Flower cluster, d. Fruit cluster

Woodbine

Parthenocissus vitacea (Knerr) A. S. Hitch.

Grape family (Vitaceae)

Also called thicket creeper, five-leaf ivy

Field Identification: Climbing by tendrils usually without sucker disks to a height of 30 feet, typically found sprawling over bushes and rocks.

Flowers: Late May-July, in clusters arising opposite the leaves near the end of short stems of the season; **flowers 10 to 60 per cluster**, yellowish-green; petals 5, spreading, recurved, thick; stamens 5, extending beyond the flower.

Fruit: September-October, in somewhat flat-topped clusters; stalk red, 3 to 6 inches long; berries bluish-black, sometimes with a slight whitish coating, **about 3/8 inch across**, globe-shaped, slightly flattened, smooth; seeds 4, about 1/4 inch across, egg-shaped, light brown.

Leaves: Alternate, palmately-compound with 5 leaflets; blades 2 1/2 to 4 inches long, 1 1/2 to 2 1/2 inches wide, tip pointed, base wedge-shaped, margin coarsely toothed; **upper surface green, glossy**; lower surface paler, net-veined, smooth, veins sometimes hairy; petioles grooved, 1 1/2 to 5 1/2 inches long.

Stems: Smooth, reddish- to grayish-brown, later brown to gray; lenticels (pores) prominent, somewhat grooved; **tendrils few-branched, usually without disks**.

Trunk: Bark of young trunks brown, irregularly broken into small, peeling plates; bark of older trunks dark brown, tight, with shallow fissures and ridges; wood soft, pale brown, with a wide, light-colored sapwood.

Habitat: Occurs along bluffs in rich woods and wooded slopes, thickets, stream banks and fence rows; **rarely found**.

Range: Pennsylvania, Ohio, Indiana, Illinois, Missouri, Kansas, New Mexico, Arizona and California, north to New England and Quebec, and west to Manitoba, North Dakota and Montana.

Wildlife Uses: The flowers are frequented by honeybees. The fruits are eaten by many species of birds. White-tailed deer browse the leaves and stems during spring and summer, and eat the fruits during autumn. Bobwhite quail consume the fruit, and squirrels eat the bark in winter and leaves and fruit in summer. Wild turkeys eat the young tendrils.

Medicinal Uses: The bark has been used in domestic medicine as a tonic, expectorant and remedy for dropsy.

Remarks: This species also is referred to as *Parthenocissus inserta* (Kerner) K. Fritsch by some taxonomists.

Woodbine has been in cultivation since 1800. It is sometimes used to cover rocks, arbors and bushes. The attractive foliage turns yellow or red in autumn.

Parthenocissus is from two Greek words, *parthenos* ("virgin") and *cissos* ("ivy") based on the English Virginia Creeper; *vitacea* refers to the grapelike tendrils.

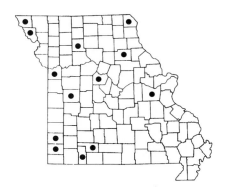

Parthenocissus vitacea 🦌 a. Growth form with fruit clusters, b. Flower

Catbrier

Smilax bona-nox L.

Greenbrier family (Smilacaceae)

Also called greenbrier, bullbrier, tramp's-trouble

Field Identification: Stout, spiny vine with angled branches, either low clambering or extensively climbing by tendrils to a height of 25 feet.

Flowers: May-June, in staminate (male) and pistillate (female) flower clusters in the leaf axils of new stem growth, cluster stalk 1/2 to 1 1/4 inches long, flattened, slender; flowers 3 to 20, yellowish-green, smooth; sepals 3, petals 3, both 1/8 to 1/4 inch long, linear; stamens 6, dropping off on female flowers.

Fruit: September-October, in globe-shaped clusters, stalks about 1 inch long, flattened, slender; berry about 1/4 inch thick, globe- or egg-shaped, black, smooth, semiglossy, usually 1-seeded; seeds about 1/8 inch thick, dark red, finely pitted, dull, with a black scar at the attachment.

Leaves: Alternate, simple, dropping in winter; blade 1 1/2 to 4 1/2 inches long, 3/4 to 4 inches wide, shape variable, heart-shaped, broadly egg-shaped, **triangular, or sometimes fiddle-shaped**, tip pointed, base rounded or ending abruptly, to heart-shaped or with lobes, **margin entire or set with stiff prickles, much more thickened than the rest of the leaf**; upper surface green, smooth, **sometimes with white blotches, veins thickened and conspicuous in a network over the leaf surface**, lower surface paler, usually with a few spines on the midvein; petioles 1/4 to 1/2 inch long, often spiny.

Stems: Canes stout, strongly angled, green; **at least the older stems more or less with tufts of small star-shaped hairs**; prickles stout, green to brown or black, to 1/4 inch long; tendrils arising in pairs at the base of leaf stalks.

Trunk: Bark green, hard, often roughened with white scales; wood greenish-white, soft, pithy.

Habitat: Occurs in rocky open woods, low ground in valleys and along streams, dolomite glades, thickets and fields.

Range: Florida to Louisiana, Arkansas, Oklahoma, Texas and Mexico, north to Massachusetts, and west to Kentucky, Indiana, Illinois, Missouri and southeastern Kansas; also in the Bahama Islands.

Wildlife Uses: The fruit is eaten by 13 species of birds, including ruffed grouse and wild turkey. The leaves, stems and fruit are browsed by white-tailed deer. In its sprawling habit, the impenetrable mass of branches furnishes good cover for small mammals and birds.

Remarks: In low lying areas, catbrier can sometimes form impenetrable thickets requiring cutting to clear a path. Native Americans made a drink from the ground tubers and ate fritters from a mixture of the ground tubers and corn meal. The hard, shiny black seeds were used as beads for necklaces. In spring, the tender growth of stems, tendrils and leaves can be eaten as fresh greens.

Smilax is a Greek name of an evergreen oak; its meaning is uncertain; *bona-nox* means "good night."

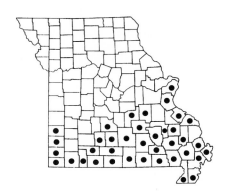

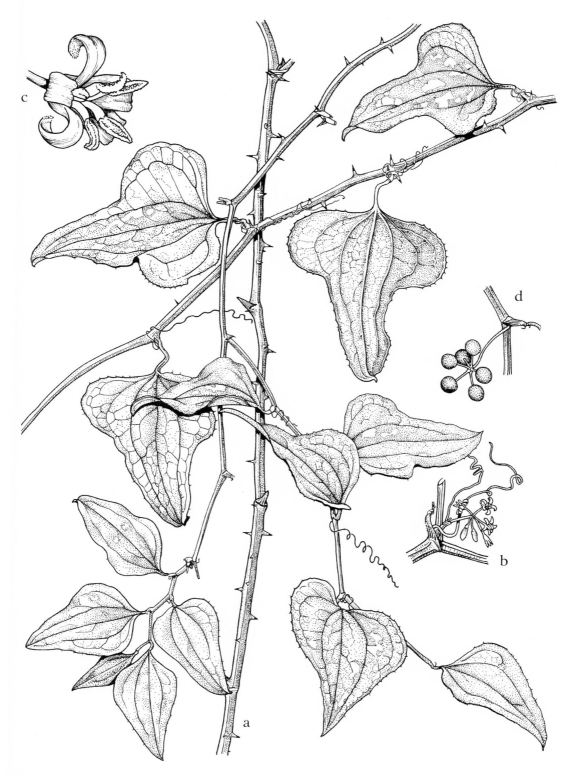

Smilax bona-nox 🐝 a. Growth form, b. Stem with flower cluster and tendrils, c. Flower, d. Stem with fruit cluster

Greenbrier

Smilax glauca Walter

Greenbrier family (Smilacaceae)

Also called catbrier

Field Identification: Slender, spiny vine climbing by coiled tendrils.

Flowers: May-June, in staminate (male) and pistillate (female) flower clusters in the leaf axils of new stem growth, cluster stalk 1/4 to 1 1/4 inches long, slender, flat; flowers 6 to 12, yellowish-green, smooth; sepals 3, petals 3, both about 1/4 inch long, linear; stamens 6, less developed in pistillate flowers.

Fruit: September-October, in small, sparse clusters; berries about 1/4 inch thick, black, with a white waxy coating, shiny, globe-shaped; seeds 2 to 3, somewhat flattened, brown.

Leaves: Alternate, simple, dropping in winter; blade 1 1/2 to 4 inches long, 1 1/4 to 3 inches wide, shape variable, broadly heart-shaped, oval to lance-shaped, tip pointed, base rounded to heart-shaped or tapering sharply, margin entire; **upper surface dark green, sometimes with lighter blotches; lower surface smooth, conspicuously whitened with a waxy coating or bluish-gray or silvery**; main veins at base 3; petioles 1/4 to 1/2 inch long, sometimes with a spine on each side at the base.

Stems: Slender, climbing by delicate **tendrils; tendrils arising in pairs at the base of leaf stalks; young stems smooth, mostly spineless**; older stems green to dark brown, smooth; spines sometimes numerous, green to reddish-brown or black, about 1/4 inch long, straight or slightly curved.

Habitat: Occurs in acid soils of chert, sandstone or igneous origin in rocky woodland, wooded valleys and moist ground along streams, open ground fields, along fence rows and roadsides.

Range: Florida to Louisiana, eastern Texas, Arkansas, and Oklahoma, north to New Jersey, and west to West Virginia, Ohio, Indiana, Illinois and southeastern Missouri.

Wildlife Uses: The fruit is eaten by several species of birds, including the cardinal, bobwhite quail, wild turkey and ruffed grouse. The leaves, stems and fruit are browsed by white-tailed deer. In its sprawling habit, the impenetrable mass of branches furnishes good cover for small mammals and birds.

Remarks: The slender stems and white under-surface of the leaves distinguish this greenbrier from the other species in Missouri. The under-surface also turns a copper color in winter. The plant is persistent, forming dense thickets and sometimes becoming weedy in sandy open ground of Missouri's Bootheel and on Crowleys Ridge.

   The roots of this species and other prickly-stemmed greenbriers are used in making a drink like root beer, in which molasses and sassafras is added. An amber-colored sweet jelly is made from boiling the roots and adding sugar to the liquid. This jelly can be mixed with water to make a sweet drink.

   Smilax is a Greek name of an evergreen oak; its meaning is uncertain; *glauca* refers to the whitened undersurface of the leaf.

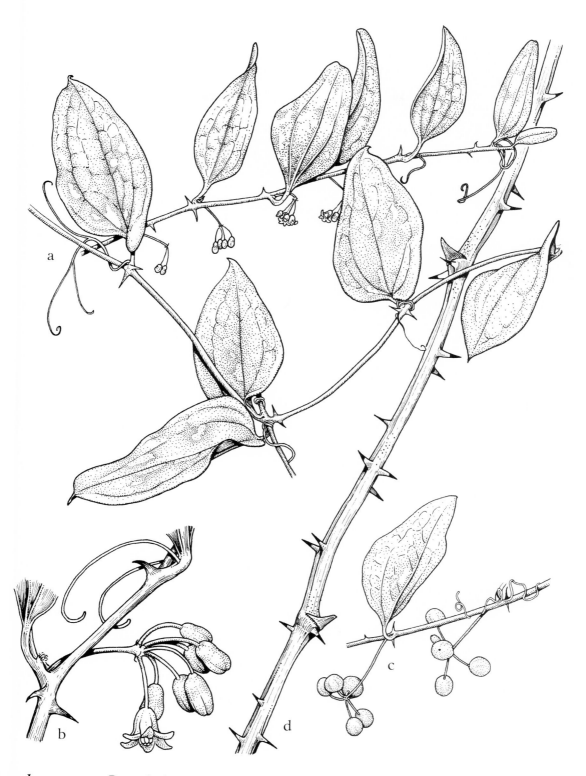

Smilax glauca ❧ a. Growth form with flowers, b. Stem with flower cluster, c. Stem with fruit clusters, d. Stem with prickles

Bristly greenbrier

Smilax hispida Muhlenb. ex Torrey

Greenbrier family (Smilacaceae)

Also called catbrier

Field Identification: A stout vine, climbing high by tendrils to a length of 40 feet.

Flowers: May-June, in staminate (male) and pistillate (female) flower clusters in the leaf axils of new stem growth, **clusters with 5 to 26 flowers; cluster stalk much longer than the leaf stalks**, 1/2 to 1 1/4 inches long, green, smooth; flowers small, green; sepals 3, petals 3, about 1/4 inch long, pistillate smaller; stamens 6, not well-developed in pistillate flowers.

Fruit: September-October, on flattened stalks 1 to 2 inches long, **stalks much longer than the leaf stalks**; berry about 1/4 inch thick, **bluish-black, usually without a whitish coating**, globe-shaped or slightly longer that wide; **seed usually solitary, sometimes 2**, round to egg-shaped, somewhat flattened, reddish to dark brown, glossy.

Leaves: Alternate, simple, persisting into winter; blade 2 to 6 inches long, 2 to 5 1/2 inches wide, shape variable, oval, egg-shaped, heart-shaped, to broadly lance-shaped, tip blunt to pointed, base rounded or heart-shaped, margin entire but sometimes minutely toothed; upper surface green, smooth, shiny, with the 5 to 7 main veins sunken; lower surface paler, smooth; petioles 1/4 to 3/4 inch long, gradually expanding into the blade, often twisted and bent.

Stems: Green with minute white dots, finely grooved, few or no prickles on the outer branches, young prickles yellow, **older prickles black throughout, round, bristlelike**; tendrils arising in pairs at the base of leaf stalks.

Trunk: Bark green to brown, hard, densely covered with prickles and hairs; prickles nearly

black, up to 1/4 inch long; wood greenish-white, soft, pithy.

Habitat: Occurs in low woods in valleys and thickets, along stream banks, and on rich wooded slopes. The most common greenbrier in Missouri.

Range: Florida to Louisiana, eastern Texas, Arkansas and Oklahoma, north to Connecticut and Ontario, and west to Minnesota and southeastern South Dakota.

Wildlife Uses: The fruit is eaten by several species of birds, including the cardinal, bobwhite quail, wild turkey and ruffed grouse. The leaves, stems and fruit are browsed by white-tailed deer. In its sprawling habit, the impenetrable mass of branches furnishes good cover for small mammals and birds.

Remarks: Bristly greenbrier also has been referred to as *Smilax tamnoides* L. var. *hispida* (Muhlenb.) fern. With proper pruning, the vine can be trained into a hedge plant. It will then provide cover for birds and small mammals, and nesting for birds—especially thrashers and catbirds.

Smilax is a Greek name of an evergreen oak; its meaning is uncertain; *hispida* is for the hispid, or prickly, stems.

Smilax hispida 🌿 a. Growth form with flower clusters, b. Flower, c. Fruit cluster, d. Stem with prickles

Greenbrier

Smilax rotundifolia L.

Greenbrier family (Smilacaceae)

Also called common greenbrier, catbrier, biscuit-leaves

Field Identification: A climbing vine to 20 feet with tendrils, sometimes forming tangled thickets.

Flowers: Late April-May, in staminate (male) and pistillate (female) flower clusters in the leaf axils of new stem growth; **stalk bearing the flower cluster shorter than or equal to the leaf stalk**, 1/4 to 3/4 inch long; flowers small, greenish-yellow; sepals 3, petals 3, linear, recurved above the middle; stamens 6, reduced and often falling off on pistillate flowers.

Fruit: September-October, in umbrellalike clusters of 3 to 25 berries; **stalk bearing the fruit cluster shorter than or equal to the leaf stalk**; 1/2 to 1 1/2 inches long; berry about 1/4 inch thick, egg- to globe-shaped, **bluish-black, covered with a grayish-blue coating**, skin, thin, flesh scanty and tough; **seeds 2 to 3 in each berry**, egg-shaped, rounded at the ends.

Leaves: Alternate, simple, blade thin, leathery, 2 to 6 inches long, 1 to 6 inches wide, shape variable, from egg-shaped to circular or heart-shaped, more rarely lance-shaped; tip blunt or rounded to pointed, base heart-shaped to abruptly tapering, margin entire or occasionally with scattered teeth; upper surface dark green, smooth; lower surface slightly paler, smooth; petioles 1/4 to 3/4 inch long, somewhat winged at the blade junction.

Stems: Bright green to brown, smooth or nearly so; **prickles pale or with a dark tip, flattened and with a broad base**, 1/8 to 1/2 inch long, scattered, stout; tendrils arising in pairs at the base of leaf stalks.

Habitat: Occurs in mostly alluvial soils of low ground along streams or in valleys, and in wet woodland and thickets; **found only in southeastern Missouri.**

Range: Florida to Louisiana, Texas, Arkansas and Oklahoma, north to Maine and Nova Scotia, west to Ontario, Minnesota, Iowa and Missouri.

Wildlife Uses: The fruit is eaten by at least 15 species of birds, and by cottontail rabbit, opossum and raccoon. The leaves, stems and fruit are browsed by white-tailed deer. In its sprawling habit, the impenetrable mass of branches furnishes good cover for small mammals and birds.

Remarks: Sterile plants of this species can be difficult to distinguish from *Smilax bona-nox* L. when the latter lacks spiny leaf margins. In spring, the tender growth of stems, tendrils and leaves can be eaten as fresh greens. The roots of this species and other prickly-stemmed greenbriers are used in making a drink like root beer, in which molasses and sassafras is added. An amber-colored sweet jelly is made from boiling the roots and adding sugar to the liquid. This jelly can be mixed with water to make a sweet drink.

Smilax is a Greek name of an evergreen oak; its meaning is uncertain; *rotundifolia* refers to the round shape of the leaves.

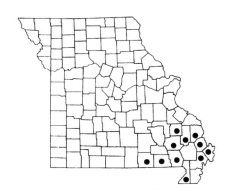

Smilax rotundifolia 🌿 a. Growth form with flower clusters, b. Flower cluster, c. Stem with fruit cluster, d. Stem with prickles

Poison ivy

Toxicodendron radicans (L.) Kuntze

Cashew family (Anacardiaceae)

Field Identification: Poisonous, a vine to 60 feet high, **trailing or climbing by aerial roots; or a low, upright shrub**.

Flowers: May-June, in clusters 1 to 4 inches long on new growth of stems; flowers small, greenish-white, fragrant; petals 5, about 1/8 inch long, lance-shaped, recurved, smooth; stamens 5, extending beyond the flower.

Fruit: August-November, in grapelike clusters, persistent, about 1/4 inch across, creamy-white, waxy, globe-shaped, indented slightly at the tip, **smooth** or rarely sparsely hairy; seeds 2, hard, striped.

Leaves: Alternate, three leaflets, variable in shape and size; end leaflet 1 1/4 to 8 inches long, 1/2 to 5 inches wide, **end leaflet stalk 1/2 to 1 3/4 inches** long; side leaflets with unequal sides, 1 1/4 to 6 3/4 inches long, 1/2 to 4 inches wide, leaflet stalks short, about 1/8 inch long; blades mostly oval to lance-shaped, tip pointed (**end leaflet with a more pronounced pointed tip**), base wedge-shaped to rounded, margin entire, largely toothed, or lobed; upper surface dull green, smooth; lower surface paler, with varying degrees of hairiness; petioles 2 1/2 to 6 inches long, hairy.

Stems: Light brown, hairy, lenticels (pores) raised, climbing by aerial rootlets. Stems trail until finding support or when lacking support often assuming an erect shrublike posture, often with single stems. Large climbing vines may have spreading branches that reach 6 feet or more from the main stem.

Trunk: Bark gray, smooth except for small raised lenticels; bark of large vines flaky; aerial roots bright red at first, becoming brown to black; wood soft, porous, yellowish-brown, with a wide light-colored sapwood.

Habitat: Occurs in floodplain and upland forests on level and sloping ground, alluvial soil along streams, thickets, along fence rows, roadsides and railroads; throughout Missouri.

Range: Florida to Arkansas, Oklahoma, Texas and Mexico, north to Canada and west to Washington and Oregon; also in the West Indies.

Wildlife Uses: The fruit is eaten by at least 75 species of songbirds, in addition to wild turkey, bobwhite quail and ruffed grouse. The plants are browsed by white-tailed deer.

Remarks: This species was formerly in the genus called *Rhus*. The leaves turn brilliant shades of red, yellow and orange in autumn. Poison ivy is not recommended for planting. An oil found in all parts of the plant is poisonous and produces an intense skin irritation. Upon contact with the skin this oil produces blisters, accompanied by intense itching and burning. Some people are immune to poison ivy, but often not for their entire lives: some have been known suddenly to become affected, when for years they had come into contact with it with no harmful results. Washing immediately after contact with cold, soapy water is the best treatment. Various lotions, including injections, are also helpful.

Toxicodendron is from the ancient Greek, and means "poison tree"; *radicans* is from the Latin "radica" or root, referring to its climbing by roots.

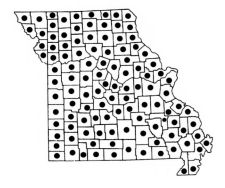

Toxicodendron radicans 🌿 a. Growth form with flower clusters and aerial rootlets, b. Stem with fruit cluster

Climbing dogbane

Trachelospermum difforme (Walter) A. Gray

Dogbane family (Apocynaceae)

Also called climbing star-jasmine

Field Identification: Slender, twining vine **with milky sap** that **often dies back to a woody base in winter**.

Flowers: Late May-July, in slender, loose clusters arising from leaf axils, cluster stalks 1/2 to 3/4 inch long; flower very fragrant, funnel-shaped, cream-colored to yellow; flower tube about 1/4 inch long, with fine-lined brown markings within; lobes 5, shorter than the tube, spreading, reflexed, egg-shaped; stamens 5, not extending beyond the flower.

Fruit: August-September, pods emerging only from one axil of opposite leaves, pod opening along one side; pods 2, slender, narrow, 5 to 9 inches long; seeds numerous, seed angled, with silky hairs.

Leaves: Opposite, simple, 1 to 3 inches long, 1/2 to 2 inches wide, lance-shaped to broadly egg-shaped to round, **tip abruptly pointed**, base heart-shaped to rounded, margin entire, blade thin; upper surface dark green, smooth, shiny, hairy along the veins; lower surface much paler green, hairy; petioles about 1/4 inch long, hairy.

Stems: Slender, twining, younger parts herbaceous, green to reddish-brown, hairy; at base, smooth and somewhat woody with age; **sap milky**.

Habitat: Occurs in swamps, borders of slow streams and sloughs, low wet woods and thickets, in the southeastern lowlands of Missouri, and along moist rocky stream banks in parts of the Ozarks.

Range: Florida to Texas, Arkansas and Oklahoma, north to Delaware, and west to Indiana, Illinois and Missouri; also in Mexico.

Remarks: The fragrant flowers emit a jasmine-like scent.

Trachelospermum comes from the Greek *trachelos,* "a neck," and *sperma,* "seed," which means "neck-seeded"; however, the seed of this species lacks a neck or a beak at the tip; *difforme,* "of two forms," refers to the two forms of the leaves.

Trachelospermum difforme ❧ a. Growth form with flower cluster, b. Flowers

Common periwinkle

Vinca minor L.

Dogbane family (Apocynaceae)

Also called myrtle

Field Identification: A low-growing, prostrate, mat-forming evergreen vine to a height of 6 inches.

Flowers: April-May, individual flowers emerge from the leaf axils of new stems; flower stalks 1/2 to 1 1/4 inches long; flowers lilac to blue, 1 inch across; petals 5, spreading, tips ending abruptly as if cut off; stamens 5, not extending beyond the flower.

Fruit: August-October, a dry capsule, 3/4 to 1 inch long, splitting on two sides, fruit is seldom set on cultivated plants.

Leaves: Opposite, simple, evergreen, 1/2 to 1 1/2 inches long, 1/2 to 3/4 inch wide, egg-shaped to equally rounded toward the ends, tip blunt to pointed, base rounded or heart-shaped, margin entire; upper surface dark green, shiny, smooth, central vein light green; lower surface paler, smooth; leaves at end of twigs often in clusters of 3 to 4; petioles 1/2 to 1 1/4 inches long, exuding a milky sap when broken.

Stems: Green, shiny, smooth.

Habitat: Commonly cultivated and sometimes escaping into woods, along rocky banks and open areas. Often planted in cemeteries.

Range: Native of Europe; introduced and naturalized in North America from Georgia to Arkansas, Missouri and Kansas, north to Nova Scotia, and west to Minnesota.

Remarks: Although not as aggressive as Japanese honeysuckle and wintercreeper, the planting of common periwinkle should be discouraged. Vines such as the native honeysuckles offer more ornamental and wildlife value.

Vinca is abbreviated from Pliny's *Vincapervinca*, the ancient name reflected in the colloquial Italian *Pervinca*; the French *Pervenche*; and the English *Periwinkle*. Minor means "smaller," referring to the size of the flower when compared to the other European periwinkle, *Vinca major*.

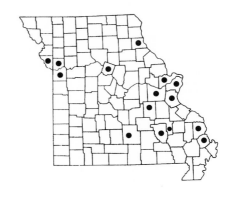

Vinca minor  a. Growth form with flowers

Summer Grape

Vitis aestivalis Michaux

Grape family (Vitaceae)

Also called pigeon grape, bunch grape

Field Identification: A vigorous, high-climbing vine to a height of 35 feet by means of tendrils, or sprawling over low bushes and trees.

Flowers: May-June, in staminate (male) and pistillate (female) flower clusters 1/2 to 3 inches long, opposite a leaf on new stem growth, cluster stalk 2 to 6 inches long, slender, loose, cylindrical, often with a short tendril; flowers minute, numerous, yellowish-green, fragrant; petals 5, dropping early; stamens 5, sharply reflexed in the pistillate flowers.

Fruit: July-October, in drooping clusters 3 to 5 inches long, 2 to 3 inches wide; fruit 1/4 to 1/2 inch thick, dark blue to black with a thin whitish coating, globe-shaped, sweet, juicy; seeds 2 to 4, about 1/4 inch long, reddish-brown, pear-shaped.

Leaves: Alternate, simple, blades 2 to 8 inches long and wide, heart- or egg-shaped to round, margin of some irregularly toothed and unlobed, **some leaves with margins shallowly to deeply 3 to 5-lobed**, lobe sinuses (cleft between two lobes) narrow and rounded, tip pointed, base heart-shaped; upper surface yellowish-green with a few hairs on the veins; **lower surface whitish, with light rusty, cobwebby hairs**; petioles 3 to 5 inch long, often red with a few cobwebby or straight hairs but later smooth or somewhat hairy.

Stems: Reddish-brown, finely ridged, woolly at first but soon smooth; **small branches round, not angled**; tendril emerging opposite the leaf.

Trunk: Bark of the branches shredding early; bark of old stems brown with long papery shreds; wood tough, porous, pale brown, with a large pith.

Habitat: Occurs in dry, rocky, upland woods, thickets, glades, and along rocky slopes.

Range: Florida to Louisiana, Texas, Arkansas and Oklahoma, north to New Hampshire, and west to Wisconsin and eastern Kansas.

Wildlife Uses: The fruit is eaten by many species of birds and mammals, including cardinal, cowbird, bobwhite quail, ruffed grouse, wild turkey, raccoon, red fox and white-tailed deer. The foliage is browsed by white-tailed deer, and the tendrils are eaten by wild turkey. The catbird, mockingbird, brown thrasher and cardinal use the long strips of bark in the middle layer of their nests.

Remarks: The grapes are variable in taste from dry and bitter to sweet and juicy, but most frequently the latter. Fine jellies and wine are made from the grape. Even the fully expanded leaves of wild grapes are used to wrap rice and meat mixtures. The vines are gathered and woven into wreaths and affixed with various ornaments of the fall and winter seasons.

Vitis is the classical Latin name; *aestivalis* means "of summer" and refers to the summer blooming.

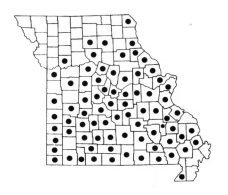

Vitis aestivalis 🌿 a. Growth form with flower and fruit clusters, b. Flower with petals dropping, c. Stem with shredding bark

Winter grape

Vitis cinerea Engelm.

Grape family (Vitaceae)

Also called grayback grape, pigeon grape

Field Identification: A high-climbing vine to a height of 50 feet by means of tendrils.

Flowers: May-July, in staminate (male) and pistillate (female) flower clusters opposite a leaf on new stem growth, 4 to 6 inches long, 1 1/4 to 2 inches wide, cylindrical, cluster stalk with a red tinge, woolly hairy, often with a tendril at the base; flowers minute, numerous, greenish; petals 5, dropping early; stamens 5, sharply reflexed in the pistillate flowers.

Fruit: September-October, in long, loose, drooping clusters 3 to 6 inches long, about 2 inches wide; fruit small, 1/4 to 3/4 inch thick, black, globe-shaped; skin tough, bitter until late autumn; seeds 1 to 3, about 1/8 inch long, reddish-brown.

Leaves: Alternate, simple, blades 4 to 8 inches long or broad, thin, round to heart-shaped, tip pointed, basal lobes broadly rounded with a narrow sinus (cleft between two lobes), **margin unlobed or with two short lobes**, irregular and finely to coarsely toothed; upper surface dark green with a few cobwebby hairs; **lower surface covered with white to gray, cobwebby, and straight hairs**; petioles 3 to 4 inches long, with both straight and cobwebby hairs.

Stems: Young branches angled, densely white-felty, green; older branches grayish-brown, striped, with white cobwebby hairs often in patches, tendril emerging opposite the leaf.

Trunk: Bark of old trunks reddish-brown, shredding into thin, long, loose strips; wood porous, lightweight, pale brown.

Habitat: Occurs in low woods and alluvial soils along streams, in thickets and fence rows; throughout Missouri.

Range: Florida to Louisiana, Texas, Arkansas and Oklahoma, north to Virginia, and west to Ohio, Indiana, Illinois, Wisconsin, Iowa, and eastern Kansas.

Wildlife Uses: The fruit is eaten by many species of birds and mammals, including cardinal, cowbird, bobwhite quail, ruffed grouse, wild turkey, raccoon, red fox and white-tailed deer. The foliage is browsed by white-tailed deer, and the tendrils are eaten by wild turkey. The catbird, mockingbird, brown thrasher and cardinal use the long strips of bark in the middle layer of their nests.

Remarks: Winter grape is the latest flowering of the Missouri grapes. The fruits are small and do not become sweet until late autumn. They are seldom used for jellies or juice because most people have forgotten about them by the time they are ready. The vines are gathered, woven into wreaths and adorned with various ornaments of the fall and winter seasons.

Vitis is the classical Latin name; *cinerea*, meaning "ashes," refers to the gray, woolly hairs of the leaves.

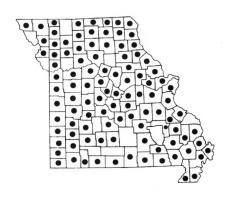

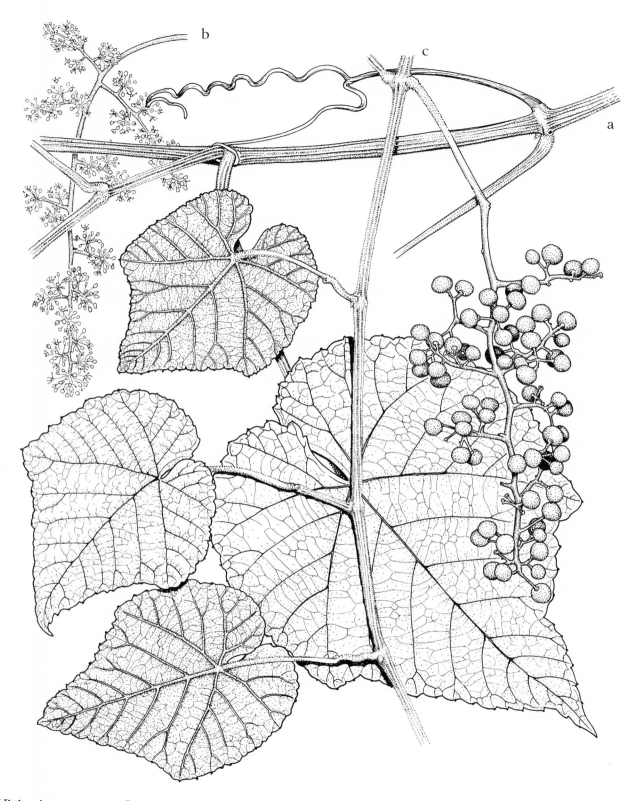

Vitis cinerea 🐾 a. Growth form, b. Flower cluster, c. Stem with fruit cluster

Red grape

Vitis palmata M. Vahl

Grape family (Vitaceae)

Also called cat grape, catbird grape, Missouri grape

Field Identification: An attractive, high-climbing, slender, delicate vine.

Flowers: May-July, in slender staminate (male) and pistillate (female) flower clusters 4 to 6 inches long, opposite a leaf on new stem growth, cluster stalk smooth, yellowish-green; flowers minute, yellowish-green; petals 5, dropping early; stamens 5, sharply reflexed in the pistillate flowers.

Fruit: September-October, in drooping clusters; fruit about 1/4 inch thick, bluish-black, round, whitish coating little or absent; skin thick, pulp juicy, sweet; seeds 1 to 2, largest of any species in proportion to the size of the berry, short, thick, about 1/4 inch long, dark brown or chestnut.

Leaves: Alternate, simple, palmately lobed (in the shape of a hand), blades 2 3/4 to 4 3/4 inches long and broad, heart-shaped or oval in outline; basal sinuses (cleft between two lobes) narrowly U-shaped, tips pointed, **margin with 3 to 5 prominent lobes with rounded sinuses**, teeth large, irregular, pointed; upper surface dark glossy green, some hairs on the veins; lower surface much paler green, smooth, some hairs on the veins; **leaf blades of flowering or fruiting branches, smaller, 1 1/2 to 3 1/2 inches broad**; petioles 1 to 3 inches long, attached at an angle to the base of the leaf, red, striped, with a deep narrow groove, hairy.

Stems: Young growth slender, tips naked or not leafy, thinly covered with whitish cottony hairs, grooved; **at maturity stems bright red or purplish-red**, finely striped, shiny, smooth; tendrils strong, red when young.

Trunk: Bark on old wood separating in wide, thin plates.

Habitat: Occurs in swamps dominated by bald cypress, sloughs and low wet woods.

Range: Georgia to Louisiana, eastern Texas, Arkansas and Oklahoma, north to Indiana, and west to Illinois and Missouri.

Wildlife Uses: The fruit is eaten by many species of birds and mammals, including catbird, cardinal, bobwhite quail, ruffed grouse, wild turkey, raccoon, red fox and white-tailed deer. The foliage is browsed by white-tailed deer, and the tendrils are eaten by wild turkey. The catbird, mockingbird, brown thrasher and cardinal use the long strips of bark in the middle layer of their nests.

Remarks: The attractive leaves and slender, delicate stems make red grape a good ornamental candidate for trellis or arbor.

Vitis is the classical Latin name; *palmata* refers to the palmately lobed leaves. Red grape is named for the color of its branches.

Vitis palmata 🌺 a. Growth form with flower cluster, b. Stem with fruit cluster

Riverbank grape

Vitis riparia Michaux

Grape family (Vitaceae)

Also called frost grape

Field Identification: A high-climbing vine to 75 feet by means of tendrils.

Flowers: May-June, in staminate (male) and pistillate (female) flower clusters 1 1/2 to 5 inches long, opposite a leaf on new stem growth; flowers minute, numerous, yellowish-green; petals 5, dropping early; stamens 5, poorly developed in pistillate flowers.

Fruit: July-September, in drooping clusters 2 to 5 inches long, 1 1/4 to 1 3/4 inches wide, stalk hairy; fruits about 3/8 inch thick, globe-shaped, **purple to blue with a white waxy coating**, sweet, edible; seeds 1/8 inch long, broadly egg-shaped, reddish-brown.

Leaves: Alternate, simple, blades 4 to 6 inches long, 3 1/2 to 5 inches wide, egg-shaped to round, **with two short side lobes,** lobes pointed, base rounded with a broad sinus (cleft between two lobes), **margin coarsely toothed, lined with fine hairs**; upper surface yellowish-green, smooth; lower surface paler, hairy on the veins and in the vein axis; petioles 1 1/2 to 2 1/2 inches long, smooth, some hairiness near the blade.

Stems: Smooth green, gray or brown, slightly ridged, tendrils opposite leaves.

Trunk: Bark reddish-brown, shredding, the strips thin, long and wide; wood soft, porous, brown, with a light-colored sapwood.

Habitat: Occurs in low woods, thickets and banks of streams in alluvial soils.

Range: Georgia to Tennessee, Arkansas, Texas and New Mexico, north to Virginia, New England and Quebec, and west to Manitoba, North Dakota and Montana.

Wildlife Uses: The fruit is eaten by many species of birds and mammals, including catbird, cardinal, bobwhite quail, ruffed grouse, wild turkey, raccoon, red fox and white-tailed deer. The foliage is browsed by white-tailed deer, and the tendrils are eaten by wild turkey. The catbird, mockingbird, brown thrasher and cardinal use the long strips of bark in the middle layer of their nests.

Remarks: There are three varieties recognized in Missouri based on the hairiness of the leaf stalks and blades, and length of flower clusters and seed; however, there is some intergradation, and positive identification of varieties may be difficult. The vines are gathered and woven into wreaths and adorned with various ornaments of the fall and winter seasons.

Vitis is the classical Latin name; *riparia* means "of river banks," and refers to its habitat.

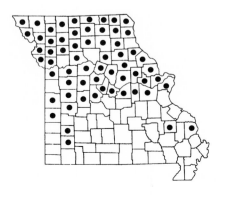

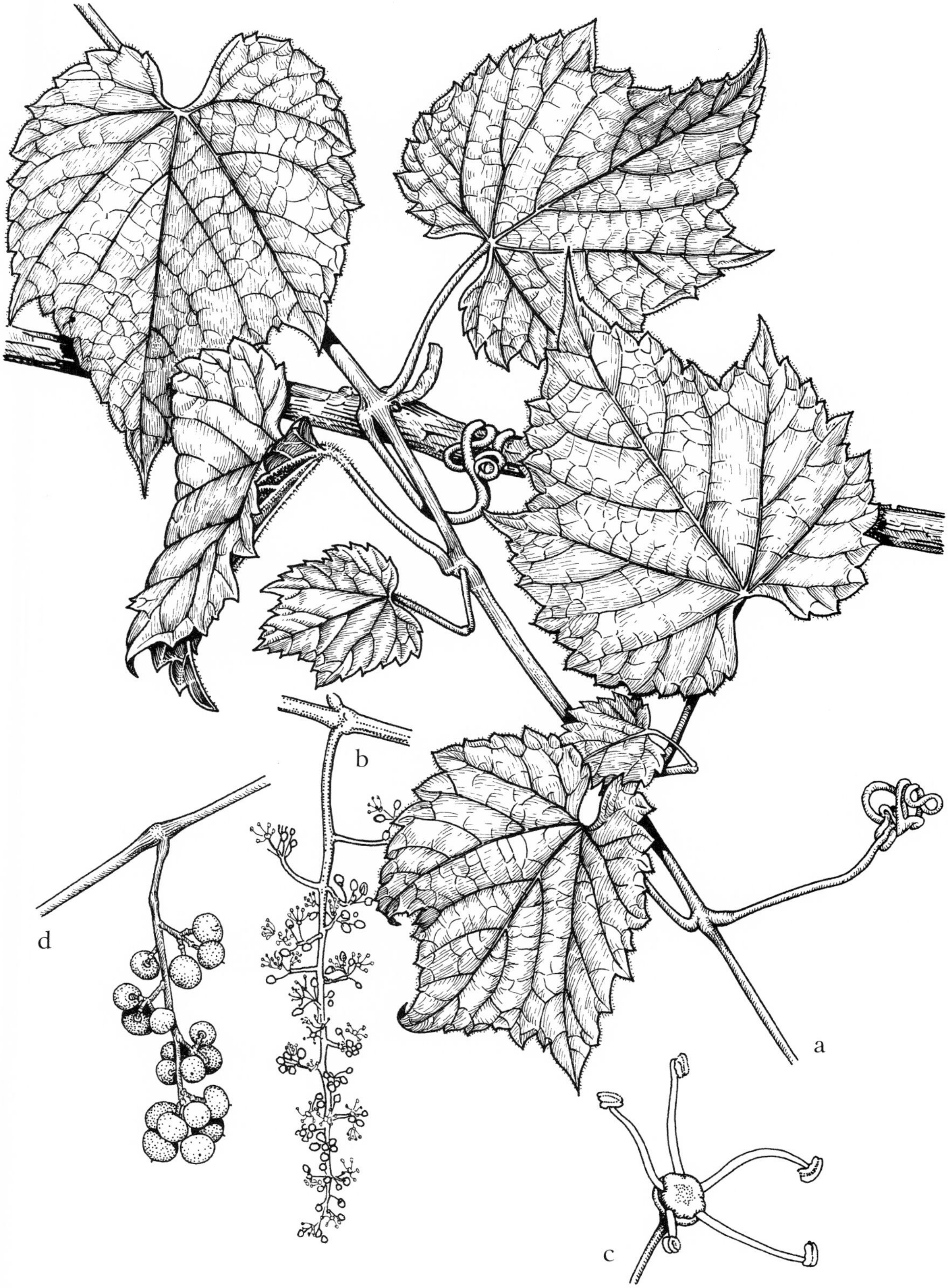

Vitis riparia ❧ a. Growth form, b. Flower cluster, c. Flower with petals shed, d. Fruit cluster

Sand grape

Vitis rupestris Scheele

Grape family (Vitaceae)

Field Identification: Vine, bushy, sprawling or trailing over rocky stream beds or along gravel bars, rarely climbing but may reach a length of 8 feet.

Flowers: May-June, in staminate (male) and pistillate (female) flower clusters 1/2 to 2 inches long, opposite a leaf on new stem growth; cluster stalk 1 to 2 inches long; flowers minute, yellowish-green; petals 5, dropping early; stamens 5, poorly developed and recurved in pistillate flowers.

Fruit: July-August, soon dropping, 1/4 to 1/2 inch in diameter, black, globe-shaped, often somewhat doubled as if two berries are grown together, skin very thin and tender; pulp tender and sweet; seeds 3 to 4, about 1/8 inch long, light chocolate-colored.

Leaves: Alternate, simple, blades 3 to 4 inches wide, sometimes to 8 inches, **usually broader than long, sometimes shaped like a kidney bean, blade folded upward or trough-shaped to expose the pale green lower surface**; basal sinus (cleft between two lobes) very broad and sometimes flattened; margin with large teeth, tip pointed; upper surface light green, smooth; lower surface yellowish-green, smooth; petioles deeply and broadly grooved, striped, green to dark crimson.

Stems: When young very leafy at the ends due to short distance between nodes, finely grooved, **red; tendrils absent or opposite only uppermost leaves or at tips of flowering or fruiting branches; thin, smooth, crimson.**

Trunk: Bark dark cinnamon, growing darker with age, scaling off in broad plates after the second or third year; wood dense, not very hard.

Habitat: Occurs along rocky banks and gravel beds along streams.

Range: Texas, Arkansas and Oklahoma, north to Tennessee, Kentucky, Illinois and Missouri.

Wildlife Uses: The fruit is eaten by many species of birds and mammals, including wood ducks, catbird, cardinal, bobwhite quail, ruffed grouse, wild turkey, raccoon, red fox and white-tailed deer. The foliage is browsed by white-tailed deer, and the tendrils are eaten by wild turkey. The catbird, mockingbird, brown thrasher and cardinal use the long strips of bark in the middle layer of their nests.

Remarks: A similar species, muscadine, *Vitis rotundifolia* Michaux, differs by having a continuous pith through the nodes; bark of branches and main stem tight, not shredding off; tendrils simple, not forked; and rare, occurring in low wet woods and borders of swamps and bayous in southeastern Missouri.

Sand grape is often found only in the vegetative state, making flowers and fruit difficult to find. The sweet-tasting grapes are large, considering the plant's growth habit. The plant is sometimes used as a grafting stock in vineyards out of its natural range, which may explain reports of the plant growing on the East Coast. Europeans use the rootstock extensively for grafting favorite wine-producing varieties. With its low growth habit, attractive leaves and red stems, sand grape makes a good ornamental for rock gardens.

Vitis is the classical Latin name; *rupestris* means "of rocks," and refers to this species' habitat preference for stony ground.

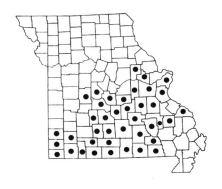

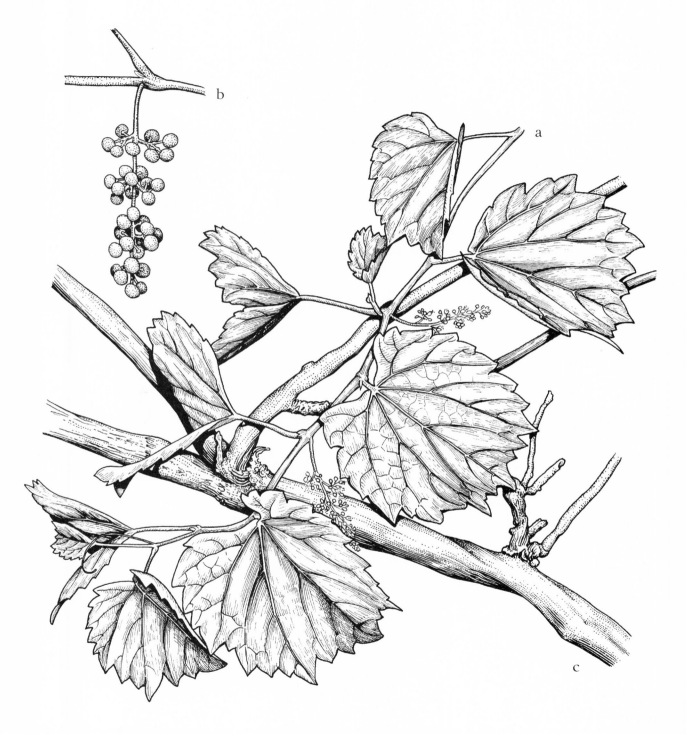

Vitis rupestris ❧ a. Growth form with flower clusters, b. Fruit cluster, c. Stem

Frost grape

Vitis vulpina L.

Grape family (Vitaceae)

Also called winter grape, chicken grape

Field Identification: A vigorous vine climbing high by tendrils to 60 feet.

Flowers: Mid-May-June, in staminate (male) and pistillate (female) flower clusters 3 to 5 inches long, opposite a leaf on new stem growth; flowers minute, numerous, green; petals 5, dropping early; stamens 5, poorly developed in pistillate flowers.

Fruit: September-October, in drooping clusters 4 to 6 inches long; berries about 1/4 inch thick, black, glossy, covered with a white waxy coating when ripe, globe-shaped; skin thin; pulp juicy, turning sweet after frost; seeds 2 to 4, about 1/4 inch long, grayish-brown.

Leaves: Alternate, simple, blades 4 to 6 inches long, 3 to 6 inches wide, heart- to egg-shaped or round, tip pointed, base with a broad to narrow U-shaped sinus (cleft between two lobes), **margin with large teeth, irregular, or if lobed, the 2 side lobes short, shoulderlike, leaves of flowering or fruiting branches not 3-lobed;** upper surface dark green, smooth; lower surface paler, with short, straight hairs on the veins and small tufts in the vein axils; petioles 1/2 to 3 inches long, smooth.

Stems: Smooth, grayish-green becoming reddish-brown, finely ridged; tendrils up to 8 inches long, appearing opposite leaves.

Trunk: Bark grayish-brown, furrowed, very little shedding; wood very soft, light tan.

Habitat: Occurs in alluvial soils along streams in low wet woods, low wooded slopes, base of bluffs and thickets.

Range: Florida to Texas, Arkansas, Oklahoma and New Mexico, north to New York, and west to Pennsylvania, Ohio, Indiana, Illinois, Missouri and Kansas.

Wildlife Uses: The fruit is eaten by many species of birds and mammals, including wood ducks, catbird, cardinal, bobwhite quail, ruffed grouse, wild turkey, raccoon, red fox, striped skunk and white-tailed deer. The foliage is browsed by white-tailed deer, and the tendrils are eaten by wild turkey.

Remarks: The vine was first cultivated in 1806. It apparently endures cold better than any other grape species; however, its ability to withstand severe summer heat and long drought is rather poor. The rootstock is extensively used in Europe for grafting favorite wine-producing varieties. The vines are gathered and woven into wreaths and adorned with various ornaments of the fall and winter seasons.

Vitis is the classical Latin name; *vulpina* pertains to the fox, which is fond of the fruit.

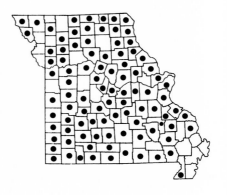

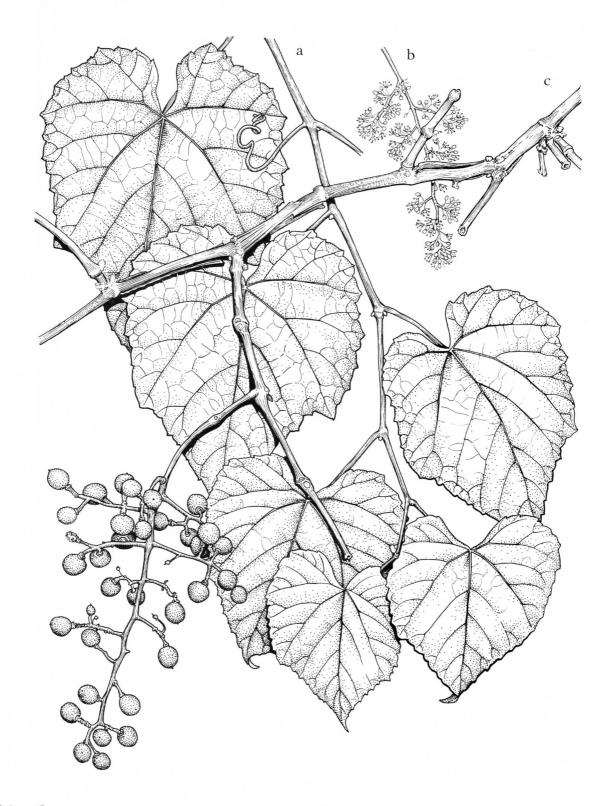

Vitis vulpina 🌾 a. Growth form, b. Flower cluster, c. Stem with fruit cluster

Wisteria

Wisteria frutescens (L.) Poiret

Bean family (Fabaceae)

Field Identification: A twining, woody vine reaching a length of 40 feet.

Flowers: April-May, flowering before the leaves fully mature, in hanging, slender clusters 8 to 12 inches long, 1 1/2 to 2 inches wide, on short side branches; flower stalks about 1/4 inch long, hairy, hairs sometimes gland-tipped, **very fragrant; flowers bean-shaped**; petals 5, upper petal reflexed, about 1/2 inch across, varying in color from white through blue to lilac or purple; side petals about 3/8 inch long, white to purple; keel petals 2, somewhat joined, about 3/8 inch long, upcurved, purplish; stamens 10.

Fruit: October, in long, narrow pods 2 to 5 inches in length, flattened, constricted between the seeds, reddish-brown; seeds large, black, shiny. The drying pod splits on both sides with a cracking sound, propelling seeds in all directions.

Leaves: Alternate, **pinnately compound**, 5 to 12 inches long with 5 to 11 leaflets; leaflets 3/4 to 2 1/2 inches long, 1/2 to 1 inch wide, egg-shaped to half as broad as long to lance-shaped, tip pointed, base rounded or slightly heart-shaped, margin entire; upper surface dull green to partly shiny, smooth; lower surface paler, bearing white hairs, especially along the veins.

Stems: Twining and climbing without tendrils; young stems green, with dense white hairs; older stems smooth, reddish-brown to gray, becoming stout and branched.

Habitat: Occurs in low wet or swampy woods and along the borders of swamps, sloughs and slow streams; sometimes cultivated and escaped from cultivation.

Ranges: Florida to Texas, north to Virginia, and west to Illinois, Missouri and Oklahoma.

Wildlife Uses: This is a popular bee plant for its nectar.

Medicinal Uses: None, the seeds are reported to be very poisonous.

Remarks: Native wisteria is not to be confused with other wisterias introduced from Asia which have escaped from cultivation. *Wisteria sinensis* (Sims) sweet, the Chinese wisteria and *Wisteria floribunda* (Willd.) DC., the Japanese wisteria, differ with the former and have 7 to 13 leaflets, the latter 13 to 19 leaflets. Both flower clusters are twice as long as the native wisteria and more loosely arranged. They are aggressive and not recommended for planting.

The native wisteria has been in cultivation since 1724. It does well on trellises and other supports. Wisteria contains wistarin, a poisonous crystalline glycoside. However, it is recorded that pioneers used the fresh flowers in salads and mixed them with batter to make fritters.

Wisteria honors Caspar Wistar (1761-1818), a distinguished Philadelphia physician and scientist; *frutescens* refers to the shrubby or woody character.

Wisteria frutescens 🌿 a. Growth form with flower cluster, seed pods and seed, b. Flowers

Appendix A

List of Families and Species

Agavaceae
  Yucca glauca
  Yucca smalliana
Anacardiaceae
  Cotinus obovatus
  Rhus aromatica
  Rhus copallina
  Rhus glabra
  *Toxicodendron radicans**
  Toxicodendron toxicarium
Apocynaceae
  *Trachelospermum difforme**
  *Vinca minor**
Aquifoliaceae
  Ilex decidua
  Ilex verticillata
Araliaceae
  Aralia spinosa
Aristolochiaceae
  *Aristolochia tomentosa**
Berberidaceae
  Berberis canadensis
  Berberis thunbergii
  Berberis vulgaris
Betulaceae
  Alnus serrulata
  Carpinus caroliniana
  Corylus americana
  Ostrya virginiana
Bignoniaceae
  *Bignonia capreolata**
  *Campsis radicans**
Caesalpiniaceae
  Cercis canadensis
Caprifoliaceae
  *Lonicera dioica**
  *Lonicera flava**
  *Lonicera japonica**
  Lonicera maackii
  *Lonicera reticulata**
  *Lonicera sempervirens**
  Sambucus canadensis
  Sambucus racemosa

Symphoricarpos occidentalis
Symphoricarpos orbiculatus
Viburnum dentatum
Viburnum lentago
Viburnum molle
Viburnum prunifolium
Viburnum rafinesquianum
Viburnum recognitum
Viburnum rufidulum
Celastraceae
  *Celastrus orbiculatus**
  *Celastrus scandens**
  Euonymus alatus
  Euonymus americanus
  Euonymus atropupureus
  *Euonymus fortunei**
  Euonymus obovatus
Cornaceae
  Cornus alternifolia
  Cornus drummondii
  Cornus florida
  Cornus foemina
  Cornus obliqua
  Cornus racemosa
Cupressaceae
  Juniperus ashei
Elaeagnaceae
  Elaeagnus umbellata
Ericaceae
  Gaylussacia baccata
  Lyonia mariana
  Rhododendron roseum
  Vaccinium arboreum
  Vaccinium pallidum
  Vaccinium stamineum
Euphorbiaceae
  Andrachne phyllanthoides
Fabaceae
  Amorpha canescens
  Amorpha fruticosa
  Robinia hispida
  *Wisteria floribunda**
  *Wisteria frutescens**
  *Wisteria sinensis**
Fagaceae
  Quercus prinoides

Grossulariaceae
  Itea virginica
  Ribes americanum
  Ribes cynosbati
  Ribes missouriense
  Ribes odoratum
Hamamelidaceae
  Hamamelis vernalis
  Hamamelis virginiana
Hippocastanaceae
  Aesculus glabra
  Aesculus pavia
Hydrangeaceae
  Hydrangea arborescens
  Philadelphus coronarius
  Philadelphus pubescens
Hypericaceae
  Hypericum hypericoides
  Hypericum prolificum
Lauraceae
  Lindera benzoin
  Lindera melissifolia
Leitneriaceae
  Leitneria floridana
Loranthaceae
  Phoradendron flavescens
Malvaceae
  Hibiscus syriacus
Menispermaceae
  *Calycocarpum lyonii**
  *Cocculus carolinus**
  *Menispermum canadense**
Mimosaceae
  Acacia angustissima
Oleaceae
  Chionanthus virginicus
  Forestiera acuminata
  Ligustrum ovalifolium
Poaceae
  Arundinaria gigantea
Polygonaceae
  *Brunnichia ovata**
  Polygonella americana
Ranunculaceae
  *Clematis virginiana**
Rhamnaceae
  *Berchemia scandens**

Ceanothus americanus
Ceanothus herbaceus
Rhamnus caroliniana
Rhamnus cathartica
Rhamnus lanceolata
Rosaceae
  Amelanchier arborea
  Aronia melanocarpa
  Crataegus pruinosa
  Crataegus uniflora
  Malus angustifolia
  Malus coronaria
  Malus ioensis
  Neviusia alabamensis
  Physocarpus opulifolius
  Prunus americana
  Prunus angustifolia
  Prunus hortulana
  Prunus mahaleb
  Prunus mexicana
  Prunus munsoniana
  Prunus persica
  Prunus virginiana
  Rosa arkansana
  Rosa blanda
  Rosa carolina
  Rosa X damascena
  Rosa multiflora
  Rosa palustris
  Rosa setigera
  Rubus argutus
  Rubus flagellaris

Rubus enslenii
Rubus invisus
Rubus mollior
Rubus occidentalis
Rubus ostryifolius
Rubus pensilvanicus
Rubus procerus
Rubus trivialis
Spiraea alba
Spiraea tomentosa
Rubiaceae
  Cephalanthus occidentalis
  Mitchella repens*
Rutaceae
  Ptelea trifoliata
  Zanthoxylum americanum
Salicaceae
  Salix caprea
  Salix caroliniana
  Salix discolor
  Salix humilis
  Salix interior
  Salix petiolaris
  Salix rigida
  Salix sericea
Sapotaceae
  Bumelia lanuginosa
  Bumelia lycioides
Smilacaceae
  Smilax bona-nox*
  Smilax glauca*
  Smilax hispida*

Smilax rotundifolia*
Solanaceae
  Lycium chinense
  Lycium halimifolium
Staphyleaceae
  Staphylea trifoliata
Styracaceae
  Styrax americanum
Thymeleaceae
  Dirca palustris
Ulmaceae
  Celtis tenuifolia
  Planera aquatica
Verbenaceae
  Callicarpa americana
Vitaceae
  Ampelopsis arborea*
  Ampelopsis cordata*
  Cissus incisa*
  Parthenocissus quinquefolia*
  Parthenocissus vitacea*
  Vitis aestivalis*
  Vitis cinerea*
  Vitis palmata*
  Vitis riparia*
  Vitis rupestris*
  Vitis vulpina*

*Woody Vines

Appendix B

Regional Sources for Native Shrubs and Woody Vines

Insist that nurseries purchase or grow plants from this region so that they are better adapted; also, make sure the plants are nursery-propagated and not dug from the wild.

Arborville Farm Nursery
15604 County Road CC
P.O. Box 227
Holt MO 64048
(816) 264-3911

Bluebird Nursery Inc.
P.O. Box 460
Clarkson NE 68629
(402) 892-3457

Bowood Farms
RR1, Box 90
Clarksville MO 63336
(573) 242-3840
(Wholesale only)

Dabney Nursery
5576 Hacks Cross Road
Memphis TN 38125
(901) 755-4037

Elixir Farm Botanical
County Road 158
Brixey MO 65618
(417) 261-2393

Forrest Keeling Nursery
P.O. Box 135
Elsberry MO 63343
1-800-356-2401
(314) 898-5571

Genesis Nursery Inc.
23200 Hurd Road
Tampico IL 61283
(815) 438-2220

George O. White Nursery
Department of Conservation
P.O. Box 119
Licking MO 65542
(573) 674-3229

Gilberg Perennial Farms
2906 Ossenfort Road
Glencoe MO 63038
(314) 458-2033

H.E. Nursery
RR3, Box 4
Litchfield IL 62056
(217) 324-6191

Johnston Seed Co.
P.O. Box 1392
Enid OK 73702
(405) 233-5800

LaFayette Home Nursery Inc.
RR1, Box 1A
LaFayette IL 61449
(309) 995-3311

Longview Gardens
11801 E. Bannister Road
Kansas City MO 64138
(816)765-5664

Missouri Wildflowers Nursery
9814 Pleasant Hill Road
Jefferson City MO 65109
(573) 496-3492

Native Gardens
Columbine Farm
RR1, Box 494
Greenback TN 37742
(615) 865-3350

Ridgecrest Nursery
U.S. Highway 64 East
Rt. 3, Box 241
Wynne AR 72396
(501) 238-3763

Sunlight Gardens Inc.
RR1, Box 600A
Andersonville TN 37705
(615) 494-8237

Trees by Touliatos
2020 Brooks Road
Memphis TN 38116
(901) 346-8065

Walker's Green Space
2699 53rd St.
Vinton IA 52349
1-800-837-3873

Selected References

Bir, R.E. 1992. Growing & Propagating Showy Native Woody Plants, University of North Carolina Press, Chapel Hill, North Carolina. viii, 192 pp.

Crawford, H.S., C.L. Kucera, & J.H. Ehrenreich. 1969. Ozark Range and Wildlife Plants, Forest Service, U.S. Dept. of Agriculture, Washington, D.C. 236 pp.

Fernald, M.L. 1950. Gray's Manual of Botany, edition 8. American Book Co., New York. lxiv, 1632 pp.

Foote, L.E. & S.B. Jones Jr. 1989. Native Shrubs and Woody Vines of the Southeast, Timber Press, Portland, Oregon. 199 pp.

Gill, J.D. & W.M. Healy. 1973. Shrubs and Vines for Northeastern Wildlife, Northeast Forest Experiment Station, U.S. Dept. of Agriculture, Upper Darby, Pennsylvania. 180 pp.

Gilmore, M.R. 1977. Uses of Plants by the Indians of the Missouri River Region, University of Nebraska Press, Lincoln, Nebraska. xviii, 109 pp.

Gleason, H.A. 1952. The New Britton and Brown Illustrated Flora. New York Botanical Garden, New York. lxvii, 3 vols.

& A. Cronquist. 1963. Manual of Vascular Plants of Northeastern United States and Adjacent Canada. D. Van Nostrand Co., Princeton, New Jersey. li, 810 pp.

Great Plains Flora Association. 1986. Flora of the Great Plains. University of Kansas Press, Lawrence, Kansas. vii, 1392 pp.

Henderson, C.L. 1987. Landscaping for Wildlife, Minnesota Department of Natural Resources, St. Paul, Minnesota. 149 pp.

Hunter, C.G. 1989. Trees, Shrubs, & Vines of Arkansas, The Ozark Society Foundation, Little Rock, Arkansas. viii, 207 pp.

Kindscher, K. 1987. Edible Wild Plants of the Prairie, University Press of Kansas, Lawrence, Kansas. x, 276 pp.

1992. Medicinal Wild Plants of the Prairie, University Press of Kansas, Lawrence, Kansas. xi, 340 pp.

Krochmal, A. & C. 1973. A Guide to the Medicinal Plants of the United States, The New York Times Book Co., New York. vi, 259 pp.

Martin, A.C., H.S. Zim, and A.L. Nelson. 1951. American Wildlife & Plants, Dover Publicans Inc., New York, ix, 500 pp.

Mohlenbrock, R.H. 1986. Guide to the Vascular Flora of Illinois, revised ed. Southern Illinois University Press, Carbondale, Illinois. viii, 507 pp., 2 maps.

Stephens, H.A. 1973. Woody Plants of the North Central Plains, University Press of Kansas, Lawrence, Kansas. xxx, 530 pp.

Steyermark, J.A. 1963. Flora of Missouri. Iowa State University Press, Ames, Iowa. lxxxiii, 1725 pp. (Pp. 1726-1728 [errata] added at second printing, 1968.)

Stokes, D.W. 1981. The Natural History of Wild Shrubs and Vines, Harper & Row, New York, New York. viii, 246 pp.

Tehron, L.R. 1942. Native Illinois Shrubs, Illinois Natural History Survey, Urbana, Illinois. 307 pp.

Vines, R.A. 1960. Trees, Shrubs, and Woody Vines of the Southwest, University of Texas Press, Austin, Texas. vii, 1104 pp.

Yatskievych, G. & J. Turner. 1990. Catalogue of the Flora of Missouri, Missouri Botanical Garden, St. Louis, Missouri. xii, 345 pp.

Index